ONE NATION UNDER GOD

RUS WALTON

The Plymouth Rock Foundation

Published in Marlborough, NH, by Plymouth Rock Foundation, Inc.,
and distributed throughout the world by Plymouth Rock and the
Christian Committees of Correspondence, Marlborough, NH.

Printed in the United States of America by Lithocolor Press, Inc.

Scripture quotations are from THE KING JAMES VERSION
of The Holy Bible.

Library of Congress Cataloging-in-Publication Data

Walton, Rus
    One nation under God.

Bibliography:p.
1. Church and state—United States. 2. United
States—Church history. 3. Christianity and politics.
I Title.
BR516.W35   1993   261.8'0973   86-28585

1 2 3 4 5 6 7 8-93 92 91 90 89 88

To

ILA

My
forever
love

Appreciation!

I take this opportunity to express my thanks
to some key individuals who, under great pressure of time,
helped revise and update this third edition.
Together, we made the printer's deadlines!
To Tim Duskin, our research assistant,
who dug and probed and delivered;
to Al Knight who helped cut through the smoke
of the great Soviet deception,
to Gavin Quill in Boston and
Adam Webb at Harvard who searched and found,
to the Sandfords at Fairwood Bible Institute,
to artist James Talmage who brought back to life
the powerful front cover, and
to my loved and lovely wife
who typed and edited and typed again —
to all of you and to each one of you,
my gratitude and deep appreciation.
Agape!
Let's do it again, sometime!

CONTENTS

PROLOGUE

Just a Few Words in the beginning ...

This is a book about Christianity. Applied Christianity. Applied to every area of life.

It is a book about taking a stand for Christ.

A book about following God's laws and Christ's teachings in all of our affairs, personal and public, spiritual and civic.

This is a book especially for Christians — particularly, Christian Americans.

A book hopefully helpful to those who live in this land and walk in the laws and the light and delight of the living God — those who are committed to the love, the truth, the power, and the path of Jesus Christ as Savior and King.

And it is a book for those who desire to reclaim America for Christ.

There is no pretense of neutrality in these pages. Nothing lukewarm. This book refuses to hide the light of Christ under any bushel, under any ballot, or under any pork barrel. It does not seek to please man; it seeks to honor God.

It suggests, it proclaims, that God is Supreme, that He is Sovereign, that He is Omniscient — and that His Word is relevant for today and for always.

This is a book about the great American Republic. About its genesis and its foundation. About its dreams and its purpose. Not man's purpose but God's purpose.

And it is a book about the false gods and strange prophets who have led this nation astray. Coupled with some thoughts

7

about what must be done if America is to be once more one nation under God.

This is a book about freedom. Individual freedom.
Not the fractured, constrained, regulated, and restricted freedom we witness and feel in this land today. But freedom in its truest and fullest measure.
Freedom under God.
Freedom through God.
Freedom because of God.
Freedom for each and every individual.
Freedom in a land and in a society where all individuals are at liberty to do the best (or the least) that they can do to pursue any calling, any trade, any profession as long as they do not trespass on the equal liberty of any other person to do likewise.

This is not a book about license or anarchy.
It is a book about the rights and responsibilities of liberty.
It does not propose or condone license — that which permits one to do what others may not do; that which leads to licentiousness. Licentiousness leads to anarchy. And anarchy is the jungle.
Some readers may be surprised at some of the concepts and proposals set forth, some of the applications and responsiblilities of freedom set forth. If so, perhaps that is because freedom is a startling concept; it finds its origin in God and its sustenance in Christ and the Christian idea of man in and under God. Such freedom has dimensions and demands we too often overlook.
It has been a long time since we have truly had freedom in this nation. Whole generations have grown up not knowing freedom as it was and is not now *but as it can be once again.*

This is not a book about groups or sections or segments or blocs. It is a book about individuals and individuality.
About the God-likeness of each and every individual. The uniqueness with which God, the Creator, has endowed each of His children. The importance with which each individual has been cloaked.
Many Christians have preached and written this truth: The gound is level at the foot of the Cross. And so it is. And so it should be in all areas of life. (Not the levelling of the anthill, but the oneness in the sight of the Lord

8

— and the equality before the law of the land.)

This book refuses to engage in segregation of any kind — inverse, reverse, converse, or perverse — other than that based on God's injunction that Christians be not unequally yoked.

Each individual must seek his or her own salvation through Christ Jesus and each must attend to his or her own earthly duties. Each must be accountable for his or her personal actions. Each must be entitled to the reward of his or her labor; each is responsible for the consequences of his or her wrong-doings.

No person is beneath the law; no person is above the law. There should be no rubber yardsticks, no double standards, no improper barriers, no special favors. All men are endowed by their Creator with the alienable rights of life, liberty, property and the pursuit of happiness. Conscience is the most valuable property of all; let no man steal your conscience!

Finally, the writings in this book are offered with love and faith and concern and conviction — and prayer. The fervent prayer of righteous Americans could save this nation — *can save it if we will!*

The purpose of this book is not to promote conformity; its purpose is to stimulate prayer, meditation, and thoughtful study of God's Word. And, to sound a call to Christian action. For applied Christianity. For faith and works! In the home, in the church, in the community, in the nation, in the world.

Go! Go forth into the world! Preach the Gospel through your words, your works, your love. Teach all things whatsoever Christ has commanded you. Forward! Forward let His banners go.

May the good Lord bless you and keep you and may the Holy Spirit guide you as you walk with The Living God.

Marlborough, New Hampshire - March, 1993

CHAPTER ONE

The Christian Idea of Government

*"For God so loved the world that He gave
His only begotten Son, that whoever
believes in Him should not perish
but have everlasting life"* (John 3:16)

In the beginning...

At that point in God's perfect timing, when the Constititutional Covention had completeted its work...
The lady sidled up to old Ben Franklin.
"Well, Dr. Franklin. What have you given us?"
Dr. Franklin turned to her and replied:
"You have a republic, madam ... if you can keep it."

So it was, after thousands of years of false starts and forbidden fruits and wrong turns and tyranny and license, man finally made a true beginning in civil government.
No more graven images.
No more state shepherds.
No more kings, or empires, or emperors.
No more unrestrained authority or state religion or sanctioned appetite or mob rule.
No more tyranny
The Great American Republic.

Self-Government with Union

Other governments before had gone by that description-republic.
But, those were different. Different in origin. Different in nature. Different in structure. The best of the past was incorporated into this new and true republic. the rest — the evil, the excess — was rejected.
This new creation stood unique. A system of self-government. A government of and by and for the people. A government by the

11

consent of the governed. With union.

Not with uniformity. With union. With unity.

One out of many. Mortared with the blood of patriots and constructed by the Spirit of the Lord wherein lies liberty.

A constitutional republic with individual liberty, elected representatives, and limited government. A government resting squarely on Biblical principles and limited by the inherent rights of the governed.

A government with its powers nailed down, chained and bound by the Constitution, fastened and confined to the proper defense of the individual's pursuit of life, liberty, and happiness — those inalienable rights endowed by the Creator.

A republic in which the power to govern was checked and balanced by devices designed to stop the tyrant in his tracks.

Four Fences

Those early Americans, those individualists, had no easy task agreeing on government. Each in his own way and in his own freedom worshiped Almighty God. Had they not come to these shores "to enjoy the liberties of the Gospell in purities with peace"?[1] They were not about to submit to another king, or men or mobs. These subjects-turned-citizens were not only mindful of their rights, they were jealous of them; determined that never again would their inherent freedom be usurped, abused, misused, or denied.

And so these cagey sons of liberty joined to erect four fences around their government.

Four fences, so government could not get out of hand or out of bounds:
- the Executive
- the Legislative
- the Judicial
- the Individual

Each was to be a check and balance to the other. The final fence, the individual, was to be the greatest check of all. No despot, no tyrant, not even a majority or a mob was to separate him from his individual rights. In the individual's hand was always to be the power to bring government to heel.

After God, the individual came first. Only by his consent could government govern — and then, only to protect his life, his liberty, and his property

Not just his, but all mens' — equally.

It is important to note that such toleration (of each individual's rights) comes about through Christianity - because only the Christian idea of man honors all men be they Greek, Jew, barbarian, Scythian, bond or free. Christianity respects each individual because it honors God and gives supremacy to Him (see Col. 3:11).[1]

A Republic!

And so the Founding Fathers created a republic.
A monarchy? No way!
They had just been down that bitter road. They knew all about the misuse of those so-called "divine rights of kings." And, they knew the Scriptures. They were mindful of the Prophet Samuel's warning when the nation of Israel had demanded an earthly king:

And he said, "This will be the behavior of the king who will reign over you: He will take your sons and appoint them for his own chariots and to be his horsemen, and some will run before his chariots. He will appoint captains over his thousands and captains over his fifties, will set some to plow his ground and reap his harvest, and some to make his weapons of war and equipment for his chariots. He will take your daughters to be perfumers, cooks, and bakers. and he will take the best of your fields, your vineyards, and your olive groves, and give them to his servants. He will take a tenth of your grain and your vintage, and give it to his officers and servants. And he will take your manservants and your maidservants and your finest young men and your donkeys, and put them to his work. He will take a tenth of your sheep. And you will be his servant. And you will cry out in that day because of your king whom you have chosen for yourselves, and The Lord will not hear you in that day" (1 Sam. 8:11-18).

The Founding Fathers knew the Bible. And they knew, first hand, the striking parallels between the excesses Samuel had prophesied and the bill of indictments against the King of England as set forth in their Declaration of Independence. They were not about to go down that road again.
Collectivism? Communism? Absolutely not!
"Ye taking away of propertie, and bring in comunitie into a comone wealth."[2] The first Pilgrms had been forced to make that false start -- communism invoked by the financial underwriters of their venture. It was collectivism "under the most favorable conditions,

among a people consicentious and bound together by strong religious enthusiasm."[3]

And it failed miserably. During the winter of 1620-21 it had almost done them in. "It resulted as such sinking of personal interest must ever result, in dissensions and insubordination, in unthrift and famine."[4]

No more of that!

A democracy? Not on your life!

Democracy? Where half plus one can squash the rest? Where a fanatical majority apart from God can deprive the individual of his rights, his life, his property? Not for these people.

They knew democracy with its excesses, its leveling processes, its inherent seeds of destruction.

Democracy? Wherein the people see themselves as gods, sovereign over men and nations? The early Americans brought no such idea to this new world. John Cotton, one of the great preachers of the colonial period, put it this way: "Democracy? I do not conceive that God ever did ordain it as a fit government for church or commonwealth. If the people be governors, who shall be governed?[5]

Pastor Cotton was not arguing for an aristocracy. He understood the democratic philosophy, with its emphasis on the sovereignty of the people; clearly aristocracy was a fundamental contradiction to the biblical doctrine of the sovereignty of God.

The very essence of democracy depends upon the absolute sovereignty of the majority. Unbridled, capricious, born of appetite and envy. Our Founding Fathers could never accept such tyranny. They recognized the seed and foresaw the fruit of humanism. For them there was but one rightful sovereign over men and nations — The Lord God. And under God? The individual — not the State, not the collective, not the majority. The individual. Self-governed with union in Christ.

Historian C. Gregg Singer reminds us that Governor John Winthrop also warned his fellow citizens of Massachusetts Bay Colony that a doctrine of civil rights, which looks to natural, sinful man like a source and guardian, would destroy the very liberty they were seeking to preserve and protect. Dr. Singer wrote:

> True freedom can never be found in institutions which are under the direction of sinful men, but only in the redemption wrought for many by Jesus Christ. Christ, not man, is the sole source and guarantee of true liberty.

This two-fold indictment of the democratic philosophy of government is one of the enduring testimonies to the keen insight which these leaders of Massachusetts Bay had into the theological practical aspects of an effective type of government.[6]

Consider this statement: "Each religion has a form of government, and Christianity astonished the world by establishing self-government ... the foundation stone of the United States of America."[7] The Great American Republic!

A government of law, not of men. Laws based on the laws of God.

With a Constitution that set down certain definite ground rules. This was the law of the land:

- the rights of the minority protected,
- the rights of the majority upheld but not permitted to be destructive,
- the process of change provided for but in a manner that prevented capricious act or wanton revision.

And, wonder of it all, the safeguard of representative government and division of powers to filter passion and emotion through the checkgates and the balances and divisions of local, state, and federal government.

Further excursion into the field of metaphysics would only emphasize what is too much ignored by contemporary Americans -- that their Republic is a far more than an administrative mechanism. The authors of the constitution were eminently practical men. but to consider this political achievement critically is to see that they realized the distinction we have drawn between the condition of freedom and the urge to liberty;

That they realized the impossiblility of maintaining freedom unless those who were "at liberty" were able to exercise self-restraint;

That their consequent objective was a political system permitting a happy balance and conciliation between the dynamic and the static.

In short, the problem to which they resolutely addressed themselves was how to integrate a liberty of divine origin with an order of human manufacture.[8]

The Golden Mean

Article 4, Section 4, of the Constitution of these United States of America states: "The United States shall guarantee to every State in this union a republican form of government."

There it is! Proposed, adopted, and ratified: "a republican form of government."

Do you think for one moment the founders of this nation would have guaranteed a republican form of government for the states without having the absolute intent of providing the same for the nation as a whole?

A republic!

A form of government under a constitution which provides for the election of (1) an executive and (2) a legislative body who, working together in a representative capacity, have all the power of appointment, all power of legislation, all power to raise reven-ues and appropriate expenditures, and are required to create (3) a judiciary to pass upon the justice and legality of their governmental acts and to recognize (4) certain inherent individual rights.[9]

That's it — the golden mean, the dynamic balance!

All through the realm of nature and of human activity we find examples of the trinity classification - the two extremes and the golden mean. A few of the more striking classifications [in government] are charted below in order to emphasize this fundamental truth and to illustrate the importance and the soundness of the law of the golden mean.

Extreme	Golden Mean	Extreme
AUTOCRACY	REPUBLIC	DEMOCRACY
Tyrants	Statesmen	Demagogues
Bondage	Liberty	License
Oppression	Reason	Impulse
Arbitrariness	Arbitration	Agitation
Submission	Contentment	Discontent
Coercion	Justice	Anarchy
Reaction	Progress	Chaos
Feudalism	Property rights	Socialism[9]

To my mind, the most important event that has occurred since creation was the coming of Christ, for He came to establish the standard of right living for all mankind. The next important event was the founding of this Republic under the constitution, because it provided for the standard of right for government.[10]

God gave His only begotten Son, so that those who believe on Him should not perish but have life eternal. Yes! Praise God! But is not Christ to be our King even as He is our Savior? And if He is our King, are we not to be governed by Him, according to God's laws? We are indeed! James Madison wrote:

> We have staked the whole future of American civilization, not upon the power of government, far from it. We have staked the future...upon the capacity of each and all of us to govern our-selves, to sustain ourselves, according to the Ten Commandments of God.[12]

Chained to the Constitution

That embryonic power, which had so boldly proclaimed its independence from an empire — and backed its words with blood and fortune and sacred honor, firmly relying on Divine Providence — would not readily hand the keys of freedom to another tyrant, regardless of the guise. Even one homegrown. They were tight-fisted with their liberty, jealous of their rights. And they meant to be.

They gave to federal government just enough power to serve, to defend. Just enough and no more. The citizens were to be the master; the State, the servant.

Even then, with all the checks and balances and fences of that constitutional document inspired by Holy Writ, it was not until the Bill of Rights was tacked on that the states would consent to union. Then and only then would they ratify the federation.

Those precious first ten amendments to the Constitution. Freedom of religion. Freedom of speech and press. Freedom to assemble. The right to trial by jury. The right to bear arms for defense and security. The prohibition against unwarranted search and seizure. The right of speedy and public trial by impartial jury. The prohibition of excessive bail or fines or cruel and unusual punishments.

Point by point those vital caveats detailed what government could do and what it could not. Then, with a final whack of their hammer, those representatives of a free and independent people capped their holy affirmation.

The Ninth Amendment:

The enumeration in the Constitution of certain rights shall not be construed to deny or disparage others retained by the people.

And, the Tenth Amendment:

The powers not delegated to the United States by the Consti- tution, nor prohibited to it by the States, are reserved to the States, respectively, or to the people.

Take heed, all would-be Caesars!

Government and men of government would be bound, and kept in bounds. Chained to their proper role by the Constitution. A government of laws, not men! Of principles, not passing fancies!

Bedrock

All those fences, all those checks and balances were vital. Are vital. Vital to the core of the Republic.

Yet in a way they were superstructure. A wrought-iron superstructure anchored in a master rock.

A greater spirit.

A greater law.

A higher authority.

An eternal truth. A light unto the way.

The rock — the power, the beauty, and the light — that was the spirit of the American Republic, and its Constitution existed even before time began.

It was there when Christ with God created the heavens and the earth and man.

It was there when Christ with God the Father gave man dominion over the land and the sea and the plants and the beasts -- but not over his fellow man. In the image of God created He man. A free agent with a free will. Not a robot, not a vassal; a steward only a little lower than the angels. In the final reckoning, man's accountability is to God. Man's dominion is not unto himself but under God as His vice regent.

The genesis — the spark — it was there, too, when Christ with God established civil government, when He ordained it after the flood through Noah (Gen. 9:5,6).

The power: it was there when God gave men the law through Moses. There on Mount Sinai and in the days that followed. The law and the statutes and the ordinances to govern man's comings and goings on God's earth (Exod. 19-20).

And surely it was there through the manifested power and

purity and love and light and sacrifice of Christ Jesus, our Savior and our King.

Free!

Christ died and rose to make men free.

Whosoever will! Praise God!

Through Christ we are freed from the wages of sin. Eternal freedom. Free if we choose to be.

Free from the bondage and ravages of appetite and self. Internal freedom. Free if we choose to be.

Free from the savagery of demagogues and the tyranny of kings. External freedom. Free if we choose to be.

Just as Christ Jesus brought us internal freedom (and a rebirth into a new life in Him) so He also brought us a new direction for our external freedom (and a new purpose for our civil government).

Internal and external freedom. Self-government with union in Christ.

For if Christ would die to make man free, how dare Caesar to force men to live or die for him?

There! There was the spark, the flame, the beacon light of the American idea. The power of the Great American Republic. The sense and the spirit of the Declaration of Independence and the Constitution of these United States of America.

The concept of a secular state was virtually non-existent in 1776 as well as in 1787, when the Constitution was written, and no less so when the Bill of Rights was adopted. To read the Constitution as the charter for a secular state is to misread history, and to misread it radically. The Constitution was designed to perpetuate a Christian order.

Let us consider the obvious rebuttal to such a statement, for it needs to be met: Why then is there, in the main, an absence of any reference to Christianity in the Constitution?

The response must be equally blunt: There is an absence of reference because the framers of the Constitution did not believe that this was an area of jurisdiction for the federal government. It would not have occurred to them to attempt to re-establish that which the colonists had fought against, namely, religious control and establishment of the central government. The colonists would not have tolerated power in the Federal Union which they had rebelled against when claimed by crown and parliament.

The freedom of the first amendment from federal interference is not freedom from religion but freedom for religion in the constituent states.[13]

Separation of church from State control? Absolutely!
Divorcement of God from government? Not so!
Both the church and the civil government were ordained by God -- each institution with a distinct division of labor. The ministry of the church is grace; the ministry of the State is justice.
Both are answerable to God, the Supreme Sovereign.

Next to the Christian religion, of which America is the most influential advocate, the American government and Constitution is the most precious possession which the world holds, or which the future can inherit.
This is true: True because the American system is the political expression of Christian ideas...a nation founded upon the rock of religion and rooted in the love of man [emphasis added].[14]

So it was that John Quincy Adams, fourth president of the Republic, could utter these words backed by truth:

Is it not that, in the chain of events, the birthday of our nation is indissolubly linked with the birthday of the Saviour? ... Is it not that the Declaration of Independence first organized the social compact on the foundation of The Redeemer's mssion? That it laid the cornerstone of human government upon the first precepts of Christianity and gave to the world the first irrevocable pledge of the fulfillment of the prophecies announced directly from heaven at the birth of the Saviour and predicted by the greatest of the Hebrew prophets 600 years before?[15]

The Christian Idea of Government

Christ's Great Commandment?
"Love one another: just as I have loved you so too you should love one another." [13]
That is the very tap-root of self government and individual freedom under God. His Golden Rule for life?
"Do unto others as you would have them do unto you." [14]
That is the power which can make men free and force governments to seek their proper place ... and, live within those bounds.

Christ's Great Injunction?

"Seek you first the kingdom of God and His righteousness and all these things shall be added unto you." [16]

There it is. Once and for all. The established balance and order for civilization, for peace and prosperity.

"For what will it profit a man if he gains the whole world, and loses his own soul?" (Mark 8:36).

And what does it profit a nation if it gains the world and rejects the Lord?

These were the ideals, the ideas, the principles and precepts, the spirit of the men who founded this republic.

This nation was founded, its government was conceived and formed, by men who knew God's Word, men who had a strong, abiding faith in Christ Jesus. They were men who embraced without hesitation the Christian idea of man and, for the first time in man's history, made it the foundation of civil government.

The Christian idea of man!

Not some pagan idea of man.

Not some proposition that man was an accident of biochemistry.

Not the claim that man was simply some higher form of ape.

But this: The Christian idea, the Christian truth concerning man -- his origins, his purpose, his worth.

The truth that in the image of God made He man.

And this:

"For God so loved the world that He gave
His only begotten Son, that whoever believes
in Him should not perish but have everlasting
life!" (John 3:16).

God gave His only Son! He gave His Son to die for us. For each one of us. For you. For me. If God loved each man, each woman, each child that much...

... if each individual counts that much in the eyes of TheGod, the Supreme Sovereign, the Creator and Sustainer of all that is...

... how can the individual count for any less in the eyes of men and nations?

What our Savior's blood on Calvary's tree purchased was not a group life insurance plan. The ransom paid was a one-for-one covenant between God and the individual sinner who believes on His son.

There we have the root, the source, the origin, and the power of the Christian idea on which this Republic was founded.

If each indiviual counts, then each indiviual is accountable. And because each individual counts and is accouantable, God sent His Son the Lamb, perfect, without spot or blemish, to pay the wages of man's sin.

That is the crux of the gospel of salvation.

Consider this also: It is the core of the Christian idea of man and the Christian methodology of government!

What was it John Quincy Adams said, on that July Fourth, back in 1837?

> "Is it not that, in the chain of events, the birthday of our nation is indissolubly linked wiuth the birthday of the Saviour?"

These were the ideals, the ideas, the principles, the spirit of the men who founded this Republic.

> "These texts, and many others of similar import, were as guiding lights to the resolute men and women who came to America not merely to worship as they wished, but even more to live, so far as humanly possible, in the manner Christ ordained."[16]

John Locke, the English theorist and philosopher of the 17th Century was one who had a great and positive influence on the framers of our Constitution. Hear his words:

> "Our Saviour's great rule, that we should love our neighbors as ourselves, is such a fundamental truth for the regulating of human society, that, by that alone, one might without difficulty determine all the cases and doubts in social morality."[17]

Years later, in 1851, when Daniel Webster was reviewing the history of this great American family, he reaffirmed the need and role of God in government:

> Let the religious element in man's nature be neglected, let him be influenced by no higher motives than low self-interest, and subjected to no stronger restraint than the limits of civil authority, and he becomes the creature of selfish passion or blind fanaticism.

> On the other hand, the cultivation of the religious sentiment represses licentiousness, incites to general benevolence, and the practical acknowledgment of the brotherhood of man, inspires respect for law and order, and gives strenth to the whole social fabric, at the same time that it conducts the human soul upward to the Author of its being.[18]

More than one hundred years after Webster, Charles Malik, then ambassador to the United Nations from Lebanon, put it this way:

> The good (in the United States) would never have come into being without the blessing and the power of Jesus Christ.
>
> Whoever tries to conceive the American word without taking full account of the suffering and love and salvation of Christ is only dreaming.
>
> I know how embarrassing this matter is to politicians, bureaucrats, businessmen, and cynics; but, whatever these honored men think, the irrefutable truth is that the soul of America is at its best and highest, Christian.
>
> When the tears and joy of Christ come to perfect fruition in this land, then America will utter her word.[19]

God First!

Christ did, indeed, command us to render unto Caesar that which is Caesar's (Matt. 22:21).

Just what belongs to Caesar?

We are not to render unto him those things that belong to God. Our body, our spirit, our soul, our conscience - those are not Caesar's. they belong to God; God has made us - not Caesar.

God had a clear and definite purpose when He ordained civil authority. Civil authority was and is to serve God and to protect the life, property, and well-being of men and women from those whose lack of moral responsibility and disobedience to God's laws turned them to crime and violence. Human government was instituted by The Lord God as a protective, defensive agency. Civil government was ordained to serve The Lord God by being a protector -- not a provider -- of the people. Its laws were established to be in concert with God's laws.

And what of those laws and the purpose of those laws and statutes and judgments? Those laws that God handed down to man through Moses? They were given to make clear the imperative doctrine of man's responsibility to God and thus his responsibliity to his fellow man. They were given to define and to dilineate the purity and the holiness that should characterize the life of a people for whom the lof the nation was, at the same time, the law of God.

Therefore you shall love The Lord your God, and keep His charge, His statutes, His judgements, and His commandments always (Deut.11:1).

Christians know that civil government is ordained by God. We know that civil magistrates (elected and non-elected) are to be "servants of God to the people for good"(Rom. 13:4). We also know that it is His will that we pray for those in authority and ask that they be receptive to God's guidance as they conduct our civil affairs.

In his book shaping *History through Prayer and Fasting*, Derek Prince reminds us that "Christian citizens of the United States should be forever thankful that the basic charter of their nation agrees so exactly with the purposes and principles of government ordained in the Holy Scriptures."[20]

Remember Paul's counsel in 1 Timothy 2:2? Roughly translated, Paul's counsel boils down to this:

"Good government is the will of God."

In Christ's teachings and in the writings of His apostles, we find the keys to good government and to its reformation and reconstruction should government cease to be good:

- the Law (Matt.5:17)
- the Great Commandment (John 15:17)
- the Golden Rule (Matt 7:12)
- the Great Injunction (Matt. 6:33)
- the Whole spectrum of Love (1 Cor. 13:1-13)
- the Whole Armor of God (Eph. 6:10-18)

Clearly it is affirmed and reaffirmed: Man is God's servant. He is God's steward, not Caesar's.

The State is to serve the law-abiding and punish the lawbreaker. Not vice versa.

Under God, the individual is to be self-governing. "Christianity is a stranger to despotic power."[21]

The First Christian Congregations

What dynamic ideas, these Christian precepts found in God's Word!

These divine precepts and principles, which had been from the beginning, burst forth as the Master walked and talked on earth. Truths that were propagated as His disciples and apostles spread the gospel.

As these ideas spread from individual to individual to family to group, a secondary transformation began to occur. The power of the

Holy Spirit, first internal, took external shape and form and practice. It manifested itself in the Christians' daily lives and in the structure of the early Christian congregations.

Consider the spirit, the structure, the lovely work of those early Christian churches at Galatia, Philippi, Antioch, Thessalonica, Ephesus, Colosse, Corinth, and Rome.

There was true self-government. Christianity applied.

The seed and fruit, the patterns for other to follow — to modify, perhaps, but to maintain.

In the beginning Christianity was simply Gospel. Ecclesiastical organization was not the cause but the effect of life.

Churches were constituted by the spontaneous association of believers. Individuals and families, drawn toward each other by their common trust in Jesus, The Christ, and their common interest in the good news concerning the kingdom of God, became a community united, not by external bonds, but by the vital force of distinctive ideas and principles...in every place the society of believers in Christ was a little republic.[22]

"Christianity, in its essence, its doctrines, and its forms, is republican."[23]

Republican.

Not in any narrow partisan sense or meaning of the word.

Certainly not in any reference to the politics of this day.

But republican meaning "that form of government which derives all its powers directly or indirectly from the body of the people and is administered by persons holding office with the consent of the governed."[24]

Consider the republican features of the early churches.

These churches had officers, which were to be regarded and observed, in their proper spheres, as much as officers of any other republic. But the manner of their ruling was not to be as "Lords over God's heritage"[25]

"Whoever desires to be first among you," said the Savior, *"let him be your slave"*(Matt. 20:27).

The churches instituted by the apostles were local institutions. Each local church was complete in itself and was responsible to Christ for its character and the character of those in its fellowship. The members of the congregations elected their elders and deacons.

Through prayer and study, they sought God's will in their lives and in the affairs of their church. They sought to imbue themselves with the love and light and spirit of Christ. In all things. The whole suit of armor!

Matters of congregational polity were attended to by the members through their chosen elders and deacons. If, upon occasion, the church sought the apostle's advice or opinion, that was their decision.

As Daniel Neal wrote in his "History of the Puritans":

If the Apostle Paul, who was an inspired person, had not dominion over the faith of the churches, how came the Roman emperor, or other Christian princes, by such a jurisdiction - which has no foundation in the law of nature or in the New Testament?[26]

One Mind in Christ

No regional body, no state board, no national council, no self-anointed hierarchy enforced dictums or edicts or decrees or tributes. Christ was Lord, Master, and Governor of individual congregational affairs, because faith was strong, vibrant, alive! (Dr. C. Greg Singer has pointed out: the weaker the creed, the stronger the hierarchy!)

Hundreds and hundreds of miles stretched between those far-flung churches. But the churches were united. There was no central control, but there was a common bond. Many members, one body. Out of many, one!

It was a new heart, a new mind, a new love through Christ. It was the power of the universe, the seed of Creation, the blaze of souls on fire. And it spread!

Against all adversity it spread. In hidden rooms. By quiet shores. Through the market place. In the darkest catacomb. Through martyrs and through persecutions. Even when the score read "Lions, ten; Christians, zero," it would not die. A glorious, unyielding, lifting faith which would not — could not — be denied.

Tyrants would try to snuff it out; hierarchies would try to smother it; emperors would try to subordinate it; demigods would try to pervert or divert it.

But it would not die and it would not yield and it would not compromise.

Its truth, its purity, its power would prevail.

And in God's good time it would find its form.

Westward to America!

Others have documented the westward movement of that Christian light. Other volumes detail to rise and fall, the contributions and inquisitions of the dark Dark Ages.

Suffice to mention here that each regime and every transit added to man's constantly expanding sum: Pythagoras and Euclid, Aristotle, Socrates and Plato, Galileo and da Vinci; language, laws and logarithm, politics and science, arts and architecture; the outwad reach of navigation and the inward quest of introspection - the ability to examine and define the concrete, the intellect to conceptualize the abstract. All increased man's knowledge of the Creator and His universe, and all were preparation for the development of man's republican capacities.

The Christian light moved westward through the epochs. Persisting like a blade of grass that shatters through the boulder to flourish in a virgin land an ocean span away.

It came through John Milton's *Paradise Lost* and through his *Pro Populo Anglicano Defensio*:

> Our liberty is not Caesar's. It is a blessing we have received from God Himself. It is what we were born to. To lay this down at Caesar's feet, which we derive not from him, which we are not beholden to him for, were an unworthy action, and a degrading of our very nature.

It came through Wycliffe, the "morning star of the reformation," whose love of truth, of freedom, and of independence compelled him to give his English countrymen the open Scripture as their best safeguard and protection during "the thickest darkness of anti-Christian idolatry."[27]

Wycliffe published his conclusions "that the New Testament or Gospel is a perfect rule of life and manners and ought to be read by the people." He then proceeded, before his martyrdom, to translate the New Testament into the English language.

This light spread, too, through Tyndale, the father of the English Bible. Through Martin Luther, John Knox, John Calvin, John Wesley, and Thomas Cartwright, and the Presbyterians. God moved in wondrous ways His mysteries and His majesties to perform!

> That mysterious influence of that Power which enchains the destinies of States, overruling the decisions of sovereigns and the forethought of statesmen. A Genovese adventurer, discovering America. An

obscure German, inventing the printing press. An Augustine monk, denouncing indulgences, introduced a schism in religion and changed the foundations of English politics.

A young French refugee, skilled alike in theology and civil law...entering the republic of Geneva, and conforming its ecclesiastical discipline to the principles of republican simplicity, established a party of which Englishmen became members and New England the asylum.[28]

The Christian light came with the growing thunder of a new age dawning in the West.

First the Pilgrims, then the Puritans. Followed by the Quakers, the Huguenots, the Catholics the Dutch Reformed, the Lutherans, the Presbyterians, the Methodists, and the Baptists. Joined here in this uncharted land by the Anglicans of Virginia who would raise their voices and lend their arms and give their sons as presidents.

It came on the written wings of Locke and Montesquieu, of Sidney and Blackstone, of Mason and Paine, and of Adams and Franklin and Henry — and the Committees of Correspondence. And it rang out from the pulpits of New England, New Jersey, the Carolinas, Georgia.

It came through the crimson tyrannies of king and parliament, through Stamp Acts, writs of assistance, and quartered troops. Impelled by the Sons of Liberty in Boston, triggered by the shot at Concord, impassioned by the words of young Patrick Henry, member of Virginia's House of Burgesses, speaking at St. John;s Episcopal Church in Richmond:

"Is life so dear or peace so sweet, as to be purchased at the price of chains or slavery? Forbid it, Almighty God! I know not what course others may take, but as for me - give me liberty or give me death!"

Thus, in the course of human events, the Christian light formed and marched and moved

"...with a firm reliance on the protection of Divine Providence."

And on that day a Boston man, Sam Adams, stood in Independence Hall as the Declaration was signed and proclaimed:

"We have this day restored the Sovereign to Whom all men ought to be obedient. And, from the rising to the setting of the sun, let His kingdom come!"

The Pagan View of Man

So it arrived — the Christian light.

Not a birth, but a rebirth!

A continuation, after so long a time, of the seed and fruit, of the courage and persistence, of preceding Christians. A propagation of that liberty wherein Christ has made men free.

> Christianity then appeared with the central doctrine that man was created in the Divine image, and destined for immortality; pronouncing that, in the eye of God, all men are equal. This asserted for the individual an independent value. It occasioned the great inference that man is superior to the State, which ought to be fashioned for his use.
>
> This was the advent of a new spirit and a new power in the world.[29]

And Christianity met head-on another value placed on man: The pagan view.

The old world view "that the social order rested on the unatural inequality of men"; that the individual was "of value only as he formed a part of the political fabric and was able to contribute to its uses, as though it were the end of his being to aggrandize the state."[30]

Such a humanistic, nihilistic philosophy could not and would not abide the Christian truth that man is created in the image of God, for His glorification; that man is not a political unit or an economic digit; that man is not an end unto the State. That man is unique, distinct, important — and God's!

> "Socialism's government is the external control of the parts, as opposed to Christianity's internal control of the individual."[31]

Thus the battle was joined.

It continues in this day — at home as well as abroad.

- Shall we have controlled citizens or a
controlled government?
- Is the individual the master or the slave?
- Is man created in the likeness of God, accountable to his Maker?
- Or is he a means to an end,
subservient to the State?

The eternal struggle; part and parcel of the eternal war.

"For we wrestle not against flesh and blood, but against principalities, against powers, against the rulers of the darkness of this age, against spiritual hosts of wickedness in the heavenly places" (Eph. 6:12)

Our Father, which art in heaven,
halowed be thy Name.
Thy kingdome come
Thy wil be donne even in earth
as it is in heaven.

Go, therefore, and teache all nacions,
baptizing them in the name of the Father,
and the Sonne, and the holie Gost.
Teaching them to observe all things
Whatsoever I have commanded you,
& lo, I am with you alway,
until the ende of the worlde.

(Matthew 6:9,10 and 28:19-20
from the Geneva Bible, 1560)

CHAPTER TWO

False Gods, Strange Prophets

*"Beware of false prophets, who come to you
in sheep's clothing, but inwardly they are
ravening wolves. You shall know them
by their fruits"*(Matt. 7:15,16)

Nothing of survival is inherent in a republic. Its longevity depends upon the faith, the spirit, and the genius of the people within. Remember those words by James Madison as he explained the nature of the American Republic?

We have staked the whole future of American civilization, not upon the power of government, far from it. We have staked the future of all of our political institutions upon the capacity of mankind for self-government; upon the capacity of each and all of us to govern ourselves, to control ourselves, to sustain our-selves according to the Ten Commandments of God.[1]

What if the faith is weakened? What if the spirit of the people flags? What if the flesh grows weak? When that occurs, the Republic goes unattended:

• The *checks and balances* between the executive, the legislative, the judicial, and the individual are rigged or circumvented.
• The *fences* between the federal, state, and local governments are downed. The system is then altered, subverted, ignored.

Part of the Past

It would not be accurate to say that the Republic is dead. But, it would not be far off the mark to say that its workings have been tampered with and cast aside. The form remains and is acknowledged on national holidays and in patriotic speeches. Then it is put back under glass, along with the other national relics.

31

The fact is this: *The United States of America is now more of a democracy than a republic.*

And to those who will see behind the slogans and hear beyond the chants, another truth is clear: *With the passing of the Republic comes the passing of the power and the freedom of the people.*

The Vital Difference

What's that you say?

How can that be? In a democracy the power is the people!

Not so! In its last rites, a democracy enslaves the people.

In a democracy the power that prevails is the militant. The vocal, organized minority. And, now and then, an occasional restive, frustrated majority.

Four hundred years ago Alexander Fraser Tyler, a professor in England, examined the fruits of democracy and called them bitter:

A democracy cannot exist as a permanent form of government. It can exist only until the voters discover that they can vote themselves largess out of the public treasury. From that moment on the majority always votes for the candidate promising the most benefits from the public treasury — with the result that democracy always collapses over a loose fiscal policy, always to be followed by dictatorship.

Consider Madison again:

A pure democracy...can admit no cure for the mischiefs of fac-tion. A common passion or interest...will...be felt by a ma-jority...and there is nothing to check the inducement to sacrifice the weaker party...Hence it is that such democracies have ever been...found incompatible with personal security or the rights of property; and have in general been as short in their lives as they have been violent in their death.[2] (Federalist Papers, No. 10)

There is the difference. The vital difference between a republic and a democracy.

In a republic, the government will represent the majority while protecting the minority. Because it is a government of laws. Because the checks and balances work and the fences are up. Representation is demanded and given. In a democracy, the government will yield to the group, the mob, the militant, the demagogue. The checks and balances are jimmied. The fences are down. Sound and fury can carry the day. The sound truck of the demagogues drowns out the voice of reason. The minority is in jeopardy.

That vital difference prompted the framers of our Federal Constitution to give us the Great American Republic.

We have not kept it very well.

> To put the matter bluntly, there is under way in the United States at the present time a definite and determined movement to change our representative republic into a socialistic democracy. It presents itself in many persuasive and seductive forms. It uses attractive formulas to which men like to give adhesion; but if it is successful, it will bring an end to the form of government that was founded when our Constitution was made.[3]

Dr. Nicholas Murray Butler, the president of Columbia University during the 1930s and 1940s, wrote those words in his book, *Why Should We Change Our Form of Government?* Sixty years ago he wrote them! That was some twenty years after that dark, dark, 1913 — the year Congress gave us the Sixteenth Amendment and the Federal Reserve System.

Where Have We Gone?

Only sixty years ago! A lot has happened since then. Huge chunks of the American Republic have been chipped away.

Think back. Check the politics and government in this nation for the past thirty, forty, fifty, sixty, years.

What has happened? Where have we gone?

Well, we have gone backward. We have digressed. We have left the course of freedom.

Upon occasion, and on specific issues, we, the people, have voted a reaffirmation of the American agenda.

"Get on with the Republic," we have advised.

We have voted for economy instead of extravagance. For liberty instead of license. For states' rights rather than centralism. For individuality instead of collectivism.

Has our will or our vote prevailed? Has the course changed? Or has it remained the same? Ask yourself!

During the past sixty years political party has been exchanged for political party; leader for leader; representative for representative. Yet the drift has remained. It has become almost inherent. And the power and the freedom of the people has been passing with the years.

Revolutionary Intent

Consider the 1930s under Franklin Roosevelt. Consider especially the first one hundred days under the New Deal in 1933. It was then socialism sank its roots deep into the nation's heart. It was then then the republic took its lumps.

Franklin Roosevelt was not elected on a platform of socialism. He did not run on the promises of a planned society or super-State. His proposals and promises to America went in the *opposite* direction.

The Democratic platform of 1932 would make today's conservatives stand up and cheer! It would make today's liberals froth at the microphone and scream from the tube! The first three planks to which FDR bound and pledged himself were these:

1. An immediate and drastic reduction in governmental expenditures by abolishing useless commissions and offices, consolidating departments and bureaus and eliminating extravagance, *to accomplish a savings of not less than 25 percent in the cost of Federal government.*

2. Maintenance of the national credit by a **Federal budget annually balanced.**

3. A sound currency to be maintained at all hazards.[4]

And in his 1932 campaign, Mr. Roosevelt stated repeatedly:

We are spending altogether too much money for government services which are neither practical nor necessary. In addition to this, we are attempting too many functions and we need a simplification of what the Federal government is giving to the people.

The American people loved it. They cheered in their anticipation. They asked for a New Deal.

But the promises and the speeches were sheer duplicity. Expediency at its zenith. Sham at its worst.

Garet Garrett, a giant of American journalism, laid it on the line. In *The Revolution Was,* he spelled it out:

What was concealed from the people was a general revolutionary intention — the intention, that is, to bring about revolution in the state, within the form of law. This becomes clear when you set down what it was the people thought they were voting for in contrast with what they got. They thought they were voting ...

For less government, not more;

For an end to deficit spending by government, not deficit

> spending raised to the plane of social principles, and
> For sound money, not as the New Deal afterward defined
> it, but as everybody then understood it.[5]

That is what the majority of Americans voted for in 1932. This is what they got:

• The number and the powers of federal agencies exploded into a nightmare of alphabets (AAA, NRA, NLRB, PWA, WPA), and the shrapnel cut and chewed into virtually every aspect of daily life (today much of it remains embedded in the muscle of the Republic).

• The federal budget zoomed and the national debt increased (in the first four years of the Roosevelt administration, spending increased 85 percent; the federal debt increased 72 percent, and the number of federal employees rose 48 percent).

• The United States went off the gold standard. The sound, gold-backed money was decimated (citizens and companies were divested of their gold under penalty of fine or imprisonment; the gold redemption clause in all governmental obligations (contracts) was repudiated; the dollar was devalued; and Washington pocketed a $2 billion "windfall" from the confiscated gold).

All that was done in the name of emergency, in the name of economic panic and the banking crisis. By Mr. Roosevelt's own admission in his book, *On Our Way,* the banking crisis lasted only one week: but the full meaning of that word emergency related to far more than banks. It could be cured only by a complete reorganization and measured controls of the economic structure....It called for a long series of new laws, new administrative agencies.[6]

Thus the Republic was shoved backstage and democracy moved front and center. It came to the fore in the dark of night, flying flags of freedom, chanting praises to a new shepherd.

Seven years later, after all of the confiscation of liberty and property, 14.6 percent of America was still unemployed, farms were still fallow, factories were still idle, and America was being readied to send its boys to war.

It has been much the same since then but not as concentrated, not always as blatant until recently. Consider those candidates who were elected on their promise to bring government back home. They voted instead to centralize its powers on the shores of the Potomac. Consider those candidates who were elected on their promise to reduce the size and scope and cost of government. They worked instead to fuel its fires and fan its flames.

Consider the consequences:

In only eight of the past forty-six years has the federal budget been balanced. For thirty one of the thirty two years since 1960, the federal government has run in the red.

Back in 1986, Senator William Armstrong of Colorado warned us. Stop! he urged. The explosion in federal spending is mortgaging the future. It threatens to destroy our economy and our way of life. Looking across America's fiscal Red Sea, Armstrong scolded his colleagues in the Senate:

> In 1940, the public debt of the United States was $43 billion. In 1986, the public debt exceeded $1.3 *trillion* - an increase of over 3,800 per cent in 46 years. Federal spending has increased nearly 1,000 per cent since 1960....In the last 10 years, spending has increased $615 billion — $400 billion alone since 1980.

Armstrong zeroed in on the ever-soaring federal debt. Look, he urged. The cost of interest on that debt gnaws at our economic vitals: "If you remember one statistic, let it be this: *Between 1981 and 1990, the federal government will spend $1.3 trillion in interest payments alone. This equals the entire amount of public debt accumulated from 1789 to 1984"*[7]

Occasionally a President appoints a blue-ribbon commission to tackle government spending. The outside experts come dig and probe. They reach conclusions and make recommendations. In 1982 President Reagan named J. Peter Grace to head a Private Sector Survey on Cost Control (the Grace Commission). Mr. Grace persuaded top professionals in private business and industry to volunteer their time and services to audit government operations.

The Commission concluded that, for the most part, the federal government does not know how much the government is spending. It calculated that by the year 2000, unless government operations were drastically revised, we would have a national debt of $23 trillion with a demand payment of *$1.5 trillion a year* just for the interest.[8]

Peter Grace and his auditors came up with 2,478 ways to tighten Washington's belt. They figured those cuts could save $425 billion in just three years. Furthermore, asserted Peter Grace, although the federal government said it had a $1.3 trillion debt in 1984, if it calculated its indebtedness according to accepted accounting standards, the total would actually be more like $4.4 trillion.[9]

The experts returned to their private jobs and the leviathan of government went on as usual. The Grace Commission recommendations were ignored. The blue-ribbon report was wrapped in red tape and lost in the political smog. Mr. Grace tried to get the TV networks to accept a sixty-second spot warning about the ravages of deficit spending; the networks wouldn't touch it. Since when did frugality and common sense become a no-no? It happened on the road to bankruptcy — after the Republic was junked.

It's (Only) Your Money

Since 1940, in every year except two, the value (the purchasing power) of the dollar has eroded. What was worth one hundred cents then is worth maybe seven cents now; maybe less!. And with the diminishing value of the dollar has gone the power of the people to control their own lives. It was not only the money but the principles; with the money went the principles.

It took 173 years — from 1787 to 1962 — for the annual federal budget to reach $100 billion. It took only nine more years for it to reach $200 billion. By 1976 that budget was gobbling up almost $400 billion. By 1980 it was $590.9 billion. And by 1986 it had soared to $990.2 billion, just shy of $1 trillion. Coming in fiscal 1992,3? More than $1. 25 trillion, at least.

(What's a billion? It's one thousand million! What's a trillion? *one thousand billion!* Look at it this way: laid end-to-end, one trillion inches equals sixteen million miles. That's 666 times around the earth. Six hundred and sixty-six times!)

The federal deficits for fiscal years 1990 and 1991 add up to $489.2 billion. That's $101.5 billion more than all the money Uncle Sam spent in the first 156 years of this Republic. More than all the federal budgets from the Constitutional Convention of 1787 to the midst of World War II in 1944. But, you ain't seen nothin' yet! The combined deficits for fiscal years 1992-93 are projected to total $631 billions! $631 billions!!

Some politicians commit to tax, spend, control, and elect. At least we know where they stand. Others say they are committed to fiscal sanity, to guarding the taxpayers' earnings, but they also vote to tax and to spend. Challenge them and they answer:

"You just don't understand the pressures. You folks live in a world of theory. Politicians deal with reality; politics is the art of the possible.

"Besides, half a loaf is better than none."

There's the answer and there's the problem: the half loaf they give away is yours. Not theirs, yours. And the next time they spend half of your half-loaf, and then half of that. Before you know it, you're left with one or two thin slices — and they are stale.

So much for campaign rhetoric. So much for party platforms and campaign oratory. Over the years new promises have been made and political guidons have changed, but the course has remained pretty much the same — always to the left. We vote one way, most politicians vote the other. We have wandered in their wilderness, traipsing after elephants and donkeys for more than sixty years.

Power at the Base

The structure of the Republic is pyramidal. Its base of strength is at the local level, in the counties and the states. From there the structure rises through the Congress to the Chief Executive, and even he is checked and balanced.

In the early days, for our first one hundred years or so, that was the shape of the nation. Over the first century the county formed the basic unit of this Republic. As important as the states were to the federation, they were not the basic unit.[10]

The county held jurisdiction in areas important to the workings of our civil government:[11]

• The *property tax* was apportioned and levied at the county level so that citizens could keep the lid on the supervisors and the tax assessors.

• The *criminal law* was foremost a matter of county jurisdiction and enforcement.

• *Civil law,* to a degree, was enacted by locally elected officials and enforced by local courts.

Not too many years ago elections to fill local offices were regarded as important as — if not more important than — state and federal contests. In those times the state was more or less benign, and Washington was miles away attending to its proper constitutional affairs.

But that has changed. Now Uncle Caesar calls the loudest tune; citizens are more entranced with his election than the election of his county cousins. The shift commenced years ago but did not really manifest itself until the early 1930s. In 1934, 1935, and 1936 that's when the turn away from the Republic began. Year by year you could see the power shift. You could measure it by the transfer of the people's money from the bottom to the top, from the counties and the states to Babylon, D.C.

The Pyramid Is Upside Down

In 1902 all governments in the Republic — federal, state, and local — spent $1.7 billion of the people's money. More than 65 percent of that was raised and spent by local and state governments. Only 34 percent was spent by the federal government.

By 1922 the total government spending had risen to $9.3 billion, but the lion's share was still spent at the local level:

- 46 percent by the cities and counties
- 14 percent by the states, and
- 40 percent by the federal

At that time, the base of the republic was more-or-less intact and fairly solid.

In 1936 the pyramid began to turn. For the first time, except in years of war, the federal government spent more of the people's earnings than state and local entities combined. Of the $16.7 billion in expenditures that year

- $9.2 billion (55 percent) went to Washington;
- $4.4 billion (26 percent) was spent by local governments;
- $3.1 billion (18.6 percent) was spent by the states.

That was only the beginning.

From then on Babylon became the repository of money and power. The money still came from the folks back home, but it was sent to Washington.

And with the money went the power.

In 1950 the federal government spent 63 percent of all public funds; in 1960, 64 percent; in 1970, 62.5 percent; in 1985, 65.2 percent. There was a slight decrease since then; "only" 62.4 percent of the people's went to Babylon in 1989.

But, in the continuum, the pattern was established; the pyramid that was the Republic is now inverted —

— and it casts a long, dark shadow.

The Lengthening Shadow

To get some idea of just how far that shadow has spread, how far across the land it has stretched, get a map of the United States and get a big red crayon.

Start with Hawaii and Alaska. Color those two states red.

Then start at the mainland, at the Pacific Coast. Color the states red from the Canadian border south to Mexico, color Washington, Oregon, California. Then move east across the Sierras, across the Salt Flats, through the great Southwest, across the Rockies, across the Great Plains. Color red every state from the far Pacific to the Mississippi River — then to seven states beyond plus the District of Columbia: Alabama, Mississippi, Kentucky, Tennessee, South Carolina, Rhode Island, and Vermont.

That's thirty-seven states in all. Thirty-seven states plus the District of Columbia. In the red.

Approximately 115 million Americans live in those thirty-seven states. In 1990 it would have taken all the personal incomes of the 115 million persons living in those thirty-seven states and the District of Columbia to equal the total tax take in this nation. The total personal income of those 115 million people was $1.33 trillion. The total tax take of all governments was $1.35 trillion (not counting that hidden tax — inflation).

Further, almost two-thirds of all those taxes went to Washington. *Color the taxpayers blue!*

From Guns to Giveaways

This siphoning of our resources to fatten the leviathan in Washington has been a steady and increasing drain. But it has had its greatest increases during times of war — wars declared and *undeclared*. In such times the increases came: most of them stayed. After every war, government's expenditures tend to keep much of the bloat of the war-years' spending. Budgets do not return to pre-war levels. The money-spending fever may drop but never to normal or even pre-war levels. In 1916, before our boys marched off "to make the world safe for democracy", the federal budget stood at $734 million. To pay for World War I the budget swelled to $12.7 billion in 1918 and then to $18.5 billion in 1919. When Johnny was safely home, the budget dropped but stopped at $6 billion — some six times what it was before the war.

(Old John Dewey, who used his Columbia University lectern to turn generations of educators to the left, was delighted with the way World War I gave a giant leap forward to increased and centralized governmental powers. "No matter how many...special agencies for public control decay with the disappearance of the war stress, the movement will never go backward." And it hasn't. "Dewey was right," observed Professor Jeffrey Hart. "From Woodrow Wilson's war-time intervention a direct line can be drawn to the New Deal and its proliferating agencies and on through the New Frontier and the climactic Great Society of Lyndon Johnson.")[12]

It was the same in World War II. In 1940 Uncle Sam was spending $10 billion a year. In 1944, it hit $100.5 billion and in 1945, when we were going all out to rescue freedom from the Axis, federal spending had settled at $98 billion. In 1948, with most of our men back home and our planes and ships in mothballs, the budget dropped to $35.5 Billion — three-and-one-half times higher than the pre-Pearl Harbor days. It increased from there, and so did government controls.

Consider Vietnam — the *unwar*. In 1960, when we were first being sucked in, the federal budget stood at $97 billion. As our involvement increased, so did the budget. By 1968 it was $184 billion a year. The fighting was over (for us) but the budget bloat remained. And it kept on bloating. In 1980 it was $615 billion; and in 1985, $1,030 billion! By 1990, it had edged up to $1,393 billion.

Today it's not the guns; it's all that butter and the buttering-up — all those giveaways, domestic and foreign. Federal spending on national defense increased from $81.7 billion in 1970 to $299.3 billion in 1990 and most of that went toward off the "evil empire" and its quest for world domination. During that same period, federal spending on payments to individuals zoomed from $64.8 billion in 1970 to $583.8 billion in 1990.

In 1992, the amount spent on defense dropped to 20.83 percent of total federal outlays while federal spending for health and welfare, education and income security, etc., stood at 52.65 percent of total federal outlays.

In 1990, out of every federal tax dollar that once was ours, 43 cents went to social welfare and public assistance payments and twenty-six cents went for national defense and security. And that's not the whole picture. Every time Uncle Sam increased federal spending for welfare, education, or health, state and local governments were forced to up their spending too. Known as "matching funds," call it what it is: *baiting the money trap*. "Here's some money; match it and it's yours." That's free?? That's a two-way stretch for taxpayers.

Small wonder so many states and counties and cities have been in financial hot water. Small wonder the taxpayers rebel. So far, thirty-two of the required thirty-four states have enacted legislation calling for a Constitutional Convention. The people want an amendment requiring a balanced federal budget. Through constitutions and charters, citizens have already prohibited most state and local governments from indulging in deficit spending -- that sneaky method of delayed taxation plus interest. But the big boys in Washington have found a way to overcome such homegrown wisdom: it's called *revenue sharing*.

What revenue?

Uncle Sam is already up to his eyeballs in red ink. More money, more revenues shared, means bigger deficits and a staggering, soaring debt. In 1992, 14 percent of the federal budget went for interest on the debt; almost $200 billion — that's more than Washington spent to run things for a whole year in 1970.

During the Reagan Administration, the so-called Grace Commission checked to see where the federal government could cut spending and control costs. In addition to some 2,500 suggestions as to where government could cut costs and save hundreds of billions of dollars, the Commission also came to this shattering realization: By the year 1995, every penny of personal income taxes will not be enough to pay the interest on the national debt which is, now, more than $4 trillion. As things are going now, we are increasing that debt by about $1 billion each and every day. That projects to a total of $6.56 trillion by 1995 -- more than the entire industrial output of the United States.

Harry E. Figgie, Jr., CEO of a *Fortune* 500 company, was co-chairman of the Grace Commission. In late 1992, Figgie was driven to write a book, "Bankruptcy 1995: The Coming Collapse of America And How To Stop It". He said he wrote the book because virtually nothing was being done to bring this nation back from the brink of fiscal disaster. He pointed out that today 61 cents out of every dollar collected in federal income taxes goes to pay the interest on the national debt; in 1992, that interest totalled $293 billion, 20 Percent of the federal budget. Here's the kernel of Mr. Figgie's pronouncement, the substance of his conclusions:

In 1995, the United States of America, as we know it today, will cease to exist. That year, the country will have spent itself into a bankruptcy from which there will be no return. What we once called the American

Century will end, literally, with the end of the American way of life — unless you and I act now to pull ourselves and our country back from near certain oblivion.

In 1985 Congress passed the Gramm-Rudman-Hollings Act. It mandated annual reductions in the federal deficits with a target of a balanced budget by 1991 — wasn't that two years sgo? The special interest groups cried "foul"; they wanted Washington to keep on feathering their nests. They wanted all they could get and more.

Remember what Professor Tyler said four hundred years ago? When the people find out they can vote themselves money out of the public treasury, they will always vote for the politician who promises to get them the most.

That's the way it works. Look at this:

U.S. Senator Warren Rudman (NH) was one of the trio who sponsored the Gramm-Rudman-Hollings deficit reduction law. Senator Rudman chose not to seek re-election in 1992. Why? Because, he announced, after 12 years of battling in the Senate for fiscal prudence, he was "frustrated." He predicted that "the 1992 election may be our last chance to head off fiscal disaster." In concert with former Senator Paul Tsongas (MA) he formed a citizens' committee to put public presure on Congress to cut spending.

Surely, he jests! In his final session, Senator Rudman was one of the Big Spenders. He supported such piddling little items as $13.5 billion for the International Monetary Fund (IMF) to bail out the Soviets; another $$87.8 billion for the Veteran's Administration and Housing and Urban Development, $246.5 billion for the federal departments of Labor, Health and Human Services and Education, and another $14.1 billion for Foreign Aid. Senator Rudman was not alone, or even out of the ordinary: Most politicians talk one way and vote another. .As the late Senator Everett Dirksen might say, "A billion here and a billion there and pretty soon you're talking about real money"

David Stockman was budget director during President Reagan's first term. Writing on why he thought the Reagan Revolution failed, he described the anatomy of the bloated federal giant: "All the umbilical cords of dependency still exist because the public wants them and elects politicians who want to preserve them. So, they have to be paid for. That is the unyielding bottom line."[13]

Senator Dennis DeConcini of Arizona who has been active in the nation's budgetary affairs has admitted:

We have gotten into this mess because we have not had the will power
to say "No," when constituents and interest groups have come to us
with requests.

The problem is the money doesn't go on and on as do the requests
... (and) we have tried to fool ourselves and the public by not paying
for the benefits we provide. Instead, we have borrowed money or
expanded the money supply.[14]

One problem has led to another, and the problem now is that
we are left with the granddaddy of all deficits and a shrinking dollar
beside plus rising unemployment, an horrendous federal debt and
entitlement programs no one has the courage to reduce.

Even before Gramm-Rudman-Hollings was passed, the big-
spenders in Washington predicted Congress would find a way around
those restrictions on spending and borrowing. They did. After all,
Gramm-Rudman-Hollings applied to only 42 percent of the total
federal budget; the remaining 58 percent was still to be foot-loose and
fancy-free.

As for a constitutional amendment to prohibit deficits, listen to
former Senator Dan Evans of the state of Washington:

Prohibition didn't keep us from drinking and a balanced budget won't
keep us from spending. A drunk will always find a bottle and a spender
will always find a wallet.[15]

That's your wallet Senator Evans was talking about!

The Fourth Branch of Government

In his introduction to his English translation of The Bible, John
Wycliffe wrote, "This Bible was written for a government of the people,
by the people, and for the people." And, in a republic, the government
is firmly of and by and for the people. The checks and balances work.
The division of powers keeps government in bounds. The line of
authority — the flow of power — runs from the bottom, up.

In a democracy the power flows in reverse — from the top,
down. Demand exceeds duty, rights surpass responsibility, and
freedoms are exchanged for the promises of security and succor.
Somewhere along the line, the people wake up to find they have become
of and by and for the government. Those who are succored will sooner
or later be suckered.

Has that not happened?

In 1929 the ratio was one government employee for every eleven Americans working in the private sector. Today the ratio is one government employee for every four Americans working in private industry. Today there are 18 million persons employed in government at all levels; 3 million civilians are employed by the federal government.

Congress is an example of government's mushroom cloud. In 1970 Congress and its staff and legislative agencies had an operating budget $343 million. Some 20 years later, in 1990, that swelled to an annual take of $2.2 billion. Why? The population, the number of constituents, did not grow like that. Complain to the officeholders and most will tell you the increase was necessary because there are now more laws and more regulations and more services. That's a chicken-and-egg cop-out. All those eggs were laid in Congress — Congress passed that multitude of laws in the first place.

(Not too long ago, the the United States senators built themselves a $137 million office building with sixteen-foot ceilings. That figures. If there are no ceilings on the debt they pileup, why should we expect any limit on the office ceilings they admire? Empire does as empire is!)

What was it those delegates at Independence Hall said about old King George and what he did to upset them back in the 1770s? *"He has erected a multitude of New Offices, and sent hither swarms of Officers to harass our people, and eat out their substance."* That's what they declared. Imagine what those colonials would say today!

The Morgan Guaranty Trust Company once engaged in some fanciful predictions; tongue-in-cheek. Noting in one of its newsletters that the increase in public employment was about twice the growth rate in the total labor force, the bank suggested "In the year 2049 everyone in America will be working for the government." It's a laugh, but it's not a laugh. Today there are more than 83,000 governmental agencies in the United States.

A new branch of government has evolved: *the Government, itself.* Along with the executive, the legislative, and the judicial, we now have the governmental. It is an entity unto itself — no longer is it the servant of the people as much as it is a vehicle for the care and feeding of its own. Out of every dollar that goes to welfare, at least seventy cents sticks to the bureaucrats. Some welfare!

Government is now an empire. *The servant has become the master.* The prophet Samuel warned that would happen. Remember? *"And you will be his servants. And you will cry out in that day because of your king whom you have chosen for yourselves."*

Behold, the Monster!

Consider the dimensions of the federal government leviathan.

The office space it occupies is four times greater than the total office space in the ten largest U.S. cities. In 1989, the total floor area of federally owned office buildings was 2,806 million square feet. Add to that another 254 million square feet of leased office space and you come up with 3,060 million square feet of office space.

It owns more acreage than all the land in the states east of the Mississippi plus Texas. In 1989, the federal government owned 662,158,000 acres of the total acerage of 2,271,343,000 land acres in the U.S. That comes to 29.2 percent ... and, if the Environmental Protection Agency and other federal agencies have their way, the total will increase dramatically during coming years.

It owns 17,000 computers and has a computer work force of 250,000 persons — many of the computers are obsolete and incompatible ... which may actually be a blessing for the citizenry.

It spends twice as much per bed for hospitals and four times as much per bed for nursing homes as do private enterprises.

In 1990 the federal government consumed 23.3 percent of the gross national product (GNP). Add to that the amount consumed by state and local governments and it amounts to 37.3 percent of the GNP.

It collects and spends $8 billion each and every workday — about $1 billion every hour. In 1990, the federal government collected $1,154,596 million — that is $1 trillion-plus!

In 1990 the federal government borrowed $423.5 billion — 56.5 percent of all the money borrowed in the U.S.

And on and on.[16] Want more exciting data? Get yourself a copy of the U.S. Dept. of Commerce *Statistical Abstract of the United States for 1992* and curl up in front of the fireplace. You won't need a sweater -- you'll have your ire to keep you warm.

Years ago when this governmental Godzilla was still an adolescent monster, Senator Paul Douglas of Illinois said there were *three* parties in Washington, D.C.: the Democratic party, the Republican party, *and the Government party,* which represents the agencies, bureaus, departments, and divisions. Senator Douglas asserted that "no pressure group was more persistent and skilled in techniques of getting what it wants."[17]

Civil service employees receive from three to six times the total pension benefits provided to workers in private business.

Congressmen do pretty well themselves; Senator Edward Kennedy has more than $1.5 million of accumulated benefits in his congressional pension fund; former Senator Tim Wirth of Colorado was elected in 1975; when he left in 1992, he had something like $2.456 million in his pension fund. Congressman Bill Anderson of Arkansas started in the House of Representatives in 1969; as of November, 1992, his pension fund totalled $2.9 million. Congresswoman Pat Schroeder, she who sought the Presidency in 1988, her pension fund is upward of $3 million. Nice work if the taxpayers will stand for it. And so far they have.[18]

Private sector workers contribute 33 percent to the total costs of their pension plans, civil service employees contribute only 19 percent — the taxpayers put up the rest.

Nearly two out of every three civil servants retire before the age of sixty-two (the ratio is one in five in the private sector).

Fringe benefits for federal employees cost more than $49 billion a year; $26.7 billion for civilian workers, $22.9 billion for military.

Federal employees take 64 percent more sick leave than employees in the private sector.

On the average, federal employees are paid 11 percent more than workers in private business and industry.

The list goes *on and on*.[19]

The Founding Fathers never dreamed it would turn out that way! They should have known. Empires are like that! But, then, they built a republic — others came along afterward and erected an empire.

The Junking of America

The shift from republic to democracy was subtle. It was cumulative. Sometimes by accident, mostly by design. An avalanche that gathered size and speed and power.

What brought about this junking of the American idea? What permitted it to happen? What permits it to continue today?

Is it a weakening of the individual will? The loss of self-reliance; the abdication of self-government? Is self-governance really too hard, too demanding; have Americans grown too lazy, too soft? People do, indeed, get the government they resemble.

Listen! Once this was the American creed:

I do not choose to be a common man; I choose to be uncommon, if I can. I seek opportunity, not security. I do not wish to be a kept citizen, humbled and dulled by having the state look after me. I want to take the calculated risk; to dream and to build, to fail and to succeed.

I refuse to barter incentive for a dole. I prefer the challenges of life to guaranteed existence; the thrill of fulfillment to the stale calm of utopia. I will not trade freedom for the beneficence or my dignity for a handout. I will never cower before any master or bend to any threat. It is my heritage to stand erect, proud and unafraid and act for myself; to enjoy the benefits of my creation and to face the world boldly and say, "This I have done."

All this is what it means to be an American! .[20]

What ever happened to that soul song? Was that not truly the voice of a past America?

Whatever happened to the uncommon common man? And to his faith?

Have we lost the faith? Replaced it, perhaps, with the "new" faith that goes with the "new" politics and the "new" economics in a "new" world order? Dr. Ivan Bierly, former head of the Volker Fund, suggests that is what has happened:

A new faith has arisen opposite to that which inspired our country's beginnings. It is a faith in man, as man, and in man's reason, as the regulator and the determiner of right and wrong. In biblical terms, man has turned from Christian orientation to anti-Christian, man-oriented, secular leadership. The problem there is: Which "man" is "right"?

In the process of the transition we have kept the "language" of freedom under God but the roots have been severed. We have lost conscious contact with our historical Christian roots. While we have kept the language we fail to realize that we have lost the spirit that those roots require. this is the source of our "tower of Babel" today.

Parenthetically, it is also the reason we find it difficult to understand that the Russian dialectic with respect to freedom is practically the opposite from that on which this nation was founded. Is it any wonder we come out second-best in "detente" situations?[21]

The Pagan View Exhumed

The intolerance of those who put God first did not bring about the change in the Republic. Indolence, perhaps, and excessive tolerance, *but not intolerance.* In fact, it was the intolerance of those who hold to the pagan view that brought the change. Those to whom the State is king and human reason the holy Grail. Those to whom a man's value rests in his contribution to the State and to its institutions. When they slammed the door on the Christian idea of man — that which holds that each individual is created in the image of God and is unique and special — they opened the gates to paganism.

By belittling God they paved the way for Caesar.

> In proportion as Americans let go of faith in the absolute power of God, they accepted the belief in the all powerful state. This is true of peoples, of nations, for their idea of God determines the form of their civil, political, religious and social institutions.[22]

There are those who hold, perhaps with good intent, that if Christ Jesus were on earth today He would be a socialist. *Be not deceived.* Socialism is anti-Christian; it is paganism. It makes the State an idol, a graven image, a golden calf; it puts the state above God. Thus, over-and-above socialism's other sins, it commits a greater sin: it violates God's First Commandment — *"You shall have no other gods before Me."* None!! (Exod.20:3).

God or Caesar?

Who could say in honesty that God's laws are now the laws of the land? That they are the basis of the workings of our institutions? If that were so, how could we account for the rise of Caesar and his hordes, and the growing glorification of the State? Or how could we explain the growing view that the Christian faith is the biggest enemy of good government?

Who could say with honesty that the state schools advance the cause of freedom under God or promote, let alone condone, a bedrock faith in God and an obedience to His laws and standards?

If that were so, how could we account for the ungodly theory of evolution being given pre-eminence and the truth of Creation being cast aside as myth and fable? Or, for the textbooks now adopted by the state which ignore religion as an historical fact and a vital element in American history and contemporary society? Or, for the condoms distributed and made available instead of counselling for abstinence? For self-control? For chastity?

Thus, to the young who sit at the feet of Caesar's instructors, man is but a super-ape, a high-grade animal, an accident of biochemistry. On the basis of such a theory, communism expands its trade routes to the youthful hearts and minds. For if man is a super-ape, his values and his functions are more easily defined, controlled, and charted: to serve the herd, the group, to be a vassal of the State.

Thus, the two tramp hand-in-hand across the Constitution: *Super-ape and Super-state.*

Choose You This Day

A reconstructed faith for the reconstructed man. That is the new offering, the new dialectic. The new world order.

From each according to his ability to each according to his need. Forget the spirit; forget the soul: the mind and the belly — that's what counts.

God is dead. Let Big Brother be your shepherd. He will lead you beside new waters; he will prepare your table; he will care for you.

Come dwell with him; his rod and his staff will succor you.

Listen.

Listen to Whittaker Chambers in *Witness.*

Chambers knew communism from the inside out. He was one. He crossed the line from light to darkness,

But he made it back into the light to warn us:

Communism is what happens when, in the name of Mind, men free themselves from God. Economics is not the central problem of this century. It is a relative problem which can be solved in relative ways.

Faith is the central problem of this age. The crisis of the Western world exists to the degree in which it is indifferent to God. Religion and freedom are indivisible. Without freedom the soul dies. Without the soul there is no justification for freedom.

Faith in God, or faith in man? That is the challenge.[23]

That is, indeed, the challenge facing our nation: Faith in God, or faith in man?

"He who is not with Me is against Me, and he who gathers not with Me scatters abroad"(Matt.12:30).

Choose! *"Choose you this day whom you will serve"* (Josh. 24:15).

As for you and your house? Will you serve The Lord?

CHAPTER THREE

God's Bedrock Laws for Freedom

*But he who looks into the perfect law of liberty
and continues in it, and is not a forgetful
hearer but a doer of the work, this one will be
blessed in what he does* (James 1:25).

Some see freedom as that state or condition in which the individual is released from all restraints, free of compunction or moral standard.

To them, freedom is a no-holds-barred opportunity for the big rip-off and the easy ride. No obligations, no discipline — just freedom to do their thing and let the other fellow take the hindmost.

Such persons are not libertarians; they are libertines. The product of their error is licentiousness.

The apostle Peter makes it clear that we are not to use our freedom *"as a cloak for vice, but as servants of God"*(1 Pet. 2:16).

Paul tells us that *"where the Spirit of the Lord is, there is liberty"* (2 Cor. 3:17). Paul also cautions us to *"not use liberty as an opportunity for the flesh, but through love serve one another"* (Gal.5:13).

Freedom, as Christians know it and Thomas Jefferson recognized, is one of our precious gifts from God.

God who gave us life, gave us liberty. Can the liberties of a nation be secure when we have removed a convictiton that these liberties are a gift from God? 1a

Spiritual and Physical

There are essentially two forms of freedom: *spiritual* freedom and *physical* freedom.

Spiritual freedom is that personal inner state of being which comes through the Spirit of God. It is that internal freedom that breaks the bonds of appetite and greed, that makes us servants of God rather than slaves of self or other men.

"Therefore if the Son makes you free, you shall be free indeed" (John 8:36).

There! That is true freedom! It is the freedom and the faith that overcomes and sustains, even in the meanest state and the severest bondage, as it did the apostles Paul and Peter and so many of our fighting men who were held long months and years in the utter degradation of enemy prison camps.

> The spirit of liberty remembers that not even a sparrow falls to earth unheeded. The spirit of liberty is the spirit of Him, Who, nearly 2,000 years ago, taught mankind that lesson it has never learned, but never has quite forgotten; that there is a kingdom where the least shall be heard and considered side by side with the greatest.[1]

Physical freedom is that outer state of the individual; the external condition that is "the absence of force, the absence of co-ercion, the absence of restraint and constraint."[2] "Sociologically," freedom on the physical plane is "man not playing God, either individually or collectively."[3]

> To every man the right to live, to work, to be himself, and to become whatever thing his manhood and his vision can combine to make him.[4]

In other words, physical freedom is that condition, that situation, in which individuals live harmoniously and do not seek dominion over each other.

The Nature of Freedom

The nature of freedom is personal, private — *individual.* The individual is free — not the group, not society. The term *free society* is a misnomer and a dangerous one. Given full application, a free society can result in the glorification of the system or the State and the diminution of the individual. The proper term, then, is a *society of free men and women.*

Freedom is also *uniqueness.* It means something different to each individual. It means each individual is free to be distinctive, to be himself or herself, to be unique. If a person is simply free to be as others are, or to do as others do, or to conform to a set and predetermined pattern, that person is clearly not free.

Freedom must, by its very nature, *be available to all — equally*. There is no true freedom where there is inequity, no freedom where there is special favor or false barrier. God is no respecter of men; all men are equal in His sight. Thus it follows that freedom can make no distinction, can practice no discrimination except on the grounds of obedience or disobedience to God's laws and Christ's teaching.

"Liberty and Tyranny"

It is important to think long and deep on the nature and properties of freedom. Abraham Lincoln said in his address to the Maryland Sanitary Commission in Baltimore, MD, on April 18, 1864:

> The world has never had a good definition of the word liberty, and the American people, just now, are much in want of one. We all declare for liberty, but in using the same *word* we do not all mean the same *thing*. With some the word liberty may mean for each man to do as he pleases with himself, and the product of his labor; while with others the same word may mean for some men to do as they please with other men, and the product of other men's labor. Here are two, not only different but incompatible things, called by the same name - liberty. And it follows that each of the things is, by the respective parties, called by different and incompatible names - liberty and tyranny.5a

Freedom and Atheism

Maximum individual freedom is generally found in nations where the laws of men are based on and in harmony with the laws of God.

That is not to say that an atheist cannot subscribe to the concept of personal freedom or the practice of liberty; many do. Yet without adherence to the bounds of God's laws, they are devoid of the restrictions that prevent freedom from becoming license.

The late Leonard Read wrote: "Yes, you can be an atheist and, at the same time, believe in freedom. But, a society of active militant atheists will not be a free society."5

Many atheists today, while denying God, adhere to the (letter of the) laws God set forth. But consider this:

Only those who truly comprehend the source and nature of freedom can understand its parameters and its requirements. Without a knowledge of God they cannot recognize the rudimentary purpose for which freedom was ordained — *to give man, through Christ Jesus, the opportunity to regain that eternal life lost by Adam and Eve and thus be regenerated for a life of union in and service for Him.*

The Most Exacting Form of All

Freedom is the most exacting form of civil government. It is, in fact, the most demanding state for man.

Freedom demands -- depends upon -- self-discipline from both the governed and the governors. The foundation of freedom is self-government, and the foundation of self-government is self-discipline, *self-control.*

The very essence of Christianity, as taught by our Savior and our King, is self-discipline.

Christ did not come to earth to force faith or good works upon us; such attributes of a Christian walk must come through voluntary choice. The Christian life unfolds through conscious decision and continuing commitment. "Those who can thus govern themselves have little need for managerial government."[6] (Translation: *The greater one's self-government in union with Christ, the less the individual's need for the restrictions of civil government.)*

No other form of civil government demands as much from each individual as freedom because in no other form of government is the individual so important. In other forms of government, the State or system is the central force; in the nation where freedom under God prevails, the individual is the central figure.

In her landmark two-volume work on *The Christian History of the Constitution of The United States,* historian Verna Hall emphasized:

> Each religion has a form of government, and Christianity astonished the world by establishing self-government. With the landing of the Pilgrims in 1620, Christian self-government be-came the foundation stone of the United States of America.[7]

Rights and Responsibilities

Many people, when thinking of freedom, think of "rights." Freedom is not only a matter of individual rights; it is also a matter of individual responsibilities. In fact, true freedom is a dynamic balance of rights and responsibilities; for each right there is generally a corresponding responsibility. When rights are demanded and responsibilities are denied, self-government is on its way out. *When this essential yoking of rights and responsibilities is understood, it becomes clear that in a society of free individuals each person not only counts but also is accountable.*

Other forms of government are often powered by appetite (either the personal appetite of the despot, the centralized appetite of the State, or the collective appetite of the mob). A government of the free men and women can survive only on the basis of *self-restraint;* it has no longevity if it permits appetite to overrule con- science or greed to violate equity.

In other societies — those fashioned by tyrants or non-elected hierarchies — the individual may find reason to duck responsibility for the errors and the evils and the excesses of civil government. *But, not free men!* In a system of self-government, wherein the governors are elected to represent the people, the individual is responsible for the acts of State — no matter who holds office or who exercises the authority. For the citizen to think otherwise is to deny his responsibilities and to abdicate his power. (For a development of this point, see Chapter Four, "Coercion —By Proxy".)

Civil Laws

Freedom has certain laws.

Such laws are not simply — sometimes not even — the statutes, codes, ordinances, and regulation of social control. Those laws are *civil laws*, extensions of the State derived mainly from the Roman system. Civil laws now, as then, attempt to spell out every detail and cover every situation. Such laws are evident in our lengthy civil codes, which seek to govern virtually every area of our lives and pursuits. Civil laws (and administrative regulations having the effect of laws) give life to the thousands of regulatory bodies, agencies, departments, bureaus, and hordes of officeholders, which seek to control the citizen from the womb to the tomb.

Civil (and criminal) laws, in proper degree and application, are essential to the maintenance of domestic tranquility and personal security (Christians are not anarchists; we are instructed to pay tribute for proper civil government -- Romans 13:6). But we must always be alert; civil laws can become a dangerous weapon. They can be proliferated, misused; their purpose can be twisted, distorted, perverted. Civil laws can be - and upon occasion have been - employed to restrict the very freedoms they were enacted to uphold. In such instances they magnify not liberty but license; they expand the excesses of the State at the expense of individual liberty and general well-being.

"The Laws of Nature"

Another kind of law exists called *common law*. It has its origins in the laws of nature.

George Mason of Virginia, the great Christian statesman who can rightly be called "the author of the Bill of Rights," defined what was meant by the laws of nature:

> The laws of nature are the laws of God, whose authority can be superseded by no power on earth.

Our Founding Fathers called upon these laws when, in 1776, they made their Declaration of Independence to assume "the separate and equal station to which the laws of Nature and Nature's God entitled [them]."

Noah Webster's 1828 American Dictionary of The English Language define the "Law of Nature" as "a rule or conduct arising out of the natural relations of human beings established by the Creator."[8]

Today Webster's takes a different line. It defines natural law as "designating law discernible by *reason* as distinguished from law laid down in codes by state, church, etc."(emphasis added). Thus is Nature's God now denied and man's reason glorified!

"Organized Justice"

In essence, common law had its genesis in the laws of God set before the ancient Hebrews through Moses the lawgiver. Civil, or Roman, law is the external code and control which originated in one of the world's great pagan nations.[9]

If we are to be free — truly free — the spirit of our laws must be in harmony with the spirit of The Lord, and the letter of our laws must be consistent with the letter of God's laws (Deut.11:1). If such is not the case, the laws will violate our persons, our liberty, and those extensions of self — our property and our pursuit of happiness.

The laws of freedom are established to preserve a system or organized justice; their proper purpose and function is to protect the individual against injustice.[10] Most basic laws spell out what man must *not* do to his fellow man (*You shall not kill; You shall not steal*), and what government must *not* do to the governed. Thus, these laws are "negative" in the sense that they are defensive not aggressive. Consider, for example, the Constitution of these United States of America (and the constitutions of most of the sovereign states):

"Congress shall make *no* laws ... The right of the people shall *not* be abridged ... or denied ... or disparaged."

Toward that same end of freedom, most of our basic laws did not tell the individual what he or she must do — decisions were left to individuals with the proviso that the exercise of their freedom would not interfere with the equal freedom of others. Now that has changed. *"There have arisen generations that know not the Lord"* or His requirement of obedience or the wonders of what obedience to Him can produce.

Fundamental Laws of Freedom

Consider these bedrock laws of nature and nature's God to be fundamental laws of freedom. There are others, but count these as basic:

"`*You shall love The Lord your God with all your heart, with all your soul, and with all your mind*'" (Matt.22:37).

That is the Great Commandment: God first, God always. Were we to obey that commandment, we would obey all God's commandments.

"In all your ways acknowledge Him And He shall direct your paths" (Prov. 3:6).

On our own, we go astray; with Christ as our shepherd, we may seek the more excellent way.

"You shall have no other gods before Me" (Exod.20:3).

No other king but Jesus! (Acts 17:7). Christ is Savior -- and King. Lord, and Master!

"For the kingdom is The Lord's And he rules over the nations"(Ps.22:28).

Government is necessary; God ordained it. He established His laws to govern it so that it would be a blessing to the godly and "an avenger to execute wrath on him who practices evil"(Rom.13:4).

"Thy kingdom come. Thy will be done on earth as it is in heaven"(Matt.6:10).

The earth is the Lord's and fullness thereof! We may look toward His hereafter, but we are to live for Him in the here and now. We are to work to advance His kingdom on earth.

"So shall I keep Your law continually, Forever and ever. And I will walk at liberty, For I seek Your precepts"(Ps.119:44,45).

Those are laws concerning the sovereignty of God.

And these are laws concerning the brotherhood of man in Christ Jesus:

You shall love your neighbor as yourself"(Matt.22:39). For the godly Christian, there is no cop-out, no easy ride. We are our brother's keeper; that task is our's, not Caesar's.

`*And as you would that men should do to you, do you do to them likewise'"*(Luke 6:31). This is the balance between rights and responsibilities.

If you love Me, keep My commandments (John 14:15).

Those are the laws which make men free. Those are the laws which put man and his will and his ways and his laws in harmony with the Lord God and His laws.

"But whoso looks into the perfect law of liberty and continues therein, he being not a forgetful hearer but a doer of the work, this shall shall be blessed in his deed" (James 1:25).

If you love God, if you love others as yourself, you will not covet, you will not steal their possessions, you will not bear false witness, you will not injure their person. No murder; no assaults; no undue infringements on the lives of others; no violations of their rights; no trespassing on their freedom.

Freedom! Freedom is in the spirit of the Lord — not only *is* there, but *lives and moves and has its being* there. And, what are the fruits of the spirit?

Love. Joy. Peace. Long-suffering. Gentleness. Goodness. Faith. Meekness. Self-control. (Gal. 5:22,23).

"But seek you first the kingdom of God and His righteousness, and all these things shall be added to you"(Matt. 6:33).

So it is with individuals. So it is with nations.

"Blessed is the nation whose God is The Lord, And the people whom He has chosen as His own inheritance" (Ps. 33:12).

Freedom And Christian Economics

Certain immutable basics should govern freedom-seeking Christians in their economic activities, their stewardship responsibilities. These are the source laws founded upon God's laws and

Christ's teachings (which were always in harmony with His Father's laws). They provide for the application of the Christian ethic, which gives free enterprise its purpose, its power, its rudder, and its boundaries.

"Man shall not live by bread alone, but by every word that proceeds from the mouth of God"(Matt. 4:4).

In today's world, as F. A. Harper wrote, "It seems correct to say that economics pervades the entire problem of liberty."[11]
Since that is so, godly Christians must examine some of the basics of Christian economics — *stewardship*.

Some Christian "Laws" of Economics

These basics should be practiced in concert with God's mandates and Christ's examples of true love and Biblical charity (Bible-directed economic activities make possible material expression of love through charity).

It is vital to keep in mind that all things are His, that all things come from Him, and that we as His stewards are to use what He has entrusted to us to serve Him and to advance His kingdom.

1. *The Law of Dynamic Balance (The Law of Harmony)*. When God created the heavens, the earth, and man, He put everything into perfect balance. Not into some static, stagnant limbo, but into a dynamic balance. There was harmony, life, growth, and abundance.

"Then God saw everything that He had made, and indeed it was *very good"* (Gen.1:31).

It will be so again when the King of kings and Lord of lords returns to establish His kingdom here on earth. Then each man will sit under his fig tree and be secure in his property, unafraid. For Christ will teach us His ways and we will live by His Word. Until that time, we, being His, should seek always to obey His Word and to spread His Word throughout the world — yes, even in the marketplace.

Consider the dynamism and the perfect balance of the Golden Rule. If we obey Christ's instructions and *"do unto others as we would have them do to us"* (see Luke 6:31), we achieve a dynamic balance between our rights and our responsibilities to Him and to others. There is harmony in the give and take of our workaday world. We do not take that which we do not want taken from us; we give as we wish to receive.

It is the dynamic balance of the Golden Rule that gives free individual enterprise the thrust and equilibrium to create, to produce, and to achieve yet keeps it from becoming an unrestricted hunting license. Properly maintained, that balance enables competitive enterprise of freemen to out-produce other systems while avoiding the excesses of greed, control, and coercion, whether it be by multinational conglomerates, centralized government, or labor monopoly.

A dynamic balance assures the workman a fair (honest) wage, the entrepreneur a fair profit, the investor a fair return on his capital, and the consumer a fair price in the market place.

When that balance is upset — when one facet of the relationship takes or receives more than it should take or receive — the dynamic balance is destroyed and stagnation takes over. Cooperation dissolves into dissension; harmony breaks down into discord; decay replaces growth; loss wipes out profits; job security fades into unemployment; and sufficiency becomes shortage.

The opposite of dynamic balance is *distortion* — greed, ruthlessness, monopoly, and coercive violence. The headstrong, self-centered desire to seize special privileges at the cost of others has deprived the human race of untold treasures because of uncreated wealth.

Extreme distortion in our economic relationships often takes the form of exploitation, strikes, or wars; these oppress countless individuals and depress man's material welfare.

Consider a stereophonic tape player: proper adjustment between the components creates a perfect, dynamic balance between the speakers. The result is brilliant harmony and beautiful music. But turn the controls so that one set of speakers overpowers the other. What happens? The balance is destroyed; the dynamism is gone. One speaker prevails to the detriment of each of the others and to the whole. Music degenerates into noise; the full spectrum of harmony is lost.

Our economic affairs are much the same. Let one party take more than it gives, and distortion results. The dynamic balance is gone; the totality of harmonious production is destroyed; negative forces prevail. Everyone involved is the loser.

2. *The Law of Productivity*. The law of productivity is always at work as is the law of gravity. Neither has been repealed!

If we work and produce, we have; if we do not work and do not produce, we do not have. Or, we turn to taking from those who do produce. *"He who is slothful in his work is a brother to him who is a great destroyer"*(Prov. 18;9).

If no one works, if no one produces, there is nothing for anyone. If we produce at marginal levels because of indolence, or undue interference, or controls, or work restrictions, or lack of capital and tools, productivity diminishes and there is less to go around.

(Consider Christ's parable of the talents, Matt. 25:15-28: we are to do the very best we can for Him with what He has placed in our trust.)

The Law of Productivity functions best where individual freedom prevails. When men and women are free to use their talents and their energies to create, to increase and employ their skills, they are able to provide more goods and services for the greatest number of individuals at the lowest possible prices.

Everything man produces involves three basic elements: natural resources, human energies, and tools. The fundamental formula for man's productive capacity is $MMW = NR + HExT$:

> *Man's Material Welfare equals Natural Resources plus Human Energy multiplied by the Tools at his disposal.*

Natural resources are gifts from the Creator. There is much we can do — much we as Christians should do — to conserve the natural resources God has provided. As His stewards, we are responsible to develop and use these natural resources wisely and to replenish them whenever possible. But we cannot create natural resources; thus, in a very real sense, they are limited.

Human energy is also one of God's gifts to man. Energy is one of His attributes with which He has endowed His creation. Each individual is blessed with certain mental and physical energies. As good and faithful stewards, we are responsible to develop these to their maximum. But, human energies are also limited.

Tool's are man's creation. They are extensions of himself that enable him to increase his potential and his productivity. (Wheels and wings are extensions of man's limbs; computers are extensions of his mind; hammers, cameras, telephones, surgical instruments, drill presses are extensions of his hands and fingers, his sight, his hearing, his touch, his speech.) Tools enable man to multiply the effectiveness of his energies.

Tools are acquired (made possible) through the savings and investments of individuals. Such savings and investments occur most readily when law (government) protects the individual's right to control his property and his right to use that property as he wishes provided he does not interfere with the legitimate rights of others to do the same with their tools.

The more owners of tools (the means of production), the greater the total production and the greater the choice of products for the greatest number of people. When the State, or any central power, controls (confiscates) savings and investments and controls the means and types of production, total productivity declines and the individual is robbed of his freedom of choice. Nations under communist rule are prime example of such tyranny.

3. *The Law of Distribution.* We cannot distribute more than we produce; we cannot give what we do not have; we have no right to distribute (give away) what we do not own. That is the law of distribution. Translated into the vernacular, that reads: *Before we can sell we must produce; before we can give we must earn; before we can teach we must learn.* Is it possible to produce enough to meet man's needs? Yes:

> Then God blessed them, and God said to them, "Be fruitful and multiply; fill the earth and subdue it; have dominion over the fish of the sea, over the birds of the air, and over every living thing that moves on the earth"
> (Gen. 1:28).

That is God's dominion charter, His cultural mandate, to man. God, The Creator, did not create a barren world or an unproductive man. Fallow fields and empty mines and starving people have been brought about by the sinful, depraved nature of man. Ample production to meet the needs of society is achieved through the efforts of free and industrious people acting as God's good and faithful stewards.

Producing more than man wants is virtually impossible. What we term overproduction (surplus) is actually unbalanced production: too much of one commodity. What we call under-production (shortage) is also a sign of unbalanced production. If the dynamics of supply and demand are permitted to prevail, overproduction will be adjusted and the surplus will be consumed or converted. In the same manner, in a free market, underproduction will be corrected and the shortage will be alleviated. (Few will continue to produce what is already overproduced; many will be quick to produce what is in great demand but in short supply.)

Decisions of production and distribution are best made in the marketplace by the consumers. The consumer is best qualified to know what he needs and what he can afford to pay. Permitting consumers to apply the law of distribution is one application of individual freedom. Permitting government (the worst of all monopolies) to make such decisions through centralized controls violates personal freedom. It also leads to surplus on the one extreme or shortage on the other; it promotes waste, inefficiency, increased costs, and higher prices.

Quantities of goods remaining undistributed (unsold) is not necessarily due to a lack of money. *Production generates pur-chasing power.* The money paid for production (salaries, wages, fees for services, materials, and equipment) flows into the marketplace for purchases, savings, or investments. The lack of sales indicates products are unsatisfactory (not acceptable to or wanted by the consumer) because of price, quality, need, or desire.

There are two ways to move unsold goods. The natural way is to lower the price until a market is created — the consumer cannot resist the bargain. The unnatural method is to freeze the price (and the wages and the costs involved in production) and to pump fake money into people's pockets, prodding them to buy (the impression of cheap money creates the illusion of cheap merchandise). The latter way is a controlled and ersatz economy. In the long run, the consumer pays much more through inflation, taxation, and the loss of liberty. (See Chapters Eight and Eleven, "Controlled People and Uncontrolled government" and "Inflation Is a Sneak Thief!")

4. The Law of Compensation. This may be termed *the law of returns* or *the law of sowing and reaping.*

"Do not be deceived, God is not mocked; for whatever a man sows, that he will also reap" (Gal. 6:8)

"Give, and it will be given to you: good measure, pressed down, shaken together, and running over ... with the same measure that you use, it will be measured back to you" (Luke 6:38).

Give refers not only to acts of love and charity but also to a full day's work for a full day's pay. *Give:* earning full value for dollars received for the products or services we sell.

What is the proper basis for deciding what share those in-volved in the production of the goods or the performance of the service shall receive? There are two ways to answer that question:

. first, in terms of *free market economics;*
. second in terms of *Christian stewardship.*

Those two answers should be completely compatible (if they are not, then someone is bending or breaking the rules).

First, the answer in terms of *free market economics.*

In a regimented society (with a controlled or managed market), who gets what is decided by the State or sub-State or by the power sources which control the State. The masters of such unfree (enslaved) people decide their lot. The government acts as controller rather than as an impartial agent defending the citizens from those who would do them harm or injustice. In such a society, the individual exists between a floor and a ceiling impressed by the State. There is little, if any, room to grow; no latitude for choice, no freedom to accept or reject or withdraw.

In a society of free men and women, the laws of nature prevail to insure that each party has a free choice and receives a proper (fair) share. What is that fair share? The impartial and equitable laws of the free market will determine what is fair as long as they are permitted to operate. That means, among other things, no restrictions that prevent the employee and the employer from deciding between themselves an equitable wage, and an acceptable working environment; no restrictions that prevent the employer from designing, producing, and pricing his goods or services; no restrictions that restrain or constrain the consumer in his free choice of purchases (the expenditure of his personal property).

All of that is essential to the workings and justice of the free market — the best system for achieving and maintaining economic justice and providing the maximum amount of goods and services for the greatest number of people. Those who deny the efficacy of any or all of those requirements imply that all employees are stupid, greedy, or weak-kneed; that all employers are stupid, greedy, or incompetent; and that all consumers are stupid or without recourse. The day-to-day, years-long record of what free men and women can accomplish through the dynamics of the free market disproves such insinuations.

Now, the answer of the fair (proper) share in terms of *Christian stewardship (the Christian economic ethic).*

. Practice Christ's Golden Rule: it will produce the equilibrium of equity in our economic dealings.

. Obey the Biblical rules for proper employee-employer relations as set forth by Paul in Colossians 3:23-4:1.

And whatever you do, do it heartily, as to the Lord and not to men, knowing that from the Lord you will receive the reward of the inheritance;

for you serve the Lord Christ. But he who does wrong will be repaid for the wrong which he has done, and there is no partiality (no matter what a person's position may be — employe or employer) (Col. 3:23-25).

Employers, for your part, deal with your workmen justly and fairly, knowing you also have a Master in heaven. Consider this wisdom from God's word:

There are many members, yet one body. And the eye cannot say to the hand, "I have no need of you"; nor again the head to the feet, "I have no need of you" ... If one member suffers, all the members suffer with it (1 Cor. 12:20-26).

Together as one. Together in Christ, one body working for Him! Would that not work wonders in this tired old world? If men and women would work together in The Lord God and in obedience to His laws, harmony, and dynamic balance, they could bring peace, well-being, and true prosperity to the nation.

Is that not our task? Our witness? To be an example!

5. *The Law of Private Property.* Implicit in God's commandments (Exod. 20:15,17) is the right of the individual to own personal property — the right to have and to hold and to use it for himself and his purposes as long as he does not infringe upon the equal rights of his fellow man. What he does with his property, whether or not he employs it to serve the Lord and to glorify His name, will be weighed and measured in due time (Matt. 25:31-46).

In Acts 4:31-37, we read how the members of Christ's church in Jerusalem voluntarily held all property in common and shared with each other. Some would have us believe that such voluntary pooling of possessions, born of Christian love, was an endorsement of socialism. That is not so. There is nothing voluntary about socialism: it enforces the sovereignty of the State above the sovereignty of God and denies the freedom of the individual.

In fact, it was upon this occasion that the apostle Peter underscored the right of private property. Ananias and his wife Sapphira, members of the church, sold some property. They kept part of the proceeds and gave the balance to the church with the inference that it was the whole amount. Now listen to what Peter said:

But Peter said, Ananias why has satan filled your heart to lie to the Holy Ghost and keep back *part* of the price of the land for yourself? While it remained, was it not your own? And after it was sold, was it not in your own control? Why have you conceived this thing in your heart? You have not lied to men but to God. And Ananias hearing those words fell down and gave up the ghost. (Acts 5:3,4).

Ananias's sin (and Sapphira's too, for she also lied) was not in owning and controlling the disposition of the property but in lying to God.

Hannah, the prophet Samuel's mother, reminds us that God is the source of all wealth, that He decides to whom it will be distributed. If that is true, and it is, then who is Caesar or even a majority by vote to second-guess God and overrule His decisions and redistribute His wealth?

Christ had the opportunity to play socialist, to take from one and give to another: Remember? Luke told us about it:

> Then one from the crowd said to Him, "Teacher, tell my brother to divide the inheritance with me." But He said to him, "Man, who made Me a judge or an arbitrator over you?" And He said to them, "Take heed and beware of covetousness, for one's life does not consist in the abundance of the things he possesses. (Luke 12:13-14)

The legal recognition and protection of each individual's right to acquire and hold property is essential to law and order; it is one of the necessities of freedom. Property, in a temporal sense, is an extension of self. To destroy or control a man's right to own and use his own property is to diminish the individual and his God-given right.

In diminishing the individual, we diminish freedom for all and injure society. When the individual is not free to grow to his potential, society is not able to improve and grow to its maximum. Thus, both the individual and society suffer.

Consider how society has benefitted because men have been free to search for and to discover God's laws of science, to harness those laws, to earn, own and invest by those laws. Look at the by-products of such freedom: electricity for heat, light, and power, automobiles, antibiotics, frozen foods, dried foods, canned foods, petrochemicals, movable type and the printed word, radio television, telephones. The list is endless, as is the list of jobs and benefits created and the amount of support created (taxes) for public services. All of this has ultimately flowed through the release of such personal ingenuity and private investment for research and development, manufacture and distribution of the fruits of private ownership of property.

Laws that confiscate, restrict unduly, or aggressively control — or that permit others to infringe upon or control — the free use, exchange, sale, purchase, or development of private property (including conscience, abilities, talents, and tools) violate the individual. They destroy untold benefits and opportunities for countless individuals throughout God's world. He will not hold guiltless those who engage in such destructive pursuits that make life more difficult for so many.

6. *The Law of Uniqueness.* Sometimes called the law of (infinite) variation, this law underscores the wonders of God's world.

Each individual is equal in the sight of God, the creator. But each person is unique, distinct, special. No two persons are equal in all respects. There is an enormous difference in the talents, desires, abilities, motivations, and physical characteristics of each individual. Praise God! What a dull place this would be if we were all stamped from the same mold. Nothing about a clone is distinct, interesting, or attractive.

The magic of the society of free men and women permits each individual to be different and provides each individual the opportunity to develop his or her uniqueness.

The United States, because of its Christian origins and foundation, was the first nation in history to put this magic to work by releasing it! By defending and protecting the right of every individual to fly as high as his vision and his abilities could take him.

That is the promise and the secret of America under God.

When God made man in His image, He endowed him with a free will and sent him forth as a free agent. He did not create robots on a string. Thus, we know that we are in harmony with God's purpose and God's laws when we defend and protect man's freedom to be what he wants to be; his accountability is, in the final reckoning, to God. Glory to God for His wisdom: the freedom of uniqueness provides us with a range of choices and decisions, an infinite variety of products and opportunities not to covet or worship but to use as His fruitful stewards, for His glory.

There is also a scientific explanation for the superior economic progress of freemen (another one of God's laws of science). It is called the results of *divergent phenomena:* the progress generated when two or more things are combined without any prior knowledge of what will happen. Also termed "the alchemy of cooperative individuals," it is a synergistic relationship. Each distinct and independent part contributes to the whole and the sum total is greater than the combined contributions of all the parts involved

Essential to the recognition of individual uniqueness is the recognition of the proper role of incentive and reward. He who works harder, achieves more, and contributes more, is entitled to receive more. What he does with what he receives is up to him.

Some would deny God's law of uniqueness — if they could! But they do attempt to enforce sameness; they attempt to legislate equality of reward for inequality of work. This is counterproductive, leading to equal performance at the lowest level. When that happens, everyone suffers. The first attempts at communal living by early Christians (and the communism forced on the Pilgrims by the underwriters during their first years in America) ended in utter failure and general misery. Results are always disastrous when men attempt to deny God's law — including His laws of uniqueness and individual freedom.

7. *The Law of Predictable (Sound) Money.* Money is a commodity, a medium of exchange. Regardless of the form or shape it takes — whether it be beads, chickens, pineapples, dollar bills, or precious metal — money is *a medium of exchange.*

Money is our receipt for selling something (services or products). We spend that receipt at a later time when we purchase someone else's products or service.

That money is best which does not lose its value between the time we receive it and the time we spend it. Money that depreciates in value diminishes the worth of the individual, his energies and his abilities. Money that depreciates steals from the worker, the consumer, and the investor. (However, it "benefits" government. When the value of the dollar declines, the wage-earner must be paid more money, pushing him into a higher tax bracket and increasing Caesar's take.) Such money is an immoral medium of exchange; it plunders the fruits of the individual's labor and/or savings.

The monetary system that most nearly achieves the ideal of predictable money is the *gold standard.*

Under that system, gold is given a fixed value, and the amount of money issued is tied directly to the amount of gold in hand or in circulation. Under the gold standard, the holder of money (receipts backed by gold) knows that his holdings have a constant (predictable) value and that no one will steal part of his earnings between the time he is paid and the time he spends his money. Most politicians and bureaucrats and speculators/manipulators detest the gold standard.

They fight against it because it enforces a monetary discipline that curbs their appetites and clips their wings. But the gold standard protects the freeman from monetary exploitation; it guards him against the thievery of inflation.

Inflation is the cruelest tax of all: it is deceptive. It confiscates the *value* of your money while leaving the money in your pocket. The actual value (the purchasing power) of your money is no longer predictable. Your worth (the worth of your labor and talents) is subject to the whims of those who rewrite the value of those receipts (paper money) you receive from the sale of your goods and services.

Inflation is not possible when the value of the money is protected and assured. Conversely, it is impossible to have predictable money when inflation occurs.

Rising prices and wages and costs are not the cause of inflation; they are the consequences. Inflation is an increase in the money supply (currency and credit). Only government can cause inflation.

Government policies which permit or encourage an increase in the money supply are the root cause of inflation. Thus, government is the perpetrator of inflation

. when it *prints money that is not backed by gold (that is fiat or fake money, which has no true backing); and*
. when it *permits banks and lending institutions to "create" money by loaning what they do no have on deposit.*

Created (fake) money reduces the purchasing power of all money in circulation; that loss in purchasing power is one measure of the tax of inflation.

Inflation is an economic cancer; it is deadly; it ravages the entire economic and social body of a nation. Scientists search for a cure for cancer in the human body. We already have the cure for cancer of the economic body. God gives us the answer in His written word:

You shall not steal, nor deal falsely, nor lie to one another ... You shall do no injustice in judgement, in measurement of length, weight, or volume. You shall have just balances, just weights, a just ephah, and a just hin: I am The Lord your God'" (Lev. 19: 11,35-36).

The prophet Amos took the civil authorities to task for *"making the ephah small and the shekel large, Falsifying the balances by deceit"* (Amos 8:5).

If we are to obey the Biblical laws concerning money (the medium of exchange), we will

- . halt the increase of fake money and ersatz credit;
- . return to the gold standard;
- . reduce government spending to those functions which are constitutionally provided for;
- . balance the federal budget; and
- . prohibit deficit spending.

(For a more detailed examination of the cause, consequence, and cure of inflation, see Chapter Eleven, "Inflation Is a Sneak Thief!")

CHAPTER FOUR

Coercion — by Proxy

*"Therefore, all things whatsoever you would
that men should do to you,
do you even so to them:
for this is the law and the prophets."*
(Matt. 7:12).

Christians, especially, should know that the use of force or
violence is a no-no — something to be condoned or employed only as
a last resort to protect their families, their selves, and sometimes their
physical property.

Christ, our Savior and our King, commanded us to love one
another. Paul instructed us that love is the fulfillment of the law.
That's true love we're talking about — not some maudlin, squishy, of-
the-moment, needlepointed passion, but deep-down love that moves
us to do to others as we would have them do to us (or, not do to others
what we would not want them to do to us).[1]

*How is it, then, that every day we engage in coercion? That every
day we force others to act against their will and violate their lives and
their liberty?*

Sic Semper - By Proxy!

What's that? You say you do not do such things? That you do
not resort to coercion or violence against your fellow man? Well, take
a good look at what you are doing every day. Consider these acts of
coercion.

Millions of Americans are forced each day to subsidize govern-
ment-financed murder — *abortion* — even though that violates their
religious beliefs and moral convictions.

Millions upon millions of Americans are coerced into paying for
public school materials (books, films, reading aids, television programs)
which offend their sense of decency and their religious faith and their
patriotism.

71

Millions of American working people are forced to join labor unions in order to acquire or to keep their jobs.

Hundreds of thousands of employers have lost their right to hire and fire their own employees or set their own standards, and many employers have lost the right to go out of business when they choose.

Young people are kept out of jobs and many are prevented from earning the money for their education because minimum wage laws shut them out of the job market.

Businessmen in every state and every community are daily coerced into serving, without fee or free will, as government bookkeepers, accountants, and file clerks.

There's more!

Under the cover of "zoning laws," pastors and lay-leaders are prohibited from holding Bible classes in their homes.

In the name of "education," children are torn from the arms of their Christian parents, taken out of their Bible-based homeschools, and placed in foster homes.

In the name of "the law," church services are invaded, pastors are carried bodily out of the sanctuary, and churches are padlocked.

In a twisted interpretation of the First Amendment, some school authorities refuse students the right to hold Bible classes on school property before or after school hours (while all sorts and types of other extracurricular meetings have "equal access" to school facilities despite the court's findings that Christian students have an equal right to "equal access").

In the name of "art" and "culture," taxpayers are coerced into subsidizing theaters, painters, orchestras, and dance groups (some of which reek with blasphemy and obscene language and engage in filthy performances and unnatural pursuits).[2]

In the name of "equality" and "balance," millions of youngsters of all colors and creeds and family backgrounds are coerced into wayward buses which haul them to schools outside their local neighborhoods and far from their parents.

In the name of "social security," millions of young couples are taxed to the point they find it virtually impossible to save enough to buy a home or to make a start toward a nest egg.

In the name of providing "public service," hundreds of thousands of our elderly are driven from their homes through arbitrary and ever-rising property assessments and taxes.

In the name of "spread-the-work," millions of Americans, thousands of employers, and hundreds of thousands of unemployed are coerced into subsidizing featherbedding, deadheading, and other wasteful make-work practices.

In the name of "fair trade," citizens are forced to forego the benefits and energies of the free and open market.

This list could go on - and it does. It grows day after day.

How Does This Come to Be?

You may object to such coercion. You may insist that you have given government no such proxy for preying on the lives of other individuals, let alone your own. You may even stoutly proclaim your belief that every individual should be free to "do his own thing" as long as he does not interfere with any other individual's right to freedom.

Well, then, if citizens never vote their proxies for such governmental excesses, how do these things come to pass?

They come to pass when citizens refuse to consider all the consequences of their proxied actions. They come to pass

- when appetite is greater than conscience, when apathy is stronger than conviction,
- when convenience or comfort overrides *"You shall not covet"* (Exod. 20:17) and ignores *"You shall not steal"* (Exod. 20:15) and shrugs off *"Do unto others as you would have them do unto you"* (Matt. 7:12).
- They come to pass when government is misused to cater to pressure groups and special-interest blocs rather than to defend the rights of all the people.
- They come to pass because we fail to work for and support candidates who are committed to the cause of freedom.
- They come to pass because we do not hold those candidates to task after they have been elected.

Remember? In a society wherein the people hold the power of election and recall over their representatives in government, the people are as responsible as the representatives. In our acquiescence by silence, we become culpable. We do indeed get the government we resemble.

Liberty Vs. Coercion

There are always those who will be quick to justify collectivized coercion; coercion by proxy. They can find one thousand and one excuses to defend such use of force. Yet not all their arguments are equal to the weight of the one fundamental reason to oppose such coercion:

the violation of individual liberty.

Generally, but not always, the defenders of coercion are those who benefit the most: the recipient of the subsidy, the beneficiary of the taxpayers' funds, the person who is pushed to the front of the line, the businessman who profits from government's favors while preaching "free enterprise".

And when their spoils are challenged, they are quick to respond: "You just don't want government to do anything. You must be against government!" "You're selfish!" "You're a far-right nut!"

Not so! Such accusations are unwarranted. It is the misuse of government, the shredding of the Constitution, the improper expenditure of the taxpayer's money, the illicit application of power — that is the issue.

Government is necessary; it need not be evil. As F. A. Harper wrote, "For liberty to be at its maximum, there must be some government."[3]

For Mutual Protection

We, the people, ordain and establish and perpetuate government and "loan" it certain powers to provide for the common defense, to insure domestic tranquility, and to achieve a general well-being (a society of law and order). Such loans are our voluntary actions, freely taken to secure the blessing of liberty. Since the powers reside in government by the consent of the governed in return for specific services enunciated in the Constitution, there is no coercion involved. We act in concert for mutual and equal benefit; *to have government be our servant.*

The apostle Paul assures us that *"rulers are not a terror to good works, but to evil"*(Rom 13:3). The apostle Peter advises us that the proper function of government is *"for the punishment of evildoers and for the praise of those who do good"* (1Pet 2:14). In other words, to protect the law-abiding from the law-breaker.

Godly Christians support good government. We recognize our obligation to uphold the civil authorities and to pray for them that they may exercise wisdom and equity in the fulfillment of their duties. Government, however, has an obligation to us. It must stay within the bounds we have established; it must not abuse the powers we have loaned it.

Our Constitution makes some 80 grants of power to the federal government and establishes 115 prohibitions ("Thou shalt nots") against it. It gives Congress 20 grants of power and places it under 70 restraints.[4] And "the powers not specifically delegated to the United States, not specifically prohibited to it by the States, are reserved to the States respectively, *or to the people*".[5]

To Protect and Defend

Thanks to our God-directed Founding Fathers,[6] the powers and functions of government are (at least, were) severely restricted and essentially defensive: they were to protect and defend the individual — his life, liberty and property — from those who might engage in violence, including the government itself.

In 1850, French economist and statesman Frederic Bastiat wrote "The Law," a truly historic pamphlet. Consider his words:

Life, faculties, production — in other words, individuality, liberty, property ... in spite of the cunning of artful political leaders, these three gifts from God precede all human legislation and are superior to it.

Life, Liberty, and property, do not exist because men have made laws. On the contrary, it is the fact that life, liberty, and property existed beforehand that caused men to make laws in the first place.

What, then, is law [government]? It is the collective organization of the individual's [God-given] right to lawful defense.[7]

Consider the essence of Bastiat's contention:
• Each person has (from God) the right to defend his person, his liberty, and his property.
• It therefore follows that men have the right to organize and support a common force (government) to defend those rights in equal measure for all men.

Limited Government

Leonard Read in "Meditations on Freedom" drew a line between the good and evil in government.

Governments — assuming a proper limitation of their activities — are necessary and not evil. Their evil begins when they step out of

When does government step out of bounds? When does government cease to be good? When does it begin to practice evil?

To paraphrase Bastiat, since no man has the right to force his will upon another man (or to act aggressively against that person's life, liberty, or property) no man or group of men (or government) can lawfully employ such coercion against other men.

These are the bounds, the fences, that contain government in a society of free individuals. Let's go over them again.

By mutual consent we may assign (or loan) government certain of those God-given rights (powers) which we possess. Thus, government becomes an extension of ourselves.

But we cannot give to other men or to government rights that we as individuals do not possess -- any more than we can give property we do not own to someone else.

We may not do that. Not even by common consent; not even by majority vote. To violate another individual's unalienable (God-given) rights via the ballot box is really not much different than violating him with a fist or a gun; it simply legalizes the law of the jungle.

And consider this: To enforce the violence implicit in the suggestion that "might makes right" is to deny God's commandments and God's laws.

So government is evil when it
  • ceases to be a defensive instrument and becomes a coercive
        destructive force;
  • engages in violence against the peaceful;
  • restricts the liberty of the law-abiding;
  • confiscates a citizen's property for its own or
        someone else's profit

When government engages in such acts, it is evil. It ceases to be in harmony with God's purpose and God's law and God's judgments. *"You shall not covet"* is swept aside; *"You shall not steal"* is ignored; and Christ's Golden Rule is revised to read, *"Do unto others before they do unto you — and if you can't do it yourself, get the government to do it for you."*

The Roots of Coercion

Coercion most often finds its roots in greed and selfishness, in looking for shortcuts to get what is wanted without working for it and earning it. Sometimes coercion takes the path of "getting a law passed" to give one industry an edge over its competition; what cannot be achieved through brains, initiative, energy and skill is acquired by "using" the law. Sometimes such legalized coercion is employed to avoid the disciplines of the free market for labor or for product. When businesses or unions demand such rights, which are not government's to give, they are no different from the able-bodied individual who demands welfare or a government "entitlement" as a "right".

Legalized coercion is not always generated by greed or selfishness. Sometimes it is motivated by good intentions — by a desire to protect the individual from his own stupidities. (In such instances it is generally the "other fellow" who is considered stupid.) Social Security is an example of good intention. It was spawned on the argument that the average American did not have enough foresight or self-discipline to save for a rainy day or for retirement. Thus, legalized coercion enforced the good intention of helping Joe Bagadonuts put something aside for his old age. Individual decision (personal choice) was shoved aside in favor of coercion — all under the banner of good intention. Thus, another road to you-know-where was mapped out, paved and steamrollered.

Sometimes someone's desire to "improve our culture" — to bring us the "finer" things in life generates legalized coercion.

The millions upon millions of taxpayer dollars spent each year on the National Endowment of the Arts (and the millions more coerced through matching funds at the state and local levels) is an example. The proponents of such "improvement societies" assume that the average person will not, of his own accord, spend enough to keep the opera or the ballet or the art gallery in business. Instead, they complain, he spends his money on such foolishness as fishing tackle, bowling balls, and hot dogs at the ball park — or contributions to his church. Thus, he must be "educated" (that is, coerced through mandatory taxation) to support the arts and culture because such finer things are "good" for society. Art can be uplifting but it should not be coercive. There is no need for coercive utopians in a society of free people.

How to Recognize Coercion

If we were to witness one man physically (violently) forcing another individual to act against his will, we would recognize that as an obvious and direct use of coercion; we would consider the act immoral and illegal. Hopefully, we would come to the aid of the victim and hopefully we would demand that the lawbreaker be punished.

Legalized coercion is not always so obvious. Often it is cloaked in the folds of the law. Yet, the violence is there and the perpetrator is seldom held accountable or punished. Usually, we rise to object and to demand justice only when legalized coercion is employed against us. Nonetheless, "It is important to remember that government interference always means violent action or the threat of such action."[9]

How does one recognize the signs of legalized coercion? How does an individual who does not want done to others in his name what he would not want done to himself detect subtle coercion and compulsion on the part of Caesar?

Try this yardstick for size:

1. Any law or government action which forces a peaceful individual to act against his will or his best legitimate interests is coercive. It employs coercion.

2. Any law or government action which restricts an individual in his peaceful pursuits and free choice is coercive.

3. Any law or government action which takes from one individual that which rightfully belongs to him (confiscates his property) and gives it to someone else who has no proper claim to it is coercive. It is coercion.

4. Any law or government action which does on behalf of an individual that which he does not have the right to do on his own or for himself is coercion — legalized but still coercion.

"Legalized Plunder"

An individual can acquire an income in basically two ways:

1. By applying himself (his energies, his talents, his capital) to provide a service to others or change the form, condition and location of a natural resource into a product of value to himself or others. Thus he acquires property — either goods, or money (a medium of exchange which he may use to purchase the necessities or even the luxuries of life)

2. By seizing (stealing) what belongs to another individual.

Ever since Adam disobeyed God and was expelled from the Garden of Eden, man has been required to earn his bread by the sweat of his brow (Gen. 3:19). And, ever since then, men have been looking for shortcuts to get around the thorns and thistles — to find ways to get what they need or want without working for it or obtaining it with a minimum of labor. Some, through ingenuity, have harnessed the energies of nature (the sun, wind, water) to expand their own energies and thus ease their work. Others have discovered or invented or purchased machines and systems to amplify their efforts and multiply their productive capacities.

And some just steal, rob, or embezzle or plunder. Plunder is often the purpose of coercion. There are two types of plunder: illegal, and legalized. It is not difficult to recognize illegal plunder.

Suppose a crook walks into a store and forces the owner to hand over the money in the cash register. Or suppose he robs a bank and walks off with the cash people had there on deposit. That is illegal plunder; it is punishable by law. If caught, the thief goes to jail.

But suppose someone knocks at your door, or walks into your place of business, and compels you to hand over a certain sum of money by threat or by force (fine or imprisonment). Perhaps the individual walks into your store and forces you to give him all or part of the money you were planning to use to buy more merchandise or new equipment or to build an addition to your shop. That is also plunder, but it is legal. No, "legal" is not quite the correct word; make it "legalized." There's a difference.

Why "legalized"? Because the fellow is an agent of government. He is acting for you and me by proxy. You and I, through our elected representatives and their unelected legions, have empowered that agent to confiscate that citizens' property. It's called taxation.

Take another example of legalized plunder — one more difficult to detect.

Suppose you manage to save some money over a period of time. Let's say you save one thousand dollars to buy something the family needs or you want. You go to the store to make the purchase and the clerk informs you that what you want to buy no longer costs one thousand dollars. The price is now fifteen hundred dollars. You are five hundred dollars short. Why? Because your dollars are no longer worth what they once were. While you were saving them, government was spending them; it spent about one-third of the value of your dollars. That's inflation. And that also is legalized plunder.

Misuse of "The Law"

Such legalized plunder is not always recognized and is often promoted. Tariffs, subsidies, progressive taxation, minimum wages, deficit spending, guaranteed jobs, guaranteed profits and wages, wage and price controls, the "right" to welfare — these are a few examples of legalized plunder.

They are not prohibited by law; in fact, they are sanctioned by law — the laws which we (you and I) enacted by proxy. The actual perpetrators of such plunder are not punished; they are protected. Usually they are elected and re-elected to office or kept on the bench. Thus, the law ceases to defend the citizen or to uphold justice; it becomes a system for the care and feeding of Caesar and his nephews and cousins through organized injustice. Some might see it as organized crime.

Not All Taxation Is Plunder

Are all taxes legalized plunder? No!

We are instructed to *"render unto Caesar that which is Caesar's"* (Matt. 22:21). Jesus instructs us to pay tribute (taxes) for the support of godly government. The money required to enable government to perform certain necessary and legitimate functions (as established with the consent of the governed) is not plunder. It is a voluntary assessment, a commitment willingly made to contribute a certain part of our property to support the proper and Constitutional, defensive activities of the law (government).

The plunder begins when government takes powers and functions never given to it by the people; when it acts without the consent of the governed; when it takes from one individual and gives to another; when it wastes the taxpayer's money through mismanagement or slothfulness.

Nothing in the Constitution empowers government to redistribute wealth. That is stealing. It is the misuse of the power to tax, and that, indeed, is legalized plunder — unconstitutional, but "legal" in the eyes of the officeholder.

"Predatory Practices"

The Chinese scholar, Chang Hsin-hai, in "The Moral Basis of World Peace," asserted that this disease of our society stems from a double standard of morals. He said that the root of our troubles, both national and international, lies in the acceptance of moral standards of government totally different from those accepted and demonstrated as necessary for a good society so far as individual conduct is concerned. At the root of the double standard of moral conduct, to which Chang

Hsin-hai referred, is the accepted belief that many forms of predatory practices, when conducted under the name of government, are honorable acts. On that premise has been built a cumulative encroachment on the liberty of individuals, which passes as "progressive" in politics.[10]

Which Choice?

As Frederic Bastiat suggested, we should settle the matter of legalized plunder once and for all. He outlined the three ways we could go about it. We can decide by law that:

- a few may plunder the many.
- everybody can plunder anybody.
- no one may plunder anybody.

To select the first choice would be to maintain many aspects of our so-called democratic system under which we are now governed. The problem with that is it's nothing more than "nascent socialism": such an arrangement cannot remain static. In such a "thieves market," those who want more plunder will always have license to barter with those who want some plunder and those who are in power or want to get in power. And, as Lord Acton emphasized, "Power corrupts and absolute power corrupts, absolutely".

Thus, the cancer breeds and grows until it becomes choice number two.

Choice number two is communism (the virulent form of socialism). The State takes all and gives all; it becomes the alpha and the omega. In such a society the State makes of itself a god and competes with The Lord God in the workings of the world.

The third choice? *The third choice is liberty!*

It is the way things should be in a society where men and women are free — a system wherein the law (government) is truly an instrument of organized justice upholding the rights of each and every person.

Which choice is yours? In which nations, under which systems, and through what uses of the law have individuals prospered most in terms of personal liberty and material welfare? Where do we find the most peaceful, the more moral, and the happiest people?

Those people are found in the countries where the law least interferes with private affairs; where government is least felt; where the individual has the greatest scope and free opinion the greatest influence; where administrative powers are fewest and simplest; where taxes are lightest and most nearly equal....

...where individuals and groups most actively assume their responsibilities and, consequently, where the morals of admittedly imperfect human beings are constantly improving ... [and] where the inventions of men are most nearly in harmony with the laws of God.

In short, the happiest, most moral and most peaceful people are those who most nearly follow this principle:

Although mankind is not perfect, still, all hope rests upon the free and voluntary actions of persons within the limits of right; law or force is to be used for nothing except the administration of universal justice.

In other words, *"Try liberty; for liberty is an acknowledgement of faith in God and His works."*[11]

CHAPTER FIVE

God's "Super" Structure:
The Family

*"For this cause shall a man leave his father
and mother and cleave to his wife;
and the two shall be one flesh ...
What therefore God has joined together,
let not man put asunder"* (Mark 10:7-9)

There are few statements today about the opportunity and the obligation of a Christian home in a republic. Yet, there is no single element in America which contributes more significantly to the success of Christian Constitutional government.

It is in the home where the foundations of character are laid. It is in the home where Christian self-government is learned and practiced.[1]

The family is God's "super" structure. It was the first of the three institutions He ordained — family, church, and State. The family is His basic unit in society. Through the family God established His line of authority so that His people could live in peace, harmony, and righteousness.[2]

Love is the mortar which bonds the home into a unit; home is the building block and the very foundation of the nation; if the family unit is weakened or destroyed, the nation will decline and fall.

Superstates may be built by governments, by tyrants, and by politicians. But truly great nations — Bible-based, Christ-centered societies that free men's souls and send their spirits soaring — are built by righteous people. Righteous people come from righteous homes. *"Train up a child in the way he should go, And when he is old he will not depart from it"* (Prov. 22:6).

From Generation to Generation

The influence of home and family life preserves the "current of life from one generation to another."[3]

Like father, like mother, like son, like daughter.

The sterling worth of George Washington is a testimony of the formative power of paternal instruction. John Quincy Adams, even when his eloquence thundered through our legislative halls and caused a nation to startle from her slumber, bent his aged form before God and repeated the prayer of his childhood.[4]

When there is a Sarah in the home, there is generally an Isaac in the cradle. When there is a Eunice teaching a Timothy from the Scriptures, there will usually be a Timothy teaching the Gospel to mankind."[5]

Napoleon knew the power of the home: "What France wants is good mothers, and you may be sure then that France will have good sons."

America needs more Christian husbands and wives, more Christian fathers and mothers. Then, you may be sure that America would have Christian sons and daughters.

Strong Homes, Strong Nation

If we are to rebuild our nation we must first strengthen our homes and make sure that they are Christ-centered. Husbands and wives must assume the full responsibilities of Christian parenthood so that children are led to walk in the ways of The Lord.

Husbands, love your wives. As Christ loved the church, and gave His life for it. Love your wives as you love your own bodies. (Eph. 5:25-28).

Wives, be obedient to your husbands (Col. 3:18). Submit yourselves to him as to The Lord (Eph. 5:22). And be his helpmeet. Love him as he loves you. For the two of you are one.

Wives are not to be doormats. Sarah is an example of a model wife (1 Pet. 3:1-7). There were times when Sarah spoke her mind. As Reverend Rousas J. Rushdoony has pointed out, "Sarah, confident in the godliness of her position, gave Abraham an ultimatum (Gen. 16:5; 21:2-13), and God declared "in all that Sarah has said unto you, hearken to her voice".[6]

Yes, the husband does have authority over the wife. But that authority is not unlimited, "No superior, whether master, parent, husband or magistrate, can make it obligatory on us either to do what God forbids, or not to do what God commands." God is the highest, and the final, authority.[7]

Children, obey your parents. That is the Christian thing to do. Honor your father and your mother so that all may be well with you and you may live a long time in the land. (Eph. 6:1-3).

Parents, raise your children with Christian discipline and instruction. Do not irritate them. Teach them with love lest they be discouraged (Col. 3:21).

Finally, husbands and wives, parents and children, build up your strength in union with The Lord and stand firm by means of His mighty power. Put on the whole armor of God. You will need it to withstand the Devil's tricks and tempting snares.

Be persistent in prayer. In all things, give thanks unto Him.

Family Functions

In *The Christian in Society*, Earl E. Cairns emphasized that the family is "an institution coming from the hand of God Himself for the good of man." Cairns outlines three major functions associated with the origin of the family:

1. The moral and spiritual function
The function of the family is to develop love, forbearance, and harmony between husband and wife and to mold the character of both into the image of Christ. The fruits of the Spirit are these. Love. Joy. Peace. Patience. Gentleness. Goodness. Faith. Meekness. Temperance. Of such is the Christian home.

2. Procreation
Procreation for the perpetuation of God's children is the fruit of a deep and holy mutual love. *Then God blessed them, and God said to them, 'Be fruitful and multiply; fill the earth and subdue it'*(Gen. 1:28). "This view is vastly different from the present sensualizing of love as the basis for marriage."[8]

3. The training of children
The major share of this is placed upon the father. *Hear you children, the instruction of a father and attend to know understanding* (Prov. 4:1). Too many Christian fathers have neglected this God-given responsibility and left this task to the mother.

Included in the responsibility of educating God's children who are placed in our trust should be training in self-governance and individual accountability.

The child who is not taught to obey authority and to govern himself (his appetites as well as his actions) is not being made ready for life. He will be sent into the world without the full armor of God because the parents failed in training him.

The Christian Home

This is not meant to be a chapter on Christian family relations or a guide to family counseling. There are many outstanding Bible-based books on those subjects. There are also several Christ-centered institutes and seminars in those fields.

The purpose here is to emphasize the importance of the Christian home and family life as the foundation of good government — good self-government and good civil government. The family is the nation in microcosm; the nation is the family in macrocosm. God has given us a clear blueprint for structure and behavior at both levels. If that blueprint is followed at the family level, it is more likely that it will be followed at the national level.

Within that context, certain properties, certain duties, of the Christian home should be stressed. The points that follow are based on the 1861 writings of Reverend S. Phillips', *The Christian Home as it is in the Sphere of Nature and the Church — Showing the Mission, Duties, Influences, Habits and Responsibilities*, as reproduced in Teaching and Learning America's Christian History by the Foundation for American Christian Education.

Stewardship in the Home. Parents are God's stewards. Our children are The Lord's. He has placed them in our trust. We are charged with their care and training, for preparing them for life here on earth and for eternity. The greatest trust committed to parents is the soul of the child. Thus, the greatest responsibility of the parent is to attend to the child's salvation. (Luke 12:42; Titus 1:7-9.)

Responsibilities of the Home. God holds us accountable for what we do with what He has given us. This Biblical principle is certainly applicable to the home, to the family, and to the children. Parents are responsible to help the children grow in the knowledge and love of The Lord, mold their habits, direct their pursuits, lift their hearts, educate their minds, and train them in God's plan for civil and self-government. (Gal. 6:6-10.)

Teaching by Example. Children quickly discern any discrepancy between the parents' words (admonitions) and the parents' deeds (actions). If parents wish to bring up their children in the ways of The Lord, they must conduct themselves accordingly — by walking in the ways of the Lord.

Christ, The Master, was the greatest example of living as well as teaching; parents should follow His leadership example. (1 Pet. 2:21, 22, 1 Cor. 11:1.)

Home Government. The Christian home is a commonwealth to be jointly governed by the parents. When parents exercise loving authority and require obedience, they train the child for a future role in society and for potential leadership in civil government. In the Christian home the child learns love, harmony, self-control, respect, and order — all based on the Word of God. (Eph. 6:1-17,; Col. 3;20,21.)

Family Worship. The Christian home is sustained by faith and thrives on worship - family worship. That includes Bible instruction, family prayer, and religious education. Too many parents excuse themselves from this, claiming lack of ability or lack of time. They should not duck this responsibility. God, through the Holy Spirit, will provide them with the ability if they will make the time. (Deut. 6:6.7.)

Today's Christians should be especially faithful in this regard. There was a time when public education was primarily the responsibility of the church. That has gone the way of the humanists and the statists. God is no longer welcome in the public school. Thus, it is all-the-more important that the home be a bulwark, a reservoir, for Christ-centered education of the young. If it is possible to enroll the children in a Christian day school as an extension of the home, so much the better. However, that does not absolve the parents of their God-given responsibilities to provide a Christ-centered home and teaching for the children He has placed in their care. Those parents who turn their children's education over to the teachings of the state are placing them in harm's way; surely they will be held accountable (Matt 19:14).

Family Prayer. Every Christian home should have a family prayer time every day in addition to asking the blessing at mealtimes. This is essential to the well-being of the Christian home; it brings all members of the family together as a unit, with one mind and one heart, one faith and one hope — Christ Jesus.

We are instructed to be faithful in our prayers. Parents are the priests of the home; they should make talking with God — prayer and praise — a prominent part of the home life. (James 5:13-16; Rev. 1:6).

Family Bible Reading. The Bible is the book for family, the book of the Christian home. It should be the textbook of home education, read and studied each day. (John 20:31.)

> *Through wisdom is a house is builded;*
> *And by understanding it is established;*
> *And by knowledge shall the chambers be filled*
> *With all precious and pleasant riches*
> (Prov. 24:3,4).

Home Influence. Finally, if all of our Christian responsibilities in the home are attended to, it can have a growing influence in ever-widening circles. It can serve to bring others to Christ and to strengthen the community and the nation.

"The Christian home has its influence also upon the state. It forms the citizen, lays the foundation for civil and political character, prepares the social element and taste, and determines our national prosperity or adversity."

There's No Place Like Home!

Philosopher Jose Ortega y Gasset observed in *The Revolt of The Masses*: "Public life is not solely political, but equally, and primarily, intellectual, moral, economic, religious; it comprises all our collective habits, including our fashion of dress and amusement."[9]

The genesis, the foundation, for all of those habits and all of those values is the home. How important it is that we, as Christian parents, be diligent, holding fast to the Word of God, guiding our children.

For as the twig is bent, so the branch will grow.

And as the arrow is aimed, so it will go.

Walking in His Light

In such times as these, as in the early days of Christ's church, the Christian home should be a holy refuge — a place of peace pleasing unto The Lord; an enclave of loving authority and godly guidance and truth.

The Christian home should be a "nursery for the soul."[10] Its mission is the spiritual growth of each member of the family so that all become one with God through Christ Jesus. Thus the home becomes, in fact, a family unit with the members united in Him. That means keeping hearts and minds on Jesus. Being Christ centered. Seeking first the Kingdom. Practicing the Christian virtues. Walking in His light. Following His way. Building a Christian core, a nucleus of Christian love, within the home.

And reaching out to others.

Society can have no greater foundation than this! No finer training ground for those, now young, who will someday go forth into the world to lead and rebuild this nation, to restore it to His way and to His blessings.

When Does Life Begin?

He was born in the back room of a run-down restaurant. The illegitimate son of a waitress who gave him to a childless couple.

Even in his ghetto world he managed to get an education. Somewhere in the depths of his soul and the corner of his mind he developed a fascination for microbes, molecules, and the agents of disease. After he had worked his way through his formal education, he got a job in a medical research laboratory. It was there that he discovered the first link in what became a ten-year chain of discovery that led to the cure for cancer.

Today, thousands live because of that one life.

But, it never happened...

... because his was a life that never was — at least, not very long.

He was aborted. Terminated in the twentieth week. What God had created, man destroyed. A therapeutic abortion. Approved by the state, sanctioned by the courts, okayed by the medical profession, and funded by the taxpayer. Not because of rape, or incest; not because the life of the mother was in jeopardy — but simply to satisfy the desire of the would-not-be mother.

What is outlawed by switchblade, or gun, or club, is condoned when performed by syringe and curette.

Many — perhaps most — Christians oppose abortion. If they seek to obey God's word they do. They know that abortion is murder, homicide, the taking of human life. Thus, it is a violation of God's sixth commandment: *You shall not murder!* (Exod. 20:13).

Some would argue that abortion is not murder if performed before the fetal heartbeat starts, approximately the twenty-fourth week of pregnancy. Some posit that abortion should be permitted until the brain begins to show signs of "self-awareness." Still others insist that abortion is permissible at virtually any stage of pregnancy — that life does not begin until the infant is delivered from the mother's womb.

Thus, a central issue in the controversy is this: When does life begin?

Two sources of information should be considered: God's Word and secular knowledge, the Scriptures and science. First things first: God's Word. What does the bible say?

Scripture makes it clear that life begins at the moment of conception. That God and God's divine spark of life are there at the beginning. That when the sperm and the egg join to form the zygote (the "genesis" cell), life begins.

Speaking to the prophet Jeremiah, God said: *Before I formed you in the belly I knew you; And before you came forth out of the womb I sanctified you; And I ordained you...* (Jer. 1:5).

Isaiah reiterates that truth: *And now says The Lord, Who formed me from the womb to be His servant...* (Isa. 49:5).

David, the psalmist, is even more explicit:

> *For You have possessed my reins;*
> *You have covered me in my mother's womb.*
> *I will praise You, for I am fearfully and*
>   *wonderfully made;*
> *Marvelous are Your works,*
> *And that my soul knows very well.*
> *My substance was not hid from You,*
> *When I was made in secret,*
> *And curiously wrought...*
> *Your eyes did see my substance, yet being unformed.*
> *And in Your book all my members were fashioned,*
> *When as yet there was none of them*
>   *(Ps. 139:14-16).*

What a vivid and detailed description of procreation and the beginning of life — from the start, from the conception. In the beginning, God created!!

The unformed substance. The sperm and the egg fusing to form the zygote. There contained were all the genes, the chromosomes, the DNA; the genesis of all his parts — the organs, the limbs, the mind and muscles. Fashioned in continuance, even before they took form and shape.

Consider the words of Job (measure them against what science now knows about the forming of the fetus — the development of the child in the mother's womb).

> *Have you not poured me out as milk,*
> *And curdled me like cheese,*
> *You have clothed me with skin and flesh,*
> *And have fenced me with bones and sinews?*
> *You have granted me life and favor,*
> *And Your visitation has preserved my spirit.*
>   (Job 44:24)

Or, consider that joyful day when Mary the mother of Jesus visited Elizabeth, who was pregnant with John. Elizabeth's babe *leaped in her womb* (Luke 1:41). Is it not wondrous that the Bible told man almost two millennia ago what medical doctors have recently learned: preborn babies feel, experience, react. Isn't it a tragedy that man will not listen!

> *Thus says The Lord, your Redeemer,*
> *And He who formed you from the womb:*
> *"I am The Lord Who makes all things"*
> (Isa. 44:24).

If God created the first man, Adam — and He did — then surely His hand and His breath were in the life of Adam's offspring — and they are, in everyone.

Who, then, is man to destroy the handiwork of The Lord? Who, then, in a court of law or a chamber of government or an abortuary dares to murder His creation?

At the Fusion of Egg and Sperm

Medical research confirms the Scriptures. When science progresses far enough, it always validates the Bible. Scientific studies reveal that life begins at the formation of the zygote.

Dr. Thomas L. Johnson, professor of biology and embryology at the University of Virginia, is one who is quite definite about the beginning of an infant's life.

> This individual organism [the zygote] cannot be a part of the mother ... It has an entirely different set of chromosomes ... it is a separate and unique life.[11]

Dr. Bernard Nathanson performed some five thousand abortions after the U.S. Supreme Court opened the floodgates with its 1973 *Roe v. Wade* decision. Dr. Nathanson had a drastic change of heart; for several years now he has been fighting against the abortionists as fervently as he once was fighting for them. He substantiates Dr. Johnson's findings:

> We have very sound data which have demonstrated that the fetus is not part of a woman's body. It is an uneasy tenant ... immediately

distinct, biologically distinct ... it is not in fact a part of a woman's body.[12]

Could it be, then, that each woman who carries a child is God's chosen vessel to bring a new life into the world? She is, indeed!

To those who suggest that life begins as the infant leaves the birth canal, Dr. Johnson asks:

> Is it possible that by some magic, at the time of birth, this alleged potential being is somehow, within a matter of minutes, transformed into an actual human being? To rational individuals the answer is incontrovertible. Both the unborn child and the newly-born child is an actual human being and at the time of birth the child is merely moving from one required environment (gaseous) so that it can continue to develop into the succeeding stages of life.[13]

Thus it is that medical science now knows what David well knew thousands of years ago! Life begins at conception and continues — from the zygote to the embryo, to the fetus, to the infant, to the child, to the teenager, to the adult. That very special and God-created moment when the egg and sperm are joined, life begins — one life in continuance.

Yet some continue to argue that prior to certain biological or physiological indicators of "viability", the fetus is simply a mass of tissue — something to be torn out, sucked out, thrown into a surgical bucket, and tossed into a garbage can.

Does not God's Word tell us that each reproduces after its own kind? That the fruit of the seed is in the seed itself?

Dear Lord, forgive them for they know not what they do!

Abortion on Demand

The sad and awful record of abortion in this nation is an American holocaust. These United States fairly drip with the blood of aborted babies.

During the year 1988, acccording to the Alan Guttmacher Institute (an arm of Planned Parenthood), there were 1,590,750 abortions in the United States. That figures out to 4,358 each and every day — 182 an hour, three per minute!

According to the American Life Lobby, the latest available data from the federal Centers for Disease Control indicate that during 1990 there were 1,429,577 in the U.S..A.[14]

That's an average of 109,666 a month!

Almost 27,417 a week.

Almost 4000 a day ...

... 163 each and every hour around the clock.

Every minute, on an average, almost three tiny lives are snuffed out!

Yet who stands convicted before men?

In this nihilistic, humanistic age of situational ethics and convenient decrees and rubberized laws, such murders are legal. They are passed off as simple surgical procedures — "therapeutic" abortions. The purposeful, premeditated termination of human life. Justified by "science" and absolved by the legalities of court and legislature.

Since that dark, dark day in 1973 when the highest court in this land okayed abortion (*Roe v Wade*), more children have been slaughtered than all the men who lost their lives in all our wars. More than in the war for Independence, the War between the States, World Wars I and II, Korea, Vietnam and Desert Storm — all those wars combined.

There were 1,160,581 combat-related deaths in all of the wars from 1776 through Vietnam. Since abortion was legalized in 1973, more than 28,000,000 babies have been slaughtered. Twenty eight million babies. They never had a chance!

The "safest" states for unborn babies based on the ratio of abortions to live births are South Dakota (82) and Wyoming (90). In the nation's capitol in 1989, death outpaced life; there were 1,257 abortions for every 1,000 live births. New York ranked second on that death row, 634 abortions per 1,000 live births.14a

This nation is awash with the blood of innocent babies. God will not be mocked.

So you shall not pollute the land wherein you are; for blood defiles the land, and the land cannot be cleansed of the blood that is shed therein, but by the blood of him that shed it (Num. 35:33). But your iniquities have separated you from your God; And your sins have hidden His face from you so that He will not hear, for your hands are defiled with blood, and your fingers with iniquity (Isa. 59:2,3).

That was His warning then; that is His warning now. Who dares challenge God? God holds nations as well as individuals responsible for such acts. We pray that the Lord will bless the United States. Will He really bless a nation that murders some 1.5 million of

His babies each year? Lots of folks are in danger of a millstone!

> *Behold, children are a heritage from The Lord, the fruit of the*
> *womb is His reward.* (Ps. 127:3; see also Matt 18:6).

Yet abortions continue on demand. Not abortion to undo rape
or incest; only one percent of abortions are performed to undo the hell
of rape or incest; maybe eight or nine percent are done to protect the
health and life of the mother. About ninety percent of all abortions
performed in the United States are performed for convenience — for
the convenience of the would-not-be-mother who wishes to escape the
consequences of sin or the responsibilities of parenthood.14b

"What is Truth?"

During recent years, state after state has enacted liberalized
abortion laws.

On January 22,1973, the United States Supreme Court handed
down a key decision regarding abortion (*Roe v. Wade*). That decision
is virtually more controlling than state laws since the Court established
certain guidelines the states must follow.

Justice Harry Blackmun wrote the decision for the seven-man
majority. Decreed Justice Blackmun: At any point during the first
trimester (the first 12 weeks) of pregnancy, a woman has the right to
end the baby's life. The state, he said, has no right to invade the privacy
of the relationship between a woman and her physician. He ignored
the question of whether the state has a duty to protect the life of the
preborn child (under the Fourteenth Amendment).

The court set the twenty-four to twenty-eight-week period as
the outer limit for abortions but held that the states had the right to
establish certain controls and restrictions to cover the second and third
trimesters of pregnancy. Mostly, those restrictions dealt with the
mother's health, including the escape hatch of mental health, which
provides a wide open door for interpretation and implementation.
Millions of babies have been murdered through the excuse of "mental
health."

The Court's decision related more to matters of health than to
the right to life. Justice Blackmun observed that there was a strong
difference of belief about when life begins. But, asked the justice, how
can the court be expected to know the truth in such a debate?[15] Thus,
he washed his hands of the central issue and consigned millions of

babies to the scalpel, the curette, the suction tube, and the trash can.

Is there not a similarity between Justice Blackmun's evasion and Pontius Pilate's cop out? You remember Pilate, the Roman governor. Christ was brought before him for trial. Pilate could find no fault in Jesus. He said as much. But he had no desire to get caught in the middle, so he let the mob decide.

He washed his hands of the whole affair.

Well, hands cannot be so easily washed in such decisions. Not then in Jerusalem; not then in 1973 in Washington, D.C and not now in 1993. There is a higher law; there is a higher court.

The Death Toll Mounts

As a direct result of that Supreme Court decision, the liberalized laws that followed, and the Court's five-to-four decision in June 1986 which virtually licensed abortion at any time during the nine months of gestation, abortions continue virtually uncontrolled. The death toll continues to climb.

In 1972, before Justice Blackmun's decree, the national total for reported abortions was 586,000.

In 1973 it was 745,000.
In 1974 it was 900,000.
In 1980 it was 1,554,000.
In 1983 it was 1,574,000.
In 1985, 1,574,000.
In 1988, 1,590,750.
In 1989, 1,396,658.

And in 1990, according to the Centers for Disease Control, 1,429,577.

Abortion is the number one killer in the United States of America. Cardiovascular disease is second. They don't tell you that when they report vital statistics on the boob tube. They ignore the murder of the preborn. But, this is fact: the mother's womb is the most dangerous place for a baby.

Abortion is a big business in this country. There are now, some 2,800 aborturaries in the nation; their total take is estimated at more than a half billion dollars a year.[16] (And that does not include the revenues gained by the sale of the bodies of those unborn babies! [17] The sale of aborted preborns brought the Washington, D.C., General Hospital $68,000 in the ten years from 1966 to 1976. The money was used to buy television sets and cookies for visiting professors.[18]

"There is no business in the world other than the oil business that produces more financial return per square inch than abortion," said Dr. Barnett M. Rhett, describing the business of abortions. He should know: he claimed that he had performed more than 25,000 abortions from 1947 to 1974.[19]

This Murder Is Subsidized!

In 1990, 162,418, of the abortions performed were financed by state governments (their taxpayers) through Medicaid.[20]

The bill for those subsidized murders came to approximately 65,180,000 of the taxpayers dollars.

Thus does Caesar compel millions of Americans to be party to the violation of their conscience and their convictions. A large part of those Medicaid funds come from taxpayers who are strongly opposed to abortions on religious and moral grounds. When tax money is arbitrarily used to violate the firmly-held religious beliefs of those who paid those taxes, Caesar goes too far.

Where does he get off forcing God's people to be party to the violation of God's handiwork — and God's commandments?

In 1777 Thomas Jefferson wrote in the Virginia Declaration of Religious Liberty, "To compel a man to furnish funds for the propagation of ideas he disbelieves and abhors is sinful and tyrannical." It was true then. It is true now even more so. Caesar not only propagates the idea; he and his legionnaires take your taxmoney to finance the evil deed.

Abortion and Welfare

Some politicians claim a strange benefit from abortions on demand. They see it as a method of relieving the swollen welfare rolls. "It is cheaper to abort than to support." That's their slogan. In 1984, vice presidential candidate Geraldine Ferraro stated, "The cost of putting an unwanted child through the [welfare] system far outweighs the cost of these abortion procedures." She told her colleagues in the U.S. House of Representatives, "It's a simple matter of economics. Unwanted children so often end up in the criminal justice systems ... it is very expensive to take care of them."

What a price to pay! How cheaply is life valued by such reasoning. What if such an "economic justification" were to be extended to other areas of life in our society. Would it not do away with due process? Wouldn't that save money? Or what of the constitutional guarantee of trial by jury? Or presumed innocence? Think of the money that could be saved by doing away with the courts and the prisons.

Take such thinking even further. If life is held so cheaply and termination in the tenth or the twenty-seventh week is a way to save on welfare costs, how long will it be before such a mentality suggests that it will also save money to do away with people over seventy or sixty-five or sixty?

In the Days of Hitler

In an issue of "New Wine", Arne Christenson, legislative aide to then-Representative Vin Weber of Minnesota, wrote that under Hitler's regime students were encouraged to calculate the cost of medical care for the chronically ill and to compare that with the cost of more "useful" expenditures. Patients were referred to as "useless eaters." The ensuing euthanasia resulted in the murder of some 275,000 individuals.[22]

When the Pandora's box of abortion was flung open, all sorts of evil things began to emerge. The American Medical Association (AMA) has voted to condone the denial of food and water to terminally ill patients. The AMA strongly opposed Dr. C. Everett Koop, Surgeon General of the U.S., when he pressed for a law to stop this practice after a baby was starved to death in an Indiana hospital. The nurses had been instructed to hang a sign above "Baby Doe's" crib - DO NOT FEED.[23] On June 10, 1986, the United States Supreme Court sided with the AMA. So much for holding life in reverence; so much for caring. The Supreme Court seems to be one of the most dangerous of places for the preborn and the malformed.

The answer to the soaring costs of welfare is to clean up the system — to end the clerical nightmare and the bureaucratic excesses that cost billions of dollars — and to remove the greedy who prey on the needy and the taxpayers. Straighten out the system. Stop promoting and subsidizing abortion clinics. Outlaw the practice of euthanasia.

Further, if the value of life is based only in economic terms, consider this: "At the present population growth, it is estimated that by the year 2000 half of the population will be over fifty years of age and a third over sixty-five, living on Social Security. If we think Social Security is in trouble now — wait until the turn of the Century. Who will support our elderly then?"[24] (For many young people, Social

Security (OASI) taxes already exceed their federal income taxes. With a shrinking younger generation in the years ahead, the employed and employing blocs face a gigantic increase in their FICA taxes unless something is done to change the way Social Security is administered. Now is the time for providing alternative private investment plans.

Freedom to Control

The most militant supporters of unlimited abortion are the women's liberation groups. Their major argument is this: A woman should be free to control her body and her reproductive processes.

That is a valid argument. Women should have a right to control their own lives. And, in a word, they do. That word is "No". That's all it takes. "No". Only about one percent of all abortions in the U.S. are performed because of rape or incest.

Further, there can be no question about a woman having the right to do what is essential to protect and sustain her life. If it can be medically determined that carrying a child to term will result in the mother's death or cripling injury, then she must make a hard decision. Certainly she has the right of self-defense. That is her decision, and it should be respected.

But no woman has the right to destroy a life — any human life — to serve her own convenience or to escape the consequences of her indiscretions. That right is no more hers than is the right to murder an individual standing in the way of her career ambitions or other of her personal desires.

The right to life is a basic right. It is *the* basic right. From it stems all other human rights. When that right is set aside by vote or by court decree and life at one particular stage of development is held to be of no value, then the value of life at any stage is in danger.

"Dear God! What Have We Done!"

Commenting on the apparent ease with which some can write off human life, Dr. Thomas Johnson wrote:

In the dark cavity of the womb, out of sight, older humans find it possible to pretend these younger humans are not living or are not human. If the growth of the child were to be observed by the mother, the issue of abortion would most likely never have become a matter of worldwide concern. For, what psychologically healthy mother,

One Uses for a Dead (or Alive) Baby

Most people do not realize that babies sometimes survive the ordeal of abortion. Dr. C. C. Murry, pathologist at the Winnepeg General Hospital, told of finding a baby boy whimpering in a garbage bag about to be tossed into the incinerator. Thousands of such incidents have been recorded across the nation.[25]

Dr. Olga Fairfax of Methodists United for Life wrote a powerful indictment of the manner in which unborn babies are disposed of: "They are treated like trash!", shuddered Dr. Fairfax. Consider these excerpts from her article, *One Thousand and One Uses for a Dead (or Alive) Baby*

• In Milwaukee police found children in the parking lot behind Mill Medical Center playing with plastic jars containing human fetuses. They told the officers they were "throwing little people".
• In Richmond, Virginia, an abortion center used a trash compactor to mash 100 babies' bodies which were tied in plastic bags and tossed in a trash bin. Dogs dragged the bags away and fought over the contents.
• In California, babies aborted at six months were submerged in jars of liquid with high oxygen content to see if they could breathe through their skin [they couldn't].
• In Massachusetts, the State Supreme Judicial Court ruled goldfish could not be awarded as prizes because that would violate the State's anti-cruelty laws. The same court upheld mandatory State funding of abortions.
• Dr. Jeronimo Dominguez wrote, "On any Monday, you can see about 30 garbage bags with fetal material in them along the sidewalks of abortion clinics in New York."
• In 1974, 47 U.S. Senators voted to protect dogs from experimentation with poisonous gas; then they voted against an amendment by Senator Jesse Helm to prevent federal funds from being used for abortions.[26]

So much for life in the United States!
"Indeed, I tremble for my country when I reflect that God is just." (Thomas Jefferson).

seeing the unborn child within herself, would choose to destroy it?[27]

But destroyed they are. Some 1.5 million in 1990. More than 28 million since 1973.

As the attending nurse cried when the doctors aborted a perfectly developed twenty-week-old fetus and dropped it into a surgical bucket:

"Dear God! What have we done?"

Murder most foul. That's what was done.

They Keep Repeating Their Error

A coalition of women's liberation groups — feminists — and liberal forces headed by the National Organization for Women (NOW) continues to push for a so-called Equal Rights Amendment. Even though the original 1972 ERA couldn't make it through the thirty eight required state ratifications — and even though that attempt was aided and abetted by a slight of hand change in the seven-year time limit rule — they are busy down in Washington, D.C., pushing for yet another try (HJRes 1: Edwards (CA), Schroeder (CO), Hall (OH), Frank (MA).

Thus, the attempt to tack an ERA to the Constitution is still in the works. And NOW is also busy in the states, pushing to amend state constitutions. (Seven states have adopted amendments to their constitutions, granting a a type of equality similar to the equality of ERA. Six of those states have ERAs with language similar to the proposed federal amendment. In November, 1992, an attempt at a state ERA was defeated mainly by ladies who went door to door pointing out the dangers in the proposed amendment.)

The key section of the proposed federal Equal Rights Amendment contains these twenty-four words:

"Equality of rights under the law shall not be denied or abridged by the United States or by any state on account of sex."

If such a proposed amendment gets through both houses of Congress and is ratified by 38 states, it would supposedly create guarantees of "equal rights" for women.

But in their passion to be "equal" the liberationists forge their own chains.

Ask the average male chauvinist. He'll tell you: Women are not equal; most of them are superior, to be treated with deference (when

they are ladies) and to be protected (when they are in need).
Abraham Lincoln put rather nicely:

> This woman was not taken from Adam's head we know;
> To show she must not rule him 'tis evidently so.
> This woman was not taken from Adam's feet we see;
> So he must not abuse her the meaning seems to be.
> This woman, she was taken from under Adam's arm;
> So she must be protected from injuries and harm.

An ERA would bring the women down a peg or two. Down to mere equality. And if that's what they want, that's already on the books.

. The Fourteenth Amendment (equal protection under the law).
. The Civil Rights Act of 1964.
. The Equal Employment Opportunity Act of 1972 and various and assorted anti-discrimination statutes.

The laws are all there. On the books. Bound and binding. Each and all of those federal laws can be applied anytime women feel they are not being treated "fair and square," whether they want to belly up to a men's bar in Manhattan or drive a garbage truck in Los Angeles.

On top of all that and the myriad rules and regulations those laws have spawned, most states already have their own laws on the equal rights of women. If those are not enough, most of the Lotharios in the state legislatures would probably fall all over themselves to please the gals and pass more laws.

But that apparently would not serve the liberationists' purpose. They use ERA as a banner to rally their forces nationwide: they figure that they can get more gals nationwide to be on their side — to be part of a national movement to free themselves from home and family. Some would then be free to be gay, to be loose, to be libertines.

- We must destroy love ... Love promotes vulnerability, dependence, possessiveness, susceptibility to pain and prevents full development of woman's human potential.[28]
- Marriage has existed for the benefit of men and has been legally sanctioned method of control over women ... the end of the institution of marriage is necessary.[29]
- Christine Downing, head of San Diego State University's religious studies department estimates that many — if not most — spiritually

sensitive women in the women's movement are willing to replace the
Biblical God with a frankly pagan and polytheistic approach.[30]
• By the year 2000 we will, I hope, raise our children to believe in
human potential, not God."[31]

The liberationists may speak for their kind, but not for their
gender. Certainly not for God-fearing, Bible-believing Christian
women. Not for the ladies that rock the cradle and wipe the freckled
noses and fry the chicken and nurse the wounds of their men who
return from daily battle in the world.

Equal Smarts, Equal Pay

There is little legitimate quarrel with equality in the work-a-
day world whether it be business, entertainment or recreation, trade
or profession. If a woman does the same work as a man, and does it as
well, she should receive the same pay. If she is qualified mentally and
physically for a job, she should have the same opportunity as the next
guy in her particular skill or occupation. Equal smarts, equal pay. By
the same token, if her smarts or skills are superior certainly she is
entitled to a higher position and a higher pay.

But that is not what the ERA pushers aim for. They want equal
everything. And that can be demeaning. The ERA could turn out to
be more of an equal burden, more of an equal obligation, than equal
rights. In many instances ERA-type laws have already forced women
to pay equal child support. What's next? Equal alimony? In Maryland,
the Court of Special Appeals held that a statute making it a crime for
a husband to fail to support his wife was unconstitutional. Why?
Because the statute "establishes a distinction solely on the basis of sex"
and "such distinctions are absolutely forbidden" by the state of
Maryland.

In Pennsylvania all legal distinctions based on the male or
female role in marriage were thrown out by the state's ERA; that was
the decision held by the court in *Albert Einstein Medical Center v.
Nathans*. Further, the Pennsylvania Supreme court ruled that child
support will be the "equal responsibility of both mother and father."

As the Concerned Women of America noted, "The traditional
role of the father as provider was deemed archaic."

What of equal conscription into the armed services? And equal
assignment to duty in combat zones? Michael Farris, a Constitutional
lawyer and former legal counsel for the Concerned Women of America

wrote, "An ERA would eliminate all flexibility on questions of gender discrimination ... The principal example of this is the drafting of women for military combat. An ERA would require the drafting of women on the same basis as men."[32] (When one young woman in the armed services brought suit against the U.S. Army because she had been raped while on duty, the judge dismissed the case on the grounds that rape was one of the risks of the job.)

And, one must ask, would that also apply to assigning women to combat duty? Would this nation so cavalierly send its women or their daughters into the path of shot and shell, through jungle trails and minefields? Are we really willing to see our women subjected to the savageries of prisoner of war camps? The feminists — the Gloria Steinems and the Patricia Schroders may be, but not the men of this republic ... if they are truly men. Not if they know their Bible and honor The Lord.

Some have suggested, the ERA might even require women to share equal living quarters in prisons and other public institutions. The courts have already decreed that separate is not equal and the pro-ERA groups demand equality. No exceptions, right?

Finally, as Attorney Farris warned, "The ERA also has some areas of extreme uncertainty. There is a serious question concerning the meaning of the word, 'sex.' Several have suggested that it could be interpreted to include homosexuals. That is an open question."[33] In *Lapino v. Rizzo*, the court proclaimed a Philadelphia ordinance prohibiting heterosexual massage parlors "invalid" because it violated the state ERA.

No Law Means NO Law!

Senator Orrin Hatch of Utah, who was chairman of the Senate subcommittee on the Constitution at that time, heard pro and con testimony on the impact of ERA on federal law. He came to this measured conclusion: the amendment's words "mean what they seem to mean — that NO law establishing disparate treatment for men and women will be constitutional."[34] No law means NO law.

Dr. Donna Shalala, President Clinton's Secretary of Health and Human Services, was Chancellor of the University of Wisconsin when she testified in support of the amendment before Senator Hatch's committee. She suggested that it would require the integration of all single-sex private schools and colleges, require all single-sex fraternities and sororities to accept members of both sexes, require all school policies to be "sex neutral." For example, a rule related to clothing or the length of hair, would have to apply equally to both sexes.[35]

Professor Jeremy Rabkin, director of the Program on Courts and Public Policy at Cornell University, testified that tax-exempt institutions, including religious organizations, would also be required to admit members of both sexes.[36] Thus, Catholic and Jewish seminaries could be required to admit women or lose their tax-exempt status. (Bob Jones University had already lost its tax-exempt status because the courts held its racial policies "violated fundamental national policy." Thus, the basic precedent has been established. If the ERA is passed, a fundamental national policy is in place.)

Professor Rabkin told the Senate committee,

> My own view is that there is something terribly wrong with a Constitution that puts the sexual exclusion of a Catholic seminary or a traditional women's college on the same plane as racial bigotry ... I will simply record my strong impression that Americans now share this sense that sexual differentiation should not be regarded with the same intolerance as race discrimination.[37]

More Centralized Control

Additional cause for legitimate opposition to the federal ERA idea is this: If the Equal Rights Amendment were to become law, it would invalidate, pre-empt, supersede, and throw into the trash can one more chunk of states' rights.

Automatically upon ratification of the ERA, all state laws dealing with women's rights and protections would be blanked out by Caesar's statutes. On one more parade ground we would be forced to march to his beat.

It says so right in the implementation clause to that proposed amendment: "The Congress shall have the power...." And, when Congress has the power, believe it: the federal government moves in and takes over. Power does as power is.

That's centralism. That's control. Whether you wrap it in striped pants or coveralls or miniskirts. Centralism is the antithesis of freedom, another slide away from the Republic. Another snag in our checks and balances. An anathema to freedom loving people.

It is hard to believe that the legislators in thirty-four states so quickly gave Caesar's palace more power. If they keep on giving away their store, the states' rights cupboard will soon be bare.

And the liberationists? They should take care. A doctor in England reported that women who assume the role of the male lose their femininity—something to do with neuro-hormonal consequences. Such women often go bald, says the doctor.

Maybe the women go bald, but a lot of men go elsewhere. Doubtless one reason for the increase in the break-up of the home — and the increase in homosexuality — is the increasing "maleness" of women, the competitiveness between the sexes, and the loss of femininity in the militant movement Rush Limbaugh calls "feminazism".

Women traditionally have been more compassionate, more tender-hearted, than men. That has helped to create a vital balance in the home and in society. Little of compassion and gentleness exists in the NOW movement. When God created Eve, He intentionally created a "gender gap". Women are to be women — helpmeets, feminine counterparts to men, stabilizing influences. In a sense, men are the muscle of the family, women the soul. When women take on the attributes of men, when they become men in women's clothes, that unity and that balance and that beauty is gone. And, so is the soul.

Lonely, Desperate Wives

Not all of the women involved on the fringes of the women's liberation movement are wild-eyed radicals. Not all of them seek freedom from responsibility or restraint. Not all of them are anti-home or anti-family. Some join the feminists out of sheer frustration, desperation, and anger.

They are victims of today's world. Women who want to be homemakers and helpmeets and mothers but whose husbands live submerged in the things and the ways of the world and spend little time at home — and far too little time with their wives and their children.

Thus, the wife and mother is too often and too long alone, without her mate and without the needed help and guidance in rearing their young. Too often in today's high-pressure world, business keeps husbands apart from wives and parents apart from children. Yet where is the profit if the husband gains the business world, or wins the big promotion, and loses his wife and family?

The family is God's basic unit, the first responsibility of the parents. Both parents. The husband, the father, according to God's plan, is to be the head of the household. All through the Scriptures that is crystal clear. The father's hand is as vital as the mother's heart. Too many children suffer from a lack of masculine authority and presence in the home.

It is unfair, it is unwise, for the mother to carry the burdens of the home and family by herself. Raising a family is a joint venture (Mark 10:7-9). The Christian home is a commonwealth, remember. The father and mother together. As one. That is God's plan and pourpose.

Too Great a Price

The way things work these days is often not at all according to God's plan but according to man's system—the ways of a materialistic, often soulless, humanistic world. The system weakens families, destroys marriages, and sacrifices children in the name of success, prosperity, and a higher standard of living. We keep building bigger barns. Are we not in danger of having our souls "this night deprived" of us?

Yes, the race today is hot and heavy. Yes, inflation steals and cheats and undermines our financial stability. Taxes erode the future. But take care lest the drive of the world rob us of our family and their love.

Small wonder more and more families seek other means of earning a living and get out of the rat race so they can be together as a unit, in love if not in luxury. For where your treasure is, there will you be also.

Let's get one thing straight: there is nothing wrong with a Christian man or a Christian woman being successful in his or her chosen vocation or profession — so long as it does not come at the cost of breaking up the family, destroying the home, and losing the children.

That is too great a price to pay.

Some years ago a survey of corporate wives found that most of them were lonely, lost and unhappy. With few exceptions they agreed they would prefer to have their husbands spend more time at home, even if it meant a smaller income and a lower standard of living. Laying up treasures whose dust and rust corrupt the family unit is no substitute for a happy marriage.

Another survey among young people found absentee fathers to be one of their major gripes. They repeatedly complained that their parents, primarily their fathers, "never had enough time to spend with me." In lieu of his presence he sent presents; instead of time, he sent money.

That is no way to build a home!

Love Your Wives!

The Scriptures spell it out. *Husbands love your wives* (Eph. 5:25). *For this reason a man shall leave his father and mother and be joined to his wife, and the two shall become one flesh.* How can two be one when one is seldom home? Parting can be more than sorrow. It can be devastating.

Love is being with each other. Love is caring for one another.

Love is patient and kind; not jealous, preoccupied, or conceited; not ill-mannered, self-centered, or irritable; and never unfaithful.

Love is giving, love is constant; love is always.

Love is loving as Christ loved us. As men love their own bodies so they should love their wives, for are they not one in Christ?

Husbands, love your wives as Jesus loved His church. Care for her. Be with her. Sacrifice for her. Protect her and sustain her.

And the two of you be with your family.

Wives, Love Your Husbands

And what of wives?

Wives, love your husbands and respect them, and obey them (Eph. 5:22-24). For that is God's Word. Knowing that love fashions love in its own loom and weaves its pattern in joyful respect.

In the Christian home obedience becomes the joy of fulfilling the wishes of a loved and loving husband and a loved and loving wife. The complete Christian woman has no greater joy, no greater fulfillment, than to love and serve her Christian mate — that man who loves and cherishes her.

Christian wives: make the home a haven, a refuge. A place of God's peace and warmth and love and prayer. An island of serenity and support and understanding in a hectic, plastic, avaricious, often vicious world. A Christian oasis far from the madding throng and godless towers of Babel.

Blessed be the homemakers, for they shall help their husbands raise their children in the love and light of Christ Jesus.

There! That is the secret of a happy home!

CHAPTER SIX

Public Schools Are Ruining Our Children

*Beware lest any man spoil you through philosophy
and vain deceit, after the tradition of men,
after the rudiments of the world,
and not after Christ* (Col.2:8)

Consider the tribulation of Barbara Jacquelyn Hoag.

Mrs. Hoag got into deep trouble with the law. Her crime? Trying to do right by her children.

Her two daughters, Sasha and Jamie, were students in the public schools of Sacramento, California, and Mrs. Hoag was mightily upset by some of the goings on in those schools and on those schoolyards.

Finally, she could take it no more. Mrs. Hoag stopped sending her daughters to the public schools.

"Schools are not a fit place for kids to be.

"There is a clear and present danger to all children attending public schools. That danger is widespread drug usage and addiction. Added to that is the danger of pre-adolescent sexual promiscuity and experimentation.

"As a parent, it is my duty and my obligation to protect my children from such dangerous environs."

Mrs. Hoag advised the school authorities that unless the situation were cleaned up at the assigned school, or her children were transferred to an acceptable school, she would keep them at home. That put her in violation of the compulsory education laws: kids will attend school until age sixteen, or else.

The school officials would not transfer the Hoag girls to another facility. The principal, the school board, and the district attorney warned Mrs. Hoag to get her kids back in school, public or private, posthaste.

Her limited income would not permit Mrs. Hoag to send her children to a private school. But don't equate income with moral values or courage of conviction. Mrs. Hoag stood firm: a self-educated black lady, she was determined to stand her ground.

She was not out to change the world. She was out to protect her children. The Hoag girls did not return to the public schools.

"Sending my girls to that public school is synonymous with sending them out to play in 'Sunset Strip' or any city's red light district, with one exception. If I permitted my children to play in a red light district I would be charged with neglect and with corrupting the morals of a minor."

Mrs. Hoag was not anti-education. Her first husband had earned his Ph.D. at Harvard. Her second husband had been graduated from Sacramento State University with a degree in education. On her own she had already taught her four-year-old son to read and spell at the second-grade level.

"I'm all for education. That is another reason I took them out; I saw what those schools were doing to my children. They were stifling their creativity. I intend to teach my children at home as long as the public schools remain the way they are."

The school board and the district attorney's office advised her that would be unacceptable and against the law. She had no "credentials" to teach her own children. In this day and time and public mentality, one must have credentials — be certified, approved by Caesar — before one can teach one's own children in the prescribed courses.

Mrs. Hoag fought back.

One of the women in her neighborhood, who had been accredited by the state, offered to tutor the Hoag girls at home. The officials said, "No."

Mrs. Hoag took her case to court and lost. The Caesar that runs the public schools and writes the laws also controls the courts.

That was no surprise. It was expected. As Reverend Rousas J. Rushdoony wrote in his *Messianic Character of American Education:*

> Early in the history of the United States, the courts had no doubt that education was a function of the parents and no more a function of the State than is the begetting of children. Education was seen as an aspect of child-rearing. With the birth and development of State schools, however, the courts steadily invaded the area of parental authority, and the schools came to be seen, not as an aspect of parental authority, but of civil government.[1]

The state had its victory of sorts. Mrs. Hoag departed Sacramento. It was the only way she could keep her children and avoid sending them back to what she termed "a cesspool of drugs and sex."

Whose Children Are These?

Mrs. Hoag's story may be disturbing, but it is not unique.

Every day Christian parents wrestle with Caesar over the care and control of their children.

On any given day, drive past a school and contemplate the children. Or better yet, look across the table at your own and ask yourself this question:

Whose children are these?

Are they yours from God?

Or do they belong to the State?

Surely most parents, and certainly all Christian parents, will answer:

By the grace of God, these are our children! Parents are not incubators for the State!

A few may answer differently; they subscribe to a foreign ideology.

Since it is true that children are of their parents and of God, then follow this:

Whose responsibility are these children?

The parents' under the admonition of God?

Or the State's under the injunctions of Caesar?

Most parents, and surely all godly Christians, will reply:

Children are the responsibility of parents!

"Train up a child in the way he should go, And when
he is old he will not depart from it" (Prov. 22:6).

God did not issue that command to the State. He gave it to parents — to those to whom He entrusts the care and feeding (physically and spiritually) of the child. God instructs parents to educate the child. As His stewards.

Christians who seek to obey the Lord are not anti-education. Far from it.

The first schools in this land were Christian home schools. The first educational institutions were Christian schools, founded and operated by Christians mostly through voluntary association with local churches. One hundred and six of the first 108 schools in America were founded on the Christian faith, with the Bible as the primary textbook. Their purpose and their curricula were to educate children to be devout Christians.

The eminent constitutional attorney, William Bently Ball, is actively engaged in litigations concerning religious and educational freedom. His expertise comes in part from years of research into the roots and precedents of religion and education in America. Consider his words:

> The colonial schools all had the teaching of religion as their chief aim and their main component. Massachusetts, in 1647, adopted what they called the "Old Deluder Act." The Act said: "It being one chief project of ye Old Deluder, Satan, to keep men from the knowledge of The Scripture, it is therefore ordered that every township in this jurisdiction, after ye Lord hath increased ye number to fifty householders, shall henceforth appoint one in their town to teach all children.

"In other words," wrote Mr. Ball, "the aim of education in the colonies was to bring children to The Scriptures and to God."[2]

Harvard University, for example, set its purpose in these words: that the student

> be plainly instructed, and earnestly pressed to consider well, the Maine end of his life and studies is, to know God and Jesus Christ which is eternal life, John 17:3, and therefore to lay Christ at the bottom, as the only foundation of all sound knowledge and Learning.[3]

For the first two hundred years in American history, from the middle 1600s to the middle 1800s, public schools as we know them were virtually non-existent. In these two centuries, America produced several generations of highly skilled and literate men and women who laid the foundation for a nation dedicated to the principles of freedom and self-government.

Dr. Lawrence A. Cremin, distinguished scholar in the field of education, has said that during the colonial period The Bible was "the single most important cultural influence in the lives of Anglo-Americans."

Thus, the cornerstone of early American education was the belief that "Children are an heritage from The Lord." Parents believed that it was their responsibility to not only teach them how to make a living, but also how to live. As our forefathers searched their Bibles, they found that the function of government was to protect life and property. Education was not a responsibility of the civil government.[4] When Christian parents gradually relinquished their re-sponsibilities and Caesar took over, the foundations of the nation began to crack and crumble.

"Compulsion," wrote Robert A. Peterson, "has turned schooling into a 'bad' rather than a good."[5]

Anti-Christian, Anti-family

It is not simply that public schools fail in their educational mission (consider the rising level of functional illiteracy). As Mrs. Hoag observed, so many of them are "cesspools" of drugs, sexual promiscuity, and violence. It is also that so many of them are anti-Christian and anti-family.

Small wonder so many Christian parents are turning to Christian education — home schools or church schools — to train their children. As Reverend Rushdoony has stressed:

> One of the reasons for Christian schools is to preserve the priority of the family in the life of the child. The state school undercuts the Christian family and is antifamilistic and thus is the poorest kind of training ground for marriage.[6]

Today, godly Christians are just as concerned with the affairs of education as are those early American Christians, even though the State has pressed hard — and continues to press hard — to exclude Christ and control the field for Caesar. Christians know that the education of the child is not only their God-given right but their God-given responsibility for which they will be held accountable.

In his tremendous book "Is Public Education Necessary," Samuel L. Blumenfeld concludes:

> Educational tyranny is the natural and inevitable result of a govern-ment school system controlled by monopoly-minded bureaucrats and educrats. The people of this country must soon decide what is more important to them: Parents' rights or compulsory schooling; educa-tional freedom or educational tyranny. Clearly we are reaching the point where these questions will have to be decided one way or another.[8]

In his review of Blumenfeld's book, Dr. W. David Gamble, founder of the American Reformation Movement, laid it on the line:

> The early Christian Church was faced with a life-and-death issue: Who is Lord — Christ or Caesar? Its confession: 'Christ is not under Caesar but Caesar is under Christ.' The modern Caesar is again offering a rival means of salvation and man must choose whom he will serve. To choose statist education is to deny Christ.[9]

As followers of Christ, we must stop sacrificing our children on the altar of Baal. As long as Christian parents continue to turn the education of their children over to Caesar and his legions, the State will grow as a god.

The Widening Gap, the Deepening Conflict

Unfortunately, many Christian parents cannot or will not remove their children from Caesar's schools. They may feel they cannot afford to send their children to a Christian school, and because of the taxes they pay to finance Caesar's education apparatus, to do so would indeed be a heavy burden. Only they can answer the question, Where is your treasure? And, what price are you willing to pay?

Many believe that public education has advantages smaller Christian schools or home education cannot provide. So they establish their priorities; they gain the fancier buildings and equipment — and they place their children in harm's way. They thus consign to Caesar a major part of the education of their children.

Sooner or later they face a widening gap and a deepening conflict. By what standard, in what moral values, shall the child be trained? In the nurture and admonition of the Lord? Or by the yardstick and dictates of the State?

Those who worship the Living God believe that *"the fear [respect] of the Lord is the beginning of knowledge"* (Prov. 1:7).

"God first," they insist. In education as in all else.

The State says "No." The State must come first. God can come along after hours. The Bible? It may be considered as an "historical" document and discussed along with other competing "theories". Creation? That's a myth; evolution is the word today.

God's Word says *"Fathers ... bring them up in the training and admonition of the Lord"* (Eph. 6:4).

What if the indoctrination of the classroom undermines the teaching at home or church?

What if those classes negate worship and faith? What if they become a divisive instrument to separate the child from God and from his parents? Is there not a risk that such conflict between school and parental authority can create a weakened faith and a schizophrenic child? Whom shall they believe?

As attorney Bill Ball points out, "Consistency between the home and school is crucial to moral and religious training, otherwise you will have conflict and anxiety within the child."[10]

James 1:8 tells us that *"a double-minded man [is] unstable in all his ways."* Surely that is not what we would wish upon our children!

And what of moral values?

Those who hold firmly to their faith know that God's Word is the only acceptable guide for life; the only true foundation for right moral values and ethical standards. They also know that morality must be maintained at the highest level if the child is to be in but not of the world and, on a larger scale, if this nation is to survive. More than 200 years ago John Adams spelled it out:

> Statesmen may plan and speculate for liberty, but it is religion and morality alone which can establish the principles upon which freedom can securely stand.[11]

Dr. Nicholas Murray Butler, that giant of an educator of the 1920s and 1930s, said:

> To exclude religious teaching altogether from education ... is a very dangerous and curious tendency. The result is to give paganism a new importance and influence.

Gresham's law of economics is this: Bad money drives out good money. Consider this: bad morals drive out good morals. Is that not happening today in this land? Switch to any TV channel; pick up any newspaper; look at the marquee on any theater. Bad morals drive out good morals.

We stand at the brink of disaster.

Americans Are Religious!

For a short while it appeared that there might be a slight glimmer of reawakening to what our Founding Fathers knew right well. For three years the secular Brookings Institution studied the American scene. Its scholars concluded that the future of America depends upon the strength of its religious institutions. Announced the Institution, government "depends for its health on values that over the not-so-long run must come from religion."[13]

Not in Schoolbooks!

Indeed it does. As God's word proclaims, *"Blessed is the nation whose God is The Lord!"* He also tells us, *"When the righteous are in authority the people rejoice: but when the wicked rule, the people mourn."* But, such a vital truth in the lives of individuals and nations is not reflected in the schoolbooks used in public (government) schools across the nation. As far as those book are concerned, religion in America is nowhere; a no-no.

> Textbooks used in America's public schools virtually ignore religion as an element in American life, as well as playing down traditional family values, according to a government-funded study of public school texts.[15]

New York University Psychology Professor Paul C. Vitz studied sixty books used in elementary grades in the public schools for the U.S. Department of Education. An estimated 87 percent of the nation's elementary schools use the books Dr. Vitz audited. Professor Vitz's conclusion?

> There is not one text reference to characteristic Protestant religious life in these books ... The dominant theme is the denial of religion as an actual part of American life.[16]

In referring to the Pilgrims and that first Thanksgiving in America, no mention was made of God to Whom the thanks were given. It is not strange, therefore, to note that Thanksgiving is becoming strictly a meet and eat and watch a football game event. Gratitude for God's manifold blessing? "Oh,somebody say a quick 'grace!'"

And, said Professor Vitz, history texts gave Muhammed, the founder of the Muslim faith, "much more coverage" than they gave to Christ.

On rare occasions when the textbook authors mentioned religion at all, the references were almost entirely to Amish, Catholic, Jewish, and Mormon faiths. Vitz found this very curious, indeed.

> It strongly suggests a psychological interpretation of the motivation behind the obvious censorship of religion present in these books. Those responsible for these books appear to have a deep-seated fear of any form of active contemporary Christianity, especially serious, committed Protestantism."

Syndicated newspaper columnist and television commentator James Kilpatrick commented, "It wasn't the Supreme Court that expelled God from our public school classrooms. It was the textbook publishers."[17]

A similar audit of high school textbooks was made for Americans United for Separation of Church and State. That survey found that "The American tradition of religious liberty is virtually ignored." Dr. Charles C. Haynes, a religious scholar who conducted the survey said: "The concept of religious freedom is largely ignored in the curriculum of our nation's public schools." He reported that the textbooks he audited gave little or no attention to the religious liberty clauses of the First Amendment to the U.S. Constitution.[18]

Gary L. Bauer, then an Undersecretary of Education challenged the members of the Association of American Publishers to give the United States a fair shake in the history textbooks they produce. As an example of distortion, Bauer said five of the history books widely used in high schools "gave the impression that the Soviet invasion of Afghanistan 'was essentially defensive or vaguely compassionate.'"

"And," he complained, "each text 'waxes eloquent' about the founding of the United Nations."[19]

Of such is the kingdom of Caesar and his propaganda in the state-controlled schools. It is hardly the place or the program for parents who seek to bring their children up in the Word and the ways of The Lord, let alone the truth about the world.

So the Battle Line Forms

Many parents will protest that the school is (or should be) an extension of the home, an arm of the parents and their responsibilities. Therefore, they insist, the parents should have the final say in morals taught and standards set; they should prescribe the directions and the values of the institution.

Not so! say those who run the system. The schools are an extension of the state, the exclusive pastures of the National Education Association. What suits the State and the NEA is what will be taught. Caesar will monitor the values; he will set the moral standards. You think that's an exaggeration of the situation? Read this statement from the NEA's teacher training manual and judge for yourself.

"Although they [the children] appear to behave appropriately and seem normal by most cultural standards, they may actually be in need of mental health care in order to help them change, adapt and conform to the planned society in which there will be no conflict of attitudes or beliefs."

That, wrote Dr. Robert L. Simonds, president of Citizens for Excellence in Education, "is a fascist brain-washing technique if you ever read one."[20]

Statist education increasingly assumes that (1) the child is the child of the state or the property of the state, which can therefore interfere extensively with parental authority. (2) The state "priesthood" of educators is best able to rear the child and prepare him for life ... (3) Statist education is alone "objective" and hence true, the state having the impartiality and transcendence of god.[21]

But, say Christian parents, these are our children! And we are not impartial; we are followers of Christ!

So it is the battle line forms for the soul of the children

In Maryland, in West Virginia, in California, in Wisconsin, in Texas, in Florida ... North, South, East, West. All across the nation, some dare to stand for Christ and challenge Caesar and his fellow-traveler, the National Education Association (NEA) — that which was once a reputable professional organization but is no longer. Today, the NEA is mostly a far-left pressure group and perhaps the major roadblock to real reform of the nation's education system.

The Weight of the Institution

And what of those who wrestle Caesar? How do they fare? Some have lost their battles. Some have won.

Jonas Yoder won. He bested Caesar.

Jonas Yoder is a member of the Amish sect. Those quiet, gentle folk who work their farms and raise their families in isolated serenity of worship free from crime or juvenile delinquency. The Amish folk reject formal education beyond the eighth grade. From that point on, their faith calls for the child to be educated through life in the Amish community — farming, carpentry, animal husbandry, homemaking, tending the various and daily affairs of faith and enterprise.

When Jonas Yoder's children had completed their eight years of state education, he refused to send them on to high school. He defied Wisconsin's compulsory education laws and the state brought suit against him. Wisconsin claimed first call upon the Yoder children. Mr.

NEA AGENDA: ROADBLOCK TO REAL REFORM OF EDUCATION

A major roadblock to reform of the public education system is the 2.2 million-member National Education Association (NEA). From July 3-8, 1992, NEA held its annual convention in Washington, DC. Among the resolutions delegates adopted were these which:

* Condemn as detrimental to public education and thus should be eliminated: tuition tax credits and voucher plans.
* Oppose home schooling as failing to provide a "comprehensive education experience"; if permitted, instruction must be by a person licensed by the State and use curriculum approved by the State.
* Urge public schools to assume an increasing role in teaching sex education. Teachers must be protected from censorship and lawsuits. Program should include school-based health care clinics, family planning and instruction in birth-control methods, confidential counselling on AIDS and reproductive (abortion) rights, etc.
*Fully-funded mandatory early childhood education programs for children from birth through age eight.
* Equal opportunity public school employment for "gays" and lesbians. Counselling for students and an NEA Gay & Lesbian Caucus training program to improve sensitivity of local elected leaders to issues of concern to homosexuals.
*Support ratification of Equal Rights Amendments (ERA); endorse use of neutered ("non-sexist") language.

*Take a "pro-active" stance in support of abortion rights.
* Urge legislation to provide funding for multicultural/global education.
* Oppose censorship of books and school curricula; support the right of teachers and librarians to select instructional/library materials without censorship or interference.
* Oppose legislation or regulations which permit teaching of religious doctrines.
* Call for political action programs and training to oppose local and state school board candidates who threaten intellecutal or academic freedom.
* Support federal funding of "creative" arts and freedom of expression for those receiving such grants; deplore any effort to suppress creative freedom regardless of content.
* Support statehood for the District of Columbia.
*Oppose legislation to make English the official language of the U.S.

Noted author and educator Samuel Blumenfeld's assessment of NEA's agenda: "It is obvious that the delegates to the NEA convention represented nothing but the narrow self-interests of a politically driven monopoly ... 'academic excellence' is an empty phrase ... [which] they wouldn't recognize if they walked into it."
A survey of members by Michigan Education Assn. (NEA affiliate) found that "the majority of their members do not support the political and ideological agenda of the union heirarchy."

Yoder insisted parental rights and religious convictions came first.

The question was this: Does the State have a right to force children to receive their education at Caesar's knee? Who has the right to direct the upbringing of the child — especially when religious convictions are at stake? The parent? or the State?

The Wisconsin courts found against Brother Yoder, but he persisted. Finally, the United States Supreme Court found for Mr. Yoder. His children were, in fact, his own. The method of education was his to decide.

And why not? Didn't the United States Supreme Court hold in 1925 that

> The child is not the mere creature of the State; those who nurture him and direct his destiny have the right, coupled with the high duty, to recognize and prepare him for additional obligations(*Pierce v. Society of Sisters*). (And did it not go on to say that) The fundamental theory of liberty upon which all governments in this Union repose excludes any general powers of the state to standardize children by forcing them to accept instruction from public teachers only."[22]

Ah, but that was sixty years ago. The Republic and its highest court have done many an about-face since then!

Now, lest you consider the Yoder decision an across-the-board victory for freedom, consider the rest of the case.

The Court went on to say that Mr. Yoder's rights — and the rights of the Amish — do not apply to all. Over all others the laws of the State shall prevail. For them, Caesar's will shall be done. Thus, in fact and in decree, the Court established a religious test: to be free as Mr. Yoder was set free, one must be Amish!

To License Is to Control

The Foursquare Church in Santa Monica, California, was hardly a threat or pressing danger to that city or its people. No motorcycle gangs hang out in its parking lot. No pot was smoked in the tidy white building or its Lighthouse Christian School next door. No one was shooting heroin in its restroom. It was no den of thieves; there have been no riots; no felons were sheltered; no loot was stashed in its sanctuary.

Why, then, did thirty state and local government officials descend upon that church? What was the need for the horde of police officers, fire inspectors, social service workers and members of the district attorney's office? What heinous crime had been committed? Where was the public peril?

As William Jasper wrote, the forty preschoolers inside the buildings were armed only with graham crackers and crayons. The women church members on duty were busy changing diapers and leading the children in games and Bible songs.[23]

Well, the "crime" was this:

The church was operating a weekday Sunday school.

It was providing a peaceful haven, a caring, Bible training facility for the children of members and mothers in the area who must work to make ends meet.

The state charged that the Foursquare Church was operating a child care center. In California, church sponsorship or not, day care centers will be licensed. That is the law and that is the root of the conflict.

Pastor Ron Norris and the members of the church devoutly believe that the weekday Sunday school is an integral part of the church's ministry just as is the regular Sunday school: all the days belong to The Lord.

As Bob Jones, Senior, used to say, "There can be no distinction between the sacred and the secular. All ground is holy ground. Every bush is a burning bush; every house a house of worship."

The Christians of Foursquare Church and Lighthouse School refused to apply for a license. Pastor Norris insisted, "We are licensed by the Lord Jesus Christ."

And that, in California, is indeed a crime! Apparently a horrendous crime. It's not nice to mess with Caesar's social services.

Said Pastor Norris:

> The teaching of our children as directed by the Holy Bible is an integral part of our church and the exercise of our religion. It is our further belief that the power to license is the power to control. The power to control is the power to prohibit.[24]

Christian congregations do have a responsibility to insure the safety of children in their care. Fire, health, and safety standards are Caesar's proper domain and concern. Was the church lax in its safety standards? No, said Pastor Norris. "Our standards exceed those of the state. But, by submitting to state licensure, we become subject to ... the State code which has some fifty pages of regulations, many of which violate our religious principles."[25]

Pastor Norris and his wife chose to stand on Biblical principles, for which they were hauled into court and indicted. They join the ranks of Reverend Levi Whisner of Tabernacle Christian School in Bradford, Ohio. Reverend Whisner fought the battle of licensure and won. The Ohio State Supreme Court ruled that the state of Ohio and Dark County had overstepped their bounds in trying to force the Tabernacle Christian School to bow before its "minimum standards" — many of which were humanistic.

The Norrises also walked with Dr. Everett Sileven of Faith Baptist Church in Louisville, Nebraska, who went to jail rather than forsake his religious convictions. They marched with Pastor Robert McCurry of Calvary Temple in East Point, Georgia; with Pastor Royal Blue of North Valley Church in Redding, California; with Reverend Bob Gelsthorpe of North Platte, Nebraska. Pastor Gelsthorpe and his family watched sheriff's deputies seize his household furniture and personal belongings as a lien against a court-imposed fine.

These men and their congregations walk with Jason and the others who proclaimed, *"We ought to obey God rather than men"* (Acts 5:29). They, like the apostle Paul, refuse state control of their ministries. Others today seek to obey God rather than Caesar. Like the early Christians, they pay the price.

As Matthew Henry noted in his commentaries centuries ago: "The favorites and heirs of heaven have never been the world's darlings."

There is a hue and cry these days about the garbage that infests our cities and the trash that fouls our land. We are rightly concerned about the smog and smoke that contaminate our air. We must attend to these critical problems. We demand a rational, realistic environmental protection. But there is a pollution problem more crucial: The garbage that is being dumped into the mind and the smut that is polluting the soul in so many of our public schools.

History attests that when morals decline and obscenity and vulgarity are glorified, nations are soon buried in their own waste.

A Different Kind of Garbage

In 1992, Dr. Joseph Fernandez, Chancellor of the New York school system, tried to dump a load of "politically correct" garbage on the city's 31 school districts. Fernandez came up with his "Children of the Rainbow" curriculum — a 416-page sex education guide for teachers — starting out with the first grade and going on from there through grade 12. Mind you, this was not some program presented as a choice or local district option; there was no parental notification or approval involved; it was compulsory, a mandated program "woven into" all subject matter including math, science, etc.

Dr. Fernandez boasted that his sex education program was setting "the pace for the rest of the nation". Critics argued that the purpose of Fernandez' "multi-cultural" curriculum (written in the main by homosexuals) was indoctrination of New York city's 600,000 public school students "into believing that homosexuality — far from being a vice — is actually one more form of virtue." The course explained again and again that homosexuality was an acceptable alternate lifestyle; that sodomy has its "positive" aspects and that sodomites ("gays" and lesbians) "must be respected and appreciated".

The curriculum included several controversial books for the six-year-olds: "Heather Has Two Mommies," "Jenny Lives with Eric and Martin," "Daddy's Roommate," and "Gloria Goes to Gay Pride Day."[26]

The left-wing media in New York, supporting Fernandez, claimed the purpose of the "rainbow curriculum" was to promote tolerance for homosexuals. But, a look at the text reveals that the material goes far beyond that. For example, it describes some of the techniques and devices involved in sodomy. (In grades four through six, students were to be taught the use of condoms and contraceptive creams; in addition, anal and oral sex was described for the edification of the nine to 11-years-olds.)

If Dr. Fernandez thought the school districts in New York would just roll over and go along with the controversial program, he overlooked Mary A. Cummins, chairman of local District 24 school board in the borough of Queens. Mrs. Cummins, a fiesty widow and grandmother, led the members of district 24 to an outright, absolute refusal to adopt the Fernandez "rainbow"curriculum. Mrs. Cummins said it was an insidious package "shot through with dangerously misleading homosxual/lesbian propaganda". And, District 24's nine-member board, elected by the folks in Queens, agreed; they refused to compromise their stand. Fernandez managed to coerce most of the other New York school districts into going along. He agreed to delay use of the curriculum until the fifth or sixth grades. But, Mary Cummins and the District 14 Board wouldn't buy that, either. In fact, they organized what was hailed as the first mass demonstration against homosexuals in New York city. Some 2,000 angry parents carrying hundreds of anti-gay posters gathered outside of Fernandez' office and listened to 20 speakers angrily protest his sex education curriculum. There was a complete radio news blackout of the demonstration. Only one TV station aired the demonstration (a 10-second quickie look-see). And, the *New York Times*? Apparently such news of the protest would not fit their philosophy or print; *The Times* completely ignored the citizens' outrage.

Finally, in a fit of anger Fernandez suspended the entire Community School Board 24 even though the members had been duly elected by the citizens of Queens.

The fortitude and persistence of Mary Cummins and the members of Board 24 paid off: the NY Central School Board voted (6 to 0) to reverse Fernandez' suspension. As a result, other districts rose up and also rejected the Rainbow garbage. The whole "Children of the Rainbow" curriculum is probably as dead as Chancellor Fernandez' chances of having his contract renewed. All because the members of one district school board out of 31, led by a fiesty grandmother named Mary Cummins, had enough courage to say, No," and mean it.

As Mary Cummins put it: "I would never give up on a principle. I found out that wars are lost because people are not persistent. You have to be persistent ... These are our kids."27

An interesting point: it wasn't the "effete elite" from Park Avenue or the "politically correct intelligentsia" from highbrow areas that fought and won the battle; they took no stand against the perversion of education in New York city. It was the parents and concerned citizens from a middle-income, blue collar, working community who bearded the lion in his den — and won. Maybe there's a lesson there?

Christian parents should not only be willing to take a stand in regard to such matters, they should also assume their full parental responsibilities and train up their children in the facts of life and faith in the Lord God. In that way, sex will find its proper role and its true beauty — an expression of deepest love between husband and wife whom God has joined together, a provision of His grace which permits those He has joined together to share in creation — to be procreators

Modern Ape in Modern Schools

According to the Holy scriptures

... God said, 'Let Us make man in Our image, after Our like-ness: and let them have dominion over the fish of the sea, and

over the fowl of the air, and over the cattle, and over all the earth, and over every creeping thing that creeps upon the earth.' So God created man in His own image, in the image of God created He him; male and female created He them (Gen 1:26,27)

But according to the State, this is the gospel:

Man is the result of a purposeless and materialistic process that did not have him in mind. He was not planned; He is a state of matter, a form of life ... a sort of animal.[28]

That is the word approved by Caesar.

Thus millions of American Christians are forced to violate their personal spiritual convictions by subsidizing the cult of evolution in the public classrooms.

Those who see in man a higher origin — that man has been made in God's image, an integral part of God's master plan —cannot abide the materialistic and ungodly teachings of the State.

Creationism is central to the Christian faith. Christ is in Genesis. In the beginning, He was there, One in the Trinity, One in the Godhead. At the creation He was, and all things were made by Him (John 1:1-3).

God did not send His only begotten Son to save some superape or "state of matter". Christ came and died and rose again to reclaim God's fallen handiwork. If there had been no creation, there would have been no need for Calvary.

Yet, the State persists in giving franchise to the theory of evolution, which blasphemes God and insults His people. Many who believe the Genesis account, therefore, present their public school authorities with this request: Handle the subject of evolution for what it is, a theory, and give creation equal time and equal weight.

Aside from whatever personal religious beliefs that may be involved, fair is only fair. But, whenever equity for creationism is proposed, the National Academy of Science is one of the first groups to rise up in protest. In resolutions aimed at school boards considering the request for such even-handedness, the Academy has boldly stated that creationism is "an appeal to the super-natural causes ... a concept not susceptible to validation by objective criteria." Contends the Academy, the story of creation does not belong in the classroom.

Vernon Gross, a member of the National Academy of Science, did not go along with his colleagues. Mr. Gross suggested that the

Academy, through its "all or nothing" demands for evolution, hoisted itself on its own petard.

"By the Academy's definition of scientific attitudes and methodology, the evolution theory is not an observable fact. Thus, by its own standards, evolution should be excluded from textbooks and classrooms." The Academy insists it opposes giving creationism equal classroom time because "it could affect the study of science for a generation." So error is condoned lest the myth of evolution fall.

Gunther Stent, a molecular biologist at the University of California at Berkeley, in his book *The Coming of the Golden Age: A View of the End of Progress*, states that science is already on the decline because young students entering the sciences are no longer convinced that true knowledge is possible. Speaking as a secular observer, Stent feels that since God has been dethroned, there are no longer any clear-cut standards or values; and so, feeling that correct discriminations are no longer possible with regard to human aspirations and behavior, the pleasure principle becomes the highest value in men's lives.[29]

A Form of Worship

Mr. Gross believes the members of the Academy, in their fervor, come close to raising the theory of evolution to a form of worship. They do, indeed. Scratch an evolutionist and see!

Dr. Henry Morris, former chairman of the Department of Civil Engineering at Virginia Polytechnic Institute and head of the Institute for Creation Research, expressed the same contention:

> Creation can be shown to be a more effective scientific model of origins than evolution, and evolution can require a higher degree of credulous faith than creation ... In fact, the exclusive teaching of evolution is not constitutional, legal or proper, since belief in evolution requires at least as much faith as belief in creation and is therefore a religious belief.[30]

Evolution is, in following if not in fact, a form of worship. It is a companion to humanism; an offspring of atheism.

It worships the creature rather than the Creator. It cannot be validated by objective scientific criteria.

Evolutionists supply ample evidence that the fossils "are invariably either of apes or men, with no true and unquestioned intermediaries between men and apes."[31] "Scientifically, something cannot come from nothing and there is no scientific evidence for one basically different type of organism becoming another type." So wrote D. L. Cuddy, Ph.D., a senior associate with the National Council on Educational Research.[31]

Dr. Cuddy cites several scientific evidences against evolution.

1. There is absolutely no scientific evidence that simple forms of life came from dead matter.

2. There is no scientific evidence that life's basic elements formed by "chance" and "evolved" over time. Statistically, the mathematical odds against one protein molecule forming by chance would be 100, carried to the 160th power.

3. Evolution violates the principle of required immediate functionality of specialized organs. For example, land plants could not have simply evolved from marine plants, as the former immediately need a vascular system not needed by marine plants.

4. There is no scientific evidence of transitional life forms. The fossil record shows only perfect kinds (for example, turtles, but no semi-turtles).

One of the world's greatest living biologists, Dr. Pierre P. Grasse of France laid bare the fraud:

> The explanatory doctrines of biological evolution do not stand up to an objective in-depth criticism ... Through use and abuse of hidden postulates, of bold, often ill-founded extrapolations, a pseudo-science has been created.[32]

What is it The Bible says? *"Professing to be wise, they became fools, and changed the glory of the incorruptible God into an image made like corruptible man — and birds and four-footed beasts and creeping things"* (Rom. 1:22,23).

David Raup, curator of the prestigious Field Museum of Chicago, asserts that fossil evidence does not support gradual, step-by-step evolution:

> We are now about 120 years after Darwin, and knowledge of the fossil record has been greatly expanded ... Ironically, we have even fewer examples of evolutionary transition than we had in Darwin's time."[33]

Evolution is a chain of missing links. It is "a theory in crisis." Why, then, does the state insist on giving prime time to such a myth-stake? In many states evolution has virtually exclusive franchise in the public classroom.

Creationism in the Classroom

In his *Introducing Creationism into the Public Schools*, Dr. Morris wrote:

> Evolutionary philosophy is the foundation of atheism and humanism, which are nothing less than non-theistic religions. Exclusive teaching of evolution has the effect of establishing religious systems of this sort as state-endorsed and state-supported religions.
>
> The political reservation (about teaching creationism) is, therefore, not only invalid but actually applies in reverse. That is the very reason there is so much concern about this question around the country.[34]

Thus, the issue is joined, even on a secular basis: Is religion to be separate from the State? If so, does that dictum apply to all? Or are some to be favored while others are excluded? Why does the state compel the parent to subsidize Darwinian dogma to the exclusion of creationism?

Why does it? Consider this:

The child who knows that he is bought with a price and is God's own, is not likely to accept the role of slave to any man or any State. But, those who are indoctrinated that man is just "a sort of animal" will, when they are grown, be more likely to accept the state as keeper.

Does that make sense?

It does to Caesar ...

... and to those who hold in common the humanistic, pagan view that man is born to be a servant of the State, an economic unit of the masses.

Wasted Money, Wasted Minds

Since the end of World War II we have more than doubled the percentage of the gross national product (GNP) that goes to schools and learning.

Since the end of World War II, total annual expenditures for education in the United States have increased from $8.8 billion to $343 billion. $343 billion. The taxpayers of the United States spent in 1988 for all schools, public and private, kindergarten through higher education. That's almost $1 billion a day. According to the latest data available for 1990, total expenditures for public education, elementary and secondary, came to $203.8 billion.[35] (Add another $86.9 billion for public-supported higher education, and it figures out total government expenditures for all education in 1990 totalled $290.7 billion of the taxpayers' money.) The average cost per student, kindergarten through twelfth grade, jumped from $294 in 1956 to $2,726 in 1982 and $5,600 in 1990.[36] Even allowing for inflation, that's some jump.

In 1990 we, the taxpayers, spent more on public-funded education than we paid out for the entire federal budget in 1970.

The number of teachers increased from 1.3 million in 1956 to 2.3 million in 1989.[37] As expenditures and personnel increased, enrollment in public schools was 45.9 million students. By 1985 it had dropped to 40.5 million in 16,000 independent school districts and 110,000 public and private schools.[38]

Americans have seldom been stingy when it comes to the education of their young. The reason for taxpayer revolts in school tax and bond elections is basically two-fold.

1. Taxpayers are not convinced that the money is being spent wisely or efficiently.

2. Voting on school financing is often the only direct opportunity the taxpayer has to vote "No" to increasing taxation.

Often, the outlay of money for education does not bother the taxpayers as much as the way the taxes hit (primarily through the property tax).

And often, they perceive the great waste involved. Not just wasted funds but wasted minds.

When taxpayers read about drugs and drunkenness and obscene literature that is assigned reading, when they read about pornography disguised as "sex education," when they read about classes in basket-weaving and pottery-making, when they read of guns and knives and assaults on students and teachers, they tend to turn against the schools — not against education, against the system, and against those responsible.

Can anyone truthfully say that Johnny and Jane are more capable of reading or writing or computing than their older brothers and sisters were ten or twenty years ago? Can the general caliber and expertise of the "new" teachers compare with the caliber and dedication of the generation of teachers ten, twenty, or thirty years ago? Or, has all of this kept pace with the increase in costs and taxes?

On the contrary.

Moral standards as well as academic requirements and the teaching of basic skills — simple skills such as reading, writing, computing, communicating — seem to have declined as rapidly as the amount of money spent on public education has risen.

In fact, during those years when expenditures for public schools went up by leaps and bounds, test scores and achievement ratings dropped drastically. Scholastic Aptitude Test (SAT) scores steadily declined from 1967 through 1991 while American College Test (ACT) scores also showing a continual decline through 1989 and then a slight rise in 1990 and 1991.[39]

Samuel Blumenfeld warns that "the dumbing down of America is taking its toll even among our 'best and brightest.' In 1972, 2,817 students achieved the highest verbal score of 750 to 800. In 1990 the number was down to 1,226. America is literally losing its brains." Blumenfeld also pointed out that while the students in public schools had an average SAT verbal score of 421, students in parochial schools had an average of 436, and those in non-religious private schools had an average of 467.[40]

According to Paul Copperman, a member of the National Commission on Excellence in Education (NCEE), the average student of the 1980s is assigned about one-half the reading and writing required of students a generation ago. They take 35 percent less government and civics (call it "social studies"), 30 percent less geography, 20 percent less math and science.[41]

Concluded Mr. Copperman,

"For the first time in the history of our country, the educational skills of one generation will not surpass, will not equal, will not even approach those of their parents."

Why is that so?

"Four years of research ... have convinced me that the federal government bears significant culpability ... With the passage of the Elementary and Secondary Education Act of 1965, the philosophical and political logjam preventing federal aid to education collapsed ... each year has seen new federal education programs ... the twin historical anomalies of extensive federal involvement in public education and the declining academic achievement are not coincidental."[50]

Small wonder the NCEE, in its report on the state of State education, assessed the situation this way:

"If an unfriendly foreign power had attempted to impose on America the mediocre education performance that exists today, we might well have viewed it as an act of war."[42]

Samuel Blumenfeld, in NEA: *Trojan Horse in American Education,* has news for them: It was an act of war. He charges that the hierarchy of the National Education Association (NEA) purposefully set out to eviscerate literacy in the United States. Why? Because a literate people, a moral people, will not accept socialistic humanism as the new order.

Most Christians could have seen it coming — in fact most of them did: When God is shut out of the classroom and morality is tossed out the window, immorality, chaos, and calamity come in.

Accountability

Several years ago the executive vice president of a manufacturers association was asked by government officials what the public schools could do to prepare students for jobs in industry. His answer was curt and to the point.

"Send us young people who can read and write and do simple math."

Tests in literacy skills and reading scores revealed that less than half of the 1985 high school graduates had an ability to locates information in a newspaper or almanac, could follow directions to travel from one location to another using a map, or enter deposits and checks and balance a bankbook. Of the 2.8 million high school graduates in 1984, about 12 percent were classified as "functional illiterates." Another 15 percent were considered barely literate.

Two-thirds of the 260 major companies, banks and utilities surveyed by the Conference Board in 1990 listed education as their number one community concern. One American corporation spends from $200 to $2,000 per employe to bring its stateside employes up to technical proficiency. In the companies plant in Japan, it spends an average of $1 (the cost of a tech manual).[43]

Industry spends millions of dollars each year teaching new employees who were graduated from, but were not taught by public schools. Three out of four businesses and industries find they must retrain such high school graduates before they can effectively employ them. Many, if not most, public colleges have special classes for freshmen students who need help in basic grammar and math before they can go on to other courses.

Schools should be held accountable for their performances. Accountability. The same type of accountability we demand in other areas of life. If we buy a car, we expect it to operate properly. If we buy a dozen eggs, we expect them to be fresh and edible. If we buy a piece of furniture, we expect it to hold together. We get what we pay for, or we hold the merchant or the manufacturer accountable. But in the public school system in too many cities, the parents pay their taxes and send their children to school and take their chances, hoping their school is one of the "good" ones.

As the chairman of a bipartisan commission assessing the American work force warned when noting the skills of workers in foreign countries competing for domestic and world markets, "We can't afford to play around with this problem for another decade."

The Voucher System

There must be ways to let the fresh air of accountability, innovation, and competition into the closed shop of the State-controlled public educational system. And there are.

One way is called the voucher plan — or, system.

The voucher system would introduce the dynamics of the free market — the energies of customer-producer relationships — to public education. Accountability would become the rule rather than exception.

Under the voucher system, now being tested in some school districts, taxpayers would "subsidize" the student rather than the educational establishment. The parents of the school child would receive a voucher from the local school district worth a predetermined amount of money, depending upon the child's grade level. Generally, the higher the grade level, the higher the cost of education, and the larger the dollar value of the voucher.

Parents would "spend" their voucher at a public school of their choice, generally in the district where they reside. If one school were delivering a better "product," educating the students better, the parents would probably decide to send their children there. Other parents might choose another school that was stronger in the arts or vocational education or science or math.

If such a plan were implemented on a general basis, those schools doing the poorest jobs (as rated by the parents' selection process) would quickly experience a drop-off in students, revenues, and job opportunities for teachers and administrators. Faced with such a reasonable and direct impact from the open market, school boards, administrators, and teachers would be forced to shape up — to work harder and deliver a better product. Failure to do so would bring the consequences of their substandard performance crashing down on their heads. The voucher system would throw open the closed doors of the public educational establishment and could hasten the return the control of the schools to the parents. Consider the voucher plan in this light: When you want a physician, you search for the best one available. When you want an auto mechanic, you look for the best one you can find. It's the same in other areas — attorneys, architects, engineers, grocers, druggists, carpenters.

Should not the same dynamics and the same opportunities apply when it comes to seeking the best education for your child?

Controversy

The voucher system is controversial.

Its most passionate opponents are some of the largest teachers' organizations — the National Education Association, for one. That is understandable. Their empire would be threatened.

That, of course, is not the argument they use against it. Generally, their opposition comes on two fronts:

1. They claim it would violate the First Amendment.
2. They charge it is a device to promote segregation.

Both arguments are specious; they are without merit or foundation.

As to the first, the voucher plan would not and should not be used to subsidize student attendance at Christian (parochial) or other private institutions. In fact, this should be emphasized, pointed out, stressed in letters writ large and loud:

Any Christian school willing to participate in such a plan would be walking into Caesar's lair. Once tied into the voucher plan, it would soon be controlled by the State -- controlled in both its academic and religious programs. **With government funds go government control: control of the curriculum; control of standards and moral values; control of policies; control of the child.**

For a Christian school to participate in the voucher system or any similar plan would mean the end of the Christian school or its take-over by the State. The purpose of the voucher system is not to bring the private school down to the State school level; the purpose of the voucher plan is to improve the public school system, to break the chains of monopoly that now enshroud it — in fact, to bring the academic standards of the public school up to the standards of the Christian schools!

As to the second charge that the voucher plan is a device to perpetuate segregation in the public schools, that is neither the design nor the purpose of the proposal.

The "purchasing power" of the educational voucher within the school district would be the same for each child regardless of his residence or location of the school. Thus the plan would work to equalize educational expenditures and opportunity. Implementation of the voucher plan could and should be coupled to a requirement that no child be excluded from or compelled to attend any school on the basis of his color, creed, or ethnic background.

Clearly, not all Christian parents believe they can afford to enroll their children in Christian schools (although they should). Many churches do not feel they can provide low-cost, high-standard, Christ-centered education for the children of their congregation (although they should.) Thus, despite God's mandate for a Bible-based education, there no doubt will be a large number of children from Christian homes in the State school system. Such plans as the voucher system would be of some benefit to those families by applying pressure to raise the level of excellence and morality in the public schools.

Tuition Tax Credits

Another way to help break the monopoly of the State and NEA educational establishment is the Tuition Tax Credit Plan. Through such a plan, parents take as a tax credit (subtract from their federal income taxes) all or part of the tuition paid to send their children to a private school. Enactment of such a proposal would provide a measure of equity for families which do not use the State school facilities but pay taxes to fund them.

Among the arguments raised by opponents to the bill is the claim that tuition tax credits benefit only the upper-middle and upper classes. The contrary is true: of those parents who send their children to private schools, 62 percent have an annual income of $25,000 or less. And in the inner city, where mostly minority parents send their children to private schools, such as Marva Collins' in Chicago, 72 percent earn less than $15,000 a year. (CORE — the Congress on Racial Equality — charges that the State school monopoly locks black children into inferior schools in the inner-city districts.)

Teachers' unions strongly oppose tuition tax credits. They insist it will destroy the State school system. But the plan is not tied to any reduction in funds for public schools. The proponents of the tuition tax credit plan point out that the dual education system (public and private schools) in Western Europe forced the State-supported schools to maintain a higher level of excellence.

The average per student expenditure in public elementary and high schools in 1989 was $4,620; in 1990 it was more than $5,600.43 In 1990 approximately 5 million students attended private schools. (About 4.3 million of those students were enrolled in sectarian (mostly Christian) schools.) If those 5 million students in private schools were suddenly to enter the public school system, it would add some $30 billion a year to the costs and the tax take of the State's tax-supported system. And, that does not include the capital outlay required for additional classrooms and other facilities.

Thus, while the parents of private school children are relieving the State system (and the taxpayers at all levels) of billions of dollars in expense, they receive no relief in return. That is unfair; it is unjust. It amounts to a compulsory double levy for the right to exercise free choice.

Those who oppose the tuition tax credit plan argue that the State should not help finance parochial schools. The tuition tax credit does not propose such a subsidy. It simply holds that parents who support private and religious schools should not be compelled to carry a full share of the support of public schools.

Opponents to the tuition tax credit also argue that parents who wish to send their children to private (non-public) schools should be willing to pay the extra costs, over and above the tax for the State schools.

What that adds up to is this: Only the wealthy are to be accorded free choice.

Caesar's tax take leaves most middle and lower income bracket families no option. They are forced to send their children to State-controlled schools.

What Neutrality?

Civil government should practice strict neutrality when it comes to religious matters. But existing tax laws (and court decisions regarding such laws) violate religious liberty.

Where is the neutrality when Caesar erects extra hurdles and enforces double burdens on those who wish to send their children to non-State schools?

The issue here is not so much a question of church and state. What is at stake is the matter of equity and free choice. The law now operates as an economic sanction against millions of Americans. Some can afford to pay the tax of free choice; most cannot. They must submit the care and mental feeding of their children to Caesar. The tuition tax credit plan would help to put a stop to such inequity.

However — and it is an important "however" — even though Christians might wish to push for tuition tax credits as a matter of fairness, Christian parents and Christian schools or churches should not — repeat, Not! — take advantage of it if it ever becomes tax law.

Why? Because, as Senator Orrin Hatch of Utah warned, tuition tax credits could well become a "lever" to gain federal control of private education.[44] Again: with public funds goes public control.

Ah! you say. A tuition tax credit is not a matter of providing federal funds. Oh? Consider this: politicians and bureaucrats are increasingly insisting that a tax credit is the same as, and should be considered the same as, a grant of government funds. They assert that by providing a tax exemption/credit the government "allows" the recipient to keep monies that belong to government.

Does that sound far-fetched? Consider the case of Bob Jones University. It lost tax-exempt status because its rules concerning interracial dating did not conform to "national policy." The U.S. Supreme court held that "entitlement to tax exemption depends upon meeting certain common law standards ... namely that an institution seeking tax-exempt status ... not be contrary to established public policy."

Without doubt the same mentality would be applied to the granting of tuition tax credits. The Christian schools which enrolled students whose parents filed for the tuition tax credit probably would be forced to open their books and their policies to federal control. That's what happened, in effect, to Grove City College.

Grove City had neither sought nor accepted federal funds. But because a very small number of students received veterans' educational grants, the federal government demanded that the college toe the federal line and bow to federal policies. So, *caveat emptor* -- or, whatever!

Barbara Morris, in *Tuition Tax Credits: A Responsible Appraisal*, raised a big red flag: "TTCs are the camel's nose under the private school tent."[45] With public funds go public control. So the courts have said.

Thomas Shannon, executive director of the National School Board Association, was honest enough to admit a fact of political life:

Tuition tax credits for private elementary schools would profoundly change the character of private education. A simple fact of political life is that public regulations follow public money.[46]

No doubt those parents who scrimp and save to send their children to Bible-based Christian schools would welcome some financial relief. But they must ask themselves if such financial aid is worth the risk of turning the Christian school into another one of Caesar's holding and their children into one of Caesar's hirelings. And as they do, perhaps they should consider what our Lord and Master said in Matthew 18:6 — millstones can give you that sinking feeling!

State Controls

Court decisions, and various state statutes, require that every child within a state be given equal educational opportunities in terms of public expenditures — meaning that no matter where the child may live, and regardless of the relative wealth (tax base) of the school district, the same amount of tax money must be spent for each and every child's education.

Equal opportunity is a commendable goal, but the policy carries with it some frightening specters for those who believe in keeping the administration of public education close to home.

Most states now wrestle with these problems, which will become more onerous as the educational establishment presses its demands. One solution that keeps popping to the top is the advocacy of a statewide property tax. That is a horrendous solution. It would be a giant leap backward ravaging both education and the taxpayer. To shift the property tax to the state would be to transfer even greater (complete) control of public schools to the state level and destroy what little local control remains.

That's the way it is: the bigger the government, the smaller the people. Big government always comes at a tremendous cost to the little people.

When the state starts doling out the money for salaries and books and supplies, the state will also control the textbooks, the curricula, the employment and salaries of teachers.

Further, once the states move into property taxation, what little control the property owner now has over assessments and rates will vanish.

Property owners would be like plums on a tree, ripe for picking — plucked at the whims and ways of the taxers and spenders at the state level, away from city hall and far from the county seat.

The Root Evil

It would take a volume, at least, to consider all of the issues that concern most parents and taxpayers about public education.

All are pressing problems that demand attention and solution. But, those problems, each in its own way, stem from a central cancer, a root evil: *Compulsory education*. As the late Leonard Read suggested, "All the furor now going on against our schools, if carefully diagnosed, would be found to stem from this one evil."[47]

If we are to solve the crises in our schools and the public school system, we must have the courage and the intelligence and the honesty to face this root issue head-on.

Just when did Caesar grab so much power over the lives of our young? It did not start with our Founding Fathers; they knew better. They feared God. And they respected the individual and the family unit. They did not make the State a keeper of the child. That was reserved for the parents and the church as proxies for The Lord God.

Coercion and compulsion — Caesar's come-ons and controls — started when American Christians stopped using The Bible as their textbook for life, for learning, for living, and for self and civil government.

One of those most responsible for the sowing of foreign seeds within American schools was Horace Mann, secretary of the Massachusetts Board of Education in the early 1800s. Mann issued a series of reports which led to state-financed, state-directed programs of education which superseded the local, usually church sponsored, schools. Mann's plan called for standardization, for uniform goals and uniform demands. Call it what it was: lock-step education controlled by the state. And, because it was presented as a way to cut costs and save money, the Christians of Massachusetts let it happen; that was the greatest sin!

Goodbye "faith of our fathers." No longer would The Bible be the textbook; no longer were children to be taught Christian character and conscience. "Humanitarianism," and "benevolent inclinations" and state programs replaced Christ's Sermon on the Mount.

There were clergymen and laymen who saw what was happening; they saw through to the root evil of Horace Mann, the Unitarian. One who dared to speak out was Rev. Matthew Hale Smith:

The principles of piety, as you illustrate and enforce them, exclude all that treats of human depravity — the atonement and the sanctions to a good life drawn from the world to come. All these common truths, held by nine-tenths of all in this state, who profess any form of Christian faith, are ruled out of schools by the high authority of the Secretary of the Board of Education; they are declared sectarian and unconstitutional.... You have settled by the authority of the Board, or without that authority, what Piety is, according to statute ... through you, the people are told what they must receive and be satisfied with, as a construction of the Constitution. All towns must hear — all districts obey, else incur the penalty of forfeiture of their portion of the school money."[48]

It was proclaimed that education is good. And it can be. Thus, it was suggested, education under the wing of the State is even better. But it isn't. Coercion never is. One compulsion leads to another; Mr. Mann's compulsion culminated in The Bible being bounced from the public schools. Rev. Matthew saw it coming; but for his temerity he was tagged an "extremist."

The goal of educational opportunity was commendable; the short cut was deadly. Education without The Bible, knowledge without prayer, may develop brilliance but it does not produce wisdom. It may generate progress but it does not build conscience. And it certainly does not propagate freedom or perpetuate faith. Only freedom begets freedom. The root evil of compulsory education spawned the revival of the pagan view that man was born to obey the State and serve the State above all else. It bore the spores of socialism in America.

I am as sure as I am of Christ's reign that a comprehensive and centralized system of national education, separated from religion, as is now commonly proposed, will prove the most appalling enginery for the propagation of anti-Christian and atheistic unbelief, and of anti-social nihilistic ethics, individual, social, and political, which this sin-rent world has ever seen."[49]

So our children develop by the numbers. Caesar's numbers. Out of the home, out of the church, into the system, march. Another six-year-old becomes a digit. Another individual an economic unit.

Gradually individuality and diversity vanish, and each is made in Caesar's mold and stamped with Caesar's mark.

"How a child, during the formative years of life, could spend a large portion of his waking hours in a socialistic institution and not emerge

with socialistic ideas, defies imagination. Many persons who believe
aggressive force to be evil, if called upon to name the one single
behavior pattern more responsible than any other for such socialism
as we now have in America, would no doubt name the aggressive
elements in our education system."[50]

This is not to negate, in any way, the many good works achieved
through education. Or to suggest its demise. Nor is it to ignore or
depreciate the dedicated efforts and accomplishments of the many fine
administrators and educators in the system. But as Leonard Read
pointed out, "The good work being done in government education is
in spite of, not because of, aggressive force (compulsory education)."

The Coercive Triad

The government education system engages in coercion in three
areas, at three levels:

- compulsory attendance,
- compulsory curriculum,
- compulsory financing (taxation).

As matters now stand, there are few avenues of escape from
such coercion for the average citizen. They must endure the heavy
hand of Caesar. Some, through wealth or sacrifice, may send their
children to private institutions. But even they do not escape compulsory
financing of the government schools. And the great number of
American parents and taxpayers must bow before Caesar's three-
tiered throne.

What is demanded by the situation is too seldom faced squarely
by most Americans: "The need to attack [the evils] by advocating the
outright abolition of all statist schools as inimical to liberty."[51]

Samuel Blumenfeld underscores that challenge:

America needs schools, but it doesn't need government schools that
drain the taxpayer, cripple the children and destroy our freedoms.
The only way to stop being "a nation at risk" is to move
education out of government hands. What we need is more
educational freedom, more private schools, and more teacher
entrepreneurs. They will give us better education at lower cost,
and all the problems created by government will simply vanish.[52]

Union Control

Now we are faced with an additional looming coercive force: the specter of even more coercion from the national teachers' unions, especially the National Education Association which has ceased to be a professional association and has entered the area of militant unionism.

Apart from demanding changes in wages, pensions, and working conditions, these unions are increasingly employing aggressive coercion against the parent and the child. They demand the power to determine curriculum, class content, and lesson plans. They demand the governance of student activities. To engage in bargaining for wages and health care benefits and pensions is one thing. But to demand authority over such policy decisions is out of line; those decisions do not belong to the unions but to the citizens and to their elected representatives and administrators to whom they have entrusted the governance of the schools.

There are now moves to lump all school management-labor relations into one giant monolithic structure — elementary, secondary, and higher education. Should that occur, labor monopoly would join government monopoly in controlling public education. Parents and students would be pawns in a power struggle that seldom, if ever, had their interests in mind.

Lest you think that an exaggeration, ponder the words of Herrick Roth. The former head of Colorado's labor council told delegates to an American Federation of Teachers' convention that the labor movement would not reach its "ultimate" until union shop signs were posted in every classroom. Roth also advised the teacher-delegates to place their union obligations first, above their professional responsibilities and above the best interests of the students.[53]

Whatever happened to the great values of the educator? The high standards which were to be passed on to students? Such talk as Mr. Roth's contained no call for professionalism. It carried the germs of coercion. Such also contains the contaminants of anti-Christian secular humanism. Ponder some other statements by the eduction establishment. First, by Dr. Paul Brandwein in his 1970 textbook, *The Social Sciences:*

Any child who believes in God is mentally ill.

And, this statement made by Harvard's Dr. Pierce when addressing some 2,000 public school teachers in Denver, CO, in 1973:

Every child in America who enters school at the age of five is mentally ill, because he comes to school with allegiance toward our elected officials, toward our founding fathers, toward our institutions, toward the preservation of this form of government, patriotism, nationalism, sovereignty... All of that proves the children are sick because the truly well individual is one who has rejected all of those things and is what I would call the true international child of the future.[54]

And this, written by teacher John Dunphy in "A New Religion for A New Age", written for *The Humanist* magazine, January/February 1983:

The battle for humankind's future must be waged and won in the public school classroom by teachers who correctly perceive their roles as the proselytizers of a new faith: a religion of humanity that recognizes and respects the spark of what the theologians call divinity in every human being. These teachers must embody the same selfless dedication as the most rabid fundamentalist preachers, for they will be ministers of another sort, utilizing a classroom instead of a pulpit to convey humanist values in whatever subject they teach, regardless of the educational level — preschool, day care, or large state university. The classroom must and will become the area of conflict between the old and the new — the rotting corpse of Christianity ... and the new faith of humanism, resplendent in its promise of a world in which the never-realized Christian ideal of "love thy neighbor" will finally be achieved.[54]

Whatever happened to those men and women who were truly dedicated to the profession of education? Whatever happened to the great values which those dedicated educators espoused? Those role models which sparked great dreams and wondrous achievements? Those high standards which were so often passed on to students? Gone — except for the few who refuse to march to the beat of the NEA.

Instant Dropouts

Yet, even in the face of all those increasing deficiencies and mounting evils, the individual who openly opposes compulsory (State/union controlled) education is scored as being selfish and "anti-education."

Such criticism is baseless; hysterical. If anything, those who have the courage to decry coercion and destruction are pro-education in the finest and fullest sense of the term. To charge that a person opposes education because he or she opposes compulsory government education is akin to insinuating that an individual opposes religion because he opposes a State-controlled church.

Some physicians raise their eyebrows at the thought of eliminating compulsory government education. Yet those same physicians rail against the idea of State control of medicine. Are they suggesting that the patient and the physician should be free from State control but that the student and the parent and the educator should be captives of such coercion? And, what of the clergy who condone compulsory State education? Are they saying that Caesar should control the classroom, that the forming of a child's mind belongs to the State and not to God and His appointed parents? Do they realize that the mind and spirit of the child cannot be made whole when those who control the classroom deny truth taught in the home or preached from the pulpit? Further, they would do well to consider this: when education is State-controlled, State-controlled religion is not far behind.

The most prevalent argument against the call for a halt to government coercion in education is this: if there were no coercion, there would be no education!

How fatuous! Pursue that line for a moment. Ask yourself. Ask your neighbor. "If compulsory education were to end tomorrow, would you have your child quit school? Would you urge your children to take your grandchildren out of school?"

The answer is, "Of course not. But, others would."

It's always "the other guy."

How does one presume to speak for that "other guy" or to prescribe his values and predict his desires? Perhaps the other guy might say the same about you.

Even if that were the reason for condoning compulsory government education, would this not be implicit in such a stance: you claim the right to compel him to act against his will, to force him to send his children to a government school. That since you think he doesn't know what's best for his children, you must force him to do what is right?

Well, who has given you the right to assume the role of a god or lord high potentate, directly or by proxy?

If aggressive force is evil — and if the end pre-exists in the means — then it follows that compulsory education is evil. If education is good, then it cannot possibly be the product of aggression. These conclusions must be correct, or one or both of the assumptions must be proved incorrect. It appears that the assumptions and the conclusions are

correct, for is not aggressive force evil? And, does not the end pre-exist
in the means? And, all of us believe that education is good.[55]

Is it not strange that those who call the loudest for academic
freedom so often fail to understand this truth?

There are those who insist that if we do not compel people to
support a public educational system, we will have no schools. Furthermore,
children of those who cannot afford private schools will be deprived of
their right to education.

That bucket has no bottom.

In 1989 Americans paid more than $280.7 billion in taxes to
finance public education. In addition, millions of Americans paid another
$65.9 billion (on top of their taxes) to send their children to private schools
and colleges. That was a total outlay of more than $346.6 billion. Others
gave billions of dollars in gifts and grants to support private educational
institutions.

Does one really believe that if those taxes or a major portion of
them were cancelled Americans would simply pocket the funds or fritter
them away and consign education to the trash heap or an occasional
endeavor? To make such a suggestion is to belittle the intelligence and
demean the values and the desires of parents and interested parties.

Most of the tax savings would voluntarily be spent for education. They
would be used to finance educational institutions, both sectarian and secular.
In addition to restoring freedom of choice and action, the tax savings would
produce a better education, an accountable education, at lower costs.

Parents are already turning from state (tax-funded) schools in
ever-increasing numbers. Christian home schooling is already the fastest
growing segment of education in the nation. One Gallup Poll found that
47 percent of public school parents would shift to a private (religious
or secular) school if costs were not a factor. Another gallup Poll
reported that 49 percent of the public believes that an increase in non-
government schools is a "good thing."

A surprisingly large percentage of public school teachers send
their children to Christian schools.

Let us suppose, for a moment, that compulsory education and
coercive school financing were ended. The following is a fairly realistic
picture of what would transpire:

Hundreds of thousands of churches, synagogues, and other
organizations would swing into action (an action many of them have
hoped for). They would establish or enlarge their own school facilities
and teaching staffs. There would be a diversity, a wide range of free

choice, a competition for excellence, and lower costs, minus the bureaucracy that now feeds on the government system. The schools would be funded voluntarily by members and friends and parents of the children in attendance.

The great majority of those schools would open their doors to children from low-income families through scholarships and work-aid and earn-and-learn programs. Many private schools do that now. Many churches which really believe that "Monday schools" are as essential as "Sunday schools" would make Christian education a part of the tithe and church ministry. In that way, they would open the doors to those who might not be able to pay the full tuition. (Many churches do that now and allow parents to contribute through their skills and time what they cannot give in money.)

Many individuals who already contribute to private schools would increase their contributions, and many who have not contributed would begin because the reduction in taxes would enable them to give.

Many companies, corporations, and foundations, freed of the burden of compulsory education taxes, would increase or institute programs to support educational institutions.

Given the open door of free enterprise, many educators, administrators, and business firms throughout the nation would support joint ventures to start schools and offer vital innovative, and responsive education at the lowest possible price. These new enterprises would attract the best of the teaching profession, who would welcome the opportunity to be free of Caesar's enervating apparatus and the labor unions' unprofessional demands.

An Idle Dream?

Some will scoff at such suggestions and predictions. They will call it an idle dream. Is it? That is up to the people. If they will, they can make it happen.

Those who question the validity of such potential should consider what would have happened if fifty years ago government had taken over the development, manufacture, and sales of such important commodities as automobiles, electricity, houses, telephone, petroleum products, or food and fiber. Where would those industries and commodities be today? Take a look at the postal service. Or the government-controlled school system. Or consider what the Soviet Union hath and hath not wrought.

There's your answer! Try freedom. It works!

Coercion and monopoly seldom result in excellence. They produce the shoddiest of goods and services for the smallest number of people at the highest cost — not the least of which is the loss of freedom.

Train Up a Child...

Even the very real possibility of higher quality and lower costs are subsidiary to the central, the vital, issue: the issue of coercion and government control of the education of our young.

Does not the contention that coercion (the use of aggressive force) is necessary for the perpetuation of the system indict the system itself? Does it not lay bare its failures as well as its coercive nature? Any apparatus which requires coercion to preserve its existence is immoral. A system which is effective and excellent does not need coercion to assure longevity.

Ask yourself: If there were no coercion involved, how long would the system stand? How soon would competitive systems gain ascendancy?

If American parents truly desire to regain control of the formal training of their children, they must have the courage to face the question of government education. Not just the courage, but the wisdom to pursue the matter to its proper solution.

"If the foundations are destroyed, What can the righteous do?" (Ps. 11:3).

Answer: They can set to work; they can rebuild the foundations. That's what Ezra and Nehemiah did.

We can begin once more to obey God's word:
*"Bring up the children in the training
and admonition of the Lord."* (Eph. 6:4).

I am much afraid that the schools will prove the very gates of hell, unless they diligently labor in explaining the Holy Scriptures, and engraving them in the hearts of youth. I advise no one to place his child where the Scriptures do not reign paramount. Every institution in which men are not unceasingly occupied with the Word of God must be corrupt. - <u>Martin Luther</u>

CHAPTER SEVEN

STEWARDSHIP OR SOCIALISM?

The earth is The Lord's, and all the fullness thereof;
the world and they who dwell therein (Ps. 24:1).
Whatsoever you do, do all to the glory of God
(1 Cor. 10:31).

We are to be God's stewards. His vice regents.

We are to be fruitful, to multiply (meaning not only to procreate but also to use our time, talents, and resources to increase, conserve, develop, and replenish the wealth of the earth for Him — because it is His).

The way we produce and the way we use what we earn are important measures of our stewardship.

God wishes for us to prosper. As a loving and bountiful Father who holds the riches of the world in His hands, He wants to bless us, both spiritually and materially.

"Beloved, I pray that you may prosper in all things and be in health, just as your soul prospers" (3 John 2).

"The desire of the righteous will be granted" (Prov. 10:24).

The key word is "righteous." The promise is provisional, not automatic. The test is whether we are motivated by the things of the spirit or by the ways of the flesh.

Wealth is not the root of all evil (wealth can and should be used to serve the Lord, to advance His kingdom, to spread His gospel); the love of wealth — putting it ahead of God, making a god of it — that is the root of evil. For that is when men build graven images and put other gods before Him.

The Scriptures are full of God's promised blessings to His people who obey Him and walk with Him — blessings both spiritual and material.

As Abraham grew in closeness to God, he prospered.

God assures us, through Moses, that *"all these blessings shall come upon you and overtake you, because you obey the voice of the Lord your God: Blessed shall you be in the city* [in your trade, profession, or industry], *and blessed shall you be in the country"* (Deut. 28:2,3).

"Blessed shall be your basket and your kneading bowl" (Deut. 28:5)

David tells us in Psalm 33:12, *"Blessed is the nation whose God is The Lord, And the people whom He has chosen as His own inheritance."*

And the apostle Paul reminds us that *"God shall supply all your needs according to His riches in glory by Christ Jesus"* (Phil. 4:19).

Yes, praise God, these blessing are spiritual, but they are also material. God is willing to bless our labors that we may be His blessing to others. How we apply ourselves and our talents is a measure of our Christian *stewardship* (Matt. 25:14-30). How we share God's blessing with others in His name and for His sake is a measure of our Christian *love* (John 13:34).

"Economics"

When you get down to the bottom line, as they say, all economic systems have the same basic components:

- Natural resources (God's earth and its riches)
- Human energy (man's attributes as he is created in the image, with the attributes, of God)
- Tools (the extensions of man's mind and body)

All economic systems are concerned with the same basic endeavor: the production and distribution of goods and services.

That is what "economics" is all about; the utilization of God's natural resources and human energy and tools to provide for man's material well-being.

The fundamental distinction between economic "systems" stems from

(1) acknowledgment or rejection of the sovereignty of God and the imperatives of His commandments;

(2) the value placed on the liberty and dignity of the individual,

(3) how that which is produced is used — does it serve God, or mammon?

In some systems, each individual counts; in other systems, the individual is simply counted. And often discarded.

Two Systems

There are, essentially, two basic economic systems in the world: the Christian idea (individual stewardship), and the pagan idea (collectivism/socialism).

The Christian idea springs from the conviction that man is created in the image of God.

Under this faith, man is a free agent, accountable to God. Man is not to be subservient to the State (Molloch worship) or to the system. Each individual is his or her own decision maker, the manager of his or her own affairs. The State is to be God's instrument (a minister of justice to the people for good); its purpose is to protect man's life and property and to govern with the consent of the governed. As God's steward, man is free to use his energies, his talents, and his property (his mind, his body, his energy, his tools) to serve God and to obey God as he is led by his conscience, so long as he does not interfere with the equal rights of others.

According to the pagan idea, the individual's value depends upon his worth to the State, to the system. The State is the master. It demands "divine rights," whether it be for monarchies, dictators, or commissars. It controls men's energies; it controls their talents; it controls the natural resources; it controls the ownership and use of tools, and it seeks to control men's minds. In a word, the State controls.

We call the pagan idea socialism (collectivism). We saw it in operation in the atheistic Soviet Union; we see it now in Cuba and Red China. Tiananmen Square is an example of socialism doing its thing.

The late Archbishop F. Sheen put it this way:

> "Socialism is the antithesis of Christianity. It is urged by people who have lost faith in God and the power of their religion to motivate men, and who have resorted to government and coercive power of the state as a substitute."[1]

We call the Christian idea of stewardship, free individual enterprise.

We use this system, in varying degrees, in the United States. At one time in this nation, free individual enterprise — like Christianity — was applied to a far, far greater degree than it is now; both the

Christian faith and free individual enterprise worked together to convert a wilderness into a bountiful society. Alexis de Tocqueville, a French statesmen and author in the 19th Century, wrote that the American settlers went forth with The Bible under one arm and a newspaper under the other. de Tocqueville travelled throughout the nation in the early 1800s seeking to learn the reason for what he called America's "greatness." He found the answer:

"It was when I visited the churches of America and saw the pulpits aflame with righteousness" that he understood the secret of America. "America," he wrote, "is great because America is good. If America ever ceases to be good, America will cease to be great."

Sad to say, it has been a long time — at least two and perhaps three or more generations — since America knew and practiced such righteousness and such freedom; for maybe sixty years, perhaps even longer, Americans have not really known what it means to live in a free society based on the righteousness of The Bible. And the cost is not simply a declining standard of morals and living, it's a growing separation from God.

Christian Economics

Spiritual freedom and economic freedom are fruits of the same root.

As Fred G. Clark and Richard S. Rimanoczy point out in "Christianity and Capitalism", the great economic reforms, as well as the great political reforms, stemmed from the Christian faith, from Biblical principles. In terms of economics, Christianity provides the foundation, the structure and the operation of the free individual enterprise system.

These may be considered the basic tenets of the free enterprise system:

• The unalienable right of each and every individual to be a free under God
• The right of the individual to own and use property without government interference ("Private property is one of the expressions of spiritual freedom because it is one of the flowerings of the essential dignity of the individual ascribed by God.")[2]
• The right of every man to consider his home his castle
• The right of the individual, alone or in concert with

other men, to own and control the use of the tools of production and distribution

• The Christian business ethic — the idea of fair competition, true value, full measure, fair wages, honest labor, integrity in dealings, a free and open market, and the morality of Bible-based human relations.

Archbishop Sheen explained the fruits of Christian economics:

Christianity would allow each man to have the use of all he earns. This encourages capital expansion, greater production, more jobs, less poverty, and increased well-being.

And, he added, "Christianity also teaches each man voluntarily to share the results of his success with those who are less fortunate."[3]

Thus, very much a part of the dynamics of Christian economics is God's law of returns, of sowing and reaping.

"Do not be deceived, God is not mocked; for whatever a man sows, that he will also reap"(Gal. 6:7).

"But this I say: He who sows sparingly will also reap sparingly, and he who sows bountifully [plentifully] *will also reap bountifully"* (2 Cor. 9:6).

"Give, and it will be given to you: good measure, pressed down, shaken together, and running over"(Luke 6:38).

In other words,

(1) God rewards works according to their measure, and

(2) if we, as His, are to complete the entire productive practice (the beneficient cycle) of Christian economics, the "Christian *love*" with which we use the fruits of our personal property is just as important as the "Christian *ethic*" we employed to gain that property.

Christ's Golden Rule must be the *modus operandi* of free individual enterprise; otherwise such enterprise is not truly Christian stewardship; it becomes a "hunting license". This distinction may often be seen as the difference in the conduct of those who practice free enterprise strictly for their own sake and the conduct of those who practice it for Christ's sake.

The former serve self; the latter serve God (stewardship).

For the former, the golden rule is "He who has the gold makes the rules." For the latter, Christ's words hold sway: *"Do unto others as you would have them do unto you"* (Matt. 7:12).

In sum, the Golden Rule is a foundational principle of stewardship. An essential ingredient of the free individual enterprise system, it prescribes the course, sets the rules, and provides the dynamics.

If you want a fair shake, you will give a fair shake; if you would want a full-day's work for a full-day's pay, you will give a full day's work yourself. If you would want fair wages as an employee, you will pay fair wages as an employer. If you do not want to be shortchanged, you will not shortchange others. If you want others to be honest with you, you will be honest with them. If you want a fair price for your product, you will pay a fair price for the products of others.

There. Has not The Christ set forth the perfect formula for a peaceful, productive, prosperous economic system? Indeed He has!

Look at the Record!

We are about to embark on a review of the results — the fruitage — of the way we were as a nation, where our heart was, and what we produced: a Christian nation of free men and women seeking to obey God's laws, to practice His love, and to advance His kingdom.

Today, in the main, this nation has changed — some areas (materialistically, physically) for the good; in areas spiritually, morally), not so good. While we were busy building the gross national product we were also building a gross national apostasy. And in large measure we who profess to be Christians — followers of Christ — must share the blame; we let it happen — and at times, if we are honest, we helped it happen. Not in any one year or decade but over a period of time. Through sins of omission as well as commission we have often rendered unto Caesar that which belongs to God.

If, for example, we had been more attentive to God's basic principles of government -- both self and civil, and His principles of economics and education, and if we had practiced what our Savior commanded in Matthew 25: 31-46, Caesar's reach and Caesar's grasp would not be so extensive, so voracious, today.

Ask yourself, is that not true? Ask yourself: during the years since -- say from 1900 on or, even from 1950 on -- have Christians in this nation really let their light shone so that others might see the good works and glorify God? During those years and even now, are Christians a distinctive people zealous unto good works?

Persisting in the works of fatih, obedient to His cultural mandate?

The Way We Were

Over America's past years -- in fact, from the early beginnings, the economic by-products of God-centered individuals in free enterprise outstripped the productivity of all other systems. That should be no surprise. When a nation walks in the light and love and law of The Lord, it prospers; when it strays from His way, things go sour. It was thus in the days of the Prophets; it is thus in these days of His followers.[4]

In the mid-decades of the 1990s, the United States of America — composed of about 5 percent of the world's population, 5.4 percent of the world's labor force, and 6 percent of the world's land mass — accounted for some 30 percent of the world's total production.[5]

There was a time, not too long ago, when U.S. labor, management, and capital working together produced

12 percent of the world's steel
26 percent of the world's energy
16 percent of the world's crude oil
31 percent of the world's corn
54 percent of the world's soybeans
23 percent of the world's coal
30 percent of the world's natural gas
24 percent of the world's electrical energy
38 percent of the world's synthetic fibers, and
about 40 percent of the world's manufactured
goods.[6]

As a result of their productivity, the people of these United States had

• more than two-thirds of all the digital computers
• 37 percent of all the motor vehicles (cars, trucks, and tractors)
• 33 percent of all the telephones
• 45 percent of all the radios, and
• 70 percent of all the television sets, and about
• 50 percent of the world's civil aviation.[7]

Free men and women produced more and better. All of this is not brag. Just Fact.

As free men and women we tried harder and produced better.

We did not achieve perfection. We were and are a long way from the ultimate. There is still much to be done. Utopia will not arrive until Christ The King returns to establish His kingdom. Even though in recent years we experienced economic difficulties, we achieved more than others, and sought ways to improve what we did and how we did it. In many ways we still do.

But, as we began to look to other gods, as we began to shut The Living God out of our schools, out of our government, out of the marketplace, out of the home and, yes, out of many "churches" — as our society did those things, both the spiritual and the material strengths of this nation began weaken and to show signs of wear and tear.

This night, thy soul ...

The Scriptures tell us of a certain rich man whose ground was producing bumper crops. He had a problem. His barns were full to overflowing and there was still a lot to be harvested.

"What shall I do? I have no room where to bestow my fruits." Here, Luke recorded the words of our Master regarding the parable of this man and his problem:

"And he said, This will I do: I will pull down my barns and build greater barns: and there will I bestow all my fruits and my goods. And I will say to my soul, Soul you have much goods laid up for many years; take thine ease — eat, drink, and be merry!

"But God said unto him, 'You fool, this night thy soul shall be required of thee!'"

And then our Savor added: *"So is he that layeth up treasure for himself, and is not rich toward God"* (Luke 12:16-21).

Nations have a soul, in a manner of speaking: the soul of a nation is the spirit of its people. Perhaps there is a message here for us. Have we, as a nation, laid up treasure (and debt and deficits) for ourselves and our children and failed to be "rich" toward God?

As we seek to repair the foundations, regain our standard of living, and restore the American spirit, here is the key:

"Seek ye first the kingdom of God — and His righteousness — and all these things will be added unto you" — or, should we say, restored unto you. Then perhaps we can once again be a city on a hill; not just a thousand points of flickering lights but a bearer of that light that is The Light of The World ... the only Light that can overcome the darkness — throughout the world, and here at home.

Poverty

There is poverty in this land. That is an unfortunate and disturbing fact. Some 2.2 million persons are homeless. They sleep in parks, or under bridges, in back alleys and doorways. They scrounge in trash bins and garbage cans; they frequent soup kitchens or go hungry. Some prefer such a life style; most of those in poverty do not. The recent sizeable and sudden increase in unemployment has caused many of us to emphasize with them — and, hopefully, to share with them.

Some seven percent of our people have annual incomes of less than $5,000. Many have no income at all. The American people have been mindful of this and have been willing to help. But, in the main, Christians — as individuals and as congregations — have fallen far short of Christ's instructions as put forth in His story of the Good Samaritan (Luke 10:33) and His admonitions concerning *"the least of these, My brothers"* (Matt 25:31-46).

What the world needs now is Christian love in action — in His name and for His sake; not our sake, not for some organization's gain or reputation, but for and in the love and name of our precious and eternal Savior and King. Then will He say to us, *"Come, you blessed of My Father, inherit the kingdom prepared for you from the foundation of the world."* Praise God!

Cold Statistics and Cold Hearts

There are thousands, many thousands — of *"the least of these"* whom we as His should be helping to reclaim their lives. That's the way to turn this world rightside up ... for Jesus.

In some areas, we must rely on government to be our agent in helping those who cannot help themselves; bit, doing so does not reduce the responsibility of the individual Christian or the local church or, in the final analysis, the local community.

The federal government should be the agent of last resort. Why? Because Caesar is a lousy steward; he has been bungling the job for decades.

In 1960, 38.4 percent of all government spending, $52.3 billion went toward social welfare. Soon after that the "war on poverty" began. When Lyndon Johnson fired the first shots in that war, about 13 percent of Americans were "poor" according to Washington's standards; unemployment was about 3.5 percent.

Since then we have been spending more money after more money to fight poverty and we have been losing the war. In 1970 the amount spent on public assistance and social welfare increased to $145.9 billion. In 1988, $886 billion was spent by federal state and local governments for public assistance and social welfare. Federal spending totalled $523 billion (59%) and state and local spending came to $363 Billion (41%). All told, that was 18.5% of the Gross National Product (GNP) and 41 percent of the combined budgets of the federal, state and local governments. In 1989, federal assistance payments to individuals were $459 billion — up from $427 billion in 1985; the costs at the state and local levels increased comparably.

And, after all those years and all those billions, some 20.2 million Americans are now on welfare. [12] In 1970, 4.3 million persons received food stamps. In 1992, 25 million were on the food stamp rolls. The cost of the program increased from $550 million to $22.65 billion and it is estimated that it will increase to $22.70 billion in 1993. The cost of the school lunch program has also increased: from $300 million in 1970 to $3 billion in 1992. The Aid to Families with Dependent Children program (AFDC), the amount spent on medical assistance programs — all have increased tremendously during recent years. [14]

These are not simply cold statistics, they speak of human need and misery as well as waste and mismanagement. Working to alleviate poverty does cost money. But money is not the entire solution, especially when it is estimated that only 25 percent of the welfare dollar goes to the poor, and 75 percent goes to the care and feeding of a "lumbering and wasteful" bureaucracy. Approximately 530,000 government employees are being paid to work on welfare programs in no one knows how many offices. Their monthly payroll alone is more than $954 million: that's $11.49 billion a year. Welfare is big business.[15]

The fact that we may be upset by Caesar's social welfare programs should not mean that we oppose helping those in need. What we do (or should) oppose is the way the system operates. It's not just the waste and cost in dollars and cents; more importantly it is the waste and cost in human lives and potential. *

Racial Solution

Not too many years ago, America's black community could be viewed as a single social bloc. That is no longer a valid view. Today there are two black Americas.

*/ For more on the Biblical (Christian) approach to the problem of poverty, see Chapter Nine, "The Greatest of These Is Love!"

One is on its way up the economic, social, and political ladder. The other remains without jobs, on welfare and often without hope.

Although an increasing number of black Americans have worked hard to get an education and increase their incomes and standards of living, about one-third of all black Americans live in abject poverty. Most of this black "underclass" exists in the inner-city areas of our nation's urban centers. They live in an "unending cycle of joblessness, broken homes, welfare and often, drugs and violence."[16]

In 1989, 43.2 percent of all black children were in poverty. In 1987, 1 million black children were in two parent households while 2.3 billion were in one parent homes. Poverty in the two parent households was 12.5 percent; poverty in the single parent households was 87.5 percent.

Consider the sorry facts of life for a youngster growing up in that black inner-city environment:

- One out of every two lives in poverty.
- One out of every two grows up without a father. (That is twice the 1965 ratio of one out of four. If present trends continue, by the year 2000, 70 percent of black families in the inner-city will be headed by single women.)
- Almost 50 percent of the inner-city black teenagers are jobless and cannot find work.
- 25 percent of all babies in the inner-city are born to teenage girls.[17] (Black teenage girls have the highest pregnancy rate in the industrial world. With each baby born, the mother gets increased public assistance benefits (AFDC).[18]
- One out of every 21 black young men is murdered.
- According to one recent survey of two thousand inner-city black teenage males, crime accounted for one-fourth of their income.[19]

What is the root of the problem?

Some blame racism. Others fault the changing job market with its increasing demands for skills.

But others insist the major cause is a moral crisis that has spawned a ghetto culture and deteriorating family values.

One prominent conservative black voice concerned about the tragic situation is Dr. Glenn C. Loury at Boston College. Dr. Loury argues that "too many blacks have become 'gimme' people, too willing to accept welfare, affirmative action, and government assistance. Civil rights," he emphasizes, "is more than removing obstacles to black achievement. Equality is the winning of respect on the basis of accomplishments."

> It's about time we stopped talking about white racism ... and start taking action against black apathy, the enemy within. We talk about economic independence but we produce no products, create no jobs. We talk about quality education, but we don't learn to read, to write, to speak good English, to guide our own youth. We rumble and mumble about the quality of life, the prevalence of crime and drugs in our neighborhoods, but we do nothing about discipline of black youths, the reduction of the number of black babies born to teenage mothers."[20]

The late John Chamberlain once suggested that the Aid to Dependent Children program "has put a premium on home desertion by the male parent. The home without a father means bigger welfare checks for mothers — and the more children the better ... in black welfare circles, 'mother's day' is the day in the month the government checks go out."[21]

After hundreds of billions of dollars in taxpayer funds were spent on public assistance, education, and housing for the disadvantaged, about one-third of the black Americans were not better off — in fact, they were worse off than before. Charles Murray, in his book "Losing Ground," reported increasing indications that the federal welfare programs of the past twenty years have not solved but have compounded the troubles they were designed to cure.

Consider these statistics:

• In 1960, 56.2 percent of America's black population was at or below the poverty line. In 1970, 29.5 percent of blacks lived below the poverty live (compared with 8 percent of whites). In 1989, 27.8 percent of blacks lived below poverty, compared to 7.8 percent of whites.
• Today the poverty rate among black Americans stands at 27.8 percent down slightly from 30 percent in 1974.[22]

In the past twenty years, a new middle class of black Americans has been taking shape and increasing in numbers. Since the mid-1960s the number of middle-class black Americans has more than doubled. The great majority of blacks are working out better lives."

Working for A Better Tomorrow

The number of black Americans between the ages of 18 and 24 enrolled in college continues to increase. In 1984 that number had risen to 19 percent.[23] By 1991, it stood at 31.8 percent.

Twenty years ago, 41 percent of the jobs held by black workers were blue collar and only 19.5 percent were white collar jobs. In 1985, 41 percent of jobs held by black Americans were classified as white collar and 32.5 percent were blue collar. The number of "household help" jobs (maids, janitors) held by black Americans declined from 12.6 percent in 1965 to 2.8 percent in 1985.[24]

In 1960 only 38 percent of black Americans owned their own homes. In 1990, 43.4 percent were home owners.[25]

Their record of achievement is heartening. During the past twenty years

- The number of black accountants, college teachers, and other professionals has almost doubled
- the employment of blacks in white collar jobs has more than doubled
- the number of black Americans graduated from college each year has almost tripled
- the number of young black people graduated from high school has more than doubled
- the number of black Americans employed as foremen and supervisors has increased more than 50 percent.[26]

From 1983 through 1991

- the number of black lawyers and judges rose 23 percent
- the number of nurses increased 32 percent
- the number holding managerial and professional specialty positions increased 48 percent, and
- the number of black Americans in the crafts and skilled trades grew by 35 percent.

There is still a way to go but the record is heartening.

In 1990 there were some 7,370 elected black officials in the United States — five times the number in office in 1970. There are 447 black federal and state legislators; 4,481 black city and county officeholders (including the mayors of such major cities as Los Angeles, Philadelphia, Detroit, Atlanta, and Washington, D.C.). There are some 1,655 black members of various educational agencies and boards.[28]

The number of Hispanic Americans enrolled in college increased from 103,000 in 1970 to 448,000 in 1990 and to 526,000 in 1991. Hispanic Americans hold an increasing number of federal and state legislative offices and have served as mayors in such cities as Denver, Colorado, and San Antonio, Texas.[30]

There is still much to be done before the ground at life's starting gate is level as is the ground at the foot of the Cross. But, it is — and should be — the spirit of America to solve these problems, to help those in need who are willing to help themselves and to care for those who cannot. That is a Christian mandate, a mandate given to us by our Savior and our King.

Minimum Wage

One of the economic categories in which blacks and other minority groups have made no progress and, in fact, have lost ground is the rate of unemployment among teenagers sixteen to nineteen years of age.

In 1954 the unemployment rate among white teenagers was 12.1 percent and the rate among non-white teenagers was 16.5 percent. The spread between the two was 4.4 percent. In 1991 unemployment was 14.9 percent among white teenagers and 39.3 percent among black teenagers.

Why the drastic increase in unemployment among non-white teenagers? Lack of education, lack of basic skills? Yes. There is a definite correlation between level of education and employment among black teenagers.

In 1989, of those black young people with only one to three years of high school, 27.9 percent were unemployed; 14.2 percent of those with four years of high-school were without work; 7.5 percent of those with one to three years of college were without jobs and 7.1 percent of those with four years of college did not have jobs.

Of those who had five or more years of college, only .1 percent were unemployed.

The message is clear: education makes a difference!

One of the greatest causes of teenage unemployment has been and is the minimum wage laws. Every time that minimum wage is raised, another door is slammed in the face of those who are trying to grab the lower rungs of the economic ladder.

Today the $4.25-an-hour federal minimum wage law keeps hundreds of thousands of teenagers — white and non-white — out of the job market. It consigns them to welfare, to the streets, to crime; it robs many of them of the opportunity to earn sufficient money to get additional education. And it prevents them from learning on the job so they can begin to climb the ladder of economic self-sufficiency.

Dr. Walter Williams in "The State Against Blacks," concluded:

> These workers are not only made unemployable by the minimum wage, but their opportunities to upgrade their skills through on-the-job training are also severely limited."[31] Professor Jacob Mincer, in a landmark study of minimum wage laws, reported: "The net minimum wage effects on labor force participation appear to be negative for most of the groups. The largest negative effects are observed for non-white teenagers, followed by non-white males (20-24)."[32]

It is a hard fact of economic life that many first-time job seekers just do not have the education or the abilities to deliver $4.25-worth of work an hour. Any businessman who expects to stay in business cannot afford to pay for something that is not produced.

As economist and author Henry Hazlitt pointed out, "The law cannot make a worker worth a given amount by making it illegal for anyone to offer him less. It can merely make it unprofitable for employers to hire workers of low skills and therefore forces such workers into unemployment."[33]

That is true. If it seems harsh, blame the consumer. To raise the hourly wage, the businessman must raise his prices. When prices get too high, the consumer cannot or will not buy. Ask yourself, "Is that not true?"

Is not the minimum wage law a violation of the unalienable rights of those young people? Yes, it is. Federal and state minimum wage laws are, as Professor Williams observed, "acts of governmental intervention in the labor market." He terms the system, "Minimum Wage, Maximum Folly."

Who are we and who is Caesar to tell young people they cannot pump gas or sweep floors or carry parcels for less than so much an hour? That is a matter between employee and employer. As long as their transaction is made voluntarily, wages are their business, not the business of some lawmaker in Boston or Sacramento, Jackson or Richmond or Washington, D.C..If we truly want to help non-white teenagers, we can repeal the minimum wage laws. Get government out of the wage-setting business and let the minimum wages seek their own levels in the marketplace. Employers can then afford to employ unskilled teenagers, and the young people can earn while they learn. What is involved in this is not just economics but psychological and sociological factors as well.

Foreign Assistance

Some people sneer at the United States and call it stingy and selfish. Yet, no nation has ever given so freely of its substance — its wealth, its production, and its resources.

During World War II, Americans sent more than $42 billion in lend-lease to sustain our Allies and help defeat the Axis. You and I are still paying the interest on a large part of those gifts that were deficit-financed.

From the end of World War II through 1989, we have given more than $319 billion in aid to other nations. That's just the tip of that iceberg. Most of those billions were borrowed money. We're still paying compounded interest on much of that foreign aid; over the years that interest has resulted in increases in our federal debt. Add the interest to the principal and the total cost skyrockets. It is manifestly clear that those billions of dollars in foreign assistance, and the subsequent and continuing interest we are paying on the principal amounts to a sizeable portion of our enormous $4 trillion debt·

Our gifts to Great Britain and France helped those nations climb back from the devastation of war.

Our economic aid rescued West Germany from the brink of economic disaster.

Our help gave Japan new life and helped make them one of the great economic and financial powers in today's world.

Our economic and technical assistance has meant the difference to many emerging nations.

From 1950 to 1953, we spent $54 billion and the lives of 54,000 of our young men to help the Republic of Korea make its fight for freedom.

All told, we spent more than $150 billion and 58,000 lives to try to help the South Vietnamese defend themselves from the tyranny and a bloodbath of communism.

Today we spend billions of dollars and station hundreds of thousands of our armed forces in foreign lands around the world in an effort to keep the Western world free and provide it with a measure of security.

We sent our men and women to the Persian Gulf to thwart the designs of an evil Saddam Hussien (and left before we made sure he had been neutralized). We have sent our Marines into that sad, sick and starving Somalia in an effort to rescue the sick and starving from the war-lords who prey like vultures on those poor unfortunate souls. It may be, as some insist, that "New World statesmen" may have other designs and purposes for the deployment of our bravest and best. But, we American citizens support such missions of mercy because it is in the nature of our Christian heritage and culture to help the oppressed and to alleviate the down-trodden.

Consider what all of this has meant to and done for the nations that have received our help.

Consider also what those sacrifices have cost the American people. Think about those men who lost their lives in the fight for freedom. Think about what might have been done with all those monies if we had thought only of ourselves, if we had spent those funds here at home while ignoring the agonies and needs of others.

Think about that $286 billion in foreign aid. Look at what those billions (just the principal without the interest) could have done here at home. They could have provided the capital investment for more than

- 3,190,000 productive jobs in industry (at an average capital investment of $100,000 per job) for plants, machinery, and equipment.
- 2,800,000 private dwellings (at an average cost of $100,000 per house)
- 31,900 miles of divided four-lane freeway (at an average cost of $10 million per mile for right-of-way and construction)
- 15,950 hospitals (at an average capital outlay of $20 million each for land, buildings, and equipment)
- 6,380 college campuses (at an average cost of $50 million for land, buildings and equipment)
- a $4,830 savings account for every one of the 66 million families in the United States, or
- millions of students loans for our young people who seek a higher education

That is just an indication of what Americans gave to other nations since 1946 through our government, with our taxes and debt. Over and above that were the voluntary gifts of individuals, churches, and other private institutions in support of missions, medical and educational relief, and various self-help programs.

All of this is what we gave. And yet there are those who criticize us for doing so little.

Well, what other nation has ever done so much? Name one!

What if There Were No United States?

Years ago John Gorton, then the Prime Minister of Australia, commented on the compassion and the generosity of the American people:

> I wonder if anybody has thought what the situation of comparatively small nations would be if there were not in existence a United States of America — with a heritage and a willingness to see that small nations who might otherwise not be able to protect themselves are given some shield. Imagine what the situation would be if there were not a great and giant country prepared to make such sacrifices![35]

This review of what Americans have done is not made to boast. It is presented to make two points:

1. We have shared God's blessings with others who were less fortunate or were in peril, and

2. We could not have helped as we did without first having worked and saved and invested to produce America's material wealth. Before we shared we had to produce; before we gave we had to earn. And the reason we able to give in such magnitude was primarily because of the free individual enterprise system which is not only the most productive but is also the economic manifestation of the Christian idea of man and society. To put it bluntly, no socialist economy could generate — and no socialist/communist government can match that record of foreign aid, period. Stewardship is better than socialism!

Pagan Economics

When the second edition of this book was published in 1987, the world was a far different place than it is now. Back then, the world was basically divided between the Communist bloc and the Free World. Despite the exaggerated claims and subterfuge on the campuses and in the media, the Communist nations had been coming unglued over the years. In fact, the economy and thus the society of Soviet Union would have crashed in pieces long ago if the West — bankers and governments, including those in the United States — had not kept propping it up. Yet even as the evil empire starting coming apart, there were those — in fact, there still are those — who boast that socialism is the way to provide the most for the greatest number. They see socialism — godless socialism — as the wave of the future. That turkey won't fly.

The free individual enterprise system produces the greatest good (and goods) for the greatest number of people.

Because there are those who refuse to learn the clear and compelling lessons of history regarding collectivism, this section on "'Pagan Economics" is printed here just as it was published in 1987. Perhaps it will demonstrate what has been clear to most thinking Christians all along:

> Humanity will reach its highest potential — spiritually, politically and economically — only when God's will and the Christ's cultural mandate — the Christian idea of man and government and economics — are the bases of society.

Check the Record

In "America's Needs and Resources", Frederic Dewhurst whacks the spike on the head: "Of all the great nations the one that clings most tenaciously to private capitalism has come closest to the socialist goal of providing abundance for all in a classless society."[36]

That's the record for all to see.

Yet, after all the years of the utter failure of socialism, some still depreciate the achievements and the aspirations of this America of basically free people. Some still persist in extolling the "virtues" of socialism. Some would have made covenant with the godless empire that was the Soviet Union. Some even now urge that we change our system to "match" the accomplishments of collectivism.

We must assume they refer to the production of goods and services — to the creation of material wealth and welfare.

Surely they would not want our nation to "match" the Soviets in the absence of individual freedom, or in slave labor camps, or purges, or the manner in which they imprisoned and raped and ravaged the captive nations.

Surely they would not want us to match the Soviet's genocide in the Ukraine in the 1930s, that dark, dark era when the Kremlin heartlessly, purposefully and diabolically starved to death some 10 million men, women, and children.

What are these collectivist achievements they would have us match? Well, putting all the ungodly horrors of that system aside for the moment, let's compare the achievements of the two systems — theirs and ours.

In order to "equal" the situation in the Soviet Union we would have to

- scrap 40 percent of our electronic equipment
- cut our coal production by 40 percent
- reduce our use of electric energy by about 42 percent
- shut down more than 70 percent of our hydro-electric capacity
- cancel 50 percent of our aluminum production
- destroy virtually all of our copy machines
- slash our natural gas production by more than two-thirds.

Just to "keep up" with the Soviet Union, we would have to

- rip up 18 of every 20 miles of paved highway
- junk 18 out of every 20 cars and trucks
- destroy 95 out of every 100 computers
- discard about 100 million TV sets; close down 2 of 3 major TV networks and let the government take over the remaining one; close down all the cable TV; outlaw the local TV stations; virtually destroy all the newspapers and magazines except those owned and operated by the central government
- rip out 8 of every 10 telephones
- tear down 7 of every 10 private homes
- dump one-third of all our refrigerators, 75 percent of all our radios and 80 percent of our vacuum cleaners and almost all of our microwave ovens, and
- reduce our gross national product by $2.5 trillion

At the same time, we would cut our standard of living by more than 50 percent.[38]

And, oh yes, increase the number of men and women in our armed services by 65 and increase our annual expenditure for defense by $250 billion ... while doubling the rate of infant mortality and cutting six years off of our average life expectancy.

Surely, that can't be what the followers of communism would have us match. That's not progress; that's atheistic madness.

Our Daily Bread

In 1989, with a total population of about 288 million, the Soviet Union had an estimated gross national product of $2.66 trillion. In that same year, with a population 235 million, the United States turned out a gross national product of $5.2 trillion, just about double that of the USSR.[39]

On a per capita basis, the Soviet's GNP came to $9,226; the per capita GNP of the United States averaged $20,910.

Translate the gap between the United States and the Soviet Union into some of the necessities of life:

In the United States, it takes the average worker about eight minutes to "earn" a loaf of bread; in the Soviet, it takes a worker about seventeen minutes.

In the U.S.A. it takes the average worker nine minutes to earn one dozen eggs. In the USSR it takes ninety-three minutes.

In the Soviet Union it takes Ivan about 160 hours to earn a man's suit and it takes Katrina about 42 hours to earn enough for a woman's dress. Here, Bill Bagadonuts can earn a new suit in about 20 hours and Mrs. Bill can earn a new dress in about 8.

In the United States, the average worker can earn the money for a new compact car in about six months; in the Soviet Union, it would take Dimitri at least four years to earn a new car, if one were available.

Those are just a few of the material differences. The spiritual gap — the chasm between individual freedom and socialism — is a Grand Canyon. The Soviet Union is a slave state; slave states cannot compete with free men. Not for long.

Charles Horton examined socialism's abysmal record page by page. He let the facts show the difference for what it is (and what it isn't). His findings should sound a clear and certain warning to those who might think well of socialism.

Socialism now has a track record — a whole book of them: 40 attempts in 40 countries, and 40 abysmal failures!

It is no longer an abstract ideal but an actual system that has been put to the tests of time and use. It flunked everywhere, on all counts.

It promised social justice, but delivered tyranny.

It promised equality, but delivered privileged elites — lots of goodies for them but a grim and spartan existence for everybody else.

It promised abundance, but delivered scarcity and economic stagnation.

It promised happiness, but delivered the infinite boredom of a drab, gray world.

It promised boundless opportunity, but delivered a stifling of initiative and motivation.

It promised freedom, but delivered a massive smothering bureaucracy that dominates all aspects of economic and personal life; and functions at a pace that makes a snail look like a racehorse.

No wonder socialism is in retreat around the world. It turned out to be a cruel and tragic hoax that could not deliver what it promised.[40]

Down on The Farm

Nowhere is the failure of socialism more obvious than in Soviet agriculture. Prior to the Communist take-over in Russia in 1917, that nation was a major exporter of agricultural products. Now, year after year, there's not enough food. Time after time, the Soviet Commissar of Agriculture was bounced and a new one named. It made little difference, food continued to be in short supply.

The most obvious indication of the problem was the Soviet's annual trek to the free world to buy millions of metric tons of grain just to have bread on the table to deal with the threat of workers' protests. During one six-year period, the United States sold the Soviet Union almost 12 million metric tons of grain. During those same years, we sold the other Eastern European nations another 8 million metric tons of grain.

Most of that was financed by low interest loans guaranteed by our government. While American farmers were having a rough time and while some were going bankrupt unable to obtain government assistance to save their farms, the United States government was selling food to the Soviet Union at low interest rates and at reduced prices subsidized by the American taxpayers — including the farmers.

The Soviet authorities blamed the wheat shortage on the weather. Farmers in other nations cope with similar weather conditions and produce enough grain for both domestic and foreign sales. For years American and Canadian wheat was the staff of life for much of the Soviet population.

The fact is Soviet "agriculture under the Communist system ... proved to be both costly and woefully inefficient."[41]

The plain truth is this: free men do produce more and better.

Results of Regimentation

The Soviet Union has complete control over the people of Russia for sixty-seven years. Even with such total regimentation, it could not make socialism work. As R. E. McMaster, Jr., wrote in his excellent newsletter, "The Reaper," "The Soviet Union would probably fall flat on its face economically and militarily if it were not for the support given it both militarily and economically by the United States."[44]

To put it bluntly, for a long time we American taxpayers subsidized the Soviets and kept it going while spending more than $300 billion a year to defend ourselves from the Soviet threat. We drained ourselves to stay free and the bankers pocketed the money.

The Soviet Union has had, over the years, billions upon billions of dollars of help from the United States government ever since New York bankers helped to bankroll the Communist takeover of Russia in 1917. We, the people, gave the Soviets $11 billion in lend-lease during World War II. At Yalta, through our elected representatives and our unelected State Department, we "gave" them the Eastern bloc nations — sold those people down the river — and threw in half of Berlin and permitted them to "liberate" tools and machinery from the factories of a defeated Germany.

From 1945 to 1983 we continued to give them some $600 million in foreign aid while they were busy pushing toward world domination.

American business corporations built their hydro-electric plants, their automobile and truck factories, and their pipelines. American precision micro-ballbearings made it possible for Soviet ICBMs to zero in on targets thousands of miles away, and our transfer of genetic and biotech smarts enabled them to perfect biological and chemical warfare.

Even today the banks in the free world — the U.S. banks among them — loan the Russians millions upon millions of dollars. In 1985, while the world, including the Soviets, was condemning the United States for its raid on Libya, domestic banks in the United States joined in a combine to loan the Soviet Union $427 million at 6.78 percent interest.

The giant Kama River truck plant, which made more military vehicles than any other factory in the world, was built with the help of the Ford Motor Company. About 45 percent of the costs of that plant were financed by the American taxpayer through the Export-Import Bank. The Chase Manhattan Bank in New York helped finance the rest.

Trucks manufactured at the Kama River plant saw service in Vietnam where 55,000 American boys were killed. You could have seen the trucks built at the Kama River factory any day on the roads of Afghanistan. They were there to help the USSR slaughter the freedom fighters; to transport the troops and guns that destroyed the Afghani villages; to disperse the chemicals and biological warfare weapons, which burned their children and consigned them to a slow and tortuous death.

General Electric ("We bring good things to life") supplied vital electrical generating equipment to the USSR. The Gleason Corporation trained some 300 Soviet engineers in the use of its sophisticated machine tools. General Electric, Dresser Industries and the Caterpillar Company provided virtually all the technology for the Trans-Siberian pipeline.

Lenin apparently knew what he was talking about when he said, "The capitalists of the world, and their governments, in pursuit of ... the Soviet market, will close their eyes to the higher reality ... In other words, they will labor for the preparations for their own suicide."

Senator William Armstrong of Colorado stated it best:

> The great irony for Americans who are asked to tighten their belts in order to pay for our defense needs is that much of the additional money ... is required to offset Soviet weapons that probably could not have been built without our assistance ... the U.S. and other Western nations have sold to the Soviet Union and its satellites more than $50 billion worth of sophisticated technical equipment the communists could not produce themselves.[46]

Richard Nixon warned in "Real Peace" that "By trading with an aggressive, expansionist power you are fueling a fire that could eventually consume you."[47]

"Simply put," says McMasters, "the Soviet Union today is a product of USA, Inc. The USSR is propped up today by the United States' loans, foodstuffs, military equipment and technology."[49]

Thus do our government officials and businessmen make covenant with God's enemy while taxing the citizens to build and maintain a military establishment geared to defend us from that very enemy.

The Widening Gap

In 1987, when the second edition of this book was published, this was what was being written:

> If the United States and its Western allies were to stop trading with that potential enemy, it would fall like a rotting plum into the hands of the Russian people who might then have a chance of freedom. For, even with such continuing outside assistance, socialism continues to be a failure.
>
> The gap between the achievements of socialism and free individual enterprise in terms of gross national product and standard of living is not closing: it continues to widen. In recent years, even while carrying the increasing burden of governmental costs and governmental controls, America's free individual enterprise system has continued to out-produce the socialism of the USSR.
>
> Analysts see no likelihood that the Soviet Union will match the economic achievements of the United States within the foreseeable span of years.

Archbishop Fulton Sheen told us why:

> Socialism which seizes, divides, expends and dissipates wealth is anti-Christian. It always has produced poverty. It always will, for it discourages the man who is dispossessed. Few will work hard if they know they are to be dispossessed of the fruits of their own labor.
>
> On the other hand, those who receive something for nothing learn to depend upon it. Their initiative, self-reliance and effort decline accordingly.
>
> These two factors combined are the reasons for poverty and suffering produced by socialism.[50]

A Lesson for Us

This section was reprinted virtually intact from the 1987 edition of this book so that we might examine the decline of the Soviet Union and thus prove a point:

Free men produce better.

Stewardship—free individual enterprise based on the Christian ethic — stewardship works!

That may not be acceptable to the "politically correct" but this is fact: it is historically accurate.

But ...

...there is nothing of survival inherent in freedom!

Each new generation must take a stand to protect it, preserve it, and cherish it. There is no assurance that our central government will limit or retrench its activities and confine itself to its constitutional responsibilities.

Indeed, recent years and events give us reason to fear that the Caesars of this nation — and their megabanker and multinational corporate friends — will become bolder and more aggressive. They have that lean and hungry look — that look of lust for the wealth and power of a new world order.

> A Government that manipulates the people's money and credit, that regulates and controls the people's wages and prices and rents and profits, that owns, or closely supervises numerous business activities, and that offers welfare programs from cradle to grave is a government which threatens to tax the citizenry into serfdom.[51]

If freemen want to continue to produce more and better, if they desire to be free to obey God's dominion mandate and to preach The Gospel to all nations, they would do well to get this republic back to God and back to the Constitution ...

... a serf is a serf is a slave ... not a steward, but a slave!

God desires for His people to be His stewards, not Caesar's slaves.

CHAPTER EIGHT

Controlled People
and
Uncontrolled Government

And The Lord spoke unto Moses, "Go to Pharaoh
and say unto him, 'Thus says The Lord:
'Let My people go, that they may serve Me.'"
(Exod.8:1)

Neither the government nor government spending, neither government planning nor government controls built this nation. The red tape of the petty clerks, the hot air of politicians, the schemes of demagogues, the usury of money lenders — those did not build the republic.

The prayers and the plans, the minds and the muscles, the tool and the capital of America's producers — the working men and women and investors of this nation — that's what built America!

Look at the tremendous record of the recent decades. Check these facts and figures.

In 1946 the gross national product of the United States was $212 billion. By the close of 1984 it had increased to $3.7 trillion! And, for 1991, the Gross National Product was estimated at $4.1 trillion. Even in terms of constant 1972 dollars, our GNP quadrupled in those 45 years.[1]

That spectacular increase in the gross national product has meant more for more people.

In 1947, the median income for our 37.2 million families was $3,031. In 1983 the median income for America's 62.7 million families was $26,443.[2] In 1991, the median family income was $37,783. Even in constant 1982 dollars from 1945 to 1991 (reflecting the loss in the dollar's purchasing power due to inflation during that span of years), the per capita disposable income rose from $ 5,285 to $11,328 —

Muscles, Minds, and Money

These achievements of production and distribution of wealth, did not come out of any council chamber or legislative hall. Indeed, most came in spite of most of the actions of government. They resulted from the productivity of free men and women — labor, management and investor — working together.

Since the end of World War II, American business and industry have invested trillions of dollars in new plants, machinery, and equipment. In 1960, total business and industry expenditures for new plants and equipment was $34.1 billion. By 1992, business and industry had upped their appropriations for plants and equipment to $580.5 billion.[5] In 1959, the average capital investment per productive worker was $17,528. By 1988 the average investment per worker to provide the plants, the tools, and the equipment was $197,196.[6]

In 1950, American business and industry employed 59 million workers. By 1990 the number of employees in private industry had increased to 117.9 million and average of annual earnings stood at $24,563.

From 1960 to 1990, the nation's output per man-hour in the private sector almost doubled while average compensation per man-hour increased nearly seven-fold. Workers had more leisure time as more machines and more sophisticated machinery and techniques increased their productivity. Today machines supply almost 95 percent of all the energy expended in manufacturing in America!

Today's Red Sea

This amazing productivity of American business and industry has kept this nation from sinking in the rising red tide of government confiscation, regulation, spending and debt.

Even as the gross national product rose — that is, even as management and labor increased the amount of goods and services produced in the nation, government's take of the GNP rose even more rapidly, Uncle Seizer was gobbling up a larger and larger chunk of that product. The "take" has increased year after year. According to the United States Office of Management and Budget (OMB) federal revenues (the tax take) increased from $94.3 billion in fiscal year (FY) 1961 to $599.2 billion in 1981, to $1.054 trillion in 1991 and to $1.091 in FY 1992. But, as Howard Phillips, chairman of the Conservative Caucus observed, "The tragedy is that, even as revenues increased so

GOVERNMENTS' "TAKE" AS PERCENTAGE OF GNP

Year	Total "Take"	Federal %	State/Local %
1929	9.9%	2.6%	7.3%
1947	18.5	13.1	5.4
1960	26.6	18.2	8.4
1970	31.3	20.5	10.8
1980	32.6	22.5	10.0
1990	37.3	23.3	14.0
1991	37.5	23.1	14.4

Source: *Facts and Figures on Government Finance*, 1992 Edition, p 66
Tax Foundation, Washington, D.C. 1992

dramatically, federal spending increased even more." Federal spending soared from $97.7 billion in 1961, to $678.2 billion in 1981 and then up to $1.381 trillion in FY 1992.

While the number of non-government workers rose 109 percent from 1947 to 1989, the number of government employees on the taxpayers' payroll (not including the military) tripled — an increase of 308 percent. In 1947 there was one government employee for every eight persons employed in the nation's private sector work force. In 1989 there was one government employee for every five workers in the private sector.

There were 15.79 million on the government payroll in 1989 and the total government civilian payroll (not including the armed forces) chewed away on $421.5 billion a year.[7]

What of the increase in taxation and debt to pay for Caesar's insatiable appetite? Well, the annual tax take for all government (federal, state and local) increased some twenty-fold during those years - from $55 billion in 1947 to $1.439 trillion in 1989.

Even that did not pay for Caesar's excesses. We had to go into hock to keep him in the style and programs to which he had become accustomed.

Thus, the total public debt was hiked more than ten-fold during that same period; from $237 billion in 1947 to $2.3 trillion in 1984 and to an estimated $4+ trillion in this year, 1933.

What was it The Lord had Samuel tell those Israelites when they demanded "make us a king to judge us like all the nations"? The Lord said, "show them the manner of king that shall reign over them ... he will take your fields and your vineyards and your oliveyards, even the best of them ... and he will take the 10th of your seed ... he will take the 10th of your sheep ... and you will be his servants".

Actually, they got off kind of easy; would that our government would settle for "the tenth"!

By the Rules and By the Numbers

What do all those facts and figures add up to? This:

Government is bleeding the patient dry. The faster our economic heart pumps, the faster government drains our economic lifeblood. It is consuming our increased productivity at a rate faster than we can manufacture it.

It is redistributing the wealth from the productive to the non-productive sectors of society.

Government is necessary and need not be evil or exorbitantly expensive. But after securing those necessities of public life and those Constitutional duties and functions spelled out by the Framers — maintenance of law and order, protection of life and limb and property, national defense and security, operation of the public infrastructure (roads and highways, waste disposal) — that's it, period. To go beyond that is not only unConstitutional, it results in eating away the nation's seed-corn which is essential if we are to have a growing, thriving, productive economy.

Government is not a producer; it's a taker, a taxer, and a spender and a borrower.

Every dollar spent by government is a dollar taxed and taken from the workers and earners and investors. Every dollar borrowed is a tax against the future — plus interest. It is a dollar that cannot be spent or invested by the productive sector.

Government is not only draining our economic lifeblood. In addition, the Lilliputs of politics and bureaucracy are binding our productive Gulliver with more and more controls, laws, regulations, rulings, and edicts and report forms and returns.

Former U.S. Senator Thomas McIntyre of New Hampshire once estimated that "the paperwork generated in one year in Washington alone would fill Yankee Stadium from the playing field to the top of the stands 51 times."[10]

It costs business and industry billions of dollars a year to handle the paperwork involved with government controls, regulations and reports. Government spends still more billions each year for printing, processing, stapling and shuffling and filing the forms and reports. There goes billions and billions a year for red tape, filing cabinets, copy machines, postage stamps, and wastepaper baskets.

It took 1,100 permits and approvals before the construction of the Alaskan pipeline could begin. When that project was first proposed, the estimated cost was $1 billion. After years of political demagoguery and governmental foot-dragging and paper work, the total costs came to more than $6 billion. Politicians and bureaucrats won't foot that bill; the consumers will.

The Heavy Hand of Government

When the Seabrook, New Hampshire, nuclear generating plant was first planned and designed, the estimated construction costs to get its two units on line were $1 billion. There followed almost ten years of governmental hassles, aided and abetted and exacerbated by environmental extremists. The delays and changes added about $4 billion to the costs of the installation and caused the utility company serious financial problems. The bureaucrats in Washington and the environmentalists from other states who picketed and protested will not pay those costs; the energy customers of New England will.

The Interstate Commerce Commission (ICC), established in 1887 to regulate railroads and prevent monopolies, drove most railroads into bankruptcy, has created monopolies of its own, and for decades stifled competition in the nation's surface transportation industry. Even though the industry was finally deregulated to some degree, a large number of unnecessary rules remain, most of them adding to the cost of transportation, which the consumer ultimately pays.

Under the Civil Aeronautics Board (CAB), controls and restrictions forced interstate air carriers into a form of government-controlled cartel that destroyed competition. "Excess fares" and "excess capacity" imposed by the CAB cost air passengers millions of dollars each year. When the airlines were deregulated, competition increased; new airlines entered the industry, fares were drastically reduced and the number of airline passengers increased greatly.

The Federal Occupational Safety and Health Act (OSHA) and the state OSHA laws (which must be tailored to fit the federal laws) have sent an army of bureaucrats, inspectors, and spies into business and industry. Under OSHA rules, these "safety engineers" have the authority to invade any business at any time without warning or warrant. These legionnaires for Caesar hold the power of life and death over businessmen. They can and often do act as policemen, prosecutors, judges and juries. Complaints against an employer can be made to OSHA in secret, and anyone alerting an employer to an OSHA inspection can be fined. (Occupational safety is important and the vast majority of employers are conscientious in that regard. But the police state tactics are out of place in a society of free people!)

Womb to Tomb

Government, wrote Dr. Raymond Moley, is with us from the womb to the tomb: a share of the federal debt hangs around the neck of every newborn babe, and when we are buried, we are consigned to a grave cut to government specifications.

Add it all up and it comes to this:

Controlled citizens and uncontrolled government.

And, while we are on the subject of uncontrolled government, consider those we send to Congress; those men and women who are to represent us before their colleagues from the other states of this republic. Those men and women who promise to serve, honor and represent us 'til elections or death do us part. These are they who take their annual pay hike in the dark of the night without a public vote - and butter their pension with millions of taxpayer dollars.and do what's best for the nation.

These are they who pass the laws and set the rules. Ask yourself what do these laws they have put on us have in common:

• The Civil Rights Act of 1964 (prohibits discrimination on the basis of race, color, creed, gender or national origin).
• The National Labor Relations Act (permits employees to organize or join a labor union).
• The Fair Labor Standards Act (sets federal minimum wage and standards for overtime pay).
• Equal Pay Act (equal pay for comparable work).
• Occupational Safety and Health Act (OSHA — establishes and enforces health and safety standards in business and industry).
• Age Discrimination in Employment Act (prohibits discrimination on the basis of age).
• Freedom of Information Act (gives citizens access to information regarding governmental decisions made "in the dark" by executive

agencies.

• Independent Prosecutor laws (require judges to appoint special counsel to investigate charges of wrong-doing by government officials).

• And, the 1993 Family Leave Act (mandating certain time periods employers must grant employees who want time off to attend to family affairs such as birth of children, etc.)

What do all those and many other laws have in common? This:

Not one of those laws applies to Congress. Congress has excluded itself, exempted itself from those laws. Congress has established its own Golden Rule: *"Do it to others, but not unto ourselves."*

America really does have a privileged class!

The Fat Cats

The real crisis in this land, after the spiritual and moral crisis, is the Caesar crisis — the uncontrolled, grinding growth of the costs and controls enforced by an uncontrolled and virtually untouchable federal government.

Some years ago, Donald Lambro belled the cat in his book, "Fat City: How Washington Wastes Your Taxes":

Our federal government has become a bloated, extravagant, paternalistic, remote, cluttered, disorganized, inefficient, frivolous, duplicative, archaic wasteland.

America has an excess of government. And it is getting fatter and costlier with every passing year.

Americans have more government than they need, more than they want, and more than they can afford. Like a riderless locomotive whose throttle has been pulled wide open, the federal government is running out of control.[12]

The locomotive is still running out of control.

Conservation, Yes. Extremism, No!

As God's stewards, Christians are not to waste the resources He has bestowed upon this nation. We are to husband the earth, the air, the water, and the bounties thereof. We are to be judicious in our stewardship and considerate of generations to come as well as those here now.

Conservation and development of our natural resources is morally correct and economically sound. However, extremism in the pursuit of ecology is no virtue; it is a vice.

But, there is now developing in the land another force that would be a controller of the people's lives, liberty, property and pursuit of happiness. It is becoming more and more evident that some would use, indeed have used, the current (and understandable) wave of environmental concern to advance their One World goals.

These are the ecology cops.

Patrick Buchanan issued the warning: "We all want clean air, clean water, clean beaches, the finest of our architecture preserved, the old battlefields left alone. But, there is something manic and intolerant about this (ecology) movement, about the hostility its fanatic acolytes show toward growth, development and progress. This issue needs airing before we all pay a permanent price. — the environmental movement has, in the late 20th Century, taken on the trappings of a new religion."

The Wall Street Journal, as it fretted over the goings on for Earth Day, 1990, attested "we are coming to see environmentalism as religion."

The eminent American sociologist. Dr. Robert Nisbet, saw the danger and weighed the potential consequences early on:

> Environmentalism is now well on its way to becoming the third great wave of the redemptive struggle in Western history, the first being Christianity, the second being modern socialism ... the dream, of a perfect physical environment has all the revolutionary potential that lay both in the Christian vision of mankind redeemed by Christ, and in the Socialist, chiefly Marxian, prophecy of mankind free from social injustice.

To many of the leading pushers and organizers and propagandists of the environmental movement (and the annual Earth Day ritual), the enemy is Christianity. Their pronouncements are openly and clearly anti-Christian.

"Christianity," they insist, "is destroying the environment because of God's commandment to man to subdue the earth."

Thomas Berry, a Catholic theologian, claims that "our Western industiral civilization, which emerged out of the Biblical-Christian-humanist matrix, is the cause of this imperiled (environmental) situation."

Professor Lynn White, Jr., " ... we shall continue to have a worsening ecologic crisis until we reject the Christian axiom that nature has no reason for existence save to serve man ... Christianity made it possible to exploit nature in a mood of indifference to the feelings of natural objects."

And TIME, the magazine, caps it all off by announcing that "the spread of Christianity, which is generally considered to have paved the way for the development of technology, may at the same time have carried the seeds of the wanton exploitation of nature..."

As Don Bell reported in his *Don Bell Reports,* "If the controlled communications media give us a correct reading (about Earth Day) the worship of Mother Earth (Gaia) by the people of America will greatly surpass the observance of the resurrection from the dead of our Lord and Savior."

Perhaps the most disturbing aspect of this so-called environmental heirarchy, after its open hostility to Christianity, is its nihilistic view of mankind. One John Davis, a member of the eco-group, believes that "Human beings, as a species, have no more value than slugs."

Ingrid Newkirk, a goddess of the environment, insists that "When it comes to feelings, a rat is a pig is a dog is a boy ... There is no rational basis for saying that a human being has special rights ... The smallest form of life, even an ant or a clam, is equal to a human. Six million Jews died in concentration camps but six billion broiler chickens will die this year in slaughter houses."

Some Blatant Myth-stakes

Paul Ehrlich is author of "The Population Bomb." He is also the man who predicted years ago that by now much of the Atlantic seacoast would be under water because of global warming and rising ocean levels. Dr Ehrlich charges that "The more common misconception of the population problem is that it's a problem of poor Indians who don't know how to use condoms. Actually, the problem of the world is too many rich people.

"One rich American causes 1,000 times more destruction to the planet than one person in the 3rd world."

It's small wonder that some have likened several of the leaders of environmental extremism unto watermelons: green on the outside and red on the inside. (Scientific data shows that, without exception, the "most poisonous polluters for decades" have been the socialist and atheistic nations such as the members of the communist Warsaw pact.)

As for Dr. Ehrlich's dire predictions concerning the "population bomb" — he asserts there are 120 million more people in the U.S. than any sensible analysis can substantiate — take this little test and see for yourself:

1. Divide the population of the U.S. into households of four persons. Give each household one acre of land. Now, how much of the total land mass of the U.S. (excluding Alaska) would be occupied? (Figure the U.S. population at 250 million and the total U.S. land mass at about 2 billion acres.)

2. All of the urban and built-up land use activities in the U.S. - roads and highways, airports, churches, shopping centers, factories, houses, schools and universities, golf courses, race tracks, football fields, dumps, cities, villages, etc. and etc. - all the land involved with those "living and working" spaces, would add up to what percentage of the nation's land mass? (Based on "A Forecast for Earth Day," by Dr. William A. Fischel, April 19, 1990)*/

"If I am right," wrote Larry Abraham in 1990, "What you are witnessing is nothing less than the beginning of the final stages of the drive toward the New World Order. This strategy could be described as 'the greening of the reds.' It's clever, it's powerful, it is believable. And, most dangerous of all, it's working."

President Bill Clinton has announced, he will raise the Environmental Protection Agency (EPA) to Cabinet status.

Ecological considerations are indeed important in our society, and no doubt most of those concerned about our environment are sincere and well-intentioned.

But, when environmental extremists pre-empt reality and ignore facts, they cause more damage than improvement or progress. For one thing, they are playing fast and loose with the lives and well-being of many Americans.

If you doubt that, talk to the lumbermen of the Pacific Northwest whose families struggle to get by on welfare because the spotted owl is more important than feeding children or paying the mortgage. But, to them, the *Humanist* magazine has words of comfort and solace: "Loggers put out of jobs find their reward in the immortality of the spotted owl."

And, editorialized the magazine, "If the end of DDT deprives impoverished Third World children of cheap protection against malaria, the return of the peregrine falcon still uplifts the human soul."

*/If you came up with between 3% and 4% you're a winner!
Same for the whole wide world, about 4%

Or, you might talk to the apple growers of Washington state about irresponsible environmental extremists. If you can, chat especially with some of those man who can't grow apples anymore because thy are out of business. Why? Well, here's why:

In 1989, CBS newsman Ed Bradley told *60 Minutes* viewers that the chemical Alar, which was used to keep apples crisp and prevent spoilage, caused cancer in children. The information came from the Natural Resources Defense Council. All across the nation, people stopped eating apples from Washington. School districts cancelled the apples for the school lunch menu. Medical school dean Sanford Miller hastened to assure the public that the risk from Alar was "effectively zero" — that one would have to eat something like a barrel of apples a day to raise any concern. But, the damage had been done: Because environmental extremists and television zealots had created an "Alar" crisis where one did not exist. Growers lost more than $250 million; many went bankrupt.

This Will Bug You!

Consider, as another case in extremism, the problem of the tussock moth.

The tussock moth is no big thing. From stem to stern it measures only one and one-half inches. But it can destroy giant fir trees. The great Douglas fir which nature may have taken fifty or sixty years to nourish can be ravaged in one or two seasons by that pesky moth. The little old tussock makes its home in the tops of those trees and is carelessly prolific with its eggs and larvae. Some of the larger trees can be salvaged after the moth has done its work, but the smaller trees are lost forever. There is only one chemical that can kill the insect and protect the trees: DDT.

The Federal Environmental Protection Agency (EPA), however, said the use of DDT was a no-no. It refused to let the foresters use the insecticide, claiming it might harm the environment. Thus, the trees died while the EPA "protected" the environment. Hundreds of millions of feet of lumber were destroyed in the name of ecology.

In one spectacular example of bureaucratic stupidity, the EPA okayed the use of 84,000 pounds of DDT to dust a dried pea crop but refused to okay the use of the chemical on an adjacent stand of fir trees infested with the tussock moth.

The peas survived.

The forest was wiped out.

And This Will Kill You!

So, DDT was outlawed. What did the EPA recommend as a substitute for DDT?

Methyl parathion.

What is methyl parathion? It is a highly toxic, deadly, organic phosphate. Consider the following points.

1. Years ago more than one dozen persons were killed in Tiajuana, Mexico. The cause of death? Eating bread made from flour that had been accidentally contaminated with methyl parathion.

2. The tragic wave of parathion poisonings in the South, mostly of children, raises some extremely pressing questions for the federal government.

3. "Methyl parathion is the hottest of organic phosphates. Five drops can kill 150-pound man. It is infinitely more dangerous than DDT."[15]

Parathion acts like mustard gas and paralyzes the respiratory system. Furthermore, it is not always effective. As an insecticide, it may kill the insect, but it has no effect on the insect's eggs. Farmers using the deadly chemical must spray or dust several times after each batch of eggs is hatched. That not only multiplies the hazards but it increases the cost of production. And guess who pays. The consumer.

Productivity

The soaring costs of big government, the continuing counter-productive bungling of bureaucrats, the political pandering to extremist groups: these all work to wreck the productivity of America.

The so-called new politics and new economics make it difficult — impossible in some cases — for businesses and industries to save or secure sufficient investment capital to replace, expand, or modernize their plants and equipment. Often the capital available costs so much its use is unprofitable.

For years double-digit inflation and high interest rates caused by spend-and-deficit policies of many politicians and their bureaucratic colleagues (in both major parties) blunted initiative by destroying incentive.

Those spend-free economists and politicians believe government can spend this nation into prosperity. They have made a fetish of growth at any price — not sound growth but simply growth. There is a credit card philosophy: spend now, inflate the balloon, pay later.

And pay we do. And pay and pay.

The Grace Commission warned that unless deficit spending was brought under control, by the turn of the century the federal debt could swell to more than $14 trillion. What would the interest be on a federal debt of $14 trillion? At 10 percent it would be $1.4 trillion. Based on projected population figures, that would be about $20,000 for a family of four. That's some inheritance to leave to our children and grandchildren!

Some years ago, then-President Ronald Reagan warned:

"The large and stubbornly persistent budget deficit remains as a dark and threatening cloud on the horizon. It threatens our prosperity and our hopes for continued healthy economic growth."[17]

That's no way to run a nation. It's no way to sustain an expanding economy and no way to build a stable society. It is the route to bankruptcy, disruption, and despair.

The years of strain under those spend-easy policies are beginning to take their toll. The cracks are beginning to widen.

During recent years the rate of increase per man hour in the United States has lagged behind that of the other free-world nations.

The following table compares our growth in productivity (output per man-hour) with that of a number of other industrial nations in the free world for the 1980 years.[18]

Increase in Output Per Man-Hour in the 1980s

United States	41.41 %
France	40.95
West Germany(FDR)	26.83
Italy	45.34
United Kingdom	61.40
Japan	49.95

Source: *Facts and Figures on Government Finance*, 1992 edition, p 66. Tax Foundation, Washington, D.C.

This next table compares the rise in unit labor costs during that same period, the 1980s.[19] It shows that the United States had relatively low unit labor cost increases during that decade.

Increase in Unit Labor Costs in the 1980s

Country	Increase in Unit Labor Costs in the 1980s
United States	11.30 %
France	18.21
West Germany (FDR)	45.05
Italy	47.03
United Kingdom	6.86
Japan	56.89

Source: *Facts and Figues on Government Finance,* 1992, P 66

Tax Foundation, Washington D.C.

Productivity is the key to strong growth and a vital economy. In the past several years there has been a slight decline in productivity in the United States. These decreases must be reversed if we are to insure an increasing — or even, stable — standard of living for Americans.

American workers are still the most productive workers in the world. "Labor productivity — that is the amount of output produced per employed person — is higher in the U.S. than in any other industrialized nation. But, for some key industries, we have clearly fallen behind, and overall, other nations are gaining on us despite our recent improvement."[20] Translation: the U.S. is still in the lead in productivity. But there is no room for complacency; our international competitors are closing the gap.

What's the relationship between productivity — output per man-hour — and gross national product? Well, here roughly is the magical equation: A one-tenth of a percent increase (or decrease) in productivity equals a $1 billion increase (or decrease) in the GNP.

Productivity is the key to prosperity. When productivity increases, the standard of living rises. When it falls, the standard of living drops.

Foreign Competition

The decline in output and the increase in costs are catching up with us not only at home but also in the world markets. Many American businesses are finding it increasingly difficult to compete with foreign countries.

Every year since 1976 imports from foreign nations have exceeded U.S. exports. In 1976 the foreign trade balance in merchandise was minus $8.3 billion; in 1984 that negative balance increased to $112.5 billion; in 1990, $98.8 billion. In 1990 U.S. exports of goods and services totaled $623.9 billion while imports of good and services came to $722.7 billion.[23]

The increasing trade imbalance can easily be seen in many different products: automobiles and trucks, clothing apparel, radios and television sets, textiles, oil, leather products, steel, office machines.

Many of these items are produced by what we consider slave labor. In fact, millions of dollars worth of goods imported into the United States were made by slave labor in Red China (some of it in factories financed by the capital of American corporations).

The impact of the trade deficit is hurting Americans and America. Every dollar in imports means dollars and jobs going to competition in foreign nations instead of to companies and workers and investors here at home. Industries such as automobile and steel have especially felt the brunt of the foreign competition.

What Price Free Trade?

There is a rising conflict between those who insist on letting free trade operate (which means few or no restrictions on imports) and those who demand some protection for American industries and American jobs.

The current debate concerning the North American Free Trade Agreement is about seeking a balance fair to all. This agreement, in principle, by the U.S., Canada, and Mexico will, if approved, eventually produce a tariff-free trade zone on the North American continent. Other nations in Central and South America might eventually join in a Western Hemispheree trading bloc which would surpass even the European Community in population and total trade. That potential, alone, makes it important to reach some equitable and beneficial agreement between the North American nations.

Free trade is desirable as long as it is truly fair trade. However, when foreign nations subsidize their industries while American business is forced to subsidize government, and when foreign competitors flood this country with their products but set up barriers against American-made products, that is neither fair nor free trade. The goal is not to halt trade between nations but to establish some rules of trade and to improve our own productive capacities.

During recent years, other nations have been spending a higher percentage of their GNP on research and development and modern plants and equipment; their governments have encouraged such investments. The United States must move to restore its competitive edge to the point where we can once again maintain a favorable balance of trade.

Increased capital investment and productivity and fair trade agreements are the keys to survival in the emerging world economy. Oil imports have been and continue to loom as a major cause of trade deficits. Congress has been lax — in fact, derelict — in not encouraging the discovery and development of alternate energy sources. In their lethargy or animosity regarding such development they leave us captive to OPEC and the Big Sisters of the oil industry.

Working Together

It is time for Americans to be Americans again!

Together, labor and management and capital built the prosperity of this nation. Together, we can get this nation moving again. Together, we help insure a brighter future for our children and their children. And, together we must force the government to return to being our servant instead of our master.

What are some of the steps we must take to increase our productivity? To restore our vitality so that we can continue the real war against poverty and win the battle against debts and deficits and, yes, inflation?

Well, one thing is sure. We won't do it by looking to Caesar to be our shepherd and provider. We won't win the battles at home or in foreign trade through increased government spending or bureaucratic controls and intervention.

Those who think that it is up to government to create growth and wealth overlook the fact that increased economic growth depends upon the intelligence, work and thrift and investments of individuals and corporations.

People — not government — create growth.

All the government can do is to encourage and make it possible for people to save and invest.[24] To loose the bonds on investment capital and let it go to work for all concerned -- worker, manager and investor. In other words, the best thing government can do is to tend to its own business as set forth in the Constitution and get out of the way so that the people can tend to their business.

Savings, Investments, and Tools

"There is only one way to achieve growth — that is by increased savings and by increased investment in the tools of production. In this way there is a greater flow of goods resulting from human labor."[25]

Remember the magical formula? MMW = NR + HE x T.

Man's material welfare equals natural resources plus human energy multiplied by tools.

The tools used by free men are the key to productivity. And, productivity is the key to economic growth and well-being for the greatest number of people. James Watt, inventor of the steam engine and pioneer of the idea of replacing muscle power with tool power, did more to fight a war against poverty than all the kings and emperors and politicians and bureaucrats combined. And that's a fact. Bill Gates of Microsoft, the giant in computer technology, has done more to win the war against poverty than all the legions of welfare agents scurrying hither and yon throughout the nation. And, that's a fact!

Our free individual enterprise system has enabled our people to save, invest, buy, and own the tools of production. That has resulted in this nation being able to achieve the greatest material well-being for more people than ever before in history. Thus, it is obvious that our material fruits have spiritual roots! Why? Because free individual enterprise — stewardship — is a Christian concept, a Christ-centered endeavour by free people under God.

Free men, under God, produce better.

The conservation of capital — the savings and capital of Americans now being drained off by excessive, bloated, wasteful government — will not come to pass without some real reforms.

The problems of capital and savings confiscation and some suggestions for basic tax reform are dealt with in Chapter Ten, "Taxes and the Power to Destroy."

For starters, we should return the control of our money and banking to the Congress, as the Framers of the Constitution stipulated. Get the heavy hand of the international bankers and money brokers out of the control of our economy, out of our treasury and out of our pockets: we should, in other words, get rid of the Federal Reserve System and get out of the International Monetary Fund and the World

Bank. We should move to regain and maintain the integrity of our currency. We should get back on the gold standard.

If we are to close those open, bleeding, economic wounds that Caesar has inflicted on our national body over the years, we must assume the role of attending physicians — and soon.

We, the people, should pray and work and so conduct ourselves that we can give birth — rebirth — to liberty which is found only in that nation which is blessed because God is The Lord.

Progress — and Conservation

Government is not the only source of interference with the activities and productivity of free men. Unrealistic strictures in the name of "environmental protection" are also impeding the output and the enhancement of the nation.

The desire for economic resurgence should not be an excuse for debauching our lands or fouling our nests. Yet it is reason to require and preserve the balance of environmental considerations with concern for economic well-being. What one person rejects as pollution, hundreds may see as a sign that the factory is still in business and their paychecks are secure. Food on the table and shoes on the children are just as important — in fact, more important — than an unobstructed view or a pristine field of wild poppies or snail darters in a brook.

Progress and conservation are not incompatible. It is unrestricted and irresponsible extremes which cause the conflict; it is government officials knuckling under to eco-extremists that often holds back the genius of the American society. The answer is to restore and practice obedience to God's dominion mandate and seek the proper dynamic balance between conservation and development.

The Lord's injunction, His mandate, is not simply to have dominion and multiply, it is also to replenish and protect.

Stop Featherbedding

Finally, we must remove restrictions on output (productivity) that exist as a result of industry or union monopoly.

Such work restrictions should be an anathema to free men. It is immoral and unbiblical to prevent individuals from producing to their fullest and best capabilities.

At this time when the nation and the world need increased productivity and foreign competition is growing stronger, this is not only a matter of principle but economic necessity.

Make-work rules in home building and manufacturing are counter-productive; they are wasteful and destructive. They raise costs and prices and slow down sales.

Bricklayers once laid more than a thousand bricks a day; now they are not permitted to lay half that number.

In some areas, painters are still not allowed to use brushes more than four inches wide and sprayguns are prohibited. In many industries workers who are capable of much higher output are held back. Machines that are capable of much higher production are restricted. Attempts to increase production to curb costs and compete with foreign enterprise often result in labor-management disputes and costly work stopages.

Some of these make-work (and/or slow-down) practices have already been outlawed or outmoded. Yet many persist because of bureaucratic and judicial twistings of the law. In many instances such actions are an open flaunting of the intent of Congress; this should be stopped.

Antitrust

Americans have traditionally been opposed to cartels, trusts, and monopolies that destroy competition and impose their demands on the people by controlling huge segments of the market. Yet we permit one monopoly to continue in the private sector year after year: the monopoly of organized labor, separate and apart from the great number of working men and women.

Labor unions should be brought under the Anti-trust Laws. This is essential for the protection of both the public and the working men and women of America. There was a time when unions needed the assistance of favorable legislation to get organized and stabilized. That time is past. The time for the free market in labor is long overdue. The need today is for American industry and labor to work with the Congress to achieve some proper and equitable method of making sure that American labor are not summarily abandoned in a flood of imports produced by cheap foreign labor while North American free trade agreements are developed.

Industrywide bargaining should be outlawed. Too often such negotiations are permitted to run roughshod over the rights of others and the interests of the public. Coastal and even nationwide dock strikes are certainly a case in point.

Every working man or woman should have the right to join or not to join a union, to engage in collective bargaining or not. The right to voluntary and free association is an unalienable right. But it must be just that: voluntary and practiced without duress or retribution from either union or management.

It is just as immoral for unions to force a working man or woman to join a union as it is for management to force them not to join. Voluntary association has been a traditional and honored principle in America.

There may be benefits attached to union membership; there may be detriments. Those are secondary to the primary principle of freedom — the freedom to choose and to join or not to join. Both choices should be protected without duress or undue pressures from any source.

The Measure of Wealth

*"For where your treasure is,
there will your heart be also"* Luke 12:34

A nation's wealth is not — and will not be — measured in terms of material prosperity alone.

In fact, in the long run, it will be measured more for its spiritual well-being.

Material wealth that is a by-product of spiritual growth is important, however. In addition to making it possible for us to care for our own, it enables us to feed the poor, help heal the sick, clothe the naked, house the homeless, comfort the widows and orphans, care for the less fortunate, and give tangible expression to our love for others in the name of and for the sake of Christ Jesus.

How we gain our material wealth — through the application of our God-given talents, energies, and resources, guided by His principles and precepts and how we use our wealth — freely, as individuals, through love, with compassion and concern — are the true reckoning of our riches.

The Meaning of Wealth

Thus, material wealth, productivity, is a spiritual instrument as well as a physical tool and economic measure.

It enables us, it empowers us, to use the blessings of God's love for us and His bounty to us to help not only ourselves but others. It enables us to give as well as receive.

God loves a cheerful and faithful giver, and He also loves a grateful and faithful recipient.

By being productive as individuals and as a nation, we can serve as God's pipeline, His transmission belt, God's instruments and purveyors of His blessings.

The Lord God, sovereign over all that is, could with the sweep of His hand transform this earth into an Eden. Someday He will. But for now, in this realm, He chooses to work through us. The task is ours. The choice is ours.

In the final analysis, that was what the Puritan ethic was all about — and that is what productivity in a Bible-based nation should be about; using the talents and time He has given to serve Him and be His stewards; husbanding that which He has assigned to us.

To produce so that we can not only benefit but share.

To earn so that we may give.

To learn so that we may teach others.

To love as He first loved us.

To be motivated, moved, impelled through the Holy Ghost, rather than being coerced, controlled, and compelled by the deadly hand of Caesar.

To be about His Great Commission

To pursue His Cultural Mandate.

To restore the foundations and reclaim this nation for Christ. Praise God!

What a great time this is for the followers of Christ!

Onward, Christian stewards!

CHAPTER NINE

The Greatest of These Is Love

"'You shall love The Lord your God
with all your heart, with all your soul,
and with all your mind.' This is the first and great
commandment. And the second is like unto it:
'You shall love your neighbor as yourself'"
(Matt. 22:37-39).

Christians are under the law — not the rotes and rituals of the ancients — but the law of love.

"If you love Me," said Jesus, *"keep My commandments"* (John 14:15).

This is the commandment Jesus gave us: that we love The Lord our God with all our hearts, with all our souls, and our neighbors as ourselves (Matt. 22:37-39).

Love is the fulfillment of law.

If you love The Lord, truly love Him, you will keep all His commandments. All His principles. All His precepts.

Now there is faith and there is hope and there is love. But, the greatest of these is love (1 Cor. 13:13).

Not the needlepointed, maudlin, ersatz, fleeting love of this plastic age. Not the chrome and glass computerized love of the superstate.

The real, moving, deep-down, constant love that lifts, that moves, that acts. Love that walks with God and seeks to do His work and His will. The love that never fails.

That is the mark — the stewardship, the discipleship, the more excellent way — of the Christian life, the Christian world and life view.

Charity

Love is like faith: without works it is dead. Words alone are not enough.

Charity is love in action. It is the act of loving. Without love, charity is diminished.

So you bestow your goods upon the poor. So you give your body to a cause. So you climb the highest mountain for a goal. So?

Without love, all that is nothing. Paul wrote about love in 1 Corinthians 13.

A tinkling cymbal. A sounding brass. A play to the crowd. A bid for acclaim. A boast for self-righteousness. An empty gesture.

Love is not puffed up. Love is not an empty gesture. Love is not for public acclaim. Love is personal. It's one-for-one. The Savior for the sinner. The saved for the Savior. Husband for wife. Parent for child. Christian for Christian. Love of one for another. Yes, even for the unlovely.

Crowds do not love. They acclaim. They cheer. They follow. But they do not love. And what they feel is transient. Fleeting.

Institutions do not love. Institutions are clinical. Cold. Lifeless. There is no love in inanimate objects. Caesar may act but not through love.

True love abides no middleman.

Love by proxy is a sham. A brittle thing. Sparkle without warmth. Shine without soul.

Christ had no proxy. He came. He gave Himself. He paid the ransom. There was no middle man at Calvary. No proxy. Only Jesus. And there was love: the real thing!

Do Thou Likewise!

Love! Love is an action word! A doing. A going. A giving. A blessing. One-to-one.

Consider the good Samaritan (Luke 10:25-37).

There on that dry and dusty road that ran from Jerusalem to Jericho. There in the heat of the day. There in the sweat of the noon sun.

After the goons had finished with the traveler, after they had stripped him of his belongings and his clothes, they left him for dead. A crumpled heap by the side of the way.

Several other travelers came along. A priest. A Levite. They kept right on going. They didn't want to get involved.

But, the good Samaritan. He was something else!
He stopped. He knelt down in the dust. He gave of himself, of his oils and balms and bandages. He bound up the stranger's wounds and

carried him to the village. He didn't stop to check to see if the fellow had Blue Cross/Blue Shield. He didn't wonder whether he was eligible for Medicaid. He did not run to the county hospital or the welfare office to say, "Hey! There's a guy back there who needs help."

No. He carried the stranger to the inn and cared for him.

The next morning he gave more. He paid the hotel bill and assured the innkeeper,"Whatever it takes, care for him. When I come again, I will pay you - the whole bill."

Remember that parable? Remember the message? Remember Christ's words?

"Go and do likewise" (Luke 10:37).

There! There is love.

And there is the law of love, the second part of Christ's Great Commandment:

"Love your neighbor as yourself" (Matt. 22:39).

There was a time when Christ's church was the center of charity. When the manifested glow of Christian love radiated and gathered and loved and aided those in need. One to another. Person to person. Congregation to member and to family. Church to community. A living part of a living Christian ministry.

It was so in the days of the early church. In the time of the pure and primitive understanding of the Gospel.

As the church historian Augustus Neander reported, this was the mark of the Christian: "See how they love one another!"

Say something like that these days and people raise an eyebrow. That's the way it is; those who do not know true Christian love don't understand the capacity, the nature, the attributes of love. The whole spectrum of love. Paul gave us that in 1 Corinthians 13:1-13. In those verses he laid it all out.

The Salem Story

The early American Christians knew the Scriptures. They sought to live them. Consider the Salem, Massachusetts, of the late 1700s and early 1800s. In his book, "Revolt Against Maturity", Reverend R. J. Rushdoony tells us about the Christians of old Salem.[1]

Salem was a sea town, a sailor's town. During the years 1795 to 1845, wave after wave immigrants swelled the population of Salem. In those fifty years it jumped from 2,500 to 45,000.

Given a proportionate increase today and given today's social values and mentality, Salem would be awash with federal grants and

aids and bureaucrats. But the Christians of Salem then were not
geared to Caesar. They were attuned to Christ, bound in the love and
the laws of Jesus. They were His branches and they bore good fruit.

- Christian schools were founded to care for the
  immigrant children (and no Caesar warned the
  teachers they could not teach from the Bible or
  lead youngsters in prayer and praise).
- Missions were founded to provide for the bodies
  and souls of the newcomers who were mostly
  without funds or resources.
- Hospitals were organized to care for the increase in the sick; county homes were operated
  to care for the indigent.
- Orphanages were started for the homeless children; classes in the English language were
  founded, with the Bible as the textbook.

All that and more in the name of and for the sake of Christ
Jesus!

What a witness!

How did they do all that? Not through taxation and coercive
levies. Through tithes and offerings unto God; through works for Him.
Their funds did not go to Washington or Boston to return shrunken in
value and effectiveness. Salem's was a local Christ-centered work, as
God had commanded.

Salem was not unique. As Reverend Rushdoony pointed out,
"It was the Christian community, in its zeal to bring every man under
the renewing power of God, that did more than anyone else to cope with
the central problems of American life between 1800 and 1850."

Is it any wonder that Alexis de Tocqueville, famed chronicler of
life in the United States, could write, "There is no country in the world
in which the Christian religion retains a greater influence over the
souls of men than in America."

What would de Tocqueville write about the United States and
American Christians today? Guess!

We have let Caesar take over the tasks Christ assigned to us.
Sometimes we invite, even require, Caesar to do our chores. As we have
relaxed our grasp on our Christian responsibilities, Caesar has
expanded his reach. Now he controls without invitation. Coercion has
replaced compassion. Legalities and regulations have pre-empted
love. Thus, we walk in the ways of the politicians rather than the steps

of the apostle Paul. So it is that Caesar is glorified and Christ denied.

Aside from the failure of the Christian commitment, this is fact: the welfare state is a lousy stand-in for Christ; the computer is a poor substitute for love.

Milton Mayer wrote of this in his book, "What Can a Man Do?" In his chapter on love, "Caritas," Mayer recounted the days of Hitler's Germany. He demonstrated that there is not necessarily a relationship between love and the giving of bread to the poor. "The need for bread was great in Germany and the Nazis fed the poor, but they fed them without love, and in taking over the feeding they relieved the Germans of the necessity to love one another."[3]

The State made possible the gift without the sacrifice. And without sacrifice there is no real love.

What's that you say? One must sacrifice to pay Caesar to do the job. True. But, there is a distinction between willing, loving sacrifice and confiscation. The one builds; the other destroys. The one worships God and obeys Him; the other bows down to Caesar and pays him.

As Mayer reminds us, Hitler's instrument for feeding the poor was the "Volkswohlfahrt" (the people's welfare program). That program was primarily intended to strengthen the Nazi's hold on the regime and that was hardly a regime of love.

We would do well to take a lesson from the evils of the purpose and consequences of that Nazi design.

Personal Responsibility

Welfare today is seldom an act of love. It is most often a tool of the politician, an instrument of the State, employed to pacify pressure groups and buy votes.

Things are out of whack, out of hand, devoid of The Holy spirit.

Nowhere — nowhere in the Scriptures — did Jesus teach the institutionalization of love or charity. Over and over He spoke of personal love, personal giving, personal responsibility. Of loving one another — person-to-person, even the stranger. Christ made it clear that we could not hide behind Caesar's law as an excuse to duck our personal responsibilities to the Lord God.

There is no Christianity in the concept that pressure groups, desiring material benefits, have the right to use the power of the state to take property from some for the material gain of those who have the political power. That is plunder, and it is still plunder even if Robin Hood declares that he is robbing the rich to help the poor.[4]

Good intentions are not enough. They often tread a well-known road. Compassion strained through the State is not love; it is a cop-out. Coercion that robs one to relieve another is not an act of love; it is a rip-off. Each individual is responsible. Each is accountable to God. Who says so? Jesus said so. Read Matthew 25:31-45.

In the final reckoning, Caesar's tally comes up a negative. The more he is required to do what we should have done, the more we will be held to task.

Yet there are many contemporary Christians who have reached the stage where they are willing to permit — even seek, insist upon — social control from Caesar to supplant Christian love and Christian action. How could they! There is nothing of Christian love in Caesar's coercive controls.

"The proponents of social control and income redistribution by the State collide as directly with the teachings of Christ as would two trains running toward each other on the same track."[5] That's the way Reverend Russell Clinchy put it in "Charity, Biblical and Political."

Reverend Clinchy was Pastor of the First Church of Christ in Hartford, Connecticut, when in that timeless essay he stressed that

> Jesus was so uncompromising in His insistence that responsibility be placed on the individual for both his personal life and his attitude toward others ... Jesus never suggested an institution of any kind that could take the place of such individual responsibility. Nor did He ever mention an institution or a power to which an individual could transfer such responsibility, either by acquiescence, force or plunder.

How Great Thou Art!

Why did Jesus not seek the power of institutions to provide for others?

Because He never, never would have put the coercion of the State above the Sovereignty of God! He also knew the infinite power and the infinite bounty of His Father in heaven, the Lord God Almighty! To put it in the vernacular, why fool around with a box kite when there is a Boeing 747 at your disposal!

Remember the time Jesus fed the multitude (Mark 6:38-44)? With five loaves and two fishes He fed them - five thousand plus!

There in the desert, away from the city, the crowds had gathered and Jesus ministered unto them. He healed the sick. He made the lame to walk. The blind to see. The dumb to speak. Through the miracle of God's love and the majesty of His power, He did such wondrous things.

At eventide the disciples urged that He send the people home so that they could have some supper: But Jesus said, "No."

"There is no need to send them home. Feed them here."

Feed them! With what? Five loaves and two fishes? They questioned Him to Whom all power is given — Him Who created all that there was from the beginning.

Jesus took the loaves and the fish and He blessed them and gave them to His disciples to feed the multitude. And the people ate. Every one of them - the five thousand plus women and children. They ate until they were filled and even then there were twelve baskets of food left over.

How great Thou art. How truly great are the works of the Lord! Oh, you of little faith!

How is it we turn to Caesar for the answers to our problems?

"We Must Be Practical..."

Years ago the ministerial association in one of our major cities conducted a survey to audit the needs of the poor within their area. The survey indicated some pressing needs. Need for food, housing, clothing, and medical assistance. This, incidentally, was in a city that had one of the highest levels of per capita income in the nation!

Spokesmen for the ministerial association called a press conference to announce their plan of attack.

Did they call on the Christians of the city to give of their tithes and offerings, their time and their energies to solve the problems? No. They called upon Caesar to provide the assistance required.

One cannot fault those clergymen for their concern. But one must fault them for their course of action. Caesar was their solution. They ignored God.

In their impatience they adulterated their compassion with coercion.

Every one of those ministers represented a congregation. What were the members of those congregations doing? What of their

responsibilities, their personal Christian duties? Were they praying?
Tithing? Were they putting into action the law of gleaning? Were they
going forth, doing God's work? Or was it just more convenient to let
Caesar do it?

Each person in those congregations — every pastor and member
and family — is the child, the son or daughter, of a rich and powerful
Father. He holds the wealth of the world in his hands.

Ask and you shall receive. Blessings will be poured forth that
your storehouses cannot hold. Blessings on you and your efforts that
you cannot imagine.

Had they forgotten that? Or did they not believe?

What Love Can Do!

How much more Christlike were the works of Dr. Veronica
Maz.

Here was a woman who translated her deep concern and her
Christian love into personal action. A woman who put her faith to
work.

Dr. Maz left her post as a professor at Georgetown University
to love the destitute. She became the driving force (and what a force
love is!) behind S.O.M.E. (So Others May Eat) and also Shalom House.

S.O.M.E. came first. A home where men ravaged by alcohol,
men without hope, could find a meal, clothes, a bed, and a compassionate
rehabilitation program. S.O.M.E. served some five thousand meals a
month and provided beds for those who otherwise would have had to
sleep in gutters or empty doorways.

The idea for Shalom House developed as Dr. Maz saw the
number of homeless, hopeless women, drifting into S.O.M.E., hoping
to find a meal, a safe haven and rest. There was no other place for them
except the street and the savagery of the alley. Shalom House provided
for such women — as many as it could provide for within the limits of
its income and its facilities.

What was the source of that income?

Not Caesar!

Shalom House and S.O.M.E. were supported by free-will love
offerings. By tithes. By fund-raising programs and prayers of ladies'
Bible classes in the churches of the surrounding area. By groceries
given by supermarket. By unsold food donated by drive-in restaurants
and fast-food chains, and other foods from a catering company. By all
the other avenues of giving God provided.

Because one lady cared enough to love and because others responded to her Christian example and her call, these homes were established. That is an example of Christian love. Love in action.

"In as much as you did it to one of the least of these My brethren, you did it to Me:" (Matt. 25:40).

Imagine what all those ministers could have achieved, those who went traipsing off to Caesar's trough, if they had had the faith of Dr. Veronica Maz. Faith and works.

Their God Is Dead

Speaking before the Economic Club of Detroit some years ago, Dr. Alfred Haake, a Christian businessman, recalled a situation that had occurred in Pittsburgh, Pennsylvania. In the face of some pressing needs in that city, a prominent clergyman asserted: "The improvement of mankind through religion is nice to think about; but, after all, we are dealing with sin. Religion has its place, to be sure; but we must be practical about these things."[6]

Dr. Haake commented on the clergyman's statement:

In that little talk he set forth the idea which many other men have followed, that if God won't do His job, we will have to get Caesar to do it for Him. What in many cases appears to be a splendidly-motivated approach, an approach motivated by love for one's fellow men, motivated by genuine desire for the good of men, is coupled with impatience with the speed with which God is working things out. We cannot wait for the visibleness, the availableness, of God — if you please.

"So," concluded Dr. Haake, "we set out to implement our aims by social and governmental devices. It means, in the last analysis, that those who follow this course have lost faith in God."[7]

Perhaps Dr. Haake is too kind. If he had been blunt he might have said, "Their God is dead."

No, that's not correct. God is! He lives! Better to say, "They were dead to God."

When a man is dead to God, it is just a skip and a jump to go along with the thought expressed by Reinhold Niebuhr, founder of the Fellowship of Socialist Christians:[8]

[The Marxian] analysis of the technical aspects of the problem of justice has not been successfully challenged ... The program of the

Marxian will not create the millennium for which he hopes. It will merely provide the only possible property system compatible with the necessities of a technical age.[9]

So much for God in a "technical" age. We should use Marxist means to seek Christian ends; that was Reverend Niebuhr's invitation.

Nothing could be farther from the Scriptures. Only God's means — God's laws and God's principles — will meet God's ends. The delusions of false prophets will not do the job. When men follow men's programs, they end up following men, not God.

As Reverend Edmund Opitz observed, "In sober truth we are forced to recognize that many of our most articulate religious leaders are part of the problem, not part of the remedy. I have reference primarily to denominational and super-denominational agencies, rather than to local churches and their ministers."[10]

In an address before the Maine Farm Bureau, Reverend Opitz referred to John C. Bennett, once Dean of the world's wealthiest seminary and once a member of the socialist party. Dr. Bennett, praising "the awakening of the social conscience of the churches," had asserted: "The leadership and many strategic centers, such as theological seminaries and church boards and periodicals, in most denominations, are committed to the position that Christianity demands drastic changes in the structure of social life."[11]

Commented Reverend Opitz, "These 'drastic changes' spell out into something like socialism or the welfare state — an economic order based upon the social ownership of the large sources of wealth and power."[12]

Christ's church calls for changes in the hearts of men. When that occurs and when men then go forth in the name of Christ to put faith and love into action in accordance with God's laws, then socialism will be seen for the evil, inadequate, coercive force that it is.

Seek ye first the Kingdom of God - and His righteousness!

Christians know, or should know, that the regenerative power of The Living God, not the programs of Marx or the socialized reordering of the state, changes the world. Changes it for the better, that is.

Her God Lives!

Remember the story about Salem in the 1700s? How the Christians of that town served Christ by serving their fellow man?

That's old-fashioned and out of style in these days of Caesar's social welfare programs and public assistance handouts. Or is it?

Is such a witness through Christian love and works still possible? Even in this day and age? It is, indeed! The spirit that was in Salem is the spirit of Christ Jesus. It lives!

Consider what one woman started in the San Joaquin Valley farming town of Kingsburg, California. It is the story of Mrs. Cindy Rocker. A story of Christian love in action.[13]

When Mrs. Rocker said "I do" to Christ, that was just the beginning. She decided to be more than a hearer of the Word; she determined to be a doer also. A living, working witness for Christ. His words in Matthew 25:31-46 burned in her heart; they turned her life inside out!

She was led to start a ministry to the poor of the area. Her first endeavor for the Lord was a Christmas basket project for poor families in the town, now an annual Sponsor Family Program. Each sponsor family was paired with a needy family and provided it with all the ingredients for a happier Christmas season — tree, gifts, food , clothing, and the message of Christ's love. For the first time some of those needy families had plenty of food on the table for the Holy days and hope in their hearts.

"In as much as you did it to one of the least of these My brethren, you did it to Me" (Matt. 25:40).

Mrs. Rocker had more on her heart: "It's easier to give charity than it is to look at needs and try to find ways to provide opportunities so that people can take care of their own needs."

That was the start of the thrift store, a place where the poor could shop for necessities at prices they could afford. All of the merchandise is donated by the townspeople. Proceeds from the store provide funds for other projects. Caesar's funds are not wanted or accepted in that store. Tithes and love offerings only. That's what makes that world go 'round.

Next came a Christian preschool. Mrs. Rocker realized that many of the children of the Spanish-speaking farm families were at a disadvantage when they started school. They could not speak English; they knew nothing of classroom procedures; they were not acquainted with other children in the town. These factors produced a low self-image and a negative influence as the children progressed through the grades. Because of the Christian preschool, they now learn English not only from the teacher but by mixing with preschool children from other parts of town.

Said Mrs. Rocker: "All of the students learn from each other ... the more affluent Anglo children learn just as much from the poor children as the poor learn from them."

Next project on Mrs Rocker's list? A food bank! During five months of the year there was little or no work in the fields. During those months some of the children went without food. Now, every Saturday morning, volunteers manage the food bank, stocked with donations from local farmers, churches, and individuals. Members of the needy families often help in the store, preparing the food for distribution. It is their way of paying for the food they receive and of maintaining their dignity.

"It is a beautiful thing so see — all of the families joined together holding hands in a big circle praying to the Father to thank Him for the food."

Then came Carlos! Mrs. Rocker had an abiding concern because there was no place where the Spanish-speaking people of Kingsburg could hear the Word of God preached in their native tongue. The Lord answered her prayers; He sent her Carlos. Carlos was milking cows to support his wife and four children. In his spare time, he was attending seminary and making the rounds to tell his Spanish-speaking friends about Jesus Christ. Thanks to Mrs. Rocker's prayer and persistence, seven of the local churches joined together in the Kingsburg Hispanic coalition and hired Carlos as pastor to the Spanish-speaking community. Today he works closely with the food bank and preschool, conducts Bible studies (often out in the fields with the workers) and holds two church services each Sunday.

What of the future for this lady and her Christian associates who are very much alive to their Lord and Master? "Our future plans include housing, job training, tutoring, and adult education."

Says Mrs. Rocker, "Whatever we do, we will continue to walk by faith as we follow the lead of the Holy Spirit, moment by moment. We have learned that it is important to have patience and wait for God to lead the way. Then, as we follow, we are committed to perform with excellence anything we do in the name of Jesus Christ. The poor do not need tokens of mediocrity; they need compassion and action with excellence."

Now, there is faith, hope and love.

And the greatest of these is love! (1 Cor. 13:13.)

"Go," said the Master.

"Go thou and do likewise."

And Mrs. Cindy Rocker is doing just that!

A Right? Or, A Responsibility?

> What happens when government takes over? Charity gives way to politics. [And love gives way to force.] Funds coercively collected are dispensed to individuals according to group, class or occupational category. This has no semblance of charity; it is robbery of Paul to pay Peter. Further, when government constructs a feeding trough and fills it with fruits forcibly extorted from the citizenry, it creates new claimants and aggravates the problem it set out to solve.[14]

In the early stages of a task force probe of the various social services and public assistance programs, Charles D. Hobbs, a Deputy Assistant for Policy Development, calculated that there were some seventy different programs designed to alleviate poverty. Approximately 30 million people received benefits under those programs at a total annual cost of morre than $130 billion.

Economist and author Henry Hazlitt once described the situation as "welfarism gone wild." He delineated the underling causes:

> The causes of this accelerative increase are hardly mysterious. Once the premise has been accepted that "the poor", as such, have a "right" to share in somebody else's income - regardless of the reasons why they are poor or others are better off - there is no logical stopping place in distributing money and favors to them, short of the point where this brings equality of income for all....
>
> ...If I have a "right" to minimum income sufficient to live in "decency" whether I am willing to work or not, why don't I also have a "right" to just as much income as you have, regardless of whether you earn it and I don't? Once the premise is accepted that poverty is never the fault of the poor but the fault of "society" (i.e. the self-supporting), or of the "capitalist system," then there is no definable limit to be set on relief ... the politicians who want to be elected or re-elected will compete with each other in proposing new "welfare" programs.[22]

Isn't that just about what has happened? Isn't it what is happening today?

Welfare is not a right. There is nothing in the Constitution or in the constitutions of the several states that conveys welfare payments to be a right of anyone.

Welfare is a responsibility. That responsibility starts with each individual: it is the responsibility to take care of oneself and the welfare of one's family. The apostle Paul was quite blunt about this:

> For even when we were with you, we commanded you this: If anyone
> will not work, neither shall he eat. For we hear that there are some
> who walk among you in a disorderly manner, not working at all, but
> are busybodies. Now, those who are such we command and exhort
> through our Lord Jesus Christ that they work in quietness and eat
> their own bread(2 Thess. 3:10-12).

Concerning the responsibilities of the father to care for his family, Paul wrote to Timothy: *"But if any provide not for his own, and specially for those of his house, he has denied the faith and is worse than an infidel"* (1 Tim. 5:8).

Those who can but will not accept the responsibility of providing for their own welfare have no right to demand the fruits of another man's labor, not even if they can enlist the aid of pandering politicians. Nowhere — nowhere in the Scriptures — did Jesus teach that any man had the right to coerce another man into giving or the right to steal or take another man's possessions for himself.

There is a clear distinction in the Bible between the oppressed — those in need who cannot work — and those who can but will not work.

Christians have a responsibility to care for the oppressed, to care for those in need.

The poor, said Jesus, the truly needy, would always be with us. it is our task, our privilege, to serve Him by helping them. To minister to them physically and materially, as well as spiritually. To do this in love without thought of return. To do it as unto the Lord, not as unto Caesar.

That is our responsibility. But that is not the recipient's right. No man has a right to take from another unless what is taken is offered voluntarily. Any other type of transaction is coercion that demeans the taker and violates the giver. And that includes plunder that is "legalized" by politicians as well as plunder that is prohibited by law.

Not an Easy Road

Some may retort that all this talk about love and free will is a cop out. A dodge. A position of greed and a lack of compassion.

They have it all backward.

The easy way is to pass a law. To force the gift. To coerce. To confiscate and redistribute. To let Caesar be the middle man.

Things are not so easy for the Christian who would obey His King. Love is demanding. It demands responsibility. It demands discipline. There is no cop out there. No easy road. No easy ride. No pushing or prodding from the outside. Just the burning desire from within from the flame of love.

What? Is it love to tell a man who can work but won't that unless he works he will not eat? You bet it is. It would be much easier to throw him a buck or two or a bundle. To shrug and say, "We already gave at Caesar's office."

But if you love, if you really care, you will take the time to help him get some steel in his backbone. You will try to help him learn a skill, earn his way, rebuild his life, restore his dignity. That is love.

Booker T. Washington once wrote, "In bestowing charity, the main consideration should be to help those who will help themselves."

If you really love, you help the sick, the lonely, the hungry, and you do it on your own or in concert with like-minded Christians. You don't run to Caesar or his nephews or his cousins. As the good Samaritan did, so you do likewise.

Enough of Caesar!

There are those who preach a social action gospel. They are no doubt well intentioned. However, that gospel too often turns out to be the gospel of Caesar: The State shall be the shepherd.

In certain times and circumstances, government action is required and proper. But Caesar and his agents are no substitute for Christian love.

Rather than calling for an expansion of Caesar's welfare apparatus, Christians should be working to expand the Kingdom of our Lord Jesus Christ. They should be working to get Caesar out of the welfare business. If not all the way out, then at least reduced to those bare and temporary essentials that can be and should be handled at the local level.

Heresy? Heartless? A pious protestation in the face of misery? Not at all!

An act of love and common sense.

Caesar's existing welfare system is obscene. Its obscenities can be seen in the way they violate the givers. "The Welfare State replaces charity with the confiscation and redistribution of wealth."[23] Its obscenities can also be seen in the way it demeans the recipients. It dehumanizes. It treats all claimants as numbers, according to a fixed formula that refuses to take into account individual differences and needs.

Its obscenities can be seen in the way it wastes incredible amounts of money.

The National Life Underwriters' Association once offered this as the rule of thumb between giving and receiving:

- In person-to-person giving, a dollar given is a dollar received.
- In giving through voluntary organizations, twenty-five cents goes for administrative costs and seventy-five cents reaches the needy.
- Through state government, it costs one dollar to get another dollar to the beneficiary.
- Through the federal apparatus, it takes almost three dollars to deliver one dollar.

Caesar is a lousy steward!

Bring Charity Home!

If we as Christians — as individuals, as families, as congregations, and as volunteers and supporters of Christian charities — if we as Christians, as His, would truly fulfill our responsibilities set forth by Jesus and the apostles, we could put Caesar out of the welfare business and get him back where he belongs.

We could dismantle the leviathan of public welfare and bring charity back home to the individual, to the churches, to the neighborhoods.

To humanize the process of assisting those in need, the welfare system will cease to be a function of government. The problems of determining who is genuinely entitled to aid will become a function of those groups and associations who have most consistently concerned themselves with human and charitable works.

The churches, the synagogues and temples of the world have occupied this role for centuries, recognizing that ..."the poor shall never cease out of the land; therefore, I command you, saying, you shall open your hand wide unto your brother."[24]

An impossible task? An idle dream? Not so! Not if we will obey God. Not if we will become God's hands and open them wide.

"With men this is impossible; but with God all things are possible! (Matt. 19:26).

Applied Christianity

Americans are a generous people.

The American people have a willingness to lend a hand to those in need.

According to a Gallup Poll, 55 percent of the adult population participate in some type of volunteer work.[27] More than one-third of that work was through religious groups. In addition to that, countless millions of dollars were given on a person-to-person, neighbor-to-neighbor, congregation-to-needy families basis. Those gifts were never reported, simply given.

Such an outpouring of time and money is not unusual in this nation. That money comes in big checks and small donations; in thousands of dollars and dimes and dollars, in checks and pledges. It was all in addition to the federal, state, and local taxes taken by Caesar and his nephews and his cousins.

Americans have done much. In fact, if permitted to, they would do more. If there is a natural disaster, they respond. If there is a calamity, they are there, personally and through the organizations they fund.

Years ago when floods and mud slides ravaged vast areas along the Pacific Coast, winds and rains and high waters wreaked hundreds of millions of dollars worth of damage to homes, businesses, and farms. Many families lost everything they had; few were covered by insurance.

The leaders of the various volunteer groups — the American Red Cross, the U.S. Jaycees, the Salvation Army, the various service and church and civic organizations — were called to the state capitol to form an emergency Governor's Relief Task Force. They responded with enthusiasm.

During the course of the meeting, after the devastation had been inventoried and the needs assessed, the head of a state agency addressed the group. The substance of his remarks was wrapped up in his concluding statement: "We have developed a system to take care of these emergencies. That system has obviated the need for individual assistance."

In other words, Caesar had taken over. There was no need for individuals to get involved. It was a tribute to the volunteer groups that they went ahead with good works on their own even while their taxes went to help pay the petit clerk's salary. They brought millions of dollars worth of assistance to families in need, to families Caesar never reached through "his" system. The system has not obviated the individual — it has simply made it more difficult to get involved.

If we are true to our calling as God's stewards and disciples, Christians must get involved. Not in so-called social action that turns to Caesar, but in personal action, Christian action. We are to be about our Father's business, spiritually and materially.

Estimates indicate there are between 50 and 60 million godly, Bible-directed Christians in the United States today.

Imagine the tremendous, the virtually infinite, power available for good works if those millions of Christians would plug into God's circuit. Imagine what could be done to alleviate suffering, hunger, pain, depravation, homelessness if just 30, or 20, over even 10 million went forth in His name and did works for Him. Imagine what would happen if we put God's dynamic multiplier-factor, His blessings, to work to help others in His name (remember those five loaves and two fish?). Helping others here at home; helping our Christian brothers throughout the world.

What if those 50 to 60 million Christians did these things and did them in the name and for the sake of the Lord!

What if we prayed? Really prayed!

What if we gave? Really gave!

What if we worked? Really worked!

Can you imagine the power that would be generated - the holy, Almighty power! - if 60 million Christians got down on their knees in praise and prayed to God for His direction, His help, and His blessings in solving the problems of this nation and the world? In feeding the hungry, in caring for the needy, in healing the sick, in opening the avenues of progress and self-sufficiency to the unfortunate and the jobless.

Not just some *pro forma*, weak-kneed prayer but bold, positive, assured prayer. Did not Jesus promise that whatsoever we asked in His name would be provided?

Did He not say that even before we prayed God was waiting to supply our requests — if we sought to be righteous, to be fervent, and to be His servants?

Such faith and prayer and work could change the world.

What a witness for Christ!

Not crystal palaces but living temples! Not cushions on the pews but callouses on the hands.

Precinct by Precinct

In recent years more and more Christians have become politically active. They are adept at gaining majorities in caucuses and advancing the cause of their candidate or proposition. They have in large part mastered the art of "working the precincts" and registering and getting out the vote.

That is as it should be. We do not fall into some second class citizenship when we accept Christ as Savior and King. In fact, as Paul wrote, we become citizens of two worlds — God's kingdom and the here and now. Thus, it is not only proper but necessary that we undertake the role and responsibility of active citizenship. We long for godly government. Who but the godly will restore it?

All too often that Christian power has been used to perpetuate the system, the establishment, the party. The more things have changed the more they have remained pretty much the same. And all too often the Christian witness and works have been forgotten in the heat of the political campaign.

We have been engaging in political action when we should have been concentrating on Christian action! Playing Caesar's game by Caesar's rules: polls, professionals, and propaganda. Not principles and precepts.

What if?

What if Christians were to make the effort, to take the same time and energies, to organize those precincts for Christ? For His works?

What if we went forth and audited those precincts - ascertained the needs within the precinct or the block or the apartment complex? Who is alone and lonely? Who is hungry? Who is without work? Who is in need? Who needs a ride to the clinic or the hospital or the market? Is there a farmer laid up whose crops need tending? Porch steps that need fixing? A toilet in need of repair? Is there a teenager in trouble with drugs? Pregnancy? A shut-in who needs to talk with someone? A single parent who is desperate for help with her children? Someone released from prison who longs for a helping hand and sympathetic shoulder? The list goes on because the needs exist.

Are there any such as these in your precinct? How do you know? What have you done? For them? For Him?

What if we then matched the needs with the resources God has entrusted to us —— as individuals, as a congregation, as a neighborhood Christian work crew? What if we organized "Christian Service" units in precincts throughout this nation in the name and for the sake of Jesus Christ? What if we embarked on a sustained and synchronized campaign to take back those responsibilities that once were fulfilled by Christians through works and faith? What if we then went forth in the name of the King to serve Him by serving others!

We could turn this nation around! We could reclaim America for Christ. We could. If we only would. Think about it!

What was it Jesus said?

"For I was hungry and you gave me food; I was thirsty, and you gave Me drink; I was a stranger and you took Me in; I was naked and you clothed Me; I was sick and you visited Me; I was in prison and you came to Me ... I say to you, inasmuch as you did it to one of the least of these My brethren, you did it to Me'" (Matt 25:25-36,40). *"Come, you blessed of My Father, inherit the kingdom prepared for you from the foundation of the world"* (Matt. 25:34).

Billions More for Christ!

First: the Faith!
Then: the Faith and prayer!
Then: the Faith and the prayer and the giving — the works!
"For all things come from You, And of Your own we have given You" (1 Chron. 29:14).

Consider again those 60 million Christians on the move, hard at work for Christ.

What would happen if, in concert with constant and Christ-centered prayer and faith and works, we gave more than we give now?

Christ never repealed our duty to tithe. Indeed, he reaffirmed it. When Christians stopped tithing their time and resources, the Christian community no longer served as the moving, guiding, spiritual influence in the United States. Faith weakened and the branches withered and produced fewer and fewer fruits.

What if 60 million godly Christians began to tithe and kept at it? You cannot begin to imagine the wealth God would pour into this nation if Christians embarked on a planned and constant program of tithing, returning to the lord what He asks. The Lord God would produce billions of dollars for His works; we would be His stewards, His agents, His transmission belt to the poor, the sick, the homeless, the lost and lonely.

"Will a man rob God? Yet you have robbed Me!
But you say, 'In what way have we robbed You?'
In tithes and offerings.
You are cursed with a curse, For you have robbed Me,
Even this whole nation.
Bring all the tithes into the storehouse,
That there may be food in My house,
And prove Me now in this," Says The Lord of hosts,
"If I will not open for you the windows of heaven
And pour out for you such blessing
That there will not be room enough to receive it"
  (Mal. 3:8-10).

That's a promise, man! What a covenant!

What's that? You say it all sounds good, but .... Oh, you of little faith! You don't really believe the Lord fed the five thousand with those five loaves and two fish, do you?

Ours is a living God! An all-powerful God. Right? Right!

As our young folks say, "You'd better believe it!"

How would those resources be expended? Not through some monolithic, centralized agency. No. Through the local congregations, at the local level.

Through local assistance programs. Soup kitchens, employment bureaus. Teenage pregnancy clinics. Half-way houses for drug rehabilitation and for men and women released from prison. Day care centers. Medical clinics. Schools and job training centers for the inner-city ghettos. Through the kind of love in action that Mrs. Rocker and her fellow Christians in Kingsburg have already undertaken.

You say that those things are already being done by Caesar? That you don't have time to get involved? That it's hard enough as it is to make ends meet?

How Christians respond to the needs of the hours, to the needs of the oppressed may well make the difference in how Christians fare in this land in the coming decades. Bank on that. Right now, Christians do not fare so well in popularity contests or polls. And, perhaps with good reason. Lots of talk of late. Lots of politicin'. But not much in the way of works.

One thing is sure: if we Christians had been doing God's work as we should have during the past years, there would not be the rising level of conflict and disdain that we see evidenced against Christians in the United States today. For one thing, those who had been helped by Christians, those who knew of Christian works, would rise up and set Caesar and the atheists-humanists straight. "Hands off the Christians!" That's what they would demand.

But face it. Who put on the Aid to Africa campaign? Who put on the Farm Aid drive? Who conceived and produced the "Hands Across America" promotion? Not Christians. How come? Perhaps a lot of those spectaculars were show, emotionalisms of the moment. Another opportunity to have a rock concert. Perhaps the receipts will be slow in getting to where they are really needed. But they do serve as examples of well intentioned action.

Many fine Christian organizations quietly work to help those in need both here at home and throughout the world. Those which are responsible and effective organizations should be supported with a portion of our tithes and gifts (gifts are charity over and above the tithe, incidentally).

But consider this: how many Americans outside the Christian community know about those Christian organizations and what they are doing? Let your light shine, said our Master. Let your good works be seen. Why? So that men may know and glorify your Father Who is in heaven.

And this: if there were truly too many groups, there would be no poor; no needy, no homeless. The fact that people are in need helps make it clear: there are not too many organizations; there are not enough.

It's time to reach out. Not to brag or to boast. Not to put on extravaganzas and deal in hype and hoopla. But show and tell that the Christian faith is indeed relevant today, to the here and now, as well as the hereafter. That Christians are out to change the world for the best! Is that not a part of the Great Commission — to preach the gospel and to teach whatever Christ commanded us? To teach by doing as well as by talking!

"Let your light so shine before men, that they may see your good works and glorify your Father in heaven" (Matt. 5:16). Light conquers darkness. And we are commanded by Him in Whom we live and have our being to be His light bearers in this sin-sick world.

Four Great Opportunities for God's Stewards

Paris Reidhead, who headed up Transformation International Enterprises, once suggested four opportunities to serve the Lord by helping Christians in developing nations (these opportunities could also be employed to help Christians in this nation).

1. *Christian businessmen* can use part of their business funds in joint ventures with Christian nationals overseas. This investment capital, which would be repaid, could help establish job-generating projects and provide employment on a continuing, expanding basis. A large part of the poverty in foreign lands stems from the lack of job opportunities. (This could also be done here at home in the inner city.)

2. *Christian congregations* could set up "over-and-above" revolving funds. These funds could be loaned to Christians overseas to start or expand projects which would be job-producing.

3. *Christian families* saving for retirement can earmark 15 percent of their investments to feed revolving funds established by their congregation. Such investments could be insured and bear interest.

4. *Christians in many walks of life* could make their experience and expertise available to their Christian brothers and sisters in foreign lands. Farmers, food processors, civil and hydraulic engineers, carpenters, small businessmen, registered and practical nurses have skills and talents which could be of tremendous help to their Christian counterparts or would-be counterparts in other lands.

Dr. Reidhead proposed that Christians in this land could and should help Christians in other lands build material self-sufficiency for themselves and their co-workers.

Since Dr. Reidhead advanced his proposals, some ninety evangelical organizations have been formed to undertake such endeavors in Christ's name. To date they have channeled millions of dollars into micro-economic projects throughout the world. The success rate of such joint ventures has been exceedingly high. Whereas many other multimillion-dollar projects have gone bankrupt because of waste and perfidy, most of the Christians-here-backing-Christians-there projects have succeeded.

World Hunger and Pain

Many Christian organizations already help meet the immediate and long-term needs. These efforts should be supported with prayer and financial support. The immediate (crises) calls for immediate (crisis) giving. The long-term calls for helping the needy and underdeveloped nations build an economy and a productivity that will enable those countries to become self-sufficient in the future. Who better to do this than Christian leaders in those countries aided by

Christians in the United States? Such results would be far more salutary and far more productive than the type of finagling by Caesar's State Department.

During recent years when nations have met around the world, many of them including former recipients of American aid, have lambasted the United States for being a niggardly "have" nation. They are egged on by "liberation theologists" who preach the gospel of Marx. Their solution to the world's food and production problems is for the United States to strip itself of its productivity and turn to sackcloth and ashes. This would solve little or nothing. It would, in fact, push the world over the brink to total chaos. Regardless of what some may claim, the record shows that the United states has been the major source of help in a needy world.

The solution is not to tear down the United States into a "have not" nation; the solution is to help other lands build themselves up to become "have" nations. Again, who better to do this than Christians here working with and through Christians in those nations?

The world is much in need right now. In need of Christ and in need of material help. Both here in the United States and abroad.

Is there an answer to the problems that exist? Jim Underwood of Christian Financial Services has given it:

> Christians already have the material answers to the needs of the world. But, not just by giving it away. It's by constructively taking those assets and using them — working them — in a productive and on-going manner. If we believe that we are God's stewards, then what we have are Godly treasures. The irony of the situation is that we have sought the counsel of the ungodly in how to plan and use those Godly treasures.[28]

Jim Underwood's God is not dead. He is very much alive and more than able to deal with any situation.

Unleash the Giant

The United States, through the enterprise of its free people and free capital — and up until the turn of this century, the Christian ethic — has been the giant among the productive nations of the world. This did not happen by accident; it did not come by robbing or depriving or exploiting other nations.

It occurred because we employed a system of economics based on Christian principles.

Today the giant is increasingly hamstrung, whipsawed, and controlled by the Lilliputs of the new economics and the new politics. They say they're new but they are not really: they are as old as Babylon.

Too often those who say this nation should give more to other nations are the very ones who work and vote to increase the restrictions on our ability to give, the ones who reduce our giving potential. They call for ever greater government spending and control of our productive enterprises. They insist on urging Caesar to gobble up even more of our cornseed.

That is not the way to increase our abilities to help others; it is the road to stagnation. Before we can give, we must produce. There is nothing productive about a bloated, oppressive government. Caesar turns out little but red tape and paper forms. These will not fill bellies or stem hunger at home or abroad.

We cannot control policies of other governments but surely we can control the policies of our own. Now is the time to remove the controls and costs and restrictions that hamper America's productive genius and capacities.

Let's Stop the Waste!

Some people are "embarrassed" about America's abundance. Their emotions are misspent. They should give thanks to the Lord that America has a bounty it can share with the less fortunate.

If they really want something to be embarrassed about, let them think about the waste in this land.

There is no greater wastrel than big (and often inferior) government. Consider, for example, the estimated $296 billion that will go this year, 1993, just to pay the interest on the federal debt. Imagine what that could do if it were returned to the productive enterprise of free men and women. Imagine what the fruits of such enterprise could do to help the needy help themselves. The waste of such monies is a sin. The Scriptures warn us about the costs of debt; they admonish us to refrain from debt. Caesar has this nation up to its eyeballs in red ink.

When Caesar wastes the fruits of our labors in such a manner, then we cannot share them with our brethren in other lands let alone with our brothers here at home. Remember Christ's parable about the fellow who wasted the talent entrusted to him by the master of the house (Matt. 25:14-30). There's a lesson there about wasteful, inefficient government. It's time we applied that lesson to Caesar.

Render unto God

Christian love and Christian action is not a cop out.

It is not letting George, or Caesar, do it.

It is a personal response and a personal responsibility.

It is living and giving as Christ lived and gave for us.

"Render therefore to Caesar the things that are Caesar's, and to God the things that are God's" (Matt. 22:21).

Does that now take on a new light? A new dimension? A new direction? A new mandate?

What is God's? The earth and the fullness therein. And us. We are His. We all are. Each individual.

We are to love one another. We are to help one another. Help one another grow not only in grace but also in skill and self-sufficiency as good stewards.

These things we do for Christ, not for Caesar.

Caesar has his own limited, prescribed duties to perform. And we render unto him to finance those duties.

But we are not to render unto Caesar our fellow man, our less fortunate, our friends, or our strangers. The care and feeding and keeping and loving of these: all that is ours to do.

Come! We have a nation and a world to turn rightside up!

In His name and for His sake.

CHAPTER TEN

Taxes and the Power To Destroy

*"The first of the first fruits of your land
you shall bring into the house of
The Lord your God"*
(Exod. 23:19).

Those Pharisees! Some of them were always ganging up on Jesus. They were constantly looking for ways to trick Him. Anything to get Him in trouble with the civil authorities.

One day a gaggle of them joined up with a bunch of politicians who were high on Herod. Together, they went down to see if they could talk Jesus into a box.

"Master." That's the way they started their little caper. "Master." They hadn't accepted Christ as their Master, but you know these smooth-talking politicians! Those Pharisees!

"Master, we know that You are sincere and that You teach the word of God truthfully, regardless of the consequences.

"So, tell us: Is it God's law to pay taxes to Caesar?"

Jesus knew what they were up to; He was way ahead of the.

"Why do you come here trying to trap Me, you impostors? You hypocrites! Show Me the coin you use to pay the tax."

The Pharisees handed Him a denarius - a coin similar to our penny.

"Whose face and name is on the coin?" Jesus asked. And they answered, "Why, Caesar's, of course."

"Render therefore to Caesar the things that are Caesar's, and to God the things that are God's" (Matt. 22:15-22).

At that point, according to the Scriptures, the Pharisees and their political buddies went off talking to themselves, confounded by the wisdom of the Lord.

Christians are, indeed, obliged to support civil authority, to obey the civil laws, except at the expense of disobeying God's laws.

In Romans 13:7, Paul instructed us to pay *"taxes to whom taxes are due, customs to whom customs are due, fear to whom fear, honor to whom honor."*

Why? Because civil government is an institution ordained by God. (Gen. 9:4,5; Rom. 13:1.) God instituted civil government so that we *"may lead a quiet and peaceable life* [in our external or physical state] *in all godliness and reverence* [in our internal or spiritual state]" (Tim. 2:2; 1 Pet. 2:14).

In other words, God established civil government so we could be safe and free on earth, so that we could pursue our daily endeavors in peace, to serve God and obey Christ's Great Commission and to these things without fear of men. As the Puritans said, "... to advance the kingdom of Jesus Christ and to enjoy the purities of the Gospell in libertie and peace."

For this protection from those who would violate our lives, our liberty and our property, we are to "render unto Caesar" his due.

Caesar Demands Too Much!

The question is, Just what is Caesar's rightful due?

All that we have belongs to God: our lives, our property, our liberty. We are His and all that we have is His, entrusted to us as His stewards, His caretakers.

God asks us to tithe, to give at least ten percent (actually about 16 percent) of our substance and our time to Him and His work.[1]

But Caesar is not so easily satisfied!

He and his nephews and his cousins at the state and local levels now demand about 45 percent of the nation's total personal income — the money we all earn through working, or through income on our savings and our retirement plans, other investments, etc.

In 1989, all government (federal, state and local) took in $1.86 trillion from the taxpayers. That amounted to 30 percent of the Gross National Product (GNP).

(Actually, to measure the heavy hand of government spending solely on the basis of gross national product is misleading. The GNP statistics generally presented are inflated. About 20 percent of the GNP is spent on the government apparatus and operation. It goes to support the governmental the bureaucracy and its paraphernalia — everything from paper clips and computers to trucks and warehouses; a great deal of the money is used for administrative overhead; remember those millions of government employees).

Up, Up and Away!

In 1990, government spending topped the $2 trillion mark; that was more than four times government spending in 1974, just 24 years before.

In fiscal year 1992, Washington once again spent more than it took in — by about $290 billion. That increased the federal debt by that amount and took it above the $4 trillion mark. And that also increased the interest payments on the federal debt by $10 billion to an annual total of $292.3 billion. Which means that just the interest on the debt came to more than what we spent on the entire federal budget in 1974.

Look what Uncle Seizer collected in his various grab bags in 1992:

- $476.5 billion in income taxes;
- $385.5 in employment taxes (things such as Social Security taxes, Medicare payments, etc.);
- $100.3 billion in corporate income taxes,
- another $45.5 billion in excise taxes (alcohol and tobacco, gas taxes, etc),
- $11 billion in estate and gift taxes and
- $17.32 billion in custom duties and various fees.

All told it added up to $1.092 trillion. And that was just for Babble-on-the-Potomac. State and local taxes come in addition to all that!

When you get right down to the bottom line and stop all the smoke and mirror stuff, the total cost of the federal government outlays in 1992 came to 24.4 percent of the gross national product. Add the spending by state and local governments and the share of the gross national product taken by all governments and government agencies and satellites, etc., totals about 35 percent. (As the federal debt now stands, it comes to about 67.2 percent of the GNP of $5.98 trillion. Someday, one way or another, that will have to be paid.

Government is big bucks! And that tab does not include the cruelest tax of all: inflation.

During recent years government spending has been increasing at an average rate of 12.1 percent while personal income has been rising at an average rate of 8.2 percent.

To see just how big the government's overbite has been, check the chart: "Government Spending and Personal Income." If you think a little mood music will help, try that golden oldie, "Up, Up and Away."

Remember that song? It was about a big red balloon.

Figure 6
GOVERNMENT SPENDING & PERSONAL INCOME
1902-1991
(in billions of $)

Year	Total Personal Income	Total Govt. Spending	Percentage To Govt.
1902	$ 20.2	$ 1.6	7.3%
1913	33.7	3.2	9.7
1922	62.0	9.3	15.0
1930	76.3	12.4	16.2
1940	79.7	20.4	25.5
1950	227.2	70.3	30.9
1960	402.3	151.3	37.6
1970	811.1	332.9	41.0
1974	1,168.6	455.0	38.9
1984	3,012.0	1,441.1	47.8
1989	4,474.4	2,030.7	45.4
1990	4,464.7	2,209.3	46.4
1991	4,893.1	2,448.1	50.0

Source: *Facts and Figures on Govt. Finance,* 27th Edition, p 131
Tax Foundation, Washington D.C. 1992

The Cost Per Producer

The cost of government is generally calculated on a per capita basis — so many dollars for each and every man, woman, and child in the nation. It's supposed to make the cost of government more comprehensible. On that basis, the 1991 per capita cost of government (the total expenditures - tax receipts and deficits) figures out to $9,737.

But that's sort of a con job. It does not really give a true picture of the cost-burden of government.

Take kids, for example, kids are figured along with everyone else as part of that per capita calculation. But kids don't pay many taxes. They may pay a dime here and a dollar there when they buy bubble gum or comic books or record albums. But they sure don't pay $6,128 a year. Someone else picks up their tab until they get a job, start to earn an income, buy a house and a car. It is the same for those who are unemployed or on welfare, they do not pay taxes.

So, calculate the cost of government this way. Figure it on the basis of "per producer" — per working men and women in the labor force. On that basis the cost of government in 1991 came to $19,321.

Take it one step further. Figure it the way things really are; figure it on the basis of per working men and women in the private sector (i.e. not including the government payrolls. That doesn't mean there aren't many fine government employees who are doing a good job; but it does mean that the people in the non-government, private sector work force are putting up most of the money to pay for government.) When you figure it on that basis, it comes to $20,976 per worker in the private sector labor force. Husband and wife both working to make ends meet? Two cost shares per family: $41,952.

Government costs big bucks!

The Delayed Tax of Debt

Sometimes we do not realize just how much government is spending because taxes do not keep up with expenditures. As a matter of fact, spending has exceeded tax income for twenty-four of the past twenty-five years. In those twenty-four years, the government ran up deficits totalling $2.828 trillions. That's an average annual deficit of $11 billion — year after year, good year and bad. In those 25 years, how many congressmen do you suppose were elected on a promise that they would cut government spending and balance the budget?

Those debts and deficits are a delayed tax. Sooner or later they have to be paid. We pay the interest each year; but it is our children and our grandchildren who will get stuck with the big red balloon!

Incidentally, for a quick look at how that interest has grown during the past twenty years and how much it has cost the taxpayers, check the data in Figure 7.

What was it former Senator William Armstrong warned about the rising tide of interest on the federal debt? "Between 1981 and 1990, the federal government will spend $1.3 trillion in interest payments alone. This equals the entire public debt accumulated from 1789 to 1984."

The Committee To End Waste in Government says that if Caesar keeps piling up the debt the way he's been going of late, by the year 2000, we would be paying $1.3 trillion *a year* — just for that interest!

Figure 7
INTEREST ON THE FEDERAL DEBT
(in billions of $)

Year	Gross Federal Debt	Interest on Federal Debt	Percent of Debt Federal Budget
1940	$ 42.9	$ .9	2.1%
1950	257.4	4.8	1.8
1960	286.3	28.7	7.5
1970	370.9	86.6	7.3
1980	914.3	89.8	8.9
1984	1,576.7	118.0	13.0
1985	1,827.5	130.4	13.6
1986	2,120.0	136.5	13.7
1987	2,345.6	138.6	13.8
1988	2,600.8	151.7	14.3
1898	2,876.5	169.2	14.8
1990	3,206.3	184.2	14.7
1991	3,617.8	197.0	14.0
1992	4,021.1	206.3	14.3

Source: The United States Budget, Fiscal Year 1987;
Statistical Abstract of the U.S., Dept of Commerce, 1986;
Facts and Figures in Govt. Finance, Tax foundation, 1992

Some Tax Fax

In 1895 a federal income tax was declared unconstitutional.

During the 1913 congressional debates on a federal income tax (the Sixteenth Amendment) opponents warned that the tax rates might go as high as 10 percent!

The federal withholding tax law was enacted in 1943 as a temporary measure to help finance World War II. It's still hanging around. We're reminded of that each time we look at the stub on our paycheck!

Taxes take the biggest chunk out of the average family budget — more than food and housing combined.

The total tax take in the United States is 20 times greater now than it was in 1950. (In 1950 all taxes totalled $54.8 billion; in 1991 they came to $975 billion).[6]

The tax grab during the years 1980 to 1991 more than doubled. Government is the galloping gourmet of the people's kitty.[7] Not all of that was raked in by Washington. The federal government took about 64 percent; state and local governments accounted for about 36 percent of all taxes levied.[8]

"Sure!" someone will say. "Since 1950, or even 1970, the nation's population has increased." It did: from 151 million to 236 million persons.

"And so," they will insist, "the more people to be governed, the more government must spend. You have to make allowances for growth, you know."

Sounds reasonable, right? Well, maybe. Let's look at the facts.

In 1950 the per capita tax burden was $365 — about a buck a day. (Keep in mind, reported taxes are only a part of the total cost of government. There are two more parts: deficits and inflation.)

In 1970 the per capita tax burden was up to $1,357. By 1980 it had jumped to $3,222, and by 1991 the tax burden for all governments was $9,737 for every person in the U.S.A.

If taxes had risen by a simple population growth factor of the $365 per capita of 1950, the total tax annual take today would have been about $86.5 billion, give or take a few billion. As it was, while the population was increasing about 60 percent, the per capita tax burden increased eight-fold — to $9,737.

Maybe that's not fair. Let's take the population in 1970 and apply the 1970 per capita tax burden to the 1991 population. In 1970 the per capita tax burden was $1,357 — four times what it was in 1950. If that 1970 per capita tax burden had remained constant for the next 20 years, in 1991 the total tax take would have been $347 billion. The actual tax take in 1991? $2,448 billion. That's two point four trillion!

Something's out of whack. What did Don Lambro say about government? "Voracious." "Bloated." "Out of control!"

Those Hidden Taxes

Most folks may say they don't pay that much in taxes. Some don't; but most do.

The truth is that many of us do not realize just how much we really do pay out for taxes. We forget to calculate the cost of hidden taxes and as F.A. Harper once wrote, "One cannot see what is hidden."

Figure 8
TAX TAKE & PER CAPITA BURDEN*

Year	Total Taxes	Per Capita Taxes	Federal Taxes	State Taxes	Local Taxes
1950	$ 54.8	$ 365.	$ 37.8	$ 8.9	$ 7.9
1960	126.7	709.	88.4	20.2	18.1
1970	274.9	1,357.	185.7	50.5	38.8
1980	727.9	3,222.	492.8	148.7	86.4
1984	975.0	4,146.	634.4	217.4	123.3
1986	1,123.3	4,681.	733.6	244.7	145.1
1987	1,243.9	5,110.	819.8	265.8	158.3
1988	1,322.9	5,409.	877.2	274.0	171.7
1989	1,239,6	5,832.	960.0	295.0	184.5

* All data in billions except for per capita
 Source: *Facts and Figures on Govt. Finance*, 1986, Tax Foundation

A sizeable chunk of the 47 percent of total personal income directed to taxes goes for those little old tax bites which are buried in the price of just about everything we buy and every service we procure.

  Someone once estimated that there are 502 taxes of one sort or another on a pair of shoes — each one levied at a different stage of planning, production, distribution, and sale. Along the line, a whole bunch of governmental gimmies — federal, state, and local — get into the act.

  Take a loaf of bread, for example. No matter how you slice it, a large part of it goes for taxes. (That was before most of our shoes were imported — those foreign shoemakers don't share all those little taxes; they just pay in import tax and that's that.)

  Here's how those min-taxes add up: From the farmer who works the field and fertilizes it (and who pays taxes on the land, the tractor and equipment, the fertilizer, the fuel — all of which are part of his costs and also the costs of the fertilizer company, the tractor company, and the oil company and to the trucker who hauls the grain to the elevator; from the folks who run the grain elevator to the milling company that mills the grain; from the bakers who bake the bread to the packager who supplies the bread wrapper; from the distributor who carries the bread to the market that sells the loaf to the housewife.

At every step of the way, taxes are added to taxes, and the housewife and her husband pick up the tab. Taxes on top of taxes mixed into that loaf of bread.

That's a lot of dough! Such crust!

Take VAT!

Now, the Clinton Administration and its political cohorts are looking for new sources of revenue and the Value Added Tax is tempting them. They figure that could put another $150 billion or so a year on the federal collection plate. Of course, they suggest a portion of that new income might be used to reduce some other existing taxes. Yeah, like the man said, "Anybody believes that, I have a bridge over in Brooklyn that's for sale!."

The Value Added Tax (VAT) is a regressive sales tax. It would end up putting a big crimp in sales, thus cutting production and thus increasing employment.

All the way along the production and marketing process — mining or harvesting or drilling and pumping the raw materials, processing the raw materials, manufacturing the finished products, transporting them to market, a tax would be put on the "value added" at each stage of production and distribution and marketing.

Say the VAT is 10 percent. And, say we're going to buy a kitchen table. Before that table ever gets to the furniture store a 10 percent tax is added to each step from the birch tree in the forest to the display window. A 10 percent tax is put on the value added to the value of the standing tree for sawing it down, trimming it out, maybe debarking it, etc., and delivering it to the saw mill. Then another 10 percent tax is tacked on for the value added to the basic price for planing the wood (which already carried a 10 percent value added tax from the first phase), another 10 percent of the increased value is added when the goes to the furniture manufacturer who adds yet another tax of 10 percent of the value added for turning that bare wood into a table and so on and so on. All along the way the prior taxes are included so that the purchaser ends up paying the tax on all those taxes plus the price of the commodity. That's compounded taxation.

Don't fall for that one! At least, not until the Sixteenth Amendment is repealed. There must be better ways to balance the budget without adding that VAT of problems for the taxpayer. And there is: reduce the size of government, cut out the waste, and cut the budget!

Rudimentary Tax Reform

Come election year, politicians — those in office and those who want to get into office — rush around the countryside dragging their tales about tax reform behind them.

"Nothing," they say, "Nothing is more important than tax reform." That is what we have been getting by way of real tax reform: nothing.

Once in a while a bone of tax relief is thrown to the public. Often it is done by transferring the tax burden and creating giant loopholes for special interests. Usually it is achieved by playing the stronger groups (the most militant and vociferous, those who contribute the most to political campaign) against the weaker. Since the taxpayers are seldom organized and do not have high-paid lobbyists, they are usually considered the weaker — and are generally the patsies.

Now and then there is reform via the shifting of tax levies. That is not reform; that's a sleight-of-hand. We end up paying just as much or more through different tax gimmicks and different transactions. Some taxes are reduced, others are increased; some loopholes are closed, some are created. The politicians boast of "taxing the rich." They could take all of the income of each and every person with an annual income of $100,000 or more and you know what they would have? Enough money to run the federal government for ten days. Ten days ... and no more geese to lay their golden eggs.

What we need at all levels is real reform, root reform. Not just expedient, squeaking-wheel-gets-the-grease revision but honest, bedrock reform.

Take the federal income tax laws, for example. What started out as thirty words and one percent has expanded to millions of complicated words and thousands of sections and tax rates which go as high as 31% — soon to go to 36%.

Consider the following as some suggestions for basic tax reform.

1. *Taxes should be used to raise revenues for the legitimate government functions, period.*

Taxes should not be used for social control or social reform such as redistribution of the wealth.

When tax laws and taxes are employed to fund the necessary and proper functions of government, that is a legitimate extension of civil authority.

When taxation exceeds those limitations, it becomes a license to plunder and is in violation of God's laws (*"Thou shalt not steal." "Thou shalt not covet."*)

There are those who see the instrument of taxation as a means of achieving their concept of social justice.

Where? Where in the Constitution do the so-called reformers find the power to use taxation to enforce "social justice"?

Where is that set forth, enumerated and defined?

Where does it say that redistribution of wealth is a power given by the people to the central government or to any government?

The Founding Fathers would never have bought such a socialistic thesis. It is inherent in the basic law of the land that government in its application of taxation should be blind, just as it should be in the administration of justice.

Professor Irving Kristol suggested that the average taxpayer viewed the problem differently from his self-appointed saviors.

> The average American, no matter what he may sometimes say or what is said in his name, is not rebelling against tax inequities. He is rebelling against taxes, period.
>
> He is rebelling against increased property and sales taxes. He is rebelling against the hidden tax that inflation represents. He is rebelling against all those itemized deduction from his paycheck — (against the fact) that his hard-won wage increases seem to exist only on paper and never find their way to his pocket.
>
> The American worker ... resents this whole process, which bureaucratically insists on improving his longer-term prospects at the expense of his shorter-term ones — on improving his general welfare at the expense of his specific well-being. In short, he resents the present structure of the welfare state, and his rebellion is an expression of this resentment.[40]

    2. *Taxes should be apportioned so that each citizen pays a fair share of the cost of government — no more and no less.*

Every citizen should help pay the cost of government, no matter how small the levy or how minute the share. Using the tax system as an appendage of the welfare system may seem to be efficient, but it can have deadly effect.

When government is "free", citizens seldom are. Further, as in the case of the widow's mite, each person wants to feel they have a part in the affairs of church and state.

3. *Tax rates should be proportional not progressive.*

If the cost of government is, for example, 15 percent of total national personal income, then a flat rate of 15 percent should be applied at all levels of income. That's the way God has established the tithe for the support of His work: He doesn't say the low-income family is to give two percent or whatever while those who may have more should shell out 15 or 20 or 50 percent. A tithe is a tithe is a tithe. It does not work like an escalator. (In this regard, it would seem a flat tax might be a Biblically and appropriate way to raise the necessary government funds. Loopholes and exceptions should be eliminated or greatly reduced.)

4. *Tax laws and tax forms should be simple, clear, and easily understood.*

The basic rule should be KISS: Keep It Simple, Sir! As the tax code is now, it has spawned a vast army of tax attorneys and public accountants to figure out what exactly is exactly. This not proper. The government should be direct and honest with the citizen. Remember that old adage? "Oh, what a tangled web we weave when first we practice to deceive!"

5. *The amount of taxes government collects each year should be clearly established in advance, with a cast-iron lid placed on that amount.*

The citizen has a right to know in advance that government will not take more than a set amount of his wealth and that no open-ended budgets can cause taxes to exceed the limit during that annual period.

That could be pegged as a percentage of the gross national (or state) product or a percentage of total national (or state) personal income. That would force governments to set budgets within the people's means and stay there.

6. *Property taxes should be levied at the local level, only.*

Currently, there are moves in some states to institute statewide property taxes. This would not only serve to weaken local governments, it would accelerate the growth of the "big brother state." It

would erode what little control the citizen now has over the property
    "When the power to tax leaves the county, tyranny will then begin in the United States. Socialism or communism will be only a step away."[41] Is that not so?

    7. *Property taxes should be levied for "property-connected" services only* (police, fire, sewer, water, special districts established by the voters." (See number 8.)

    Compelling property owners to pay taxes on property (real estate) to finance general governmental functions (education, welfare, justice, etc.) is not equitable.
    First, because non-property owners can vote to force property owners to pay tax for all manner of government programs which have nothing to do with the property. This, places an inequitable tax burden on the property owners while "exempting" the non-property owner.
    Second, placing such a disproportionate tax on property usually increases the tax to a level where many elderly (and usually retired) persons are unable to keep their homes — and, where many young couples cannot afford to buy a home of their own.
    "People" taxes (sales, income, etc.) should be used to finance "people" services (education, welfare, justice, etc.).

    8. *Only those who are to pay the tax should be permitted to vote on the imposition and rate of that tax.*

    "How long would Christianity last as an institution if unbelievers could vote in churches (i.e. on church policies)? Will non-property owners respect property to any greater degree?"[42] "Is not private property as an idea abolished when the non-property owner becomes legislator for the owner? The property qualification for the vote is the ultimate political form of the recognition of private property." Guess who said that? Some fella named Karl Marx.

    9. *Taxes should always be visible. No more hidden taxes. And, no more pyramiding of taxes* (taxes on a tax).

    The people have a right to know when, how and how much they pay in taxed. Hidden taxes promote hidden government.
    Further, taxing the cost of a product based on a price which already includes taxes, is improper. Example, adding a sales tax to the

price of a gallon of gas which already includes state and federal fuel taxes.

10. *Those government representatives (federal, state and local) who vote to spend taxpayer funds should also be required announce the tax impact and to levy the tax required to raise those funds.*

With the power to tax should go the requirement to answer to the taxpayer for the taxation or the deficit. No more passing the tax buck from the state to Caesar, or vice versa.

11. *All tax agencies and agents should be required to obey and uphold all Constitutional guarantees and protections* (due process, restrictions on search and seizure, presumed innocence). *Violators should be subject to severe penalties under the civil rights act.*

Social Insecurity

Income, property, and sales taxes are not the only taxes that have gone out of sight during recent years. Look at what has happened to the tax on employers and employees for Social Security — the FICA taxes.

Many economists, thousands of businessmen, and millions of wage earners, are increasingly concerned about the enormous increases in Social Security taxes and the problems threatening the financial integrity of the system. The way things are going, the increased pay outs of the system, are bound to keep requiring greater payroll deductions for both employer and employee.

It has been projected that FICA taxes would total 35 percent of all federal revenues by the year 2000 — they are just about at that level already. Those taxes are falling on the backs of those Americans earning between $25,000 and $60,000 — the middle Americans who already carry the major share of taxation and inflation.

Serious Trouble Coming?

Let's talk a bit with Mrs. Dorcas Hardy, U.S. Commissioner of Social Security under President Reagan. Mrs. Hardy, in an interview with the excellent newsletter, *Bottom Line,* was frank enough to say that "Social Security will be in serious trouble within 10 years, and the crunch will be devastating when the baby boomers start arriving at retirement age around 2010." Social Security has expanded coverage and benefits to the point where this year (1993) it will pay out $302 billion — $830 million a day to retired workers and their spouses, to widows and dependent children, and to the disabled.

It has also increased its tax take; in 1992 more than 70% of U.S. families paid more in Social Security taxes than in income taxes.

The Store Is Raided

If the public believes the Social Security funds are kept in a trust fund, they are mistaken. Payroll taxes which are received but not needed to meet current payments are "invested" in Special Issue Government Bonds; that money is spent on current federal government operations. The Treasury issues an IOU to the Social Security System. When the year 2010 rolls around and the Social Security system must have its money, to meet obligations, the Secretary of the Treasury will ask Congress to fork over — to repay the System. That means they mustr act to increase taxes or to pass new taxes.

From 1935 to 1937, when the Social Security system was being debated and enacted, Congress intended that it would be

1. purely a supplement to the individual's retirement arrangements (and not a retirement plan in and of itself) — it would provide a "floor" but not the entire pension structure
2. fully funded by contributions from the employer and the employee; and
3. operated honestly on a sound actuarial basis

The harsh reality is that the Social Security system is and has been a "wealth transfer from young to old". In the beginning the burden was easy; there were a lot more young and middle-aged workers than old folks in retirement and drawing Social Security benefits. In 1940 there were sixteen workers paying into the fund for each Social Security recipient. Today, the ratio is about two workers paying in for every recipient taking out. The increasing rate of abortion and the improved medical techniques and better health care for the elderly will skew that ratio even more. Extended life spans are placing an increasing and prolonged demand on Social Security payouts.

Since 1937, Congress has expanded the program thirteen times. Now it's called "Old-Age Survivors and Disability Insurance" and it goes far beyond the original intent of a "floor" under the individual's retirement plan. Now, in fact, it is a retirement plan in and

A QUICKIE QUIZ

Here's a quickie quiz on government taxes and spending. It was cooked up by the guys at the National Tax Limitation Committee.[9]

1. How did the average (civil service) federal wage in 1989 compare with the   average wage for private industry? The average federal wage was:
    A. 5% lower   C. 10% higher
    B. about the same as private wage   D. over 25% higher

2. To the nearest million, excluding the military, how many people worked for the federal government in 1989?

3. In which decades did the average yearly increase in both spending and taxes grow faster than the GNP?
    A. The 40s, 70s, and 80s   C. The 70s only
    B. Every decade since the 40s   D. The 80s

4. The most inflationary decade was:
    A. The 50s   C. The 70s
    B. The 60s   D. The 80s

5. The decade with the lowest productivity was:
    A. The 50s   C. The 70s
    B. The 60s   D. The 80s

6. In 1967, the Smith family budgeted $100 for groceries each month. How much would they have spent in 1984 to buy the same groceries?
    A. $240   C. $310
    B. $280   D. $400

7. In 1929, governments at all levels spent an amount equal to 10% of gross national product. Sixty years later, in 1989, total government spending had increased to what percent of GNP?
    A. 17%   C. 32%
    B. 25%   D. 37%

8. Which was larger:
    A. California's tax revenues in 1990 or
    B. all states tax revenues in 1965?

9. In the 30 years from 1960 to 1990, annual state tax receipts had increased:
    A. 500%   C. 1500%
    B. 1,000%   D. 2000%

10. During which presidency did we experience the lowest average annual inflation rate?
        A. Nixon   D. Reagan
        B. Ford   E. Bush
        C. Carter

(Check your answers with the footnotes at the back of the book.)

itself. The hope is that when those now working (and contributing) get ready to retire, there will be funds in the program to cover them. That may not be the case — not without tremendous infusions such as they forced upon the public by the Savings and Loan debacle.

If your friendly local banker or savings and loan executives handled their customer's trust funds that way, they would be holed up in Leavenworth or Atlanta or some federal pen. But too often these days what is considered unethical, immoral, and illegal in the private sector is standard operating procedure when practiced by Caesar and his legions.

The Social Security system's long-term debt (unfunded liabilities) is estimated to be about $6 trillion. The system operates on a hand-to-mouth basis. Guess what will happen by the year 2000 when more than 50 percent of the population will be over fifty years of age and the ranks of those on Social Security will have swelled proportionately.

Economist Michael Boskin has warned, "Unless honest solutions are found and commitments honored, the United States faced the greatest tax revolt and age (generational) warfare in its history."

Necessary Reforms!

Dorcas Hardy suggests these reforms, based on her service as U.S. Commissioner of Social Security:

1. Raise the eligibility age for benefits to 70. Cut or eliminate benefits for early retirement as 62 (a majority of recipients take that early).

2. Slow the growth of benefits by reducing the COLAs (Cost of Living Adjustments).

3. Privatize the system. Refund part of the Social Security taxes but require that those amounts be put into private retirement system where the beneficiary has control of the investments.

4. Invest the Social Security trust funds in private securities that would (a) generate added income, (vb) pay back the principal when needed. Other countries have been doing that quite successfully.

5. Restore the full deductions for Individual retirement accounts (IRA). Encourage the growth of private pension plans.

6. Give those entering the labor force the option of contributing a certain (flexible) amount of their earnings to a private investment or retirement fund.

Some other ideas from other sources:

Stop the congressional raids on the Security Trust fund and require Congress to enact a scheduled pay-back plan to rebuild that account. If Congress needs money to meet appropriations, let them cut other programs be honest and face up to the taxpayers

Stop the Congressional raids on the trust fund. Recognize that sooner or later the Social Security system must be bailed out — as were the Savings and Loan accounts. Start the scheduled pay-back plan and invest those the trust fund monies where they will (a) be safe, (b) bring the a good return and (c) perhaps be available as investment capital for an expanding economy.

Social Security (OASDI) is now a virtually full-scale tax-funded welfare program: 97 percent of all Americans over the age of sixty-five depend on it for all or most of their income.

The "Tax" of Social Security

In 1983, Congress passed and President Reagan signed into law a provision requiring that Social Security beneficiaries with an adjusted gross annual income of $25,000 or more ($32,000 for a married couple) must pay taxes on 40 percent of his or her Social Security benefits received (60 percent if benefits for a nonworking spouse are included). The Clinton Administration is now proposing an adjustment which would require that taxes be paid on eighty-five percent of those benefits.

Senators John Chafee (RI) and Robert Dole (KS) estimated the measure would bring in revenues of anywhere from $5 million to $200 million during the years 1983 through 1990. It was, they insisted, a matter of "equity".

Those senators and representatives are not quite so "equitable" when it comes to their own retirement plans. Members of both houses of congress become eligible for retirement benefits after five years in office. The member contributes eight percent of salary to the fund; the taxpayers put up most of the rest. The National Taxpayers Union points out that "Many congressmen (who have been at the taxpayers' trough for years) will find themselves receiving annual benefits in excess of their current yearly salaries."

Senator Robert Dole, who pushed for the tax on Social Security benefits, will have a potential accrued retirement pension of more than $2,000,000. An estimated $1,370,361 retirement fund will be waiting for Representative Dan Rostenkowski, chairman of the House Ways and Means Committee, when he retires.[14]

Congressmen take care of their own; their "own" are not always their constituents back home.

Social Security and Religion

Congress and the President did something else in that Social Security Reform of 1983.

It slapped a tax on the church and church-related organizations.

For the first time in the nation's history, the federal government put a tax on religious institutions. That's what Congress did. And Mr. Reagan agreed to go along.

Public Law 98-21 decreed that church staff members must come under Social Security. The original provisions of the bill compelled churches to collect the employee's share of the FICA tax and also pay the employer's share. The estimated Social Security taxes would have cost Christian schools, for example, about $240,000 a day.

But again, it wasn't just the money (which would have forced many Christian schools to fold); it was and is the principle. The principle of religious liberty, of separation of church and state.

Not all the politicians went along with such a violation of religious liberty. Senator Thomas Eagleton told the Senate Finance Committee

Mandating participation of religious organizations in the tax system violates Constitutional principles of religious liberty as guaranteed under the First Amendment.[15]

And Constitutional lawyer William Bentley Ball warned that Congress

has not only said in effect that churches and other religious bodies must pay if they are to carry out their God-given mandate or else suffer persecution and penalties — it has also set the stage for further taxation.[16]

Foreseeing an inevitable confrontation between church and state, the National Association of Evangelicals urged Congress to rescind their action. But the National Council of Churches, many of whose members had already cozied up to Caesar and joined the Social Security system over years past, went all the way with Congress. It claimed that the system is "a State interest that may outweigh any claims of religious liberty."

Let's go over that one once more. The National Council of Churches told the Congress taxation is "a State interest that may outweigh any claims of religious liberty."

Do you wonder why the Christian influence in the marble halls of Babble-on-the Potomac is rather weak? God's word tells us that a double-minded man is unstable in all his ways. Cannot that also be said for organizations that supposedly seek to obey the same Lord God?

Pastor Kent Kelly of Calvary Memorial Church of Southern Pines, North Carolina, had something to say about that:

> It is not the ministry of Christ's church to collect taxes for the State. Further, for the churches to comply would give the IRS access to church records and that surely would be "excessive entanglement" of Caesar's agents with church affairs.[17]

President Reagan, who got an all-important boost in the elections of 1980 and 1984 from the "evangelical Christian community" was adamant. He declared the Social Security Act of 1983 was "untamperable." The churches would pay the FICA tax, period. Hail, Seizer!

Fire in the Pulpits!

Pastors and religious leaders throughout the nation stood firm; some eight thousand of them joined in revolt.

They were not Caesar's agents; they would not collect his taxes.

Faced with the prospects of thousands of pastors and church employees being indicted and even possibly being jailed, Congress backed down. Part way, at least. It passed the Dole Amendment, which repealed the FICA tax on the church and church schools. It also declared that church employees were self-employed and shifted the entire FICA tax to them as individuals. (Not all church employees, mind you; nuns and priests and Christian Science practitioners were exempted). What the Congress did, in fact, was to shift the line of the tax from a direct tax (on the church) to an indirect tax (on the church employees).

A tax is a tax, whether it is direct or indirect. And, argued Pastor Richard Harris of Bethel Baptist, Sellersville, Pennsylvania, since the church employees are an indispensable part of the church's ministry; a tax on them is indeed a tax on the church. Pastor Harris and the Bethel Baptist congregation elected to challenge the law in court. All the way to the United States Supreme Court, if necessary.[18] As Rev. Rushdoony said years before, the same folks who pack the Congress man the ramparts in the Courts. The law stands. So much for religious liberty.

Render unto Caesar, All to Him We Owe!

In an earlier case (U.S. v. Lee), the U.S. Supreme Court held that Edwin Lee, an Amish carpenter, must pay the Social Security (FICA) tax for his employees. Brother Lee had refused to do so. He insisted that to compel him to pay the tax would violate his religious convictions. Lee was a member of the Old Order Amish. He believed and sought to obey the Scriptural injunction that families and fellowships of believers are to care for their own (1 Tim. 5:8). Neither Lee nor his employees enrolled in the Social Security system.

The IRS took Brother Lee to court. The U.S. District Court held for Mr. Lee, saying that the "free exercise" clause of the First Amendment outlawed compulsory payment of the tax if such payment violated the individual's religious faith. The IRS appealed to the U.S. Supreme Court. That's where Brother Lee lost his case.

Mr. Lee did not simply lose his case, Chief Justice Warren Burger flat out decreed that:

> Maintaining a sound tax system is of such high order, a religious belief in conflict with the payment of taxes affords no basis for resisting the tax.[19]

Further, said the Chief Justice "The State may justify a limitation on religious liberty by showing it is essential to accomplish an overriding governmental interest".[20]

That wasn't Adolph Hitler speaking. It wasn't the atheist Karl Marx. That was the Chief Justice of the Supreme Court of these United States of America.

The First Amendment reads, *"Congress shall make no law respecting an establishment of religion, or prohibiting the free exercise thereof."*

Nowhere does it say "except when such religious freedom comes in conflict with the payment of taxes" or " except in the case of an overriding governmental interest."

On what particular day did the people of this Republic amend the First Amendment? Did they really give the Supreme Court the power to junk the Constitution? When? There is nothing on the record which shows that Congress enacted and the necessary states ratified an amendment doing away with the religious liberty clause of the First Amendment.

Ripping Off The Young

For young men and women just starting out, Social Security (OASDI) is a giant rip-off. Through coming years it will force them to hand over more and more of their earnings so that politicians can continue to hand out larger and larger benefits to those already retired. That's the way votes are purchased with someone else's money. And those over 65 comprise a sizeable voting bloc.

Don't blame the retired for the mess. They tried: They worked hard. They paid their dues; many of them saved what they could. It's just that their dollars aren't what they used to be or what they thought they'd be. But that's another story — the story of inflation.

On a strictly financial-return basis, Social Security is a lousy investment. And that, no doubt that is one of the reasons the system is compulsory.

Suppose, for example, that in 1980 young Joe Everyman got a job. Suppose that he earned an average wage all his life, and retired when he reached sixty-five (by then the retirement age will no doubt be higher). During his working life he would pay Social Security taxes of more than $350,000 (the actual amount would depend on what the politicians and the pressure groups foisted upon him and his generation: the OASDI tax base is now indexed and goes up like an Otis Elevator).

When Joe retired, he would receive OASDI benefits of about $15,000 a year for himself and his wife. He would have to live to be in his nineties to receive benefits equal to the FICA taxes he had paid.

Try Freedom, It Works!

Now, suppose that instead of being forced to put all than money into Social Security, he was permitted to put it into a private retirement fund at 6 percent interest. If he did that, at age sixty-five he could retire on $45,000 a year, or he could draw on the interest at a rate of $28,000 a year and bequeath an estate worth more than $500,000 to his heirs or whatever beneficiary he chose. It would be his money. No politician would be "borrowing" it or slicing it up to redistribute his hard-earned wages and savings. No bureaucrat would be doling it out to him with strings attached. He could earn additional income, as much as he wanted to. He would, in other words, be a free man.

Try The Free Market!

Government agencies are like cats who grow up to have kittens who grow up to be cats who have kittens, and on and on. It's time to spay a few of those government cats.

More and more communities are reducing the size of government bureaucracy by contracting with private firms for such public services as fire protection, trash collection and disposal, operation of jails and prisons, and maintenance of public property. They are finding that privatization makes sense; that it saves money; that it is more efficient, and puts a damper on the inherent tendency of government agencies to expand.

Private enterprise can hold down proliferation of government workers and budgets. It can do the job and do it better — and do it for less money.

For example, we-the-people pay the U.S. Postal Service $19.11 per hour just in labor costs to deliver our parcels and express mail. The United Parcel Service handles that type of mail for $13.00 an hour — a savings of $6.11 an hour.

The Heritage Foundation, a Washington-based conservative think tank, did a study which shows how the deficit could be cut by about $40 billion. How? By contracting with private firms to perform various services at greatly reduced costs. For starters, Heritage suggested that the federal government sell its three Washington area airports to either the private sector or to local governments. That would save $2.3 billion right off the bat.[30] Where does it say in the basic charter of the Republic that the federal government should operate airports?

'Way back in 1982. the Congressional Budget Office reported that 81 percent of the federal in-house activities could be shifted to the private sector. By doing that the federal work force could be cut by 165,000 and the taxpayers could be saved more than $1 billion a year.

Federally run hospitals (Veterans Hospitals, for example) would provide better services at a lower cost if they were contracted to private health firms. Social Security would be in much better operational condition and stronger financially if it were switched to a type of individual retirement program. Public housing would be better for residents and taxpayers if it were managed by private enterprise firms.

Like the report of the Grace Commission, the Budget Office report was given the "file and forget" cold shoulder. It is not the nature of the empire builder to willingly decrease the size of domain or scope of dominion.

Prime Minister Margaret Thatcher's administration in Great Britain far out-distanced the Reagan-Bush administration in working toward turning many areas of government back to the private sector. The Thatcher administration looked at government programs from this perspective: If you can sell it, sell it. If you can't sell all of it; sell part of it. If you can't sell any of it, give it away. If you can't give it away, contract it out or get rid of it.

As Reverend Joseph C. Morecraft, pastor of Atlanta's Chalcedon Presbyterian Church, pointed out, "By following this rule, Great Britain ... transferred over 400,000 jobs back to the private sector that has generated some 7.7 billion pounds sterling in new income for the British Treasury."[31]

Further it has provided better services for the consumer and better working conditions for the employees.

Privatization can make the difference between getting the nation out of the red or going into bankruptcy.

Lewis K. Uhler, president of the National Tax Limitation Committee explains why privatization is "a favorite and effective tool for getting a handle on government." There are enormous advantages to "contracting out" certain functions to the lowest bidder — public or private.

• "It forces government to think through exactly what its goals and objectives are and to put these in writing so that someone can intelligently enter a bid on the program or project.

• "It enables elected officials to find out what particular functions should really cost and that can save anywhere from 10 to 90 percent of the cost when it is performed by government without competition (government agencies often join in the bidding and sometimes win the contract — but only if they really get a handle on costs).

• "The taxpayer enjoys savings benefits from innovation and improved service.

• "The stranglehold of bureaucracy on the political process is shattered, reducing pressure for ever-larger pay and perks which have been driving government budgets through the roof."

Some government is necessary and need not be evil or excessive. A certain number of government employees will always be needed to perform legitimate functions. In that sense, government employees are productive rather than parasitical. It is the illegitimate and the excessive in government that should concern us.

The excessive funds now siphoned from the individual (the private sector) could and would be used by the private sector to provide the greatest benefits for the greatest number of people. those benefits would be far greater than any provided by government.

Once freed from Caesar's grasp, those funds could be used to:

• Provide the taxpayer with additional disposable income and real purchasing power, creating an increased demand for goods and service and the formation of more and new jobs (thus reducing the number of welfare recipients)

• Supply additional investment capital for economic expansion and new jobs in the productive private sector (the present transition to a Hi-tech society can be as much of an economic boon as was the advent of the industrial society and will be if the investment capital is available)

• Enable individuals to save and invest in annuities and pension plans so that they need not be so dependent upon government (other taxpayers) in their later years

• Create and accelerate the natural distribution of wealth (thus broadening the tax base and spreading the tax burden)

That is the way to build a strong, expanding economy in a society of free people.

Henry Hazlitt refuted the arguments of those who advocate increased government spending and purchasing power through larger and bloated government payrolls:

Once again it is forgotten that if these bureaucrats are not retained in office, the taxpayers will be permitted to keep the money that was formerly taken from them for the support of the bureaucrats. Once again it is forgotten that the taxpayer's income and purchasing power go up at least as much as the income and purchasing power of the former officeholders go down.[33]

That's the way it would have been if the Hebrew people had listened to Samuel instead of having a king "like other nations."

That's the way it could be in America even now, if the nation had no other King but Jesus.

The Dead Hand of State Capitalism

Individual enterprise and investment build capital. State control and State spending destroy capital.

That is what is happening to this nation today

As government takes more and more of the nation's personal income and a larger and larger chunk of our gross national product, the nation's economy slows down. When government takes less of the nation's personal income, the economy speeds up.

Leviticus 17:14 tells us that "the life of all flesh is its blood." Year ago, physicians came to realize that. They stopped bleeding their patients and let the body manufacture new blood, which helped to strengthen the patient and cure the illness.

The economic lifeblood of a nation is in its working capital, whether it be the individual carpenter's investment in his tools or a corporation's investment in machinery and equipment. Such capital, such economic lifeblood, is essential to the health and growth of a nation; it helps the national body manufacture new economic lifeblood to solve its economic problems.

Yet the "government witch doctors" continue to bleed the patient. This is the hangover, the chronic debilitation with all its economic, social, and moral cancers, left in the wake of the New Deals, Fair Deals, New Frontiers, Great Societies, and New Federalism: controlled citizens, uncontrolled government and debt, inflation, and crime.[34]

A New Slavery

If someone were to suggest that this nation once again condone slavery, he would no doubt be glued together with tar and feathers and ridden out of the country on a splintered rail. Yet, consider this:

The amount of money government takes is equivalent to the total personal income of more than 100 million Americans. Compare today's "legalized" involuntary servitude with the four million slaves in America just prior to the outbreak of the War between the Sates. Those four million slaves of the mid-1800s were privately owned and worked on privately held plantations. Today's slaves are federally owned: they labor to support the federal plantation.

Since the outright enslavement of some 100 million of our fellow countrymen would provoke a rebellion, the bondage is distributed. Each of us is made part-slave, and each of us is left part-free. We can live in our own house (as long as we pay the property taxes); we can work at our own job (as long as we pay our income taxes); we can attend our own church and send our children to our own church school (as long as it complies with zoning requirements and the school accedes to state licensing standards); we can even go bowling on Friday nights (as long as the bowling alley meets OSHA requirements). We can do all these things as long as we render unto Caesar what he demands.

Such a "convenient" arrangement should not blind us to the fact of life:

Involuntary servitude is involuntary servitude, and it is being forced upon citizens by excessive government spending and arrogant government officials.

Congress: Thirty Pieces of Silver

Just plain, ordinary citizens — the kind of men who fought at Bunker Hill and Belleau Wood and Bataan and Iwo Jima and Baker Two — would like to assert that Articles IV and V of this nation's Constitution protect each citizen from arbitrary confiscation by Caesar and his men.

Article IV: the right of the people to be secure in their persons, houses, papers and effects against unreasonable search and seizure
Article V: nor be deprived of life, liberty or property, without due process of law.

While we were trusting them to serve us, Congress stole a chunk of our freedom and protection. It tore a hole in the Constitution. Consider these powers Congress gave the Internal Revenue Service (Title 26, Section 6331, U.S. Code):

• the power to seize property without a court order (in the name of the Secretary of The Treasury of the United States of America)
• the power to invade a citizen's privacy without due process
• the power to engage in electronic surveillance
• the power to use fear to force compliance
• the power to attach a citizen's wages

So much for the Constitution. so much for the blood spilled to birth it and preserve it.

When did all this happen? It happened in the darkness of 1939, when Franklin D. Roosevelt was president and Henry Morgenthau, Jr., was Secretary of the Treasury, when Americans were trying to climb out of the depression, and when the United States was edging into World War II. That's when it happened the first time.

All that was reaffirmed in 1954. And it occurred both times with the aid and consent of Congress — those men and women who were elected to represent us, to serve us, to protect us.

The courts have occasionally held the statutes valid, have held in summary that the Internal Revenue Service is above the Constitution and its powers do not violate Article IV, Article V, and Article XIV (equal protection under the law).

Peace officers, even with compelling reason to suspect a clear and present danger to public safety, cannot search or seize or confiscate without a court order. But IRS agents can, on the allegation of a computer print-out that says a citizen is delinquent in his federal taxes.

It is written in God's Word that where a man's treasure is, there will his heart be also (Luke 13:34). That should tell you something about Caesar's heart and those of his legionnaires.

Not Even King George

During the hearings on Watergate, Senators Sam Ervin and Herman Talmadge made a great issue of the precious right of a citizen to be secure in his person, his home, and his office.

The senators, in front of nationwide television, traced the protection back to its beginnings: back through the Constitution and the Bill of Rights, back through the days and laws of the early American colonies, back to English common law and the Magna Carta.

If they had chosen to go back even farther into history, they could have cited God's laws as established for the Hebrew republic in the days of Moses — laws which formed the matrix for English and American common law.

Senator Talmadge ended his effusion with a reading from the words of William Pitt, the Elder: "The poorest man may in his cottage bid defiance to all the force of the Crown. It may be frail; its roof may shake; the winds may blow through it, the storms may enter, the rain may enter — but the King of England may not enter; all his forces dare not cross the threshold of the ruined tenement!"

Yet in all their stouthearted histrionics in defense of the citizen's right to be secure, neither Senator Ervin nor Senator Talmadge mentioned the violations of such security in the name of the Secretary of the Treasury and the Internal Revenue Service. Perhaps they thought it was not germane.

But isn't freedom indivisible? Or, are expedients and shortcuts in the name of efficiency and economy more important than upholding those once-guaranteed rights of the individual citizen?

Presumed Guilt

A similar type of tax arrogance exists in many states. There, too, when Caesar's tax agents say the citizen is wrong, he's wrong unless and until he proves himself to be innocent or right.

In no other area of the law is the individual presumed guilty. In every other legal battle, the citizen is covered by the guarantee of presumed innocence until proven guilty beyond a reasonable doubt. Caesar's tax agents are above that law and in such matters the citizen is beneath it.

What America needs is a taxpayer's bill of rights, an amendment to the Bill of Rights, as it were. If men will not act on principle, perhaps they will act when their property is confiscated.

When this Republic was being birthed, Benjamin Franklin suggested this be the national motto:

"Rebellion to tyrants is obedience to God."

It was a good idea then; it's not a bad idea now.

History issues the cold, hard warning:

When government takes 35 percent or more of a people's production, individual freedom is close to the point of no return. From then on it's mostly a downhill slide.

Sir Flinders Petrie, noted British archaeologist and recognized authority on individual liberty in relation to the rise and fall of civilizations.

During his lifetime Sir Flinders studied the records of the world's six great civilizations over the past eight thousand years. His probing led him to this conclusion:

Civilizations reach their peak when liberty is at its maximum.

When economic "parasitism" sets in — when government and its allies in the special interest factions feast on the fruits of the working man's labors — civilization slides into the abyss of a prolonged "dark age."[37]

By then it's almost too late.
Few ever recover to make it back to freedom.

Cut, Limit, and Restore

Let someone suggest the restoration of individual liberty through the limitation of government, and someone else is bound to pop up with the dog-eared challenge, "Okay, wise guy. Just what would you eliminate?"

Obviously, before taxes can be cut, government spending must be reduced. Otherwise you end up with greater debt and more inflation, and that means you're not really cutting taxes at all. Before you can reduce the cost of government, you must eliminate or reduce the size and scope of government.

So, just what would you eliminate? That is not always an easy question to answer. The thicker the shell, the more difficult it is to get to the meat of the coconut. And, the government's shell is pretty thick right now. So far, there have been only feeble gestures to tackle the job. It's a job that citizens must undertake, just as the Committees of Correspondence tackled the king and his political sycophants prior to the War for American Independence.

Some congressmen are already moving in that direction. They have introduced bills that would mandate a balanced federal budget, put a cap on federal taxes, call for a constitutional amendment forbidding future federal deficits (except for temporary overspending in case of emergency), and require a gradual pay-off of the federal debt.

One of the difficulties in eliminating or reducing federal spending involves so-called uncontrollable (untouchable) expenditures. These uncontrollables are open-ended programs and fixed costs to which Congress has committed the taxpayer in the past. In many areas, such back-door spending is not only improper but deceitful. Many of the commitments were pushed through by spend-and-elect congressmen who feared that future Congresses would resort to fiscal sanity and eliminate such spendthrift programs. Thus, the congressmen foisted upon the taxpayer taxation without representation.

Some congressmen argue that these uncontrollable expenditures cannot be eliminated without violating the public trust. The public trust has already been violated by these devious tactics tailored to fit special interest groups.

At least 76 percent of all federally budgeted expenditures are "virtually uncontrollable." Unless this stranglehold on today's and tomorrow's taxpayers is broken citizens will not have representative government and will not regain the freedom to make their own decisions as to how they wish to allocate future tax receipts.

Such commitments must be undone or reduced if we are to avoid the disaster which one-time budget director Roy M. Ash foresaw. Mr. predicted that someday 66 percent of our gross national product would go down Caesar' gullet.

What has been done can be undone. If not by those now in Congress, than by representative the citizens elect to release them from such bondage.

A Matter of Principles

If government is to be restored to its proper size and scope, if Caesar is to be put back into his Constitutional restraints, it must be done on principle. It will not be done by getting bogged down in petty details or decimal points or pettifoggery. Those are the refuge of the scoundrel and the spender.

What principles? The principles of individual liberty and limited government.

The late Leonard Read, founder and president of the Foundation for Economic Education, was one of the leading expositors of such principles. For more than forty years he preached and taught those principles to countless Americans.

So, just what government would you cut? Let Mr. Read's writings and words answer that challenge:

I would favor the rescinding of all governmental action — federal, state or local — which would interfere with an individual's freedom
• to pursue his peaceful ambition to the full extent of his abilities, regardless of race or creed or family background...
• to worship God in his own way, even if it isn't "orthodox"...
• to choose his own trade and to apply for any job he wants - and to quit his job if he doesn't like it or if he gets a better offer ...
• to go into business for himself, to be his own boss, and set his own hours of work— even if it's only three hours a week ...
• to use his honestly acquired property in his own way — spend it foolishly, invest it wisely, or even give it away. Beyond what is required as one's fair share to an agency of society limited to keeping the peace, the fruits of one's labor are his own...
• to offer his services or products for sale on his own terms, even if he loses money on the deal...

- to buy or not to buy any service or product offered for sale, even if refusal displeases the seller...
- to agree or disagree with any other person, whether or not the majority is on the side of the other person...
- to do as he pleases in general as long as he doesn't infringe the equal right and opportunity of every other person to do as he pleases.

"In short," concluded Leonard Read, "instead of attempting to explain the thousands upon thousands of government agencies you would eliminate, let the author of the tricky question explain just one peaceful activity he would deny to the individual ...

"... isn't that putting the burden of the proof where it belongs?"

Indeed it is!

CHAPTER ELEVEN

Inflation Is A Sneak Thief!

Diverse weights and diverse measures,
both of them are alike, abomination to The Lord
(Prov. 20:10).

Things are not going too well for Joe Griffin and his wife.

Here they are, retired, in the golden years of their lives, and everything keeps coming up crab grass.

Some twenty three years ago, Joe and Dolly bought their home for about $50,000. They planned to live there for the rest of the days The Lord gives them here on earth. Two years ago Joe retired, and the Griffins now live on an income of around $24,000 a year. That depends in part on what their small investments pay. When Joe took out that annuity years ago, he figured that, along with their Social Security payments, it would provide them with a comfortable old age.

In 1970, when Joe and Dolly bought their home, the property taxes were $700 a year. This year their tax bill was $2,750. That's more than three times what they were paying back then and almost one-tenth of their total income.

What's going on here?

Did the Griffins add on to their house? Did they put in a swimming pool? Or a new garage? No. Aside from the normal maintenance, there has been no change in the Griffin house. Oh, a couple of flower beds and a bird bath, but that's all.

What happened was this: over the years the so-called assessed value of their home was just about tripled. And, over the years, the property tax went up right along with it.

According to the county tax assessor, the Griffin house now has a market value of $125,000, and their property tax was based on that figure.

The Griffins have had no thought of selling (although now they may be forced to). The house is their home, not a speculator's sport.

However, they are being taxed on the basis of what the assessor says they could get if they were to put it on the market.

So they have been hit from both sides. The tax rate went up to pay the inflated cost of government, and the assessment rose to reflect the inflated prices of the market. (When the house was reassessed some years back, the folks at town hall assured them the rates would go down to equal out the increased assessed value. Somehow, that got lost in the shuffle; both the rates and the assessed value went up.)

The Great Bubble Machine

All of this has hit the Griffins in their old age and right in their limited income.

On top of that, the cost of almost everything else has skyrocketed. For example, when they first moved in, it cost them about $400 a year to heat their house. Today it costs them almost $1,500. It's the same with the cost of electricity, the cost of food, and the cost of their other necessities — the car, gas and oil, clothes. You name it.

The bottom has dropped out of the purchasing power of Joe's annuity. He has received some cost-of-living adjustments on his Social Security, but he and Dolly are hard-pressed to make ends meet. In fact, Joe has taken to doing odd jobs to supplement their income and Dolly makes hand stitched quilts to sell at the local flea market. It's a struggle to keep their heads above the rising tide of inflation.

They are not alone. Most folks, especially retired folks, are in the same bind. Caesar has really done it to them. Millions upon millions of Americans have suffered, and now suffer, on the rack of inflation. They stretch and scrimp but it keeps getting harder and harder.

The economists and the politicians tell them the rate of inflation has decreased, and it has to some extent, temporarily. However, gas for their six-year-old car costs about $1.25 a gallon. If there really has been a drop in inflation, it doesn't show when they go to the supermarket. Not very much. A loaf of bread still costs about a buck. And coffee? Crazy!

Every now and then a group of housewives will whoop it up down at the grocery store. They raise Cain with the butcher and switch from roasts to chicken and fish. And then the price of fish goes through the ceiling. So, back to beans and franks and macaroni salad.

Their frustration and anger is understandable. But they raise Cain with the wrong outfit. High prices and shrinking dollars are not the cause of inflation. They are the consequences!

The ladies and Joe and Dolly should be raising Cain with the politicians. They should be boycotting the federal bubble machine, the one in Babble-on-the Potomac. The fake money and the license for fake credit comes from there.

That is the source of inflation.

And that is the cause of Joe and Dolly's and the housewives' economic woes.

Just What is Inflation?

Politicians keep passing the buck!

They say it's worth thirty-two cents based on what the dollar bought in 1967. If they were honest with us, they would at least admit that the dollar is worth maybe ten cents based on what it was worth in 1940. Or that it's worth maybe twenty cents based on what a dollar would buy in 1950.

The American consumer is being had. We will no doubt continue to be had by something called inflation.

Just what is inflation?

Inflation is an increase in the supply of money — an increase in the amount of currency and credit.

Inflation is not higher prices.

Inflation is not higher wages.

Inflation is not an increase in the cost of living or the shrinking purchasing power of the dollar.

Those are the results, the consequences, the symptoms of inflation. The disease itself, the root cause, is something else. Scratch five economists and you are likely to come up with five different definitions of inflation. Consider what these prominent individuals have to say.

Henry Hazlitt: Inflation is the increase in the supply of money and credit.[1]

Lawrence Fertig: Monetary inflation is always and everywhere the cause of price inflation.[2]

Wilhelm Roepke: It should be clear by now that the quantity of money in circulation decisively affects the purchasing power of money, an increase in the supply of money lowering its purchasing power [inflation], a decrease raising it [deflation].[3]

Professor Tom Rose: Inflation is an increase in the money supply; period.[4]

Gary North: There are two basic definitions: (1) An increase in the money supply and (2) a rise in the general level of prices which is caused by an increase in the money supply. I prefer the first definition Inflation is simply an increase in the supply of money.[5]

Harry Browne: Inflation is the issuance of paper currency for which there is no gold (or other commodity in storage) ... inflation is nothing more than the counterfeiting of paper money.[6]

Leonard Read: Inflation is nothing more or less than the printing of what government has declared to be legal tender, that is, printing ever-increasing quantities of fiat money.[7]

There you have it. Each one of those men is saying just about the same thing: Inflation is an increase in the money supply. The more money government pours into the system, the less each unit of money is worth (See table, "The Tale of The Shrinking Dollar," page 266)

Money! Money! Money!

The key word in the definition of inflation is money.

What is money?

Many people equate money with wealth.

Is money wealth? No.

Wealth is what exists, what you own, in real goods, in tangible items, in property. The market value of those items (what others are willing to pay for them) represents wealth, inherent, intrinsic wealth.

Money is a medium of exchange. In that sense, wealth is not how much money you may have but what your money is worth; what it will buy.

Let economist and author Henry Hazlitt explain:

The most obvious and yet the oldest and most stubborn error on which the appeal of inflation rests is that of confusing "money" with "wealth" Real wealth, of course, consists in what is produced and consumed; the food we eat, the clothes we wear, the houses we live in. It is railways and roads and motor cars; ships and planes and factories; schools and churches and theaters; pianos, paintings and books. Yet, so powerful is the verbal ambiguity that confuses money with wealth that even those who at times recognize the confusion will slide back into it in the course of their reasoning. Each man sees that if he personally had more money he could buy more things from others. If he had twice as much he could buy twice as many things; if he had three times as much money, he would be "worth" three times as much. And, to many the conclusion seems obvious that if the government merely issued more money and distributed it to everybody, we would all be that much richer.[8]

Welcome to the age of inflation!

Hazlitt goes on to point out the fallacy of such reasoning: simply increasing the amount of money does not increase one's wealth; it only increases the amount of money. Other factors take over from there.

Look at it this way.

Suppose you had one pitcher of milk, and you wanted to have two pitchers of milk.

You could buy another quart, or you could get your cows to produce twice as much.

Or you could mix a pitcher of water with the pitcher of milk.

The first two ways, would produce two pitchers of milk — twice as much milk as you had.

With the third way — the inflation way — what would you have? You would still have one pitcher of milk. It might look like two pitchers of milk. But you would have one pitcher of milk in two pitchers, each one half milk and half water.

The milk represents wealth; the water represents money. Inflation and dilution are virtually synonymous!

For an extreme example of what happens when money is poured into the system, look at Germany during the years 1919 to 1923. During the close of that period the German people had scads of money. They had so much money that they literally carted their Deutsche marks to market in wheelbarrows. A loaf of bread cost 1.2 trillion marks.

American tourists visiting Germany at that time had much less money. Did that mean they had less wealth? No. In 1923 one American dollar could get 11.7 trillion marks. An overnight stay at a good hotel cost one thin dime. Why? Because the American currency represented actual (real) wealth.

Legalized Counterfeiting

What occurred in Germany is an extreme example (although not an isolated one). Many nations have experienced such hyperinflation, such massive counterfeiting of currency. Yet in that extreme can be found this fact: it is not the quantity of money that counts, it is the quality. If inflation is arbitrarily increased the quality (purchasing power) of the money will automatically decrease.

In his "Introduction to Christian Economics", Dr. Gary North emphasized that inflation is counterfeiting:

> If individuals do it, the State must intervene and punish the violators, since fraud and theft are both involved. Yet, the state is also to be limited by the law of honest weights and measures; it must not force citizens to accept a unit of money which is worth less in exchange than its face value. In short, legal tender laws are immoral; currency debasement is immoral; printed unbacked money is immoral.[9]

(Legal tender laws dictate that certain specified "money" [i.e., Federal reserve notes] must be accepted at its face value for the payment of debts, public and private.)

From Merchandise to Manipulation

To give a detailed and comprehensive history of money in a few short paragraphs or even in a few short books would be impossible. Thus, let these few lines suffice to sketch money's genesis, evolution, and degradation.

1. In the beginning, the medium was the merchandise. The fish that was traded for a stone axe; the canoe that was bartered for the cave.

2. Soon the medium (of exchange) was narrowed to include various recognized and accepted commodities, beads, jewels, salt, tobacco, women — and finally, precious metals, such as gold and silver which had intrinsic (inherent) value. That metal was weighted and stamped and used as money.

3. Paper IOUs were introduced as a matter of convenience to the metal owner. The heavy coins or bars kept wearing a hole in the pocket; thus, it was easier to carry a pocketful of paper receipts (notes) than it was to haul around a bag full of gold or silver.

The metal was deposited with a reputable holder (a banker) and the IOUs were worth their face value in gold or silver, redeemable at any time. They were "as good as gold."

4. The state got into the banking business., It accepted deposits of gold or silver and issued receipts (bank notes) for the metal on deposit. The notes (IOUs) were redeemable at any time.

5. Government then arbitrarily divorced the paper (IOU) money from the metal (gold or silver). It repudiated any claim the

holder of the paper had on the gold or silver on deposit. It declared the paper itself was money (fiat). Why was it money? Because the State said it was. *Sic semper tyrannis*. Sic, sic, sick!

6. Government now prints money at will and without regard to species money (gold or silver) or existing wealth. Thus, funny money replaces sound money and the state manipulates the citizen by manipulating his money.

A Quickie Quiz!

To understand what has happened to the purchasing power (the value) of your money, keep these two things in mind: 1. Money is not wealth. It is a medium of exchange. 2. Inflation is an increase in the supply of money: it is not an increase in wealth.

Now, how about a quickie quiz?

Who can increase the supply of money (check one)?

(a) Business

(b) Labor

(c) Government

Answer: *Government.* Only government can increase the supply of money. (Actually, it's the Federal Reserve (that privately owned, not answerable to Congress or the people central bank) that does it. The "Fed" determines and manipulates the supply and thus the value of "legal tender" — its declared medium of exchange. .

Cause and Effect

One of the prevailing fallacies about inflation is the so-called wage-price spiral. That is the myth that higher wages and higher prices cause inflation. Wage and price hikes are not the cause of inflation; they are the consequences.

As Henry Hazlitt explained,

If it [the wage-price spiral] were not preceded, accompanied, or quickly followed by an increase in the supply of money, an increase in wages above the "equilibrium level" would not cause inflation; it would merely cause unemployment. And an increase in prices without an increase in cash in people's pockets would merely cause a falling off in sales. Wage and price rises, in brief, are usually the consequence of inflation. They can cause it only to the extent that they force an increase in the money supply.

Lawrence Fertig, in "Prosperity Through Freedom", underscored the point:

> It is a common misconception that increased wages always mean higher prices and inflation. This is not so unless the government acts to inflate the currency in order to support uneconomic wage rises. Otherwise the results of increases would be curtailed production and unemployment.[10]

For example, in the 1920s when Henry Ford introduced the eight-hour day and the ten-dollars-a-day wage, it did not result in inflation; it resulted in higher wages, increased production, and lower prices for his Model T. The government at that time was not into printing funny money.

So much for the argument that high prices or high wages cause inflation. Businesses cannot print money. The labor unions cannot print money. Government (or its agencies or designees) creates inflation. Its monetary policies have been and are the root cause of inflation.

Money and Credit

There are basically two ways government increases the supply of money.

First, it just plain prints more money.

It creates money out of paper and ink and printing presses and backs it up, not with a specie or wealth, but with hot-air words.

The Continental Congress did that back in the 1770s. It printed money (fiat) to help pay for the War for Independence. Without any backing, the money soon became worthles. Merchants and citizens would not accept it as a medium of exchange (thus the expression, "Not worth a Continental").

France went through a rain of paper money in the late 1700s. Before financial ruin and spiritual depravity took over, the cost of a barrel of flour soared from forty-five cents to $45. Finally, there was no bread. That was when Marie Antoinette picked up Jean Jacques Rousseau's quip "Let them eat cake." (Economic ruin and spiritual decline are companions; where there is one, there will sooner or later be the other.)

In 1947 President Harry Truman warned Congress, "We already have an alarming degree of inflation and, even more alarming, it is getting worse." And it did get worse !

Consider the anticipated federal deficit of $341 billion for the fiscal year 1993. Where will all those big bucks come from? Quite a bit of it will come from the government's printing presses. From the federal bubble machine!

As the need arises to finance the deficit, the Federal Reserve will instruct the Treasury to print and issue debt security notes. It will then sell those securities (and thus compete with the individuals and businesses trying to borrow money). Next, it will have the Bureau of Engraving print the necessary paper money and hand that over to the Federal Reserve, which will use that fiat to buy the securities from the brokers and private individuals who purchased them from the Treasury. The whole process is nothing but creating money out of thin air.

That new money will pour into the economy. No real wealth backs it. It is, in essence, worthless. But we will be forced to accept it at face value. We take our financial licking when we spend the money and find out it's worth a lot less in terms of real purchasing power.

Fractional Reserves

Second, the government can increase the supply of available credit by manipulating the requirements for fractional reserves. Most of the $341 billion for that 1993 deficit will come this way. In reality it's just another way of pumping fake money into the system. As a matter of fact, there is far more credit funny money in the economic system today than there is funny currency.

Once again, look to the Federal Reserve, that privately owned and privately controlled central bank which, back in 1913, received from Congress the power to manipulate the amount and value of our money.[11]

The Fed establishes the percentage of cash reserves its member banks must keep on hand to cover their customers' demand deposits. These are called fractional reserves.

Suppose you deposit $100 in your local bank subject to payment (withdrawal) on demand.

How much of that deposit do you suppose the bank is required to keep on hand against the possibility you will walk in and withdraw your money? $100? $75? $50? $25? $14? $3?

The answer is $3. Three percent is the required reserve amount of checkable deposits up to $25 million. Above that amount the required bank reserve varies from 12 percent to 18 percent depending upon the circumstances of the deposit and The Feds' discretion.

(If all the depositors, or even 25 percent of them, demanded their money at the same time, the bank would be in serious trouble, "deposit insurance" notwithstanding. When that happened in 1929, nine thousand banks went kaput.)

What can the bank do with the other part of the deposits — yours and all others? It can loan it out. A single deposit of $100 can be used to create about $800 worth of loans throughout the banking system.

Professor Wilhelm Roepke explained how it works. (Keep in mind that when Dr. Roepke wrote the following, the fractional reserve requirement was 10 percent. Now it averages about 14 percent):

> There is yet another angle from which we can observe how the modern banking system affects the supply of money. A businessman, for instance, may establish a demand deposit (checking account) not only by depositing hard cash, but by getting the bank to extend him a loan for this purpose. Thus, by adhering to the proportion of 1:10 between cash reserves and outstanding demand deposits, with 90 percent of the actual currency paid in being loaned out, the bank can by granting credits create new checking accounts (demand deposits) to an amount nine times greater than that which has been paid into it ....[The bank] grants credits not out of preceding savings, but from additional resources obtained by the creation of credit .[12]

Fractional reserve banking has vastly outstripped the State's printing of money as a means of inflation.

Warned Dr. Roepke, "It is of great importance that we thoroughly understand [this].... for without such understanding we cannot adequately comprehend the perils and problems which currently beset our economic system."[13]

Not only have the vast majority of Americans failed to understand the irresponsible system, they have done nothing to correct it. Thus, the perils and the problems have been and are continuing to be magnified.

The Big Red Balloon

The table ("The Tale of The Shrinking Dollar," covering the years 1940-1992) reveals how government has increased the supply of money and how the purchasing power of the dollar has been eroded. If you thought you had a hole in your pocket, that table shows why! That is a picture of inflation during the past fifty two years. It is a record of what happened to the purchasing power of your hard-earned dollars. What is happening and why. It's a big red balloon.

The bureaucrats and politicians will insist that the purchasing power of the dollar is about thirty cents. That's a con job, based on an arbitrary price index set at one hundred in 1967. But in 1967 the dollar that was worth one hundred cents in 1939 and 1940 had already shriveled to less than fifty cents.

Based on straight talk and hard figures, the dollar in your pocket today is worth about ten cents in purchasing power compared to the dollar of 1939-40.

Why the sliding scale and double talk about the consumer price index? Well, when loss in the purchasing power of the money becomes indefensible and the voters get restive, switching the base year of the index makes it appear the dollar is worth more than it really is. It's easier to falsify the balance by deceit than to enforce the discipline necessary to halt inflation.

It may be easier, but it is also deadly. It keeps adding on to the house as the foundation is being washed away.

Nine Trillion Dollars!

The American Institute for Economic Research estimated in November 1992 that inflation had robbed American families of $9 trillion during the twenty-year period, 1971-1992. That, figures the AIER,, was the loss in purchasing power, in savings accounts, insurance policies, pensions, annuities, trust funds, government and corporate bonds, mortgage loans held by individuals, and currency held in checking accounts.[14]

Nine trillion dollars!

Add to that the almost $1 trillion embezzled by inflation in the years 1940-1970. Figure that there were many families not included in the AIER data who also lost billions, if not trillions of dollars.

Now do you see what inflation has really cost the people of this nation?

Much is written about and many will recall the tremendous losses suffered during the Great Depression (1929-33). Yet those losses were mild compared to the losses Americans have suffered due to inflation.

The AIER reported, "During the early years of the Great Depression, from the end of 1929 through 1933, nearly 40 percent of the nation's banks failed [some 9,000 of them]. Loud were the lamentations when depositors lost $1.3 billion as a result of those bank failures."[15]

The losses to savers and holders of life insurance during the past years, in relation to total wealth, were more than four hundred times the relative loss suffered by depositors whose banks failed between 1929 and 1933!

Inflation robs the working man. It robs the saver. It robs the investor. It robs the person who receives public assistance, and it robs the person who pays for that public assistance.

Even those whose wages and salaries have been adjusted from time to time to make up for the rising cost of living (the declining purchasing power of the dollar) have been robbed. Why? First, because the theft has been so subtle and sustained over so long a period of time (it's chronic), few working persons realize the full extent of their losses. Second, because quite often when a person's wages are increased to cover the loss of purchasing power, it shoves him or her into a higher tax bracket with higher tax rates. Thus, there is a net loss for the taxpayer and a net gain for government. Governments thrive on inflation! For Caesar, inflation is an open-ended supply line; for the working man, it's a bottomless pit.

Lifetime Earnings - and Theft!

Take a hypothetical but entirely plausible case. In 1971, Bill Bagadonuts graduated from college. He started earning $20,000 a year. Bill's employer raised his salary periodically and by 1992 after twenty years with the firm, Bill was earning $50,000 a year —more than double what he earned when he started out.

Over the years the value of the dollars Bill was paid — the purchasing power — was just about chopped in half by inflation. Calculated on a dollar worth one hundred cents in 1971, the dollar declined in purchasing power almost every year since then. In 1991 the purchasing power of Bill's dollar was about 45 cents. Forgetting the compounding of that loss in purchasing power, Bill was just slightly ahead in terms of real purchasing power. On a base of the 1971, 100-cent dollar, he really earned $22,500 in 1992; only $2,500 more than he earned in 1971. And, with a face value (current dollar) increase of $30,000 a year in his income (which was the way his income tax had to be figured), Bill was pushed into a higher tax bracket; he paid more taxes than he had in 1974. So he was not even; he was behind!

That in itself is enough to drive a fellow up the wall. Think what it does to the wife who has to make ends meet in the home. And the kids who were counting on help from Mom and Dad when they were ready to go to college!

You may have an idea of just how much inflation steals from you and your family over a year's time. But do you really comprehend what inflation has done and is in the process of doing to your lifetime earnings?

Eight Percent Compounded

Sure, the experts tell us that inflation is down below three percent for now. It wasn't too long ago that it was running close to double digits. The way the government debt and deficits are running, it won't be long before it starts going up again.

In his essay "Is Inflation Here To Stay," Morris J. Markowitz suggested, "A 35-year-old man now earning $20,000 a year may need $200,000 a year, or more, by the time he retires."[16] Mr. Markowitz used the term "may need" — may need $200,000 a year by the time he retires. May need for what? To satisfy increased appetite? To luxuriate in some splendid new creature comforts? To amass a chunk of wealth?

No. He is saying that when the fellow retires he may need $200,000 a year just to stay even, financially speaking, with where he was thirty years earlier.

Says Mr. Markowitz, "Note that a mere eight percent annual increase [in inflation] amounts to over 1,000 percent in 30 years, when compounded." Too many folks fail to realize the tremendous price tag that comes with that little word compounded. And each year the price you pay for inflation is compounded.

Inflation Is a Tax...Is a Tax...Is a Tax!

Inflation is a tax. It is the most insidious tax of all. It's hidden. It sneaks. It compounds its evil.

Whoever cast his or her ballot for inflation?

The loss of purchasing power of the dollar is the invisible tax that pays for the increase of [government] expenditures. The inflation tends to hide the actual burden of taxation; what we do not pay for on April 15, we pay for daily in higher prices. The government cannot get

THE TALE OF THE SHRINKING DOLLAR
(in billions of dollars)

Year	Federal Spending	Federal Debt	Money Supply*	Purchasing Power of the Dollar
1940	$ 9.1	$ 42.9	$ 66.0	100c
1945	98.4	258.7	138.4	78
1950	39.6	252.7	169.9	58
1955	64.6	274.4	207.7	52
1960	92.2	290.9	217.0	47
1965	118.4	323.1	301.1	44
1970	196.6	382.6	425.0	36
1975	340.5	544.1ª	1,023.0	24
1980	615.4	914.3	1,631.0	16
1984	919.4	1,572.7	2,372.0	13
1992	1,092.0	4,021.1	3,439.0#	10

*M2 Money supply (cash, deposits in checking accounts, and nonbank travelers checks). ªshort and long term debt included Sources: *Facts & figures on Govt. Finance*, 1992, Tax Foundation; Statistical Abstract, U.S. Dept of Commerce, U.S. Treasury Debt. # 1991, latest data available.

something for nothing; when it increases expenditures the private sector must reduce its consumption or investment. Higher prices accomplish this goal: The citizens reduce their purchases as the government in-creases its purchases. That is why inflation is a tax.[18]

Inflation is a hidden tax. There are no reports to fill out, no printed forms to complete, no deductions itemized on the paycheck stub. But it is there, just as real and just as destructive as any other form of confiscation.

Inflation is an open-ended tax. There is no fixed rate of confiscation. There is no way to figure, "If I earn so much the rate will be X percent of Y dollars." What will it be, that tax? Eight percent? Ten percent? Four percent this year and 15 percent two years from now? How can you know?

How can you plan? Not even the perpetrators know; they have lost control

Inflation is a flat tax. "Tantamount to a flat sales tax of the same percentage on all commodities, with the rate as high on bread and milk as on diamonds and furs." Inflation is a regressive tax. It hits hardest those who are the least able to pay. Inflation is butchering the lower and middle income groups. Destroying not only their todays but also their tomorrows. And their children's also.

Is it not strange that those politicians who shed the biggest tears for the little people are the very champions of the spending and deficit programs which destroy the individual's earnings and savings and benefits and hopes and opportunities? You know who they are: the inflation fighters who insist that government is not doing enough; that it print more money to make up the loss in purchasing power; that it can spend and buy our way to prosperity.

We have wandered in their wilderness for more than forty years and now we know: all their glitter is fool's gold!

This gigantic swindle, this hoax, this immorality in politics and economics.

How did it happen in America?

We the people never voted for inflation.

We never passed an initiative on the proposition "Shall we employ inflation?" There was never a referendum on the matter.

Yet here it is. A national way of life. It has been with us, creeping up on us, boring in on us, accelerating its take for more than fifty years. Longer even.

Our federal representatives claim they never voted for inflation. And they didn't. Not *per se*. Not in so many words.

Many campaigned on it. Many promised it. When they were elected and re-elected, they voted for it. But not once did they utter the word except to oppose it. Not once did they say, "We are voting to destroy the value of the U.S. dollar. The one that has 'In God We Trust' on the backside."

Instead, they voted for the roots of inflation. For the cause.

They voted to knock the dollar loose from gold; to discard that measure of monetary discipline.

They changed money from a medium of exchange to a political tool.

They voted to delegate to a private banking corporation the power to manipulate the value of our dollar.

They handed that right to dictate legal tender to a central entity not answerable to the people or to the people's representatives.

Thus, they tossed the Constitution into the ash can and with the help of the Court rewrote Article 1, Section 8, Part 5 of the law of the land:

Congress shall have the power to coin money and regulate the value thereof, and of foreign coin, and fix the Standard of Weights and Measures.

Standards of weights and measures are important to a people, but what good are they if they do not also apply to money? Where is the protection to the people if a quasi-governmental, independent bank can manipulate their medium of exchange and rig its value?

The politicians voted to take billions and hundreds of billions of the people's dollars and spend them for subsidies and social programs, giveaways, and foreign aid. But seldom did they have the guts to vote the full measure of taxation to fund such spending. They hid it behind the elastic ceiling of an ever rising federal debt. So it is today that the federal debt is about $4.1 trillion - about $15,600 for every man, woman, and child in the nation. (Some compute the total federal debt to be much higher. The National Taxpayers Union, for example, once figured the federal government's long-term unfunded liabilities to be close to $13 trillion.)

We Let Them Do It!

In retrospect we may ask, "How did it happen? How did these politicians get away with it?"

Part of the answer is trickery. Deceit. Sleight of hand. The art of those economic messiahs who led us in dark directions. The other part of the answer is they got away with it because we the people let them. When we stopped believing that government was the responsibility of the people and bought the line that the people were the responsibility of the government, we gave the green light. From then on Caesar and his costs were magnified; faith in God and His abundance, obedience to His laws — these were shoved back to second or third place, or even forgotten.

"Look at the birds of the air, for they neither sow nor reap nor gather into barns; yet your heavenly Father feeds them. Are you not of more value than they?" (Matt. 6:26).

Somewhere along the line we seem to have forgotten that. Or lost our faith. And when faith dies, foolishness takes over.

The fool has said in his heart,
"There is no God."

Corrupt are they, and have done abominable iniquity;
There is none that doeth good (Ps. 53:1).

Some Said "No!"

There were those, in and out of Congress, who fought the planting of inflation's roots. They tried to prevent the rape of the working man and his family.

The people whose intelligence and integrity compelled them spoke out for monetary discipline and said that it was essential to the survival of the Republic. They preached that a nation could not go on spending what it did not have; that some day we would have to pay; that the consequences could be catastrophic.

Slow down, they urged. If government needs more money, stand up and say so. Tell the people why. Be honest with them. Tell them what the tax will be and be guided by their response.

Watch out, they pleaded. Inflation will destroy America! Economic debauchery brings spiritual degradation.

Take heed, they warned. Those who control the money system control the nation!

They were in the minority. Their words were true, but they were not popular. Some of the men who spoke out were defeated at the polls. We will punish them for their selfishness, the voters said. But, the voters were only punishing themselves, and their due bill would come. It has come.

Dupes and Do-Gooders

Most of the congressmen simply gave the people what they felt they wanted. They could read the polls. And where the public's heart was, they put the public's treasure.

To suggest that they had some evil intent or that they knew they were tearing the heart out of America's economic body would be untrue and unfair. In that regard they did not know what they were doing. They were simply dupes and do-gooders, incompetent, perhaps, and more concerned with staying in office than with preserving the nation.

They failed to realize the unholy powers of the new economics and the new politics, which were taking advantage of the situation and taking over the system. So they went along, helping to plant and cultivate the roots of that insidious inflation. Some in retrospect saw the error of their ways. Sumner Slichter of the New Deal days was one. He looked back and cried, "Who will reform the reformers?" But the damage had been done; it was eating into the soul of the Republic.

Those Who Knew

What of those elected or appointed to high office and those who served the men in high places, knowing exactly what they were doing and where they were taking America?

For them, inflation was the economic means to a political end, and the end was revolution.

This is what they knew about inflation: at the outset economic disruption is important, but in the long run monetary ruin is secondary; it is the ensuing moral decay that leads the way to raising the State above the individual.

In "The People's Pottage" Garet Garrett laid bare their purpose and design:

> Those who take the New Deal to have been the beginning of the revolutionary change in the character of the government are wont to cite its laws, and its many innovations within the law, and to forget that if it had been without the means to enforce them all of its intentions would have died in the straw. It had to have money; and not only a great deal of money, but freedom from the conventional limitations of money. It knew that. Unerringly, therefore, its first act was to prepare inflation; and this was to be a kind of inflation we had never imagined before; that is, inflation for premeditated political purpose.[19]

What would be the path and the consequences of such inflation? Garet Garrett outlined it step by step:

> When, in the conquest of power and for political ends, a government deliberately engineers inflation, all the monetary evils occur as before — and then to those you add such consequences as:
> First, that as the government expands explosively, the people will lose control of it; Second, as the people receive millions of checks from the automatic printing machines in the United States Treasury they learn to become dependent upon government for aid and comfort; Third, people are first enticed by the benefits and then obliged to exchange freedom for security, and Finally, the revelry of public money, which for a while seems to cost nobody anything, brings to

pass a state of immorality that permeates every level of society.[20]

Thus was mapped the course to change the character of American government. Thus was inflation engineered to serve the pagan view that man was born to serve the state.

The citizen was invited to finance the funeral of his own freedom; inflation bought the casket and the burial plot.

Monetary destruction breeds not only poverty and chaos, but also government tyranny. Few policies are more calculated to destroy the existing basis of a free society than the debauching of its currency. And few tools, if any, are more important to the champion of freedom than a sound monetary system.[21]

Slogans and Money

At no time, except within the inner circle, did propagators of the quiet revolution admit to such design. Publicly they talked of economic growth, of everlasting progress and full employment. They boasted that their new economics could spend the nation out of depression into never ending bonanza; a perpetual boom with ever higher plateaus. That was their promise; that was their deceit; that was their "people's pottage."

They coined new slogans the way the Pied Piper piped new tunes. They coined new money even more rapidly. Under such auspices inflation came: a thief in the night leaving behind the seeds of revolution. While the people were in their parlors counting all their "free" money, inflation crept through the back windows. While the people were listening to fireside political flimflam, inflation stole the family valuables—not just their gold and silver, but their moral fiber and the parchment proclaiming their right to be free. From then on they would gradually become more and more dependent and more and more enslaved.

P. T. Barnum was right!
One every minute!

Gross Products

It wasn't long before most people bought the line.

Why worry about the federal debt? We only owe it to ourselves. It's not as if some foreign potentate held the mortgage.

And so they went on letting government spend their tomorrows to pay for their yesterdays. Now the interest on the federal debt — just the interest — will cost $206.3 billion in fiscal 1992 and will figure out to about $1,280 for every man, woman, and child in the land — more than $5,000 for a family of four.

Well, boast the wheelers and dealers, look at the gross national product! See how it grows. Inflation hasn't hurt a bit! In fact, it helps.

That was another argument backed by error, by deceit, by duplicity.

(As the late Dr. Elgin Groseclose of the Institute for Monetary Research pointed out GNP totals have been revised to include "services." Services may contribute to our comfort, convenience, and well-being, but how much do they really add to the gross national product? Constructive, helpful, even necessary services they may be; but tangible products they are not.)

The boasters seldom pointed out that the GNP was being figured in new dollars, worth less in purchasing power each year.

Nor did they bother to consider the greater and greater portion of the GNP being taken by government: 18 percent of $99 billion in 1940; 20 percent of $2.1 trillion plus in 1992. (Not including the federal government's long-term unfunded liabilities — or those burdens levied by the locals and the states.)

Running Wild

The people largely ignored the early symptoms of the cancer.

Even when it took larger and larger doses of fake money and stretched the credit to alleviate the economic pains. Even when it took increasing hordes of the bureaucrats to staff the mushrooming agencies and departments. Even when the controls and interventions multiplied, they were slow to acknowledge how deeply the malignancy had eaten into the nation's marrow and its morrows. Who likes to admit he is sick and has to take the cure?

It was not just the economic cancer; it was also the political cancer: both were running wild. Physicians have a word when cancer goes wild, They step into the hall, close the door, and whisper, "It has metastasized!" It's all through the body. Then they shake their heads and walk away.

That's what has happened. The cancer has metastasized.

What part of the national body — what organ, what appendage, what function — is not affected? Name one!

Those Scapegoats

The symptoms are not recent. They began to show years ago. The higher prices, the economic dislocations, the shift of capital from the individual to the state, the slow and steady erosion of savings and annuities, the rising unemployment.

What about those higher prices That loss of purchasing power? The difficulty in stretching the family budget to make ends meet? What about that symptom?

After a while the people began to ask, What's going on here? We have more money but we're sliding backward. How come?

The manipulators were ready for that one. They had their scapegoats preselected; It's those greedy businessmen! That's what's causing the higher prices. Those guys aren't satisfied with a reasonable profit. We try to fight inflation and they keep raising prices.

That's right, agreed the public. It's those greedy businessmen. They keep raising prices. All they care about is profits. It's just as they taught us in school. Those guys are greedy.

(Few bothered to consider the cause for the higher prices — the rising costs of inflation. And few bothered to check the profit structure. If they had they would have found that in general and in constant dollars profits had not increased; that by and large profits were dropping; that over the years profits averaged from four to seven percent of sales.)

The public took the politicians' propaganda at face value; thus, it was no trick at all to add more controls and more shackles to free individual enterprise. That, of course, increased the costs and raised the prices even more. And so the people howled again.

In defense, the businessmen put forth a scapegoat of their own.

Look, they countered, it's the labor unions. They keep demanding higher wages. They hold down productivity. How can we keep prices down when they keep doing that?

Yes, that's true, agreed the people. The labor unions keep demanding unrealistic and higher wages. And look at those make-work rules. The high cost of labor must be part of the high cost of living.

So the public blamed both business and labor, and business and labor blamed each other, and very few blamed the government. And there, for the most part, was the culprit: the politician, the manipulator, and the money changer who kept pumping bad money after bad money and debt on top of debt.

Rising Unemployment

The people asked still later: "If this new economics is so great, how come this rising unemployment" What's causing that?"

Well, inflation caused it.

The spenders and the socializers may not like this, but it is fact: The "recession and all its symptoms — rising unemployment, falling commodity prices, lower production, and the like — are the direct results of the previous roaring inflation."[22]

When waste is rewarded and thrift is penalized, when speculation means gain and investment means loss, then capital disappears and production declines. When production declines, prices soar and unemployment rises.

> Rampant inflation [i.e., two-digit inflation such as the nation experienced in the late 1970s] destroys the capital markets which are the very wellspring of productive enterprise. Business capital, especially long-term capital, becomes very scarce, which precipitates economic stagnation and recession.[23]

What happens when such cracks appear? When recessions keep niggling at the door and unemployment rises?

> The Federal government comes to the rescue with record budget deficits and new bursts of currency expansion. After all, this is the basic recipe of the "new economics" that has shaped Federal economic policy since the 1930s and has given us "inflationary-recession," i.e., simultaneous inflation and recession.[24]

The federal government comes to the rescue. Politicians talk about tax cuts and increased deficits and Santa Claus rides down the hill of inflation, taking our dollars down to dimes. And the people cheer.

Or do they?

Are more and more of us ready to run the money changers out of the temples of government?

Only the people can raise the demands that will restore monetary discipline to the system and rebuild the value of the dollar and return integrity to our private and public contracts.

Only the people can make it clear that this nation is willing to sacrifice to halt the purveyors of inflation and economic immorality.

"The nation which permits monetary inflation to persist, as if it were not a terrible moral evil, will suffer the consequences described by Isaiah and Ezekiel."[25]

If the people do not set things straight, God will.

"I will turn My hand upon you, And purely purge away your dross, And take away all your tin" (Isa. 1:25).

"Yea, I will gather you and blow upon you in the fire of My wrath, and you shall be melted in the midst thereof. As silver is melted in the midst of the furnace, and you shall know that I, The Lord, have poured out My fury on you" (Ezek. 22:21-22).

We must put a lock on inflation — control it and bring it to a halt. If we don't we will continue down the slide to economic chaos and the social, political, and moral bankruptcy it always brings.

We cannot depend upon the politicians, the bureaucrats, or the other vested interests — the manipulators and the hangers-on to do it for us. They may toy with gimmicks, they may produce Band-Aids, but few will really dig down to the roots of the cancer.

If this Republic is to be saved, the people must do it. To be blunt, if the republic is to be saved, saved Americans must take the lead. Based on Biblical principles. Real reform, true reformation, will be achieved only through a complete and honest overhaul of the way things are being done or undone.

It will take courage, persistence, prayer, obedience to God's Word (His laws as well as His gospel), and a willingness to make some short-run sacrifices.

The Pain Without the Cure

How do we stop inflation?

Many experts are quick with advice on that. Some good. some bad.

One thing is sure: We will not cure inflation with more inflation. If that were the cure — if simply printing more money, lowering the fractional reserve requirements, and increasing government spending were the answer — we would have been whole long ago. The fact is the more government takes from the people, the deeper go the roots and the more deadly is the cancer.

There is only one way to stop inflation and that is to stop it. To chop out its roots, to lay them bare and dig them out. Lowering the rate of inflation to three or four percent is a start, but it is not the cure. As long as the germ exists, the disease spreads.

Among those who resist putting an end to inflation are those who argue, "If we take that cure, we will have serious economic dislocations! We will have recession. We will have unemployment. We will have suffering!"

Are they blind? Deaf? Dumb? Do they not see the pain that already exists without the cure? We have had inflation and recessions. We have had inflation and stagflation. The economic dislocation is already there. In the steel mills. It was brought about in large measure by inflation. By the destruction of the investment capital to modernize factories and hold down costs and increase productivity so that we could better compete with other nations.

The cure does not cause the illness. It eliminates the disease before the disease eliminates the patient.

First Things first

Advocate the end of inflation and some will respond, "Yes! Let's return to the gold standard!"

Is it necessary to restore gold as the measure of our currency if we are to halt inflation and prevent it in the future?

The answer is, "Yes, it is."

Not as a graven image or an object of worship. No. As a means of monetary discipline. To keep the manipulators and the money changers out of the temples of government.

But there are other things that should be tackled first.

"The gold standard is not important as an isolated gadget but as an integral part of an economic system."[26]

The first step we must take is to demand economy in government. Not jut demand it but enforce the steps necessary to see that it is done.

How can we do that?

Cutting the cost of government will not be accomplished by messing around with bits and pieces of the government apparatus. Trying to reduce the cost of government by tackling one department or one area of the governmental budget is like wrestling with a rubber life raft: the more you squeeze on one end, the more the other end swells up. There is only one way to really cut the cost of government: cut its "take" - reduce its revenues.

Therefore, this must be the first step: Put a limit on government spending. Slap a lid on the amount of our money the government may have in any one year.

Down to Twenty Percent?

The federal government now spends about 30 percent of the nation's total personal income. State and local governments spend another 20 percent. that brings the total of all government spending to about 50 percent of the total personal income in the nation.

Since 1940, government spending has increased almost twice as fast as the rate of growth in total personal income. The per capita cost of the federal government has increased from $77 to more than $6,000 in 1992.

"Government, as a percentage of the nation's total economic output, has increased nearly one-third since 1960, from 26% to 37%," according to a report by the Institute for Policy Innovation. Government spending per household (in constant 1990 dollars) grew from $12,790 in 1960 to more than $23,000 in 1992.

Continued the report: "For the first time, there are more civilian government employees (18.2 million) than manufacturing employees (18.1 million)."

Where do we draw the line?

What is a reasonable percentage of total national economic output to pay for the operation of the federal plantation? 15 percent? 20 percent? 25 percent? 30 percent?

The answer should be decided by the people. In a society of free men and women it would be. Those who pay the piper should call the tune. Yet seldom do the people have an opportunity to vote directly on what they want the cost of government to be.

But for the sake of illustration, let's say that the cost of the federal government should be no more than 20 percent of the nation's total economic output. That would mean that Washington is now taking about 15 percent more than it should; that Caesar's grab exceeds that hypothetical ceiling by one-third.

Those who advocate continued and increased spending go through the roof at the very thought of returning money to the people from whom it came. They insist that such a reduction in Uncle Seizure's funds is impossible. What they really mean is that such a cutback in the federal grab would make it impossible for the leviathan federal government to continue to live in the style and on the scale to which it and its sycophants have become accustomed. It would force the elimination or reduction of some of their pet projects; it would mean fewer bureaucrats and fewer extras in Babble-on-the-Potomac. Exactly! And that is part of the task that must be tackled.

One liberal Republican senator chastised conservatives for trying to force "quart-sized" problems into "pint-sized jars." That might have been a neat turn of a phrase but it was off the mark. What conservatives really object to is the propensity of the liberal to turn pint-sized problems into gallon-sized spending programs.

Over a Ten-Year Period

Why not put a lid on the cost of government and make it a chief aim to cut spending and taxes to or below that level within a period of, say, ten years?

We have to start somewhere.

If that lid on federal spending were, for example, set at a maximum of 20 percent of the nation's total exconomic output in any one year, why not require the federal government to reduce its present 37 percent by two percent a year, for eight years, and then hold it at the 20 percent ceiling?

Actually, under such a planned reduction each year during that period. How? Because even though the federal government would be taking a smaller percentage of the total national output each year, the total income would be increasing! Especially if the citizens were able to enjoy more of the fruits of their labor through a reduction in federal taxes. Part of those savings would go into investments. That would mean more capital for commercial and industrial expansion and that would build a greater total gross national product and a larger total national economic outout. Thus, the federal government would be taking a smaller piece of a growing pie.

The important point is this: The taxpayers would have realized savings that otherwise would have been confiscated, masticated, and swallowed by the federal government.

There is little chance that such root reform tax legislation would ever come out of the present Congress. It is not the nature of spend-easy politicians to cut themselves loose from the taxpayers' pockets. Thus, any such ceiling, or any real restriction on government spending and taxation, can come only through the election of congressmen truly committed to such fiscal responsibility.

That would take lots of work, sweat, and volunteers. And, it would mean holding the Congressmen's feet to the fiscal fires until the job was done. But surely it would be worth it to gain control over the expenditures and the taxing policies of taxation!

Outlaw Deficits

It is also essential to outlaw deficit spending.

Government must begin to live within a balanced budget. We can no longer abide these annual, ever greater, federal deficits.

As long as irresponsible politicians can take the easy way out by indulging in deficit spending, we shall not regain a real measure of control over our personal earnings, our take-home pay, or the value of our money.

The Gramm-Rudman-Hollings deficit reduction act was one small step in the right direction. But it was not enough. And, power blocs in both houses of Congress found ways to circumvent and then alter the provisions of that law. So much for depending on Congress.

If the people truly want to gain control of the monster that is government, and if they really want to curb its taxing and spending appetite, they must gain control of the Congress. The route to fiscal sanity, the way to restore the value of the dollar, starts in the precincts and aims toward election day, year after year. What is that saying, "Eternal vigilance is the price of freedom"? It is also the price of fiscal sanity on the part of government.

One of the commitments that should be exacted from any candidate seeking congressional office is that he or she promise to support a constitutional amendment mandating an annual balanced federal budget. No more deficits; they fan the flames of inflation and mortgage our children's future.

There will be those, there are those, who rise to say, "Yes, but..."

They will argue, "What if an emergency arises and a deficit is necessary?" "What if government needs more money in a hurry and cannot obtain it quickly enough through a tax increase?" Such an occurrence would not be likely in a well-run House or Senate. Funds can always be obtained through transfers, through reducing expenditures or appropriations for one program and increasing them for another. Then, too, through the sinful device of withholding, which has been foisted upon the people all these years, Congress could enact a tax increase and have additional tax revenues flowing into the treasury in short order if such a situation were urgent. We should not make it easy for the politician to circumvent a law prohibiting a deficit budget. It is always the better part of wisdom and best for the citizen to restrict the ease with which government can increase spending, taxes or deficits.

Monetary Discipline

Suppose, for a moment, that the people have been successful: we have put a limit on the amount of money the federal government can take from the total personal income (or gross national product) in any given year; and we have outlawed deficit spending, and forced government to live within a balanced budget.

Now comes the third step in achieving monetary discipline.

We must return to the gold standard.

Why? Because as long as the government can print funny money and rig credit, we are still short of the goal of preventing inflation.

The gold standard is "the capstone of the arch of building sound money."

Former Congressional Representative Jack Kemp of New York made no bones about the necessity of returning to the gold standard: "The choice between two systems [gold vs. fiat money] is the most crucial of our generation."[27]

The money changers and the political exploiters do not like the idea of returning to the discipline of gold. It would clip their wings and their coupons. It would tie their hands and take away the tools they have used to whipsaw the working men and women of America.

"The gold standard functions with the force and inevitability of natural law, for it is the money of freedom and honesty."[28]

Were not freedom and honesty — certainly honesty on the part of government as well as individuals — to be a part of the bedrock of the American Republic?

Should it not be so again?

The Gold Standard

The rejection of gold as the basis for freedom and honesty in our monetary system and affairs is a relatively new advent. Except for a few quirks and periods of impropriety, the American dollar was always as good as gold or silver. That came to a crashing end about fifty-three years ago. The rejection came as an illegitimate offshoot of the new economics and the new politics, those twin plagues which have torn this nation loose from its moorings and pushed it to the brink of fiscal and moral insolvency. Those unholy programs were designed to prepare for the quiet revolution. The new order.

Why do the advocates of the new in economics and politics reject gold? Because it is impossible to debauch a nation's economy as long as it is on the gold standard. And the debauching of money opens the door to inflation, which opens the door to the silent revolution, which opens the door to a one-world government with a one-world economic and fiscal system.

The new economic and political messiahs reject gold because it restricts their movements and impairs their license. It deprives them of their major weapon in the war against the middle class. They argue that the gold standard won't work in this day and age. That's a smokescreen. Vermont Royster, former editor and columnist for *The Wall Street Journal* called their bluff.

"The problem with the gold standard is not what so many allege, that is, that it won't work. Quite the opposite. It works very well indeed, forcing monetary discipline upon kings, dictators, parliaments and people."[29]

Dr. Charles E. Weber, an authority on history and monetary matters, wrote it this way:

Gold strongly restricts governmental intervention in the economy and the redistribution of wealth from the productive to the non-productive components of the population. We appreciate the role of gold as an honest, constructive monetary medium when we consider the nature of its enemies. Keynes, whom Lenin lauded before the Second Congress of the Communist International, considered gold a barbaric relic. Typically, the people who are shouting most loudly that gold is a barbarous relic are the very ones who are most adamant in their demands to suppress the monetary use of gold by force. These "experts" must know full well just how powerful gold is in spite of their public denials that it should play a role in the monetary system and in spite of their claims that it is worthless except for filling teeth and the like [emphasis added].[30]

History makes this much crystal clear: unless we resume gold backing of our currency, inflation will go on and on, and this nation will go down and down.

As Dr. Howard E. Kershner of the old Christian Freedom Foundation warned years ago, "No civilization has long survived the disappearance of trusted money."

Let a nation leave the gold standard, he admonished, and it will soon relegate God to second place.[31] The First Commandment will surely then be revised to read, "Thou shalt have no other gods before the State."

The worship of fiat money is the root of many evils.

Not "If" but "How"

The purpose here is not to attempt to detail any step-by-step or certain time plan for returning to the gold standard. Many outstanding free market economists and freedom-oriented philosophers have written on that and those works are available. For the layman, the best explanation and proposal is to be found in chapters fifteen through nineteen of Henry Hazlitt's "What You Should Know About Inflation".

However, it is important to emphasize that any overnight return to the gold standard could be counterproductive and injurious to the overall effort to restore monetary discipline to the nation.

To return to the gold standard without reflecting on the tremendous changes in our economic picture — our monetary situation and the real growth in our national product in the past fifty years — could create havoc.

What should be the price of gold if this nation were to return to the gold standard? Who should set that price? How?

It would seem obvious that the best way to determine the price of gold is to let the free market speak. As Hazlitt proposed, announce (well in advance) that on a certain date the United States will return to the gold standard. The value of gold will be at that time whatever the free market has determined it to be, and that price will be the official price of gold for conversion of dollars. After all, money is simply a commodity.

When France revalued its gold in 1975, it pegged it at $170.40 per ounce. When the right of ownership of gold was restored in the U. S. in 1975, bankers paid an average of $165.50 an ounce. (The U.S. Treasury, which set the official price of gold at $42.50, laid bare its duplicity when it refused to accept bids on gold for less than $153 an ounce!)

To repeat: the purpose here is not in any way to suggest the manner or method by which we return to the gold standard. That is left to those who have studied the problem and formulated the various plans. The point being clearly and purposefully made is this: if we are to conquer inflation, we must return to the monetary discipline of the gold standard. Lewis Lehrman, one of the few pro-gold members of the U.S. Gold Commission appointed in the 1980s by President Reagan, emphasized that history shows irredeemable currency is always accompanied by deficits, inflation, and high interest rates. Said Lehrman, "Unbacked money is the handmaiden of war, protectionism and big government."[32]

End Fiat Money!

The fact that the right to own gold (which should never have been revoked) was restored in January 1975, is good. However, it does not really restore those rights which were stolen on April 5, 1933, at the outset of the New Deal. On that day this nation went off the gold standard. On that day gold (and the gold-backed dollar) was no longer legal tender; paper was. Whatever the U.S. Treasury decided, that became legal tender.

Since then, the American dollar has not been convertible into gold. The use of gold money is a no-no. The absolute and monopolistic power of the federal government to enforce fiat money remains a darkening cloud over our heads, our homes, our economy, and our future as a nation.

That hoax should be ended.

The Federal Reserve

There are those who continue to insist that there is no need to return to gold. They will assure you that the Federal Reserve System can keep our economy stabilized through management of our money and our credit. Such reasoning is itself reason enough to return to gold! Dr Hans Sennholz, president of the Foundation for Economic Education, sets straight those "money managers":

> Experience alone would dictate an immediate inactivization of this central command post over the economic lives of the American people. In the sixty [now seventy-three] years of its existence the Federal Reserve System has presided over unprecedented economic instability — over two depressions of which one was the longest and most severe in American history, over seven booms and recessions, and an inflation that reduced the American dollar to less than one-fifth of its present Federal Reserve value. This is indeed a long record of money mismanagement [emphasis added].[33]

What America needs is not a managed currency but an honest dollar. What America needs is a vital, strong economy based on the energies and efforts of the free men and women engaged in free enterprise, employing the free choices of the free market.

Dr. Sennholz offered this truism: "Its [the Federal Reserve System's very premise of central management of money and credit is alien to economic freedom and contrary to economic stability."

Of all the major political parties, only the U.S. Taxpayer's Party takes a direct and firm position in this area. The plank on Money and Banking of its 1992 platform reads, in part:

"... we believe that, to restore integrity, credibility and stability to the nation's money and banking system we must:

1. Declare unconstitutional the Federal Reserve Act of 1913, the seizure of gold coins in 1933, and the outlawing in 1934 of private contracts that called for payment in silver and gold.

2. Disestablish the Federal Reserve System

3. Terminate the status of the Federal Reserve Notes as obligations of the United States and as legal tender for all debt.

4. Restore to the Constitutional monetary system that gold which was unconstitutionally seized from the American people and which is now held by the U.S. Treasury.

5. Revalue in Constitutional (silver) dollars all outstanding contracts now payable in Federal Reserve Notes.

6. Resume the "free coinage" of Constitutional (silver) dollars and appropriate gold coins.

7. Adopt all monetarily viable foreign silver and gold coins as money in the United States.

8. Prohibit all fraudulent "fractional reserve" banking schemes and related commercial practices.

Five-Part Program

What has been briefly outlined here is a five-step program to

- put a lid on the cost of government
- prohibit deficit spending
- restrict the printing of fiat money
- repeal the Federal Reserve Act
- return to the gold standard.

A path such as that must be followed, a course which must be taken, if we are to halt inflation, restore value to our money, and regain economic freedom for Americans.

Can it be done?

That answer rests mostly with the people.

Politicians will not embrace it until they see the people taking the lead.

The money exploiters will fight it every inch, every foot, and with every dollar at their command.

Speculators will lambast it. Easy spenders and special interest groups will blast it.

Only the "forgotten Americans" who will benefit from such a reformation will endorse it and work for it.

The working men and women, the retired who exist on fixed incomes, the young who desire a measure of security without becoming wards of the state, the emerging minorities who want to believe there is still a ladder to climb...

... for them, the restoration of the Constitutional money and banking system, the end of inflation and the return to the gold standard is the way to a future in which their earnings will have value and their holdings, no matter how small, will be secure.

The decision rests with those forgotten Americans. Those who work and pray and pay and who seldom have a spokesman at the great divide and the easy take.

It's in their hands.

CHAPTER TWELVE

These Are The Peacemakers

And it came to pass from that time forth,
that the half of my servants wrought in the work,
and the other half of them held both the spears,
the shields, and the bows ...
They which builded the wall,
and they that bare burdens,
every one with one of his hands
wrought in the work,
and with the other hand held a weapon
(Neh. 4:16,17).

As children of God, as Christians, as followers of Christ, we are instructed to be at peace.

We are instructed to seek to have within us the peace of God. Which, of course, is the only true and lasting peace.

To be, insofar as possible, at peace with our fellow man.

To love one another; to be of good will and good works.

To establish and support civil government, and to enact and support laws that foster peace among men of good will.

The apostle Paul, in Romans 13:3, assures us that *"rulers are not a terror to* [people of] *good works but to evil."* Magistrates (public officials) are to be ministers of God to the people for good.

Citizens coming together in Bible-based civil government to protect the individual and to punish those who would violate his person or his rights: that was what it was all about when our Founding Fathers formed this "more perfect union," this one nation under God.

The defense of the individual, whether it be from the front-office thief or the back-alley hood or a foreign power; that is the first and foremost function of government in a society of free men.

For that reason we willingly render unto Caesar what is rightfully his due.

287

First Things First

In recent years, things have been getting out of whack. In many of the affairs and functions of government, first things are no longer first.

For decades, government has been so involved and so embroiled in secondary, often improper, activities that it has neglected its most important function, its reason for existence: keeping the peace, maintaining law and order, upholding justice.

When government meddles in men's affairs that are not its legitimate concern, when it forcibly intrudes upon areas of private domain and personal responsibility, it tends to neglect those primary duties to which it was assigned. It spends its time and attention and the people's resources on matters of lesser importance; it gives short shrift to issues of first priority.

Such disarray in Caesar's palace tends to condone —in fact breed — disorder throughout society. More and more legislators feel free to coddle the criminal and to seek detente with the enemy abroad, all under the guise of "peace".

To paraphrase Edmund Burke: Their passions forge our fetters.

Farewell, Young Man

Consider, for example, the tragedy of young Jeff Adams.

Jeff was sixteen and full of life and laughter and all the things of a young man at the magical age of sixteen. But, there is no more laughter in Jeff Adams and no more life.

He was shot down by a felon's bullet. Struck during a gun battle between a cheap hood and police officers who were trying to apprehend him.

Jeff and his dad were driving along when a slug slammed through the door of their car and, for Jeff, life on earth was over.

He was killed as much by government as he was by the bullet.

The hood who shot it out with the police should not have been at large. At the very least, he should have been in San Quentin prison.

Charles Hein had already been convicted and sentenced for first degree murder. But no capital punishment for him. A majority of the state supreme court had hung an "Out of Order" sign on the death penalty. Life imprisonment, the court decreed, was sufficient to serve the people's purpose.

Life imprisonment? Parole authorities interpreted that to mean a few years in the pen. Hein was due for release. As a part of life adjustment prior to parole, Hein was given a twenty-four-hour pass so that he could look for a job.

Charles Hein never went job hunting. He fled to Oregon, where the police of Springfield caught up with him. That is when and where Jeff Adams paid the price:

> Here lies Jeff Adams, aged 16
> Shot down by a felon's bullet;
> But killed in part by soft-headed judges
> And a parole board's game of roulette.

Jeff Adams was made a sacrifice — one of many made — on the altar of the new morality which has a strange sense of values. It slaps the slayer on the wrist and sends him job hunting while it thrusts the innocent into harm's way.

No Law, No Peace

In this "enlightened" age — this age of humanism, in which old values are discarded and young victims die — "law and order" seems to be an antiquated term, words to be avoided lest they conflict with (or raise questions about) the semantics of some new morality.

Even a President of these United States was once prompted to skirt the issue. In a "tough" speech on violent crime, he observed: "In thinking about this problem [of violent crime] I do not seek vindictive punishment of the criminal but rather protection of the innocent victim ... [That is] why I do not talk about law and order and I return to the constitutional phrase insuring 'domestic tranquility'."[3]

Did that President really equate law and order with "vindictive punishment"? Vindictive punishment is not the pursuit of law and order; it is vengeance.

Vengeance belongs to the Lord. What the people seek is law and order, safety and justice.

How does a society preserve domestic tranquility without a foundation of law and order? How do we measure the crime and mete out the punishment without law?

If there were more attention paid to the punishment of the convicted criminal, there would be fewer innocent victims.

Sleep well, Jeff Adams.

The Plastic Jungle

The thin blue line which holds back the jungle of barbarism grows proportionately thinner as crimes increase.

These officers of the peace are not any less dedicated to their awesome task; if anything they are even more committed and better trained. However, the tide of unrestrained appetite and violence is rising, fueled by increasing narcotics traffic and growing drug abuse. Sodom and Gomorrah in quadrophonic sound and hallucinogenic color — rocked and rolled. Full blast, no holds barred. Whatever turns you on.

Hear the acrid, acid music. The blatant, blaring, bleating beat of sex and drugs and violence. Pornographic, incestuous, pervasive. Televised, romanticized, and headlined by the media which so often seems devoid of values or conscience. And, which so often puts sensationalism before civility and profits above propriety. But then, what is the standard of propriety when we are assured there are no absolutes; no rights, no wrongs?

The situational ethics and values manipulation of the public classroom, the State's owned and operated establishment, slop over into society; they permeate society. The permissiveness of a thousand homes becomes the promiscuity of a hundred streets and alleys. Narcotics flood the grammar schools and more than one-half of the nation's high school students boast they have been drunk on alcohol.

Thus does the whirlwind grow. As it is sown so does it reap. Authority is flaunted. The police are vilified. Morality goes out the window and down the drain. Justice is a sick joke; peace is a drop out. The miscreants are excused; the malcontents are pampered. And society is faulted because life does not come on a silver platter and the world is not a bed of roses.

It's society that is sick. We are all to blame. That's what the new moralists insist. The environment is behind it all!

Perhaps, in part, they are correct but for a different reason than they posit.

We have let things go too far. We should have yanked things straight long ago.

Individuals commit crimes; not societies.

Societies do not molest children. Individuals do.

Societies do not rape elderly women and infant children. Individuals do.

Societies do not murder shopkeepers for a few dollars or a quick fix. Individuals do. Society is at fault certainly in this way: it has excused and coddled too many of the individuals who commit the crimes. That is our crime. The silent majority has been voiceless, inactive, while soft-heads and bleeding hearts have cried "peace" to wage crime.

The gods of humanism measure with a rubber yardstick and the State too often governs with a double standard. Social adjustment becomes a synonym for justice.

Accountability becomes a dirty word.

Where are those who will stand and insist that every individual is indeed equal before the law and that equality includes accountability? When will we shout out that he who is not held accountable does not count — that he is thus demeaned, belittled, and considered unimportant?

And what of the so-called victimless crimes being pawned off on us these days? That term itself is contradictory. If there is no victim, there is no crime. But there are victims: the children who go hungry when the money goes for a bottle or a fix; the abandoned wife, the abandoned husband, the abandoned child; the murder victim of the drug addict. (Is the murder criminal but the cause not? What specious reasoning!) And what of those who are led astray, those who imitate, those who get hooked on drugs or are pushed into prostitution? Are they not victims?

Does no one care for them? What has happened to the soul of America?

The Righteous Mourn

The righteous mourn. But let them voice their concern, let them challenge the laxness of the law and the abdication of the courts in meting out justice, let them call for a restoration of solid values and moral judgements, and hear the retorts: "Hey, man. Who are you to force your values on us?"

"You can't legislate morality!"

All law is based on morality or the lack of it. And that's a fact they will not or cannot understand. But, at the very least, we can work to stop the legislating of immorality. The record is clear: when *Thou shalt not* is revised to read *Do your thing* the social order is on its way down and out.

Coddling the criminal, excusing the crime, making an act uncriminal, legalizing it in the eyes of the law does not beget law and order. It does not lead to domestic tranquility. It leads to crime and violence.

In that there is no justice and no peace. No peace with God. No peace among men.

Get to Work!

The immoral minority is both. We'd find that out if we had the courage to take a stand and fight.

The issue of crime and violence deserves, demands, the citizens' attention.

Law enforcement agencies at all levels, from the local police department to the FBI, have public information programs on both the causes and the cures for lawlessness. God's Word is replete with the basic truth and bedrock principles concerning such matters.

Concerned Christians should get these facts, and get to work on constructive efforts to see that the necessary laws are enacted or revised and enforced to keep the peace and protect the law-abiding. Concerned Christians should get involved in those campaigns to elect to the legislatures and the courts men and women who will not only stand for — but do battle for — law and order.

In the final analysis, the call for law and order must come from each citizen at every level and on every occasion. Only in that way can our people be free and safe and tranquil.

The problems dealing with crime and violence are sometimes complex and multifaceted. The solutions will be found on many fronts and at many levels: they start with the inner self, the inner man, reaching up to Christ Jesus! Through Him man is regenerated, transformed, made new. And the new man and woman in Christ, the person who has true faith, will go forth to do good works, to obey God's immutable laws and to promote law and order. Law and order are very much a part of the Christian world and life view.

Not all crimes are committed on the streets or in the back alleys. Refusal to enact laws that protect the law-abiding, refusal to enforce laws that give the peace officer a fighting chance; refusal to mandate appropriate penalties against those who prey upon the innocent, their lives and property; refusal of the court to enforce such laws and hand down such sentences: these, too, are crimes against society. They are crimes committed by legislators and jurists who refuse to protect the citizens; crimes by those elected to protect the citizen but who insist on coddling the criminal.

In a society of free men and women, in a republic, we insist that each individual be held accountable for his deeds and misdeeds. Should not legislators and jurists also be held accountable? Is that not a vital and proper use of the ballot box?

Capital Punishment

For those who would obey God, capital punishment is not a matter of choice or opinion, or even court decree: it is a Biblical mandate.

God's written Word, the Holy Bible, makes it clear: The death penalty is both proper and necessary.

> *"Whoso sheds man's blood*
> *By man shall his blood be shed;*
> *For in the image of God*
> *Made He man"* (Gen. 9:6).

Not just for Noah's day; but for perpetual generations (Gen. 9:12).

Further, the Scriptures distinguish between accidental killing (manslaughter) and premeditated (purposeful) murder. Capital punishment is not required for manslaughter:

> *"And this is the case of the slayer which shall flee thither,* (city of refuge) *that he may live: Whoso kills his neighbor ignorantly* (unintentionally), *whom he hated not in time past — as when a man goeth to the woods with his neighbor to hew wood, and his hand fetcheth* (swings) *a stroke with the axe to cut down the tree, and the head slippeth from the helve* (handle) *and strikes his neighbor so that he dies - he shall flee to one of those cities and live ... he was not worthy of death, inasmuch as he hated him* (the victim) *not in time past"*(Deut. 19:4-6).

But murder? That is a different matter. It requires the death penalty:

> *But if man hate his neighbor, and lie in wait for him, and rises up against him and smite him mortally, that he dies, and flees into one of these cities, then the elders of his city shall send and fetch him thence* (from there), *and deliver him into to the hand of the avenger of blood, that he may die"* (Deut. 19:11-13).

Moses also set forth the reasons for the death penalty. It was a punishment, but it was more; it was a protection to the innocent and a deterrent to those who might feel impelled to murder their fellow man. *"Then shall you do unto him as he had thought to do unto his brother; so shall put the evil away from among you. And those who remain shall hear and fear, and shall henceforth commit no more such evil among you."* (Deut. 19:19-20).

That is the law. God's law.

Ah! Some will protest. That is the law that was. That is the Old Testament. Christ, they insist, repealed the law.

Not so! Where in God's Word does it say that Christ revoked God's law? Christ did not die to save us from the necessity of obeying God's law. Christ died and rose again to save us from the curse, the penalty, of disobeying God's law. And as Paul wrote, *"What then? Shall we sin because we are not under law but under grace? God forbid!"* (Rom. 6:15).

Christ came to fulfill the law as well as the prophecies. He did not come to destroy the law, or set it aside. God's law is not null or void. His Word is eternal; it changes not.

"Do not think that I am come to destroy the Law or the Prophets. I am not come to destroy but to fulfill. For verily, I say unto you, Till heaven and earth pass, one jot or one tittle shall in no wise pass from the law till all be fulfilled. Whoever therefore shall break one of the least of these commandments, and shall teach men so, he shall be called least in the kingdom of heaven" (Matt. 5:17-19).

Remember how Paul recognized the validity of capital punishment for specific crimes. *"For if I am an offender, or have committed anything worthy of death, I do not object to dying"* (Acts 25:11).

The opposite of law is not grace; it is lawlessness.

Many who oppose the death penalty may be well-intentioned but they are also misguided. They are guilty of putting what may seem right to them above the will and law of God. Repealing the death penalty may prevent death for the murderer but not for victim. The victim still dies. Those, who argue that capital punishment is not a deterrent to murder, take a gamble. They gamble with the lives of future victims. They have no right to take such a gamble.

Professor Isaac Ehrlich of the University of Chicago was an opponent of the death penalty. After studying the records, Dr. Ehrlich wrote his studies indicated that if the death penalty were really enforced eight murders would be prevented for every murderer who was executed. Other criminologists say Dr. Ehrlich's data is low — that is, for each execution at least fifty murders would be deterred.[4]

During the ten years that capital punishment was outlawed, the number of murders in the United States almost doubled from 10,000 in 1967 to more than 19,000 in 1977. As executions ceased murders increased. Since 1976, when the ban on capital punishment, was lifted, the ratio of murders to population declined.[5]

After a prolonged study of crime and punishment, Gordon Tullock, Virginia Polytechnic Institute, came to this conclusion: "Eighty percent of the people who seriously think about crime think of punishment as a deterrent — except for the sociologists and they wrote all the books."[6]

Dr. Charles Rice, of the Notre Dame School of Law, comments

"Statistics show the number of murders that were committed in spite of capital punishment, but they cannot show the number of murders that were deterred and therefore never committed. The best evidence that the death penalty has a uniquely deterrent impact with respect to such crimes (as premeditated and deliberate homicide) is not based on statistics but is rather based on common sense and experience."

Dr. Rice concluded: "A more basic justification for the death penalty is retribution, which is often wrongly equated with vengeance. To exact retribution is to fit the punishment to the crime in accord with the requirements of justice."

And, one might add, in accord with God's law.

Clean up the Prisons

Prison reform is a pressing need.

Many of the nation's jails and prisons are overcrowded hellholes. They are breeding grounds for crime. More and more judges are refusing to sentence felons convicted of nonviolent crimes to prison because of such conditions.

Prison reform does not mean turning the correctional institutions into country clubs with tennis courts and swimming pools; it does not mean "let-the-inmates-run-the-institution" reform that so many liberals push or some experiment-minded penologists advocate. We have been that route and it doesn't work. In too many instances, those experimental mistakes were paid for in blood: the blood of prison guards, the blood of peaceful inmates, and the blood of unsuspecting citizens.

The reform needed in our prisons is the creation of decent, habitable places to house those convicted of violent crimes. An individual does not lose his basic human rights when he is imprisoned. Prisons should have adequate facilities for sanitation, medical care, wholesome meals, some measure of privacy, and personal safety.

Prisons should not be hell-holes. Too many of them are.

Consider, for example, the sixteen-year-old boy who was jailed for a minor, first-time offense. He was thrown in with vicious, depraved criminals. By the time his father learned of the boy's incarceration and retained an attorney to get his son's release, the boy had been repeatedly sodomized and beaten by drug addicts and hardened criminals.

Or, consider the thirty-eight-year-old mother who has been charged with obstruction of justice. Because she could not make bail, she was placed overnight in the Washington, D.C., women's detention center. During that one-night stay, she was sexually assaulted "innumerable times" by other inmates. Such cases are not justice; they are the savagery of the jungle for which the State or its agent is responsible and should be held accountable.

Those are not isolated instances. They occur frequently in prisons across this nation.

The vicious, the unrepentant, and the radical, must be separated. They should be kept apart from the repentant, peaceful, and defenseless inmates. If they must prey upon others, let them prey upon each other.

The Biblical Approach to Prison Reform

Increasing numbers of prisons and jails are becoming centers of violence. They are filled with racial tensions, homosexual and ethnic gangs, assaults (including murder), drug trafficking. Few prisons are really correctional institutions. More often they are schools for crime. Many repeat offenders learn to sharpen their skills from older inmates. Many first-time offenders, most of them are young (25 percent of prisoners are between the ages of eighteen and twenty-four), are thrown in with hardened criminals and emerge hardened themselves.

When you get right down to it, prisons are anti-Biblical except as they apply to Satan and his cohorts. (1 Pet. 3:19; Rev. 10:2,3.)

God's civil code does not provide for prisons. The closest thing to a prison in the Bible is a temporary holding place where bona fide suspects of a violent crime (the indicted) are held pending speedy trial and swift justice (Lev. 24:12; Num. 15:34).

Restitution, Not Retribution

Some 90 percent of those in jail and prison were found guilty of crimes against property (robbery, larceny, grand theft) rather than crimes of violence against persons. The Biblical penalty for such crimes against property is clear: restitution. Making good to the victim what was stolen. The more serious the crime, the more severe the punishment, the greater the requirement for restitution.

Under God's law the guilty person is to make restitution to the victim, not society.

Thus, God's perfect justice is employed: the guilty person is held accountable and must pay for his crime (Exod. 22:3). Instead of languishing in prison where he may learn new tricks of the trade, he is required to work and earn the money to make reparation for that which he stole. The victim has the property or its value replaced. The taxpayer does not subsidize the crime or support the criminal.

In the case of assault (committing a crime against one's person, his most precious property), the criminal is required to make restitution for the victim's loss of time, loss of income, and mental anguish.

Under the prevailing humanistic criminal code, restitution is largely ignored, and retribution (which belongs to the Lord) is preempted by the State.

Is God's law relevant to today and the problems thereof? It is, indeed! If, as God's Word requires, the men and women who have been found guilty of crimes against property were required to get a job and repay the victim, there would then be enough space and personnel in the prisons to incarcerate the perpetrators of violent crime and a true system of justice would be employed.

Our Brother's Keeper

Although circumstances are forcing jurists and some police agencies to put God's law into practice to alleviate overcrowding and rebellion in the prisons, true Bible-based prison reform will not be accomplished until God-fearing citizens work to bring it to pass. In the meantime, we have a responsibility to minister to those who are in prison.

Our Savior set the example and we have a duty to follow suit (Matt 25:36). There is comfort to be given, hope to be shared, skills to be taught, and most of all, souls to be saved. We should be about our Father's business in that regard. If we are not able to do so ourselves, surely we should support those who can and will.

The Real Peacemakers

It had been a long and acrimonious legislative hearing. The lights in the stately old capitol had burned far into the night. An endless stream of well rehearsed witnesses, including several men of the cloth (if not the Cross), argued militantly against the proposed stiffer penalties for violent crime.

As the session moved toward a close, State Senator Clark Bradley removed his spectacles and aimed his remark toward the soft-on-crime group. He knew its members well; they were always on hand to oppose any tough-on-crime bills.

"You have spoken for the criminal," he sighed. "Is there not one among you who has a word to say on behalf of the victims?"

Those who are not willing to provide protection for the innocent the defenseless and the law-abiding; those who are eager to excuse the criminal and the crime; those who work to weaken our system of law and order and justice; they are not peacemakers.

They are in effect if not in fact, party to the crime; they are, in fact, partly responsible for the increasing number of victims.

Who are the peacemakers?

They are those who walk in peace;

• those who will not violate the lives and rights of others;

• those who will stand to protect and defend the helpless, the innocent, and the law-abiding;

• those who insist that civil authorities be given the power to uphold the right of each individual to be secure in his person, his property, and his lawful pursuit of happiness;

• those who help preserve law and order and justice.

They are the builders of domestic tranquility, the providers of the common defense.

They are the peacemakers.

Blessed are they! They shall be called the children of God.

Can a Christian Be a Pacifist?

This world is engaged in a death struggle.
It is. It still is.
The forces of light against darkness.
The forces of good versus evil.
The children of liberty versus the tyrants of slavery.
The forces of peace against those who would cause war.

We, as Christ's disciples, cannot ignore the battle any more than we can ignore the criminal on our streets. To ignore either is not to keep the peace; it is to entertain the enemy, to thrust the world into darkness.

Thus, as we assess the current, unfolding affairs of this world, we must face this burning question: Can a Christian be a pacifist? Or, should a Christian be a pacifist?

If, by that term pacifist, we mean someone who prays for peace, someone who walks in peace and works for peace, someone who is willing to take a stand for a just and lasting peace and pay its price, then a Christian must be a pacifist.

But if by pacifist we mean

• those who would buy peace by enslaving themselves and their fellow man to the tyrant;
• those who are not willing to protect their loved ones;
• those who are not willing to defend the defenseless;
• those who will not keep strong this land which shields their lives and liberty;
• those who are not willing to fight, those who criticize and belittle those who do fight the battle and those who then emerge to enjoy the fruits of victory;
• those who yield, who sell out to the atheistic forces that suppress the freedom to proclaim the gospel of Christ Jesus, who would rather be red than dead ...
... then the godly Christian cannot, must not go along!

Christianity? Or Cop Out?

Are we not to love one another?
Where is such love in one's sitting back while his brothers and sisters are slaughtered by an anti-Christian tyrant just as the millions in the Ukraine were slaughtered by the Soviet regime? Where was love in one's standing by while those barbarians invaded, enslaved, ravaged,

raped, and ruined as the Soviets did in Afghanistan; where they used
chemical warfare against villages and trapped women and children in
tunnels which were flooded with gasoline and then turned into fire
bombs? Where was love in one's being mute and motionless while
others were fed into gas ovens and machine-gunned at the side of some
communal grave? Where is love in one's doing business as usual with
a regime that forced Christ's church underground and sent Christ's
followers to the salt mines and psychiatric wards?

To mutter pious mouthings in the face of such depravities, to
seek to make detente with such butchers is not love but cowardice,
total selfishness. It is not Christian. It is ungodly. It is a cop out.
Intended or not, it serves to serve Satan. And in it there is no love, no
honor, and no true peace. There are those who rationalize that such
indifference, such indolence, such capitulation, is peaceful — that it
promotes peace. Pacifism that stands by, that permits others to be
sacrificed on the altar of despotism, is not a virtue, it is a vice born of
the same stupidity which gave the world the sell-out at Munich. That
turned Poland over to the Communists. That cost 58,000 American
lives in Vietnam. (What must the nations of the free world think of a
country which spends the lives of 58,000 splendid young men and then
gives up? Just quits and walks away and says, "Sorry, fellas, it was all
a mistake." What must our young people of this day think about a
government which sacrifices such fine young men for virtually nothing?
We should never have sent them there in the first place. But, having
gone, should they not have been permitted to gain the victory? Or, is
life held so cheaply in today's Babble-on-the-Potomac?)

It spawns and is spawned the same myopic mentality that
would have us coddle the criminal in our streets and prisons and ignore
the anguish and the pain of the victim or his widow.

It promotes the distorted reasoning that we should be unequally
yoked with the forces of darkness — that we should play footsies with
our enemies and do business with those who wouldbury us.

Nowhere in the Scripture, nowhere, does The Lord God tell us
to love His enemies or to make covenant with them in any way. God
does, in fact, prohibit us from doing so!

"'Should you help the wicked and love them that hate The Lord?
Therefore is the wrath upon you from before The Lord'" (II Chron 19:2).

"Do I not hate them, O Lord, who hate You?
And am I not grieved with those that rise up against You?
I hate them with perfect [total] *hatred;*
I count them mine enemies" (Ps. 139:21-21).

Defensive Force

Let this be clear. Crystal clear. Christians are not and must not be warmongers.

There are basically two types of force: defensive force to protect and to defend, and aggressive force to attack, capture, and enslave.

As followers of Christ, we oppose the use of aggressive force, whether it be against an individual or a nation.

As Christians we have a right, however, to seek, to insist upon, defensive capabilities for our civil authorities. Only in that way can our local police department and our nation's armed services have the means by which to defend us as that need arises.

Thus, our call for military preparedness, for a strong defense, is not for aggression, or economic gain, or increased employment: it is for defense — for survival. .

Pacifism that denies the propriety and availability of such defensive capability is either misguided or subversive. It invites the use of aggressive force by our enemies at home and by evil empires abroad. It excites the barbarian and encourages the bandit. It jeopardizes the lives and liberty of all within our land. It consigns lesser nations, struggling to survive, to surrender, subjugation, and slavery.

There is no love in that.

When Do We Stand?

As long as there are men of evil intent and diabolical design, free men must be willing to take a stand: a stand for freedom under God; a stand for what is right in His sight.

A strong and vigilant defense is one of the essentials of freedom. The greater the threat of evil, the stronger that defense must be. What is right does not survive unattended; it must have its defenders.

Consider Nehemiah, used of God to rebuild the wall (Neh. 1-6).

Jerusalem was desolate. The wall was down. The city was virtually defenseless. It was also surrounded by its enemies.

Did God instruct Nehemiah to go make a treaty, to seek detente with God's enemies, the Hormites, the Ammonites, and the Arabs? No. He used Nehemiah to rebuild the city's defenses; its walls and towers and gates.

Nehemiah did not wait until the enemy was pouring through the gaps in the wall to defend Jerusalem. He moved to rebuild those

defenses before the fact, before an attack. To have waited until the
enemy came through the gap would have resulted in a bloody battle,
with many lost lives and possible defeat.

Nehemiah, used of God, made his stand.

When do we make our stand? When do we erect and maintain
our defenses?

Is it when the enemy launches his rockets? Is it when his troops
are on the way? Is it when his planes are just over the horizon? Or, when
his ships appear off our shores or show up on our sonar?

When? When do we erect our defenses and maintain them to
protect our loved ones and to defend our homeland where God can still
be worshiped in truth and safety?

When there is time to rebuild the wall? Time to refurbish the
towers of defense? Or when it is too late?

What Would You Do?

Suppose, men, that you are nearby when some thug, some
depraved maniac, some barbarian, threatens your wife or your daughter. What would you do? When would you move to protect her? Before
the attacker made his advance? When he held a knife at her throat or
a gun to her ribs? When he began ripping the clothes from her body?

What would you do? Would you yell, "Come! Let us reason
together!" Would you say, "Go so far, but no farther!" Would you shut
your eyes and hope the thug would have a change of heart?

Or would you do everything you could as soon as you realized
the threat? Would you use some half-hearted measure? Or would you
employ everything at your disposal, including your life, if need be, to
protect her?

And if, by the grace of God, she were spared would you not do
everything possible to make sure that such a barbarian were never ever
again be permitted to get into the situation he could prey upon the
helpless or endanger the peace and safety of others?

Suppose you were nearby when someone of criminal intent
threatened a friend, a neighbor, or even a stranger? What would you
do then?

Would you rush to his or her aid, to his defense? Or would you
do as the neighbors did that night when young Kitty Genovese was
brutally attacked on a dark and lonely New York street?

From house to house she ran, screaming through the darkness,
pleading for help, begging for people — someone to protect her, to let

her into their home. The murderer hid in the bushes — ready to run if someone came, ready to attack again if no one responded to her pleas.

Lights went on in the houses along that street, but no one came to Kitty Genovese's rescue. Not one person. Not one. No one even bothered to call the police.

The murderer finished his job.

Kitty Genovese was slain because the good folks on that block did not want to get involved. They would not lend a hand; they would not take a stand. They loved themselves more than they loved a stranger. Blessed are such peacemakers? No way! When the people of Athens sought freedom from responsibility, Athens ceased to be free.

The Battle for the Souls of Men

We may mourn for Kitty Genovese. But did we mourn for the captive nations? Or, for the people of Afghanistan? For the gentle people of Cambodia? For the people of Poland? Hungary? Angola? Tibet? Nicaragua?

This nation faces an enemy far more despicable, more evil, more implacable than the criminal who ended Kitty Genovese's life.

That enemy is atheistic communism.

It poses the severest threat — the most sustained threat — this nation and the free world has ever known. It still does.

In "Creed or Chaos?" Dorothy L. Sayer spelled it out, coldly, clearly:

Christendom and heathendom now stand face to face.
... The people who say that this is a war of economics or of power politics, are only dabbling about at the surface of things ... At bottom is a violent and irreconcilable quarrel about the nature of God and the nature of man and the ultimate nature of the universe; it is a war of dogma.[8]

Dr. James Roy Smith, in "God Still Speaks in the Space Age", emphasized the spiritual and psychological nature of the war that is even now upon us:

The germ of the conflict is anchored in religion, and the battle is an ideological battle between atheism and theism. It is a battle not only for the minds of men, but also for their souls. Communism is atheistic. Communist Russia is the first nation in history which has officially adopted atheism as its national belief. Its motives and its methods are the result of a denial of God. Because there is no God, there is no moral judgement and there is no personal accountability.[9]

Lest you think Dr. Smith exaggerated or that he may be unduly prejudiced, hear the words of the Communists.

If nothing else, listen to them as a Christian and know just where they would have you stand:

Radio Leningrad: The struggle against the gospel and Christian legend must be conducted ruthlessly and with all the means at the disposal of communism.

V.I. Lenin: Atheism is a natural and inseparable part of Marxism, of the theory and practice of socialism.

Josef Stalin: We have disposed of the czars of the earth; we shall now dethrone the Lord of Heaven.

The Soviet Commissioner of Education as quoted in the Congressional Record, Vol 77, pp 1539-1540: We hate Christians and Christianity. Even the best of them must be considered our worst enemies. Christian love is an obstacle to the development of the revolution. Down with love one's neighbor! What we want is hate... Only then can we conquer the universe.

The Communists have given us fair warning: "What we want is hate!" "We will bury you!"

That death sentence has yet to be recanted; the form may be gone or revised, the end goal remains. It has not been rescinded. The enemy is single-pointed. Unremitting. Subtle. And, shrewd.

Yet our leaders made covenant with them; sat down across the table and bargained with them. Because of so-called liberal and mis-guided politicians, virtually no resistance was made to forestall a Soviet beachhead in Central America; businessmen did business with them; the leftwing media was their advance team, and liberation theologians invited them to spew their propaganda from their pulpits.

How soon they forgot. Or, did they ever understand. Or, did they understand and acquiesce? Not too many years ago one of the nation's most prominent newspapers and one of the nation's most visible television commentators were hailing Fidel Castro as "another George Washington."

And in Nicaragua? We know now that the Sandinistas could never succeeded in their drive to power — with all its bloody rape and ravages and murders — if it had not been with the acquiescence, if not the outright approval, of men in the highest offices in our nation.

Those Who Will Not See

There are those in our midst and even within our churches and their national councils who assure us that the Communist drive for world domination is over. That there is a change in the Communist grand design.

There is, indeed, a change: but, it is a change in strategy.

The Soviet is gone, long live Russia and all the mini-Russian spin-offs. Witness, but do not be deceived, by its latest ploy of open society and western-style public relations. The ultimate goal remains. It is unchanged.

If there has been any softening, it has been here in the United States. Not in communism.

"We will bury you!" That threat still stands. We live in its shadow.

The Enemy (Still) Is Atheistic Communism

Take a moment. Review the theater of operation and understand conflict. Listen to the words of General Albion Knight, USA (Ret). It is important that you do. Those who refuse to learn from history will repeat its mistakes, will pay the price, and will endure its carnage.

The United States, and Western Civilization, has faced this enemy in intense materialistic and military forms under the leadership of the Soviet Union ever since the end of Word War II.

Under Stalin, the Soviet Army placed itself behind an Iron Curtain in Eastern Europe. Those formerly free nations slammed behind that Iron Curtain, became satellites of the Soviet Union and wretched under its dictatorial control enforced by occupying Soviet troops. The crushing of the 1956 Hungarian Revolution (in the face of the West's craven inaction) and its 1968 invasion of Czechoslovakia were powerful examples of how Marxist-Leninism dealt with uprisings.

Soviet Plan for Control Over The West

Since the Cuba Missile Crisis in 1962, the Soviet Union has been engaged in a three-pronged approach to gaining control over the West:

1. the build-up of a massive thermonuclear weapons superiority over the United States;

2. a series of disarmament negotiations (called "arms control")

in which the United States could be convinced to "freeze" or even reduce its own strategic nuclear forces, and

3.   the encirclement of the United States with Communist satellite nations and bases by a series of wars-by-proxy, .

One authority on Communism, Dr. Fred Schwartz, of the Christian Anti-Communist Crusade, gave us a prediction — and a description of the Soviet's plan:

> By this process the Soviet leaders plan to complete the encirclement of the USA, deprive this country of the supplies of essential war materials such as strategic minerals and energy, and finally convince an encircled, demoralized giant to make an agreement that will grant permanent Soviet supremacy on the world scene. In this way the Soviet Union will outflank the military might of the USA and all the planes, missiles, ships and soldiers will be as ineffective to preserve the freedom and security of the USA as the military might of Iran proved to be to preserve the rule of the Shah of Iran.

How well did that plan succeed?

On April 2, 1985, President Ronald Reagan stated bluntly that "The Soviet Union virtually outnumbers us in any type weapon you want to name."

David Sullivan, a noted expert on U.S. Disarmament policies, concluded that "President Reagan has publicly conceded that the Soviet Union has achieved overwhelming strategic superiority over the United States at least seven times since 1982."

How did the Soviets do this? With the combination of expensive effort, theft of Western technology, and unwise concessions by the United States in the many disarmament treaties since 1962. Call such concessions stupid. Call them naive. Call them treacherous if not treasonous ... call them what you will, this much is fact: the dagger was aimed and moving straight at the heart of our republic.

In remarks on the Senate floor on August 3, 1990, Senator Jesse Helms summarized the situation:

> It is clear that Soviet military spending has increased at a rate of almost eight percent per year from 1970 through 1988 in real terms. In contrast, US defense spending has declined each year since 1985 in real terms. US defense spending remains less that six percent of US gross national product, as compared with nearly 14 percent in the 1950s and 1960s, while the Soviet military's share of Soviet GNP has soared to about 19 to 25 percent.

As noted, according to the Department of Defense, 19 out of 28 main categories of Soviet defense production either remained constant at a high rate, or increased through 1989. Even after Gorbachev's 1988-1989 defense cut-backs, the Soviets alone were still out-producing all of NATO by about 2 to 1 in tanks, 3 to 1 in armored personnel carriers, and 10 to 1 in artillery.

And again, as President Bush stated in 1989, the Soviets continue to modernize their strategic forces at a "furious pace". For example, this year alone (1990) the Soviets are producing for deployment hundreds of three types of ICBMs, three types of bombers, and two types of SLBMs (Submarine Launched Ballistic Missiles), compared to only a handful of the one U.S. strategic program being produced for deployment, the Trident II SLBM system.

Even now, while virtually begging for loans and other types of aid to keep their economy from collapsing completely, the Soviets under Boris Yeltsin "continue to strengthen Russia's (the Soviet's) military and security forces and advances in the foreign field. The influence of Russia's entrenched and all powerful military-industrial hierarchy continues to influence Russia's military and domestic policies. Recently, the Russian president announced that his military budget for 1993, while unchanged from last year overall, would include a 10% increase for 'arms and equipment.'"

(Robert Morris, a leading geopolitical observer, is quoted in the January 1993 issue of *America's Future*: "Yeltsin's navy is now deployed on active duty with its fearsome Typhoon-class nuclear submarines. According to the chief of the North American Defense Command, Russian planes armed with cruise missiles continue regularly to test our 'Early Warning' defenses.

("Meantime, warns Morris, "there has been a resurgence of Communist influence in many of the former Soviet client states in Africa, the Middle East, and elsewhere in the Third World, as well as in the United Nations.")

The Treaty Trap

The United States government (eight administrations since Eisenhower) succumbed to the deceptions and blandishments of the Soviet Union in engaging with them in negotiations seeking to eliminate nuclear weapons from the face of the Earth. Through these treaties (from Kennedy through Bush) the Soviet Union gained ever greater nuclear superiority over the USA. The Soviet Union blatantly violated each of those eight treaties. Our government knew this. It could not (or would not) do anything about it. And, in spite of these violations, President after President returned to the bargaining table "one more time" to gain a scrap of paper that would bring us "peace in our time." They refused to admit that each treaty placed the American people in greater danger.

Why? The possibilities range from wishful thinking, to stupidity all the way to possible treason. Regardless of why or how, the fact remains:

By 1989 the Soviet Union gained a dominant first strike nuclear capability against the United States.

And that made possible the thermonuclear blackmail that was a prerequisite to the surrender of America.

Encirclement

The third prong of the Soviet Union's materialistic/military offensive was "encirclement" of the United States through wars-by-proxy in the Third World.

Through Soviet instigation, U.S. armed forces fought in Korea and Viet Nam, losing more than 90,000 lives and billions of dollars in "no-win" wars because of a series of unwise political decisions made by Presidents Kennedy, Johnson and Nixon.

With the fall of Saigon in 1975, this conclusion became clear to the Kremlin:

> The United States no longer had the courage or the will to defend free people around the world. It also raised the question as to whether America's leaders had the will to defend America in the face of thermonuclear blackmail.

As a result, Soviet world domination and influence expanded explosively through Moscow-orchestrated "wars of national liberation". Thus fell to the red flag of Communism South Viet Nam, Laos, Cambodia, Angola, Mozambique, Ethiopia South Yemen, Nicaragua (thanks to the Carter administration), Rhodesia (with the help of Great Britain and the World Council of Churches), Syria, Libya and Namibia (with the help of the United Nations).

Continuing even now under Communist threat (whether the source is called Soviet or Russian) is the Republic of South Africa (again with help from the US, the European Community and the World and National Council of Churches). Should the RSA become a Marxist state (as seems to be the desire of every administration since Nixon) the result will be a bloody tribal and civil war internally with resulting economic chaos and the loss to the U.S. of strategic minerals vital to our industrial community.

In that regard, it is wise to recall these words by Leonid Brezhnev in 1973:

> ... Our aim is to gain control of the two great treasure houses on which the West depends: the energy treasure house of the Persian Gulf, and the mineral treasure house of central and southern Africa.

The New Pathway for Communism's World

But, isn't the Cold War over? The answer is "Yes" and "No".

Yes, the Berlin Wall is gone. Yes, Eastern Europe is no longer under Soviet control. Yes, the Soviet Union itself came to an end and split into 16 of its former "republics". Yes, a free election in Russia made Boris Yeltsin (a former Communist party apparatchik) its first president and there is a freely elected parliament in Moscow. Yes, there is now an openness to Christianity in Russia. Yes, copies of The Holy Bible are flowing into Russia.

This major change since 1989 has appeared to be one of the most dramatic events in history.

In 1989, the Soviet Union had within its grasp the ability to defeat the West (and the United States) without firing a shot — by the existence of the largest military force ever created in history. The world's two nuclear superpowers faced each other and the United States "blinked" by its loss of courage in Viet Nam and its continuing concession in repeated debilitating disarmament negotiations.

What Happened?

Along the way to the surrender of the West, the Soviet Union suddenly broke apart. Some believed that it collapsed from within because of its inherent inefficiency. Some believe that the excessive cost of their military machine was too heavy for their command economy. They could not feed their own people. They were sunk in a morass of growing chronic alcoholism. Eastern Europe was a simmering political explosion. The rise of Islamic fundamentalism in their 60 million Muslim population was a foreboding omen.

The gleeful conclusion in the West was that the Cold War was over: the West had won!

One astute observe of the Soviet Union, Dr. Joseph D. Douglass, made this assessment of the fall of the Soviet Union:

> ... The breakdown in the Soviet Union was not our victory; they lost in spite of the efforts of our political leaders, bankers and multinational corporations to keep them alive. We are still doing this, although now our efforts are to keep Russia and its social bureaucrats alive. Russia is another bottomless sink hole that various private interest groups want to pour our tax dollars down. Presumably in yet another effort to salvage a socialist disaster. The Soviet Union broke down because it did not produce anything of value (other than military hardware or intelligence services) and had run out of creditors. This failure is the failure of socialism on a grandscale, but few are recognizing this and none are drawing the parallel to what has been happening in America.

Take Care! Beware!

But, there are others who warn, "No, the Cold War is not over! Do not be deceived!"

Some who have studied the history of Soviet Marxist-Leninism since 1917 believe it possible that the United States and the West are being taken for the most colossal dupes in history. Consider this evidence:

1. In the early 1930s, Dimitri Manuilskli, one of the principal Soviet strategists, said in the Lenin School for Political Warfare:

> ... War to the hilt between communism and capitalism is inevitable. Today, of course, we are not strong enough to attack. Our time will come in thirty to forty years. To win we shall need the element of surprise. The bourgeoisie ... will have to be put to sleep. So, we shall begin by launching the most spectacular peace movement on record. There will be electrifying overtures and unheard of concessions. The capitalist countries, stupid and decadent, will rejoice to cooperate in their own destruction. They will leap at another chance to be friends. As soon as their guard is down, we will smash them with our clenched fist.

2. In 1984, Anatoliy Golitsyn, a former senior KGB officer involved in Soviet strategic planning, wrote a book titled "New Lies for

Old". In it he predicted many of the dramatic events since 1989 and stated that they were part of a carefully structured KGB plan within the Kremlin. Some of the scheduled events he predicted were:

a. Yield nominal control of Eastern Europe
b. Superficially encourage democracy in Eastern Europe and the Soviet Union
c, Open the Iron Curtain and tear down the Berlin Wall
d. Allow reunification of East and West Germany
e. Declare communism dead, the Cold War over, and the Communist parties in Eastern Europe and the Soviet Union irrelevant.

What were the benefits expected by the Kremlin from these Soviet concessions? What was expected from the West in the KGB plan?

a. The United States and the West would assume the financial burden of Eastern Europe for the Soviet Union.
b. The West would permit reunification of German
c. Withdrawal of American troops from Western Europe
d. The United States and the West would finance the Soviet's devastated economy.

And, to these Western concessions would be added obvious additional ones:

a. Cause the United States and its NATO allies to make deep cuts in their military and naval forces (since the Cold War would then be over and there would be no enemy to fight). (Mr. Bush obliged and Mr. Clinton is pushing for even deeper cuts. Germany and other NATO nations are following that lead.)
b. Encourage the United States to open greater access to Western technology to help modernize Russian industry. (Our industrial and business leaders are on shuttle commuter runs to Moscow while visions of rubble plums dance in their heads.)
c. Encourage the United States to continue engaging in the same kind of disarmament negotiations which were so favorable to the Soviet Union. (Mr. Bush signed the clearly unbalanced START I and II disarmament treaties).

Have not all these predictions and actions actually become reality by 1993? But, what do we really know about what is happening in the former Soviet Union? We really do not have a clear picture. In his final testimony to the Senate in 1992, outgoing CIA director Robert

Gates described the events in Russia as "tumultuous!" The reformers make up only about one-third of the Russian parliament; in early 1993 Yeltsin seemed to have little control over events beyond 100 miles of Moscow.

In his confirmation hearings on February 5, 1993, incoming CIA director, James Woolsey, warned the Senate Intelligence Committee that the threats we will see in the future are

> less predictable but potentially more dangerous than the past. We have slain a large dragon, but now we live in a jungle filled with a bewildering variety of poisonous snakes, and in many ways the dragon was easier to keep track of.

Uncertainty. Instability. Danger. These are the hallmarks of the future.

The Hand of God

Those who remember the wondrous ways in which God moved to protect and preserve this nation in its early days — and those united 13 colonies before them ..

Those who recall how God's Hand of Providence saved General Washington's troops from sure and total capture in the battle of Long Island, for example ...

... cannot but wonder if the collapse of the Soviet Union on the very eve of its potential ultimatum to this nation was not the timing and the Hand of God in the affairs of men. Perhaps, once again, our nation was spared — given one more opportunity to repent, to reimbrace the faith of our fathers, and to reclaim America for Christ. To do it now before it is finally too late; before His final judgment.

Whatever, the calling is clear: there is still time — time to heal this land, time to save this land ...IF. If we will humble ourselves, and pray, and seek His face and get to work to turn this nation back to The Lord God, ruler of nation ... and back from our wicked ways.

The New Strategy

Golitsyn, Don McAlvany and Larry Abraham and a growing number of informed observers of the Marxist-Leninist war to the death with the West are convinced that instead of the collapse of communism, we are now experiencing a profound change in its strategy. At least temporarily, the materialist/military strategy has been given a lower priority and the war has shifted into two new directions: First, a war to undermine the culture and morality of the West, and, Second, using the United Nations as the framework to build a communist-dominated One World Government.

Destroying the United States from Within

The Old Testament is centered upon how nations are destroyed more from within than by external military threats and conquests.

The Book of Judges and the books of the prophets tell that when the Israelites turned from God, they rotted from within before they were conquered from without. Their economy was destroyed, their justice system was perverted, their governments became corrupt, their worship deteriorated into form rather than substance, they worshipped false gods, their family life deteriorated into a sexuallly-oriented society and ...

... they fell like ripe fruit into the hands of the Assyrians and the Babylonians.

History is filled with other examples of how nations and civilizations rotted from within before they were destroyed by military action. The fall of the Roman Empire is, perhaps, the most dramatic example. Back in about 500 B.C., Sun Tzu, the Chinese philosopher (and premier strategist) advanced this truth about defeating an enemy:

> ... To fight and conquer in all your battles is not supreme excellence; supreme excellence consists in breaking the enemy's resistance without fighting.

Antonio Gramsci

This was also the concept proposed by Antonio Gramsci, a Marxist-Leninist theoretician and founder of the Italian Communist Party. Back in the 1930s Gramsci studied Marxism/Leninism and concluded that the then-prevailing Marxist strategy (military/materialistic warfare) would not succeed. He argued that it could not conquer the western world as long as even a remnant of Christian culture existed.

Gramsci advocated a shrewd, subtle and total social/cultural warfare aimed at the destruction of the Christian faith and culture. In his voluminous works on political science and strategy, written during his imprisonment by Mussolini, Gramsci outlined such a total anti-Christian warfare and urged that it be pressed against the West.

Gramsci understood that religion determines culture and that culture in turn determines politics. Culture is basically the externalization of religion and a people who are religious will resist the anti-religious such as Marxism/Leninism.

Could it be that with the failure of the Communist mmaterialistic/revolutionary economic and military conflict the Marxists have now turned to the Gramsci strategy?

Is that what we see in this nation travelling under the guise of the "politically correct" and the push of the sodomites and in the flood of promiscuity, perversion, drug addiction and rise of environemtnal extremism and its worship of eco-religions — all aimed at denial and destruction of our Christian culture?

Patrick Buchanan was correct: we are in a battle for the soul of America.

There is no need for a litany of the licentious and the promiscuous and the anti-Christian that is sweeping our cities, our schools, our academies, our courts and our halls of government. Such evils are all to manifest every day.

Such depravities do not follow The Holy Bible, which was the great political textbook of our founding fathers; they follow more closely the "Communist Rules for Revolution." Those rules were found in 1919 in Dusseldorf, Germany, by the Allied Forces then occupying Germany after World War I:

A. Corrupt the young; get them away from religion. Get them interested in sex. Make them superficial; destroy their ruggedness.

B. Get control of all means of publicity, thereby:

1. Get people's minds off their government by focussing their attention on sexy books, plays and other trivialities.

2. Divide the people into hostile groups by constantly harping on controversial matters the past of no importance to the present.

3. Destroy the people's faith in their natural leaders by holding the latter up to contempt, redivcule and obloquy.

4. Always preach democracy, but seize power as fast and as ruthlessly as possible.

5. By encouraging government extravagance, destroy its credit, produce fear of inflation with rising prices and general discontent.

6. Foment unnecessary strikes in vital industries,

encourage civil disorders and foster a lenient and soft attitude on the part of government toward such disorders.

7. By specious argument cause the breakdown of old moral virtues, honesty, sobriety, continence.

C. Cause the registration of all firearms on some pretext, with a view to confiscating them and leaving the population helpless.

Those rules are 74 years old. They read like our daily newspaper; and, in fact, they smack of current legislative agendas.

The Holy Bible makes it clear: man, without God, is a sinful, raging, vicious, cruel, vindictve, treacherous, and deceitful creature. And it also makes it clear that conceptual enemy planner is not Gramsci or his ilk — but Satan, the father of lies and a murderer from the beginning.

Beware, America. Satan races to and fro looking for those he can enslave! He does so, even now.

Take care, America, this night thy soul may be required of thee!

One World, but Whose?

No one can fault the idea of a world at peace. It is one of mankind's loftiest aspirations.

Christians know that peace is coming — that it will come through The Living Word, through our Heavenly Father through Whom and in Whom men of good will will be brothers.

Then the lamb will lie down with the lion and men will beat their swords into plowshares and their spears into pruning hooks.

What a glorious day that will be !

"Nation shall not lift up a sword against nation,
Neither shall they learn war any more" (Micah 4:3).
Praise God!

But they shall sit every man under his vine and under his fig
tree, And none shall make them afraid...
For all people walk every one in the name of his god,
And we will walk in the name of The Lord our God
Forever and ever (Micah 4:4-5).

Amen! So let it be!

Surely the United Nations does not fit or fulfill that prophecy!

It does not serve God. It denies God.

It is no house of God. God is officially *persona non grata* there.

In 1945, in its beginning, the United Nations made its choice. The United Nations, it proclaimed, is man's last best hope for peace.

Oh? What happened to the Lord God?

The United Nations chose man. It chose the superstate. It rejected God.

"He who is not with Me is against Me, and he who does not gather with Me scatters" (Luke 11:23).

The United Nations does not gather with God; it does not work for God. It is the ultimate expression of humanism — the delusion that man himself can solve the problems of the world and keep the peace.

Consider this. In the United Nations park, this scripture is written on the marble of a monument:

> *"They shall beat their swords into plowshares,*
> *And their spears into pruning hooks;*
> *Nation shall not lift up sword against nation,*
> *Neither shall they learn war any more."*

Recognize that? It is taken from Isaiah 2:4. It is also taken out of context; spiritually eviscerated. For what precedes that passage gives the only hope and the only reason that "nation shall not lift up sword against nation."

> *And it shall come to pass in the last days That the mountain of The Lord's house Shall be established in the top of the mountains, And shall be exalted above the hills; And all nations shall flow to it. And many people shall come and say,*
> *"Come ye, and let us go up to the mountain of The Lord, To the house of the God of Jacob; and He will teach us His ways, And we shall walk in His paths." For out of Zion shall go forth the law, And the word of The Lord from Jerusalem.*
> *And He shall judge among the nations,*
> *And shall rebuke many people.*

There! That is what the United Nations left off of its marble slab. It denied the source, the power, the hope of the world: The Lord God!

Without that source, without that power, the age of humanism and its tower of Babel fails and fades and falls and becomes undone.

The UN is no house of God.
The Psalmist wrote years ago,
"Except The Lord builds the house,
They labor in vain that build it;
Except The Lord keep the city,
The watchman waketh but in vain"
(Psalm 127:1).

False Gods, False Starts

The United Nations does not serve God. And it does not serve men very well. Not the men of freedom, not the men of peace; not their quest for justice.

Those who are truly concerned, those who truly search for peace (not capitulation but peace) among men of goodwill, should consider the facts. Any honest assessment of the UN and its almost fifty-year pursuit of one more false god is one more false start by men who reject God and who seek to make of themselves a god.

"Peace," men cry. But there is no peace. The United Nations organization is hardly an instrument of peace. As British Prime Minister Margaret Thatcher once pointed out, since its founding in 1945 there have been more than "140 conflicts in which up to 10 million people have died." Some peace! The UN did little or nothing to prevent those conflicts or to restore the peace.

What of Hungary in 1956? The Soviet invasion of Czechoslovakia in 1968? The Vietnam war, which started in 1945? The Vietnamese invasion of Cambodia? The Soviet invasion of Afghanistan? Gadhafi's invasion of Chad in 1983? Lebanon? The Iraqi-Iranian war?

John Chamberlain wrote in one of his columns, "The UN, as it has evolved, has become the happy hunting ground of all the two-bit bully boys who talk about liberty and use stolen property to bolster their one-party regimes."[35]

Words, Words ... and Misdeeds

The UN talks of human rights and human dignity.

Since it was founded, more than one billion people have been enslaved by communism.

It did nothing when Red China practiced genocide on the Tibetans. (That practice resulted in the liquidation of some 1.2 million Tibetans — approximately one-seventh of the total population.) Yet the UN kicked out Free China and opened its doors to Communist China. In the new world, might makes rights! That's the way it is with men -- not with God, with men.

The UN declares the worth of the human person. God also declares the worth of the individual. He loved the world so much He gave His only begotten Son, that whosoever believes on Him should not perish but have everlasting life.

And the UN? It gave its blue-helmeted mercenaries and under its blue and white banner, they slaughtered and maimed and pillaged and ravaged the helpless of Katanga. They bombed hospitals, shelled ambulances, destroyed churches, murdered noncombatants.

So much for the UN declaration of human rights. The UN speaks of equal rights of nations, of self-determination. Yet it did nothing when Nigeria forced starvation on 800,000 children of Biafra. And, it did nothing when the communist dictator of Ethiopia starved his opposition and consigned them to the most desolate parts of that nation.

The UN prattles on about man's inhumanity to man.

Yet it refused to act in the face of incontrovertible proof that the Communists of North Korea deliberately machine-gunned more than 5,000 American prisoners and buried them in a mass grave. It did nothing when the Communists of the Soviet Union dropped butterfly bombs and incendiary devices and chemical warfare bombs on the helpless people of Afghani villages.

The UN talks of trust and goodwill and justice.

Yet it welcomed that pistol-packing terrorist, Yasir Arafat, to its podium and applauded as he spewed his venom. The PLO was invited to have representatives on various UN agencies; Free China is excluded.

"Peace, peace. Justice, justice." The UN babbles. Where is their peace? Justice lies bleeding in its marbled halls.

Anti-U.S.A.

There is no equity in the representation at the United Nations. No such thing as one-man, one-vote. More than one-half of the nations in the UN have fewer people than the population of New York City. One-fifth of the UN members have populations of less than two million each. Yet each of their votes in the General Assembly is equal to that of the United States, and most of the time their votes supported the demands of the Soviet Union or the want-list of the Third World.

When the United Nations voted to expel Free China (a charter member in good standing), the record of that world body was forever marred with bigotry and bias. George Bush was an ambassador to the UN then. During the debate he was moved to protest, "Never have I seen such hate!"

On the day when the free people of the Republic of China, our friends and allies, were drummed out of the UN, the United States should have removed itself from the United Nations and the United Nations from the United States. For if it had not been clear before, it was surely evident from then on: the United Nations was a tool for the advancement of the hate-America, up-with-communism campaign. But we turned our back to Free China. We have been turning our back to our friends ever since.

Ask yourself: How can hate be an instrument of peace?

Is not the United Nations dedicated to peace? Whose peace? As one-time U.S. Ambassador to the UN David Patrick Moynihan warned, the United Nations is a "dangerous place" where the United States is becoming "an endangered species."

U.S. Senator Robert Kasten reported that 159 members of the UN vote against the interests of the United States on nearly 80 percent of the roll calls in the General Assembly. Among those with high rates of voting against us are nations whose leaders were received at the White House: Algeria (94.9 percent), India (91.2 percent), Saudi Arabia (86.4 percent), Mexico (85.5 percent), Egypt (84.7percent), Brazil (84 percent), and Argentina (83.6 percent).[36]

The maddening aspect is we continue to send foreign aid and loan money to many of those nations which consistently vote against us.

The Tower of Babel

Remember the tower of Babel? The one the sons of Noah built there on the plains of Shinar? Remember how they set out to make a name for themselves? How they planned to be on a par with God?

"They refused to acknowledge God's power in the world. They thought they were wiser than God."[37] Doesn't that description fit today's humanistic United Nations?

"They wanted the security of being together. They tried to achieve security and unity through organization. But unity does not come through visible organizations. Real unity is internal, not external."[38] It's what is in the heart that really counts.

But they built themselves a tower, a temple of idol worship. Those sons of Noah put another god before God; they enthroned themselves rather than the Lord.

The result? Confusion. Chaos. A scattering of the people far and wide.

Is not the United Nations today's tower of Babel?

Is it not the same with that tower of steel and glass and stone, that monolith of humanism and chicanery, duplicity and hate? Does it not deny God and worship the false gods of men? Does it not seek unity and security in an organization devoid of Spirit and goodwill?

They have builded them a UN tower on sand, the sands of idolatry — a pagan temple which puts man above God and the State above man.

Small wonder God confuses them and scatters them and makes their big talk like chaff which the wind blows away.

Be Ye Not Unequally Yoked...

It is time for concerned Americans, especially godly Christians, to honestly and seriously and prayerfully consider the United Nations. Consider its godless no, its anti-God-roots, its anti-American record, and its anti-free nations actions in these troubled times.

We must attend to this matter if we are to protect the security of this Republic. Arkady Shevchenko, ex-KGB agent and UN under-secretary for Political and Security Council Affairs, revealed that a high percentage of Soviet's UN delegation were KGB spies. Burton Pine, when at the Heritage Foundation, charged that the UN serves as a base for Soviet espionage in the U.S.[39] It still does; today, in 1993.

It is perhaps more important in regard to our spiritual well-being as a nation. For, if we are to obey God, we surely must be mindful of His Word:

Be you not unequally yoked together with unbelievers. For what fellowship has righteousness with unrighteousness? And what communion has light with darkness? And what concord has Christ with Belial? Or what part has he who believes with an infidel? And what agreement has the temple of God with idols? For you are the temple of the living God.

As God has said:

"I will dwell in them And walk among them.
I will be their God, And they shall be My people."

*Wherefore "Come out from among them
And be you separate," says the Lord.
"And touch not the unclean thing;
And I will receive you. And will be a
Father unto you, And you shall be My
sons and daughters," Says The Lord
Almighty* (II Cor. 6:14-18).

What a tremendous promise.

What a wonderful transformation — from chaos to peace, from darkness into light.

What a mighty fortress is our God! Our shield and our buckler, our strength and our salvation. If we will be separate unto Him.

God's Strategic Agents

These hours may seem dark but from the darkness emerges a glorious light.

It is the Light, the True Light. The Christ!

He calls to each one of us. He issues His challenge. He offers His way.

It is a special responsibility to all Christians fortunate enough to be Americans, either natural born or naturalized. We who are His in this still-free land are the ones to go forth for Him!

Even now, as The Loving, Living, Gracious God has given us another opportunity to reclaim His freedom and this nation in His name and for His glory!

Let others seek to remove that great old hymn "Onward Christian soldiers" from their hymnals. Let us go forth, the Cross of Jesus going on before.

In the final analysis, He must lead us against the foe; at home and abroad. The battle is His. It has been; it is now. And His will be the victory!

In the meantime we go forth — commissioned, instructed, inspired — to seek dominion in His name and for His holy sake.

Listen to Dr. Charles W. Lowry.

He raised the banner and sounded the call:

America today has the mightiest opportunity in history. It is not merely the chance to throw back the forces of reaction and to repel the evil and demonic dream of a single, man-governed totalitarian world.

Nothing negative will suffice. Simple condemnation will not stem the tide of a dynamic advance.

The opportunity of our great country, which God has so wonderfully led and so richly blessed, is to lead faltering mankind beyond the twilight and the hovering darkness into the sunshine of a larger, happier day. It is to use our vast resources and inspiring inheritance under God to usher the whole earth into a period of abundance, freedom, and brotherhood. It is to be a strategic agent in continuing God's recreative work in Christ.

It is to extend and ever-more to consolidate in the affairs of men the Christian Revolution!.[40]

Like a mighty army, Moves the Church of God;
Brothers, we are treading Where the Saints have trod.
We are not divided, all one body we —
One in hope and doctrine, One in charity.
Onward Christian soldiers, Marching as to war,
With the Cross of Jesus Going on before!

Choose You This Day!

Some years ago a group of 120 self-proclaimed humanists hung a "Closed" sign on the world.

In their dead and deadly "Humanist Manifesto II," they intoned that it was God who was dead. They assured America that any search for Divine guidance in these troubled times was an exercise in futility, a bunch of hokum. Voodooism in twentieth-century garb.

"No deity will save us," they insisted.

"We must save ourselves!"

That was their message of hope. Their clarion call.

Religion that places God above man does a disservice to the human species.

That's what they said. Let we who are dead be your shepherds.

That was their invitation.

Well, for years this nation has been wandering in their wilderness. Theirs and their cohort, the Super-state.

And look where we are!

The whirlwind we reap is not of God. It did not come from obeying and following God.

It comes from man cut loose from God. From man denying God. From man in disobedience to God. From man playing God.

As a nation sows, so does it reap.

If we would return as a nation to God and to His eternal truths, if we would rekindle the faith of our fathers, we could get out of the fix we are in.

But the darker it gets, the louder the humanists and the statists propound their paganistic propaganda. Religion, they assert, is only an escape mechanism.

We have heard that one before.

"Religion is the opiate of the people." Karl Marx came up with that one.

Sorry, gentlemen. No sale!

Our God is not dead!

He lives! He reigns!

We tried to warn you about yours.

The unholy alliance of humanism and statism has always been a failure. It was in the French Revolution. It is in the Communist revolution. It is in the rebellion of today's humanists. and atheists and agnostics and ACLU.

The world shudders; it wretches from those errors.

As Reverend R. J. Rushdoony points out, what we now witness is the breaking up of the pagan proposition. The thieves fall out. Their order disintegrates. The more it flies apart, the more they demand control as if it were an adhesive capable of saving their day. It won't.

The question before the nation is this: What will take its place?

The light and the love and the power of Jesus Christ?

It waits to be reasserted! To be reapplied!

It, and it alone, is the power that can change men's hearts. The power that can move nations. The power that can end famines and wars. The power that can still the raging of the seas.

It is the power that makes all things possible, through prayer and faith and works.

If we are to restore America, if we are to make it a home of righteousness and freedom, we must return to God, humble ourselves, seek His face, and follow His ways. We must obey His laws, do His works, and present His whole and Holy Word for all of life and living.

Dr. Charles Malik summed up the challenge:

"When the tears and joy of Christ come to perfect fruition in this land, then America will utter her word."

There! There we are!

Christ is the answer. For each individual. For America. For the world.

America has a choice to make. That choice starts with us, each one of us. With you, beloved of the Lord.

It is the choice which God's man, Joshua, put before the people of Israel:

"Choose for yourselves this day whom you will serve".

What about you?

Have you made your choice? Do you have a personal commitment to Christ? Do you know Jesus? Really know him? As your Savior? And, as your King?

That's the first step: to put Christ first, always.

Then join with others of like mind in Him. In prayer, in praise, in study, in action.

Put your faith to work!

In your home. In your church. In your community. In your personal affairs. And in your civic duties.

Yes! Even in the affairs of civil government. Join with others.

Remember this: if Christians had not shirked their civic duties as stewards of Christ, Caesar could never have so extended his reach and expanded his grasp.

To hang back, to do nothing, is to invite Caesar to become even more powerful, to become as god.

There's the choice: One nation under God. Or Caesar's Superstate.

That is the decision American Christians must make. Now.

The children of Israel made their choice.

"Far be it from us that we should forsake The Lord
to serve other gods".

America's choice? It starts with you.

With the Christians of America.

What will it be?

Let it be one nation under God!

STUDY GUIDE

Introduction

You have been chosen to be the discussion leader—the guide—for this study series. Your role is very important. You can help make this study exciting, enjoyable, and informative. You can help the fellow-Christians in your group acquire a deeper under standing of God's will and purpose in the affairs of civil government.

As a guide you are not expected to be a teacher, or a lecturer or an expert on government or politics. Your talk is to guide your friends through the twelve chapters of this study course; to encourage each one of them to take an active part in group discussions and study, to keep the discussions on time and on track—and to do this prayerfully and thoughtfully.*

Here are a few suggestions that might be helpful:

1. **Always open and close each session with prayer and praise.** Pray especially that the Holy Spirit will abide with the group and that the

Light and Love of Jesus Christ will illumine the study. Praise God for the opportunity and the freedom to gather in His name.

We suggest that you, as the guide, give the opening prayer at each session. You might want to include in your prayer a request that the Lord bless this nation and its leaders and its people. As you know, Christians are instructed to do that.

We also suggest that you ask a member of the sutdy group to give the closing prayer. Why not rotate this each week so that during the course of the study each member of the group has an opportunity to share in the privilege of paryer?

2. **Start each study session on Time.** And end on time. Each study session is designed to last for one hour.* That should allow ample time for questions and answers and discussion of the material set forth in your study plan.

Some groups may choose to have a coffee-time before the study session begins (usually lasting 30 minutes). This helps to make sure that

---

*This book has 12 chapters and can be used for a six-week cram course (two chapters a week) or as a 12-13 week adult class (similar to a Sunday School Quarterly).

*You may want to extend this to 90 minutes but that should be the maximum time for a study session.

everyone arrives before the start of the lesson period and establishes a congenial atmosphere for the lesson study. Some people will want to stay after the formal lesson time to continue the discussion. That is fine. But, make it clear that the formal lesson period lasts for one hour* and that members of the group are free to leave at that time. This is important for those couples who have other duties, or children at home, or baby-sitters, etc.

3. **Encourage every member of the group to participate fully.** The most successful study groups are those in which there is a relaxed and friendly atmosphere—one in which all feel free to give their answers, express thier views, and take part in the discussions.

Some members of the group will probably be more articulate and responsive than others. They will help keep the sessions moving; but do not let them dominate the session to the exclusion of others. And, without embarrassing the more reserved individuals, encourage them to contribute their ideas and answers. If a member talks too much, gently switch the discussion by asking someone else a question.

One way to "open" the session is to direct the questions to each member of the group, in turn—starting with Question #1 to the person on your right. Question #2 to the next person on your right, and so on around the room. Do the same in regard to having members of the study group read aloud suggested references from the text and from the Bible.

4. **After the opening prayer, read aloud the purpose of the lesson at hand.** The purpose—the three or four major points to be covered—are set forth at the start of each session in your study plan.

Doing this will help to establish clearly the major points to be considered during the study session. It will also help you, as the guide, keep the study on track.

5. **Answers to the questions raised in the study plan will be found in the references enclosed in parentheses after each question.*** These refer you to specific pages in the book or to the Scriptures. After the group has answered a question and discussed related matters, bring the discussion on that particular topic to a close by reading (or, asking a member of the group to read) the key portion of the reference material.

6. **Guide the group so that it does not become involved in negative diatribes or discussions of a controversial nature that could get the study session off track.** Do not let the session devolve into partisan politics (in the contemporary sense) or into pro and con debates on candidates or personalities. Concentrate on the basic Christian principles of

---

*Note to Leader: The study plan purposefully includes more questions than can be answered within the time-span of the typical (90-minute) session-discussion. The leader should select those questions on which he wishes to have the group concentrate. It may be that only one or two or three questions will be developed during the lesson; that is up to you and the group. Or, you may want to deal only with the central questions and pass by the subsidiary questions; again, that is your choice. It is important to keep the discussion moving, and to stay on time; however, it is more important to create a free-and-open atmosphere so that the class feels free to enter into the sharing that comes through a Spirit-filled and congenial discussion of the points at hand.

---

*You may want to extend this to 90 minutes but that should be the maximum time for a study session

civil government as applied to the issues.

7. Decide at the outset how many sessions your group will hold; when, where, etc. Most groups will want to hold 13 study sessions—one each week for 3 months. *One Nation Under God* was written in 13 parts to fit that schedule.

Some groups may want to combine certain chapters into one study session so they can spend two sessions on another area of the book (education, social welfare, taxations, etc). That can easily be done; the program is flexible.

However, try to decide these details at the first (introductory) session so that members know what the schedule is and can plan ahead.

And, in all things, remember this:

But seek first the kingdom of God and His righteousness, and all these things shall be added to you (Matt. 6:33).

SESSION ONE

"ONE NATION UNDER GOD"

Introductory and Planning Session

Opening prayer by discussion leader

Personal Introductions:
Discussion leader should "formally" introduce self and give short personal background (including, if you wish, a short testimony.) Starting from your right, ask each member in the group to give a self-introduction and personal background.

Purpose of this first session:
- to introduce and distribute

copies of *One Nation Under God*
- to outline and discuss the purpose and basic thrust of the study course
- to discuss the Christian's role in government and politics
- to set the schedule for the study course
- to explain the lesson plan and announce basic questions to be considered in study session on Chapter One

Introductory Notes (leader should read this, or convey its message in your own words):

This is a study about God and government.

It is not the ordinary course in civics or good government *because it puts God first!*

Sadly, that is all too unusual in government and politics these days. During the next few weeks together we will undertake to accomplish several things:
- to review the genesis of civil (human) government and its purposes as instituted and ordained by God
- to trace the roots and development of the Christian idea of self-government
- to consider the Christian origins and foundation of our American Republic
- to assess how far America, as a nation, has strayed from its Christian foundations
- to evaluate some of the serious social, economic, political and moral problems that have resulted because of that separation from God, and
- to discuss what Christians can do to restore the spiritual foundations of America and to apply

God-centered principles to find the correct solutions to the issues of these times.

GOD FIRST

Just as we strive to keep God first in all areas of our lives, so let us keep God first in our study course. As we study and share together, let's keep these words from Proverbs before us; let's make them—in effect—our class motto:

In all your ways acknowledge Him, And He shall direct your paths (Prov. 3:6).

If we prayerfully pursue our studies in that light, and seek God's love and guidance, we will surely find correct answers to our questions—God's answers. . .and that is what is so sorely needed in government and politics today.

CHRISTIAN UNITY

In our study together, let us be of one mind in Christ Jesus. Working and sharing and studying and considering the issues involved in civil government in Christian love and unity.

...stand fast in one spirit, with one mind striving together for the faith of the gospel (Phil. 1:27).

Each individual, because of background, experience, previous study or prior association, may have differing views on various topics. That is as it should be in a society of free individuals. Christians seek unity, not uniformity. The sharing of differing views in Christian love will help all members of the group gain a deeper insight and understanding into the issues and problems of the day.

GOD IN GOVERNMENT

Our purpose in this course is to advance the cause of good government—and good civil government is the will of God, as we shall study in subsequent sessions.

We do not gather a political partisans; we meet as American Christians. We do not assemble to promote political labels; we join to raise the banner of Christ.

Our cause is to serve the one and Holy Sovereign, the Lord God of Hosts—and to do that in all things, including prayerful participation in the affairs of State. For some, that may raise a question: *Should Christians be involved in politics?* That is a sincere question in the minds of some Christ-centered Americans. It is dealt with in the opening chapter of *In the Spirit of '76*, by Rus Walton.

CHRISTIANS IN POLITICS

In the chapter entitled, "Politics—But Not As Usual," we are offered this counsel:

"There are some who say that Christians have no business getting involved in politics.

"If, by that, they mean politics as usual—the type of politics that seems all too prevalent these days—*they are right.*

"But, if they mean politics—the affairs of state, the process by which free men seek the balance between the extremes of anarchy and collectivism—*they are wrong.*

"And, if they mean Christians must divorce themselves from their convictions, or leave their religious beliefs behind when they enter the halls and precincts of government—*they are wrong again.*

"Christians have every right to be active in politics. The fact that we love

A-4

the Lord and have accepted Jesus Christ as our Saviour and Master does not make us second-class citizens or exclude us from the electorate.

"Furthermore, Christians have many reasons for taking part in the political processes of government. Consider at least these four:

"1. Christians should get involved in politics to restore morality and a sense of true values to public affairs. This will help to rebuild public respect and confidence in government.

"2. Christians should get active in public affairs because government is involved in virutally every aspect of our daily lives.

"3. Christians should get involved in government because Divine Guidance is the only power that can restore the soul of this nation and save it from a terrible disaster or even total destruction.

"4. And, Christians should get involed in government so that the doors might be held open for the sharing of the Gospel until Christ comes again."

IT IS NOT TOO LATE

Finally, there are some who feel that it is too late to do anything to straighten out our government or save America.

It is never too late to be about the Lord's work. Second Chronicles 7:14 holds God's promise in that regard:

If My people who are called by My name will humble themselves, and pray and seek My face, and turn from their wicked ways, then I will hear from heaven, and will forgive their sin and heal their land.

Further, the prophet Samuel tells us:

If you fear the LORD and serve Him and obey His voice, and do not rebel against the commandment of the LORD, then both you and the king [or president, or congressman, or governmor, or mayor] who reigns over you will continue following the LORD your God (1 Sam. 12:14).

IN, BUT NOT OF, THE WORLD

Let's go back to the opening chapter In the Spirit of '76 once more. Here is what it has to say:

"Christians can succeed in politics without playing dirty. They do not leave their faith and their ethics behind them when they become involved in the affairs of government. God First, always, in all things—that is the basis on which Christians get involved in any activity—spiritual or secular.

"To say that a Christian cannot be active in politics without getting dirty, or being dirty, is to belittle the sustaining power of our faith and to suggest that God can prevail in some areas, but not all.

"If that attitude were to hold sway, Christians would withdraw from the world—from commerce, and law, and sports, and medicine; from education and jornalism, and whatever esle. Politics is not the only arena in the human contest where the game gets tough and some get rough. There are unholy pressurs in virtually every aspect of life. Should we therefore refrain from entering such professions or trades or avocations? Certainly not!

Jesus said, "I do not pray that You should take them out of the world....As You sent Me into the world, I also have sent them into the world" (John 17:15, 18).

NOT TO CONFORM,
BUT TO TRANSFORM

"What we must do is participate with energy and skill and refuse to be a party to any dirty deals or questionable pursuits or practices."

Be in the world—but *not of* the world, that is our role.

Christians should be active in public affairs not to conform, but to transform.

To be effectively active in public affairs, we must first have a clearer understanding of God's purpose for civil government—and a knowledge of how His principles should be applied to the affairs of state.

In the words of the Apostle Paul, we should *"Be diligent to present yourself approved to God, a worker who does not need to be ashamed, rightly dividing the word of truth"* (2 Tim. 2:15).

That advice should apply to every area of our life—including our role in govement and politics.

And that brings us to our text, *One Nation Under God,* written by Rus Walton.

Please turn to the Prologue of this book.

Let's read together this short section. It outlines the nature and the purpose of the book.

(Ask the next person to your right to read the first eight paragraphs—ending with "...God is Supreme...He is relevant for today and for always.")

(Ask the next person to your right to read the next two paragraphs—ending with ". . .one nation under God.")

(The third member of the group should read the next paragraphs ending with "equal liberty of any other person.")

(The fourth, the next four paragraphs.)

(The fifth, the next two paragraphs and the sixth the next.)

(The discussion leader should then read the final paragraphs in the Prologue.)

Discuss plans and schedule
for study course.

Does the group want to meet once each week for the next 12 weeks? (Perhaps you should read the chapter headings (see Table of Contents) and discuss whether the group wants to spend one session on each of the chapters—or combine some, thus spending more than one session on such issues as education, taxation, social welfare, etc.)

Decide on meeting details (day of the week, time, lenth of sessions, etc.).

Preview next week's study
session

(Chapter one—The Christian Idea of Government) *and announce some of the questions that will be considered:*

(1) When earthly kings are put ahead of God, and when nations put civil sovereigns ahead of the Lord, what happens?

(2) If the Republic is the superstructure of our givernment, what is the Foundation?

(3) Who ordained civil (human) government? When?

(4) Define the Christian idea of government.

Closing Prayer:

Ask a member of your group to close the session with prayer. Make a note of the person's name so that you are sure to rotate this prayer privilege—sharing it with each member during the course of the study.

A-6

SESSION TWO

THE CHRISTIAN IDEA OF
GOVERNMENT

Chapter One

Opening prayer by discussion leader

Purpose of this lesson:
- To understand the origin of civil government and the purposes for which God ordained it
- To examine the basic tenets of the Christian idea of self-government
- To discuss what happens when man is ruled by men rather than governed by God and God's laws
- To review the Christian origins of the American system of self-government with union, including its spiritual foundations and its structure and functions
- To delineate the distinctive Christian properties and workings of a truly republican form of government, and
- To better comprehend the core of the never-ending conflict between the Christian idea and the pagan view of man and state.

Questions to be considered and discussed (page references in parentheses):

1. When earthly kings are put ahead of God, and when nations put civil sovereigns ahead of the Lord, what happens? What warning did the prophet Samuel issue to the Israilites? (p. 10; 1 Sam. 8:10-18).

a. Is there a parallel between Samuel's warning and the colonists' "bill of particulars" against King George as set forth in the Declaration of Independence? (Read, or ask a member of your group to read this section of the Declaration, starting with the next to the last sentence in paragraph two ["The history of the present King..."] and continuing through the paragraph that begins, "He has excited domextic insurrections amongst us...")

b. Our Founding Fathers rejected each of the following forms of government. Why? Where is the sovereignty in each? (pp. 10, 11).
— Monarchy
— Communism (socialism)
— Democracy

c. For the Christian, where must sovereignty (heavenly and earthly) reside? (pp. 10, 11).

d. Why is "self-government with union" a Christian concept? (pp. 10,11).

2. Describe the nature and structure of the republican form of government (p. 11-12).

a. Why is the republic called "the Golden Mean"—the dynamic balance—in civil government? Discuss the table on page 12. Give examples of the loss of balance and the existing extremes in our civil government today.

b. What is the "Bill of Rights" in the U.S. Constitution? Why is this so important to the maintenance of individual liberty? (p. 12. Have the first Ten Amendments to the Constitution read aloud.)

c. Refer especially to the Ninth and Tenth Amendments (p. 12). Discuss examples of how these provisions (guarantees) are violated in these days.

3. If the Republic (with its checks and balances and fences) is the superstructure of our government, what is the foundation? (pp. 12-13).

a. Why is there no reference to Christianity in the U.S. Constitution? Is the absence of such mention to be regarded as the exclusion of God from government? (p. 13).

b. List some of the central Christian concepts that are the basis of the American form of self-government with union (pp. 13-14).

c. Daniel Webster described the differences between a government in concert with God, and a government devoid of God's influence. Review Webster's comments and discuss. (p. 14).

4. Who ordained civil (human) government? When? (p. 15).

a. What was God's purpose in instituting civil authority? (1 Pet. 2:13-14; Rom. 13:1-3).

b. Apply each of the following to civil government, its concept and its operations, and assess their impact on society (p. 15).
— The Law (Matt, 5:17)
— The Great Commandment (John 5:17)
— The Golden Rule (Matt. 7:12)
— The Great Injunction (Matt. 6:33)
— The Whole Spectrum of Love (1 Cor. 13:1-13)
— The Whole Armor of God (Eph. 6:10-18)

5. Analyze the structure and operation of the early Christian church with regard to (pp, 15-16):
— self-government
— local autonomy and selection of leadership
— union (unity)

a. The early Christian churches have been described as "little republics." Why? (p. 16).

b. What was the bond, the cement, that gave the early church unity? (p. 16). How was that concept adopted in the founding and formalizing of our nation's governance? (pp. 13-14, 17-18).

6. Define the Christian idea of government (pp. 10-11, 13-14, 16-17).

a. Contrast that with the pagan view of man (pp. 17-18).

b. Relate the conflict between the Christian idea and the pagan view (of man and state) to the world situation today.

Closing prayer by a member of the study group

SESSION THREE

FALSE GODS, STRANGE PROPHETS

Chapter two

Opening prayer by discussion leader

Purpose of this session:

• To emphasize the vital differences between a republic and a democracy
• To trace the *devolution* of our government from a Constitutional Republic to a democracy
• To analyze some of the excesses and evils and transfers of power that have occurred as a result of that change
• To examine the rise of the pagan view (of man and government) and the resultant glorification of Caesar at the expense of God's sovereignty and God's laws and Christ's teachings.

1. What are some of the vital differences between a republic and a democracy? (pp. 19-20 and table on p. 12).

a. It has been observed that in a republic the government is "of and by and for the people" while in the democracy people gradually become "of and by and for the government (the system)." Explain how this shift occurs and why (pp. 19-20).

2. Describe the original structure (relationship of the various levels of government) in the American Republic. Where did the power reside at the outset? Why was the county considered the basic unit—the base of the pyramid? (pp. 22-23).

a. Where does the bulk of the civil power (authority) now reside? Is this in keeping with the concept of a republic? What has happened to the checks and balances and fences of self-government with union (p. 23).

b. The author suggests that the pyramid of government is now inverted. What measurements does he use to reach that conclusion? How has the advent of war been used to facilitate that transfer of power from the individual to the state? (pp. 23-25).

3. What is the "new branch" of government (some have called it "the real third party")? (p. 25).

4. Why is faith in God an essential factor in the preservation of self-government? What moves in when such faith in God is lost, weakened or supplanted? (pp. 26-27 and paragraph 4, p. 27).

a. According to James Madison, on what did our Founding Fathers stake "the future of our political institutions"? (p. 19).

5. There are some who insist that if our Saviour, Jesus, were on earth today, He would be a socialist. Why is this a patent and serious distortion of truth? (p. 27; Exod. 20:3, Luke 12:13-14).

a. Can a Christian, rightly dividing the Word, be a socialist?

6. Karl Marx offered to dedicate his *Das Kapital* to Chrales Darwin. Why was Darwin's *Origin of the Species* important to the propagation of Marx's collectivistic (paganistic) ideology? (pp. 26-27).

a. How have the theories of Marx and Darwin been combined (worked together) to promote the pagan view of man and state? (p. 27).

b. Delineate the vital distinctions between humanism and Christianity in regard to the individual, the state, and the future of this world.

7. What is the choice facing Christians today? How does this relate to civil government as well as to all areas of our lives? (p. 27: Matt. 12:30; Josh. 24:15).

Closing prayer by a member of the study group

SESSION FOUR

GOD'S BED-ROCK LAWS FOR FREEDOM

Chapter Three

Opening prayer by discussion leader

Purpose of this session:
- To gain a clearer understanding of the source, the nature and the demands of individual liberty
- To review the two basic types of law in our society and to trace their source
- To appreciate the proper role and function of "the law"
- To examine and apply some of God's laws to our daily lives

1. Ask each member of your study group to give his or her personal definition (understanding) of individual freedom.

a. Who is the source of our individual liberty? How are we to use our personal freedom? (p, 29: 1 Pet. 2:16; 2 Cor. 3:17; Gal. 5:13).

b. What are the two "forms" (or levels) of personal freedom? Discuss why and how each is dependent upon the other (p. 29).

c. Is freedom individual or collective? Why is the term "free society" a dangerous error in semantics? (p. 30).

2. Is freedom the "easy road"? Or, is it the most demanding form of civil (and personal) government? Why? (pp, 30-31).

a. Describe the "dynamic balance" between "rights" and "responsibilites" and give several examples of how this balance works. Why is this essential to the working of freedom— give some examples of what happens when "rights" outweigh "responsibilities" (p. 31).

3. What are the two basic types of law in our society? Discuss their source and their function (p 31).

a. What is meant by "The Laws of Nature"? What is their source? How did our Founding Fathers recognize these laws in the Declaration of Independence? (p 31).

b. What is the proper purpose of Law? How does this relate to God's law and God's purpose for civil authority? (pp. 31-32 and p. 15).

c. What are the dangers implicit in the misuse of civil laws? (p. 31).

4. List some of God's fundamental laws of freedom:

a. Laws pertaining to the Fatherhood of God and His sovereignty (p. 32 and noted Scriptures).

b. Laws pertaining to the brotherhood of man through Jesus Christ (p. 32 and noted Scriptures, also p. 15).

5. The manner in which Christians engage in economic activites is a manifestation of our stewardship responsibilites, our love of the Lord, and our witness to others (especially non-believers). Why? (pp. 32-33).

a. Briefly review and discuss each of the following Christian "laws" (or rules) of economics (pp. 33-38).

— The Law of Dynamic Balance (The Law of Harmony) (p. 33 and Matt. 7:12)
— The Law of Productivity (pp. 33-34 and Matt. 25: 14-30)
— The Law of Distribution (pp. 34-35)
— The Law of Compensation (pp. 35-36 and Luke 6:38; Col. 3:23-4:1)
— The Law of Private Property (pp. 36-37 and Luke 12:13,14)
— The Law of Predictable (Sound) Money (pp. 37-38 and Luke 10:7)

Closing prayer by a member of the study group

SESSION FIVE

COERCION—BY PROXY

Chapter Four

Opening prayer by discussion leader

Purpose of this session:
- To fix clearly the responsibilities and accountability for the actions of civil government in a society of free individuals
- To comprehend the nature and source of coercion—whether it is on a one-to-one basis or by proxy
- To consider the nature and ramifications of plunder—both "legalized" and "illegal"
- To help us recognize coercion (and avoid or end it) and to

clarify the choices that face us in this regard

1. It has been written that "government is necessary and need not be evil." Do you agree? Is government necessary? Must it be evil? (pp. 40-41).

a. In a society of free individuals, who—in the final analysis—is responsible for the actions of government? (paragraph 3, p. 31).

2. Define coercion. Is coercion a violation of the Christian ethic? (p. 39 and Matt. 7:12; John 15:17).

a. Are there any circumstances under which a Christian can condone coercion? If so, what are they? (p. 41).

b. Review and discuss some of the examples of coercion listed on pages 39 and 40. Can members of your group condone any of these?

c. Does the fact that these, and other, coercive acts are sanctioned by civil (man's) law make them proper or excuse the violence involved? (pp. 41-42).

d. Should a Christian refuse to be a party to "aggressive" coercion? If so, how can such repudiation be manifested? (pp. 40 and 42-43).

3. How does coercion by proxy come to pass? The author suggests six possible routes. Review and discuss (p. 40).

a. Where does coercion usually find its roots (its genesis)? (p. 42).

b. How may one recognize the hallmarks of "legalized" coercion? (pp. 43-44).

4. What is the "distinction" between "legal" and "illegal" plunder? Is there really a valid distinction (i.e., Can either type really be properly excused)? (pp. 43-44).

a. Does "legalizing" plunder make it moral? Discuss "the ethics" of Robin Hood (who stole from the rich and gave to the poor). Were such acts in keeping with Christ's teachings? (pp, 43-44 and Luke 12:13-14).

b. Are all taxes "legalized plunder"? Are some? What is the distinction? (p. 43-44 and Rom. 13:7).

c. How is "legalizing" plunder a violation (misuse) of the law? ((pp. 43 and "Organized Justice," pp. 31-32).

5. Fredric Bastiat (in his "The Law") wrote that there are three ways we can decide the issue of "legalized" plunder. What are the three choices? (p. 44).

a. Relate each "choice" to a form of government and to the situation in the United States today (p. 44).

b. Which "choice is in keeping with God's will and laws, and why? (p. 44).

Closing prayer by a member of the study group

SESSION SIX

GOD'S "SUPER" STRUCTURE: THE FAMILY

Chapter Five

Opening prayer by discussion leader

Purpose of this session:

• To stress the importance of the family and the home, God's "line of authority" in the home, and the Christian duties involved

• To demonstrate that the training and discipline in the home determines, to a large degree, the spirit and soul of the nation

• To analyze the evils inherent in unrestricted abortion

• To examine "women's liberation" movements in light of God's laws, and to discuss the

dangers to the Republic inherent in the ERA proposal
- To consider the proper role and relationship of husband and wife, father and mother, and children as set forth in God's Word.

1. What is God's basic unit in the earthly society? Why can the family be properly termed "the foundation" of the nation? (pp. 45-46).

a. What is God's established "line of authority" in the family? How should this function in the home? What responsibilities does it place on each member of the family? (pp. 45-46).

b. What is the proper relationship between husband and wife, and parents and children, in the Christian home? Why is Christian love the basis for such relationships? (p. 46 and Eph. 5:21; Col. 3:15-21; Exod. 20:12 and p. 57).

c. Discuss some of the "external" (societal) pressures working today to weaken the family structure.

2. What are the three major functions of the Christian family as set forth by Earle E. Cairns? (p. 46).

a. Who, as the head of the family, has the prime responsibility to see that these Christian duties are fulfilled? (p. 46). Why is it vital that the Christian husband (father) not let anything come before (and between) his God-given responsibilities in the home? (p. 57).

b. Why is the instruction (discipline) in self-governance at home and in the family vital to future discipline and participation in civil affairs? (p. 46).

3. Review and discuss the various duties that should be attended to in the Christ-centered home (pp. 46-48 and Scripture references).

a. The author suggests that the home is a microcosm of the nation. Explain. Relate the situation in many of today's homes to the social and political state of the nation (pp. 46-47).

4. Under most circumstances, Christians must look upon abortion as murder. Why? Why are at least ninety-four percent of abortions against God's law and will?

a. Are there any circumstances in which an abortion might be condoned? What are they? (p. 52).

b. How do government subsidized abortions violate freedom of religion and freedom of conscience? (p.51).

c. What are the inherent dangers to the right to life at any age when that right is legally set aside to permit "abortion on demand"? (last paragraph, p. 52).

5. What (federal and state) laws now guarantee "equal rights" to women? (p. 54).

a. If such laws are not now adequate, what would be the proper level of civil government at which to enact additional laws?

b. Improperly framed and applied, how could such "equal rights" laws be used to subvert God's line of authority for the family? (pp. 45-46 and 1 Pet. 3:16).

c. Analyze and discuss the dangers to the Republic implicit in the adoption of the proposed 27th (ERA) Amendment (pp, 54-56).

6. The author suggests that some women who support the ERA movement are victims of today's world—man's system rather than God's plan. Explain how such pressures and anxieties could be removed through Christian living (pp, 56-57).

a. The woman's role as wife and mother—homemaker—is one of the most important of all tasks assigned by the Lord (equal to the man's role as breadwinner). Explain why this is so. Discuss why this is so. Why, and how should husbands love and respect their wives? What is the secret of true love, joy and "liberation" for husband and wife in the Christian home? (p. 57 and pp. 46-47).

Closing prayer by a member of the study group

SESSION SEVEN

PUBLIC SCHOOLS ARE RUINING OUR CHILDREN

Chapter Six

Opening prayer by discussion leader

Purpose of this session:
- To emphasize the responsibility for the education of the child in the Christian home
- To review the evils of "situational ethics," "sex education" and the over-all secular, humanistic, anti-American and anti-God" philosophy that pervades many goverment (public) classrooms
- To analyze the growth and impact of the evolution theory as "the state religion" in most government (public) classrooms and to discuss what can be done to end this violation of religious liberty
- To consider the terrible waste (in dollars and minds) involved in government (public) education
- To get to the root evil involved in government (public) education and to analyze the possible solutions to the problem.

1. In God's plan who has the responsibility for the education and training of the child? (pp 60-63 and Deut. 4:9-10; Prov. 4:1, 22:6; Eph. 6:4).
   a. Where should the basic education and training of the child take place? (p. 47)
   b. Is it proper to say that the school (state or private) should be an extension of parental authority? (pp. 60-61).
   c. What is the prevailing attitude of the State today in regard to the schools and the education of the child? How does Rev. Rousas J. Rushdoony trace the transfer from parent to state? (p. 60 and "So the Battleline Forms," pp. 63-64).
   d. What happens to moral standards (and values) when the State sets the levels? Discuss how "Gresham's Law" applies not only to money but to moral values (p. 62).

2. Frank Fox, president of a textbook publishing company, spelled out what he termed "the gut issue" regarding state schools. What is that issue? What must be the answer to the question he raised? (p. 67).

3. What is meant by "situational ethics"? How do such rubber yardsticks weaken values and undermine morality and blur—if not remove—the line between right and wrong? (pp. 66-69).
   a. Consider the situation faced by the parents in Kanawha County, W. Va., and other school districts (pp. 67-69). Are there similar problems in your area? Have you audited the materials used in your local schools?
   b. What can Christian parents (and taxpayers and citizens) do to cure such problems in their local schools? (p. 69).

4. Why can the evolution theory, as it is being taught in state schools, be considered a "form of worship"—a non-theistic religion? How does this

violate the First Amendment to the Constitution? (pp. 69-71).

a. What has your state done to provide that public school students are given the story of man's creation? (p. 71). Is creationism being at least given "equal time and emphasis"?

b. Why is it important to the humanist and those who hold to the pagan view of man and state that evolution be taught as fact and to the exclusion of creationism? (p. 71).

5. On pages 71 through 73, the author suggests that parents and taxpayers are becoming increasingly concerned about two forms of waste in state education. What are those two types of waste?

a. Is there an "accountability" in the way state (public) schools are run? If so, is that accountability as effective as the accountability of the free market (as in the private school, for example)? What is the direct relationship between monopoly and the lack of accountability? (pp. 72-73).

b. Describe and discuss the voucher plan and tax credits. Would the implementation of one or both of these proposals help break the state monopoly on education? Would they increase accountability? How would both introduce the dynamics of the free market (supply and demand) to the education system? (pp. 73-75).

c. Evaluate the economic sanctions imposed upon those who send their children to God-centered private schools. Is such a state-imposed double burden equitable? (pp. 75-76).

d. What are the dangers inherent in a statewide property tax to finance government (public) education? Could this evolve into complete federal financing and control of education? (pp. 76-77).

6. What, in the final analysis, is the root evil of state (public) education? (pp. 77-78).

a. What are the three prongs of aggressive coercion used to perpetuate the state (public) education establishment? Is such coercion defensible? (p. 78).

b. What about the added coercion of union control of education? Is that defensible, or acceptable? (p. 78).

7. The author suggests that the compulsory aspects of education should be ended, that the removal of such coercion whould improve the quality of education and solve many of the problems now forced upon society by the education "establishment." Do you agree? What do you think would happen if such compulsion were ended? (pp. 79-80).

a. Is state-controlled education any different (in essence and ultimate effect) from state-controlled religion? Can either be condoned? (pp. 78-79).

b. Can a physician who opposes state control of medicine—or a businessman who opposes state control of commerce—logically accept state control of education? On what basis? (p. 79).

Closing prayer by a member of the study group

SESSION EIGHT

STEWARDSHIP OR SOCIALISM?

Chapter Seven

Opening prayer by discussion leader

Purpose of this session:
- To define our role as God's stewards
- To analyze the two major economic systems in today's

world (the Christian idea and the pagan proposition)
- To consider some of the economic reforms that came through the spread and application of Christianity
- To compare the records of free enterprise (stewardship) with slavery (socialism)
- To discuss the destructive impact of economic restrictions such as the minimum wage.

1. Define Christian stewardship. What is the mark of a good steward? Where does the responsibility of stewardship rest (with the state or with the individual)? (p. 83).

a. What are some of God's promises regarding material blessings? Are these provisional? What is the test? (p. 83 and Deut. 28:2,3; Prov. 10:24; Phil. 4:19).

b. Is wealth necessarily evil? Is the love of wealth evil? Can wealth be used to do God's work (i.e., to serve God)? (p. 83).

c. Discuss the interdependence of Christian stewardship and Christian love (p. 83).

2. There are, basically, two different economic systems at work in the world. What are they?

a. Define and describe the workings of the Christian idea (free enterprise stewardship))p. 84). Why is the Christian ethic essential to the proper practice of free individual enterprise? (pp. 33-38).

b. Define and describe the workings of the Pagan idea (socialism). What did Archbishop Fulton J. Sheen say about socialism? (p. 84).

3. What economic reforms stemmed from the propagation and application of the Christian faith? List these and describe how they should be applied to our personal and group economic activities (pp. 84-85).

a. What is the "law of returns" and why is Christian love essential in completeing the cycle of productivity? (pp. 84-85; Luke 6:38; 1 Cor. 3:13).

4. Based on the record, which of the two systems—Christianity (stewardship) or Paganism (socialism)—comes closer to providing the greatest good for the greatest number (in terms of individual freedom and standard of living)? (pp. 85-94).

5. How does the minimum wage operate to exclude the unskilled and the young worker from the work force? (pp. 88-89).

a. Is this a violation of the civil rights of those excluded by this arbitrary wage floor? Is it a violation of the right of free contract between employer and employee? (p. 89).

6. Describe what the bounty of Christian stewardship has allowed this nation to do in terms of foreign aid. What might these resources have provided in terms of jobs and capital if we had not shared them with others? (pp. 89-90).

a. What had to be done before these blessings could be shared? (p. 90).

b. Has any other nation, or economic system, done so much? If not, why not? Who should get the credit and the praise?

7. What have been some of the results (fruits) of paganistic systems such as the one in the USSR? (pp. 92-93).

a. How did Archbishop Fulton J. Sheen explain the reasons for the failures of socialism? (pp. 92-93).

8. What is the internal threat to the survival of our freedom and free enterprise system? What are some of the manifestations of that threat? (pp. 93-94).

Closing prayer by a member of the study group

SESSION NINE

CONTROLLED PEOPLE AND UNCONTROLLED GOVERNMENT

Chapter Eight

Opening prayer by discussion leader

Purpose of this session:
- To understand the forces that have created this nationn's material wealth
- To examine the results when government costs and controls cease to be limited and restrict the energies and talents and tools of free individuals
- To consider the assertion that productivity is the key to man's material prosperity
- To emphasize the true measurement of national wealth and the Christian's responsibilities involved in personal material wealth

1. Who built (produced) the material wealth of this nation? (pp. 95-96).

a. "And God said to them, 'Be fruitful and multiply; fill the earth and subdue it'" (Gen. 1:28, 9::1-3). To whom did the Lord issue those instructions: to man, or to State?

b. Trace briefly the record of material achievement in this nation since the end of World War II. Relate that to individual well-being (pp. 95-96).

c. Has the tremendous growth in the size and cost of government helped or hindered America's productive capacity and output? (p. 96 and pp. 100-101).

2. What is the estimated cost of government-mandated paperwork each year? What is the estimated cost of this to the consumer? (pp. 96097).

a. Review briefly some of the costs and counter-productive effects of various government regulatory agencies.

b. Did government control contribute to the energy and fuel shortage? How? (pp. 96097).

c. Ask members of your study group to cite their own examples of wasteful bureaucratic controls at your state and local level.

d. What happens to (the rate of) employement when productivity increases? What happens when productivity declines? (pp. 97-98).

3. What should be the Christian's attidtude and role in regard to conservation and development of God's natural resources? (p. 99).

a. Discuss the proper balance between conservation and development and use of natural resources; cite some examples of extremism in the pursuit of "ecology" (p. 99).

4. It has been asserted that "productivity is the key to prosperity." Is this a valid assertion? (pp. 100-101).

a. What is meant by "productivity" (output per man-hour)?

b. What is the direct-line relationship between productivity and gross national product? (p. 101).

c. How can increased productivity help combat inflation? How can it help compete with foreign enterprise and production? (p. 101 and pp. 33-35).

d. Explain and discuss the "magical" formula MMW= NR+ HE x T.

e. What happens to productivity (and freedom) when the State owns and controls the tools of production? (p. 34 and p. 102).

5. Is "union monopoly" any different from any other form of monopoly?

a. Should unions be placed under

anti-trust laws similar to those now governing industry? (p. 103).

b. What is meant by "feather-bedding"? Do such make-work practices reduce productivity and increase costs and prices? How? (pp. 34-36 and pp. 102-103).

6. What is the real measure of a nation's wealth?

a. To the Christian, why is material wealth an added opportunity (and responsibility) to serve the Lord? (pp. 103-104 and 1 Chron. 29:14).

b. Individual productivity is an essential to individual charity (gifts of love). Why is this true? Can one give that which he or she has not produced or purchased through productivity? (pp. 33-36, "The Law of Productivity" and "The Law of Distribution").

Closing prayer by a member of the study group

SESSION TEN

THE GREATEST OF THESE IS LOVE!

Chapter Nine

(*Note to leader:* This is an extrememly important chapter. If possible, your group could take two separate sessions to cover it. If that is not possible, try to spend up to ninety minutes on this session.)

Opening prayer by discussion leader

Purpose of this session(s)
- To understand the true nature and role and responsibilities of Christian love
- To examine the glories of that love in action (Christ's love reflected through us) and to

contrast it with the demeaning and costly workings of Caesar's welfare apparatus
- To stress that the Christian life is not a "cop out" but, in fact, the most demanding life of all
- To realize the boundless blessings and opportunities that are possible to all through "joint ventures" with God in loving and helping others
- To make clear Christian responsibilities to help those in need because they cannot support themselves, as well as our responsibilities in regard to those who will not help themselves.

(*Note to leader:* Start this session by asking a member—or members in turn—to read aloud 1 Corinthians 13).

1. What are the qualities (the attributes of Christian love?*

a. The author asserts that love is an "action" word; that without works love is "dead." How was this love in action exemplified in the parable of the Good Samaritan? (pp. 105-106 and Luke 10:30-37).

b. What is Christ's commandment regarding love? What did Jesus tell us regarding our love for the Lord and our fellow man? (p. 105 and Matt. 22:37-40).

c. What is the difference between love in person and love by proxy?

2 Trace the devolution of charity (love in action) from the days of personal involvement and congregational action down to today's welfare leviathan. What caused this change? (p. 106).

a. As "social" (government) action

---

*The qualities of Christian love are patience, kindness, generosity, humility, courtesy, unselfishness, good-temper, sincerity and purity of purpose.

has pre-empted personal involvement how has God been denied and Caesar magnified? What, for example, happened in Hitler's Germany when the State took over charity? (pp. 107-108 and pp. 109-110).

3. How are God's boundless power and blessings made manifest through Christian love in action? (p. 108).

a. How did Jesus feed the multitudes? (Matt. 15:14-21) Is this same power and blessing available to Christians today? (p. 108).

b. Discuss the difference in the love manifested by the actions of a ministerial association in a large city and the giving of Dr. Veronica Maz (pp. 108-109).

c. What occurs when we permit (encourage) Caesar to do the job we, as Christians, should do? Why does this violate not only Exodus 20:3-6, 12, 15, and 17, but also Christ's teachings? (pp. 109-110 and see also Isaiah 30, selected verses).

4. Why is the term "socialist Christian" a contradiction in itself? (p. 203, footnote 8, chapter 9).

5. Is welfare a "right"? (pp. 112-113).

a. What did the Apostle Paul write about those who can, but will not, work? What did he write about the person who will not care for his own family? (p. 113 and 2 Thess. 3:10-12; 1 Tim. 5:8).

b. What is our Christian responsibility to those who cannot help themselves (as contrasted with those who will not)? (pp. 112-113).

c. How does the existing welfare leviathan demean both the "receiver" and the "giver"? (pp. 113-114).

d. What should Christians be doing in regard to Caesar's welfare apparatus? What are some of the things we can do as individuals and as congregations acting on behalf of our Lord and Master? (pp. 113-114).

6. The author suggests that if the Bible-based Christians in the United States had faith and prayed and worked and gave in the light and the love of the Lord we could change this nation. Do you believe this? Where should such faith and prayer and works begin? (pp. 114-116).

a. Discuss several examples of such living faith and the accomplishments of such "joint ventures" with God (pp. 117-118). Cite examples in your community or state.

b. Some suggest we could (and should) eradicate poverty in the world by stripping ourselves and tearing down the productive capacity of our nation. Is this the solution to the world's needs? What is? (p. 118).

c. What might be done to help the peoples in under-developed countries if we could harness the resources and wealth confiscated and wasted by our government year after year? (pp. 118-119 and pp. 96-97).

7. What should Christians be doing to transform this failing worldly system into a triumphant manifestation of our living God? (pp. 114-117 and 119).

Closing prayer by a member of the study group

SESSION ELEVEN

TAXES AND THE POWER TO DESTROY

Chapter ten

Opening prayer by discussion leader

Purpose of this session:

- To distinquish more clearly just what is Caesar's due and what belongs to God

- To review the soaring size and cost of government and its increasing burden on the productive man and woman during recent years
- To evaluate the inequities and weaknesses of the Social Security system and consider some reforms and alternatives
- To emphasize the manner in which the Internal Revenue Service can and does violate the individual's Constitutional rights and guarantees
- To consider various ways in which the basic tax structure can be reformed

1. The Apostle Paul advised Christians to "Render therefore to all their due: taxes to whom taxes are due." Why should Christians willingly pay a just tax to government? (p. 121 and Rom. 13:7; 1 Tim. 2:2; 1 Pet. 2:14).

a. What is Caesar's rightful due? For what services? (p. 119 and also "The Spender and the Taxers," pp. 130-131).

b. What belongs to God? (p. 119).

2. What is the cost of today's government? (p. 122).

— In billions of dollars?
— In terms of the percentage of total personal income?
— Per capita?
— Per producer?

a. Why is the term "business tax" misleading and politically motivated? (pp. 124, 126).

b. In 1973, what was the extent of the "lengthening shadow of government"? How many states did it cover? How many people? (p. 23). Why does the author also describe this situation as "A New Slavery"? (p. 133).

3. What was the original intent and design of Social Security when it was enacted in 1935? (p. 126). What was its inherent evil?

a. How have politicians destroyed the original design of Social Security? What are the resultant fiscal weaknesses and inequities as a result of their irresponsible actions? (pp. 126-128).

b. Why is Social Security a "rip-off" for the young man or woman who is forced to participate? Could they make better use of their retirement funds? (pp. 129-130).

c. What two basic reforms are essential if Social Security is to be made (a) compatible with the ideals of a society of free people and (b) financially sound? (p. 130).

4. Has the growth of government (costs and size) kept pace with the growth in population and gross national product? (p. 131).

a. What has the Grace Committee report recommended that would save the taxpayers more than $10 billion over a three-year period? (p. 132).

b. Advocates of the "new" economy claim that government spending is essential to prosperity. Why is this a false and ruinous proposition? Where does government get "its" money? What happens when it takes (taxes) that money? (pp. 132-133).

5. How does the Internal Revenue Service violate the citizen's rights as set forth in the U.S. Constitution? (pp. 133-135).

a. Who gave the IRS these powers? (p. 134).

b. What do your congressmen (representatives and senators) have to say about such tyranny?

6. Discuss—as time permits—the eleven-point proposal for tax reform set forth in this cahpter. If you have the time, go over each point and discuss (pp. 137-139).

Closing prayer by a member of the study group

SESSION TWELVE

INFLATION IS A SNEAK THIEF!

Chapter Eleven

Opening prayer by discussion leader

Purpose of this session:
- To gain a clear understanding of the root cause of inflation
- To comprehend the vital distinction between "money" and "wealth"
- To analyze how the manipulation of money and credit has destroyed the value of our currency and increased government control over the citizen
- To consider some of the moral and social—as well as fiscal—evils of inflation
- To trace the rise of inflation in America, to identify its principle perpetrators and the ruses used, so that we can forestall them in the future
- To discuss what must be done to halt inflation before it "halts" America

1. What is inflation? (p. 142).

a. What is the root cause of inflation? (p. 142 and "Legalized Counterfeiting," p. 143).

b. What are some of the consequences of inflation (economic, moral and social)? (pp. 141-142, and "Those Who Knew," pp. 150-151).

c. What do the Scriptures say about debauching money (inflation)? What will God do if the people do not end this sin? (p. 153 and Isa. 1:25; Ezek. 22:21-22).

2. What is money? (pp. 142-143).

a. What is "wealth"? (pp. 142-143).

b. Trace the genesis and evolution of money. How did fiat (paper) money open the floodgates of inflation? (pp. 143-144).

c. How has the general confusion of "money" with "wealth" abetted the introduction and spread of inflation? (pp. 142-143).

d. Give the group the "quickie quiz" on page 144. Then stress the root cause of inflation (government monetary policies) and the consequences (loss of puchasing power, decline in value of currency, higher prices, lower quality, etc.).

3. What are the two principle ways in which government cause inflation? (p. 145).

a. What is the effect on "good" money when government prints "fake" (fiat) money? What does this do to your purchasing power? (p. 145).

b. How do the credit policies (manipulations) of the federal government (through the Federal Reserve and acts of Congress) also cause inflation? (p. 145).

4. Is inflation a tax? Why? (pp. 148-149).

a. Why do so many politicians favor the tax of inflation rather than direct (or open) taxation? (pp. 149-150).

b. Many try to place the blame for inflation on "business" or "labor." What would occur if there were a rise in prices or wages without an increase in the supply of money and/or credit? (p. 152).

c. Why is the cure for inflation difficult but easier in the long run than letting the disease run its course? What is the prognosis for unchecked inflation? (pp. 152-153).

5. How can we halt inflation? Is more inflation the answer? (p. 153).

a. What is the first step we must take? (pp. 153-154).

b. Is something like the proposed ten-year plan to reduce Caesar's spending power practical? What must we do to invoke such a plan? (pp. 154-155).

c. What is the second thing we must do to stop inflation? (pp. 155-156).

d. And, what is next? Why is it important to accomplish steps one and two (fiscal control and stability) before restoring the gold standard? (pp. 153 and 156-158).

6. How would the gold standard enforce "monetary discipline"? Why is that essential if we are to prevent inflation in the future? (pp. 156-158).

7. The author suggests a five-step program for halting inflation. Where does the responsibility for instituting such a program begin? What are the first steps toward achieving such a reform? (pp. 158-159).

a. Ask a member of the study group to read aloud Isaiah 1:25.

b. Ask another member of the study group to read Ezekiel 2: 21-22.

Closing prayer by a member of the study group

SESSION THIRTEEN

THESE ARE THE PEACEMAKERS

Chapter Twelve

Opening prayer by discussion leader

Purpose of this session:
- To assess the combined ravages of the "new" morality, the "new" politics, and the "new" justice on today's society
- To reaffirm the propriety and purpose of imprisonment and capital punishment
- To understand the root (basic and unyeilding) conflict between Christianity and Communism
- To underscore the need for a strong defense and vigilance as prerequisites for national security
- To contrast the difference between a "peacemaker" and a "pacifist"
- To analyze the foundation and the record of the United Nations and to consider God's Word regarding "one world"

1. What is the first and foremost function of government? (p. 161 and Rom. 13:3).

a. When Caesar gets involved in affairs that are not his proper or legitimate function, what happens? (p. 267 and "Limited Government," pp. 41,42).

2. What is happening in our society as a result of the pursuit and application of the "new" morality, the "new" politics and the "new" justice? (pp. 163, 164).

a. What is the situation regarding crime and punishment in your state (community)? What can Christians do to help "keep the peace"? (pp. 164-165).

3. What is the purpose of capital punishment? (pp. 165-166).

a. What do the Scriptures say about the purpose and use of the death penalty? (pp. 165-166; Deut. 19:4-6, 11-13, 19-21).

4. What is the biblical approach to prison reform? (pp. 166, 167).

a. What type of "prison reform" is badly needed in many institutions? (p. 166).

b. What is our Christian duty regarding those in prison? (p. 167). What teachings and examples do we find in this regard? (Matt. 25:36-44; 1 Pet. 3:19).

5. Is there a parallel (a com-

monality) between those who would coddle the criminal here at home and those who would appease (bow down to) our enemies abroad? ("First Things First," p. 161 and pp. 167, 168).

a. Is there a distinction between aggressive force and defensive force? Which is improper and which is essential? (pp. 168, 169).

b. Distinguish between a "peacemaker" and a "pacifist" (pp. 167-168).

c. Can a Christian be a pacifist?

6. What is the root conflict between Christianity and Communism? (pp. 170, 171).

a. Nikita Khrushchev once boasted, "We will bury you." Has there been any change in the Communists' goal? How must we judge the Communists—by their words, or by their deeds? (p. 171).

b. What has Aleksandr Solzhenitsyn said about Communism and its goals? What has he warned us about "detente"? (p. 171).

c. Briefly review what has happened to the comparative military posture of the U.S.A. and the USSR during the past few years. What must be done to restore our national security? (pp. 173-176).

d. What is S.D.I. ("Star Shield")? What is MAD? Does the U.S.A. now have any defense against ballistic missiles? (pp. 177-178).

7. What is God's promise and prophecy concerning one world at peace? (p. 178 and Mic. 4:14).

a. Is the United Nations "God's instrument" or is it today's "Tower of Babel"? Why? (pp. 178-179 and p. 180).

8. What does it mean to be God's "strategic agents" in today's world? What is the nature of "the Christian revolution"? (p. 181).

9. What choice faces America and Americans? Where does that coice begin? (p. 183 and Josh. 24:14a).

a. What choice must we make, whom shall we serve, if America is to survive and be restored as "One Nation Under God"? (p. 183 and Josh. 24:15 b. See also 2 Chron. 7:14).

Closing prayer:
Since this is the final session in this series, it is recommended that each member of the study group join in offering a prayer of praise and thanksgiving—asking God's guidance and blessing in the restoration of your nation.

NOTES

Chapter 1

1. New England "Articles of Confederation," 1643.

2. Governor William Bradford, *Of Plymouth Plantation*, 1647 (Wright and Potter Printing Co., 1901). See *The Christian History of The Constitution of The United States,* vol. 1 (San Francisco: Foundation for American Christian Education, 1966), 213.

3. Ibid.

4. Ibid.

5. As cited By C. Gregg Singer, *A theological Interpretation of American History* (Philadelphia: Presbyterian and Reformed Publishing Co., 1964),18.

6. Ibid., 19

7. Verna M. Hall, *The Christian History of The Constitution of The United States,* vol. 1(San Francisco: Foundation for American Christian Education, 1966) iii.

8. Felix Morley, *The Power in The People* (New York: D. Van Nostrand Company, 1949), 41.

9. Harry F. Atwood, *Back to the Republic* (Chicago: Laird and Lee, 1918), 28,29.

10. Ibid., 37.

11. Ibid.

12. As cited in Frederick Nyneyer, *First Principles in Morality and Economics: Neighborly Love land Ricardo's Law of Association* (South Holland, Ill.: Libertarian Press, 1958), 31.

13. R.J. Rushdoony, *The Nature of The American System* (Nutley, N.J.: The Craig Press, 1964), 2,3.

14. J.A. Partridge, *The Making of the American Nation* (1866).

15. July 4th, 1821, Fourth of July oration.

16. Felix Morley, 47.

17. John Locke, *"The Reasonableness of Christianity,"* 1695 *(The Works of John Locke, Esq.,* John Churchill, 3 vols., 1714). See *The Christian History of The Constitution of the United States,* vol. 1, *op cit,* 56.

18. Daniel Webster, *The Works of Daniel Webster,* vol. 1 (Little, Brown and Co., 1851). See *The Christian History of The Constitution of The United States,* vol.1, 245.

19. Honorable Charles Malik, Ambassador to the UN from lebanon. Farewell address to the United States upon retiring from the UN.

20. Derek Prince, *Shaping History Through Prayer and Fasting,* (Old Tappan, N.J.: Fleming H. Revell, 1973), 42.

21. Edwin Hall's *The Puritans and Their Principles* (Baker and Scribner, 1846). See *The Christian History of The Constitution of The United States,* 27.

22. Leonard Bacon, *Genesis of The New England Churches,* (New York: Harper and Brothers, 1874).

23. Edwin Hall.

24. Noah Webster, *The American*

Dictionary of The English Language (New York: S. Converse, 1828); facsimile edition by Foundation for American Christian Education, San Francisco.

25. Daniel Neal, *The History of The Puritans,* 2 vols. (New York: Harper and Brothers, 1844).

26. Ibid.

27. George Bancroft, *History of The United States,* 10 vols. (Boston: Little, Brown and Co., 1866). See *The Christian History of The Constitution,* vol.1.

28. Richard Frothingham, *The Rise of The Republic of The United States* (Boston: Little, Brown and Co., 1890). See *The Christian History of The Constitution of The United States,* vols 1,2.

29. Ibid.

30. Rosalie J. Slater, *Teaching and Learning America's Christian History* (San Francisco: Foundation for American Christian Education, 1973), 187.

31. Ibid.

Chapter 2

1. As cited in Frederick Nyneyer, *First Principles in Morality and Economics; Neighborly Love and Riicardo's Law of Association* (South Holland, Ill.: Libertarian Press, 1958), 31.

2. James Madison, Federalist Papers.

3. Dr. Nicholas Murray Butler, *Why Should We Change Our Form of Government?*

4. Platform of the Democratic Party adopted in convention, 1932.

5. Garet Garrett, *The People's Pottage* (Caldwell, Idaho: Caxton Printers, 1953), 18.

6. Ibid., 22.

7. "Balanced-Budget Amendment Loses by 1 in Senate," *Human Events,* April 5, 1986, 5,6.

8. John Rees, "Interview with J. Peter Grace," *The Review of the NEWS,* May 30, 1984, 42.

9. Ibid.

10. R.J. Rushdoony, *The Nautre of The American System* (Nutley, N.J.: Craig Press, 1965), 9.

11. Ibid.

12. Jeffrey Hart, "A Revolutionary Idea: (The Money You Earn Is Yours)," *Manchester Union Leader,* April 25, 1986.

13. As reported in "Quotelines," *USA Today,* April 18, 1986, 12A.

14. "Balanced-Budget Amendment Loses by 1 in Senate," *Human Events,* April 5, 1986, 6.

15. "Balanced-Budget Amendment Goes To Full Senate," UPI, March 6, 1986.

16. "We Can Blow The Whistle On Government Waste!" bookelt by *Citizen's Against Waste,* October 1984; "The Tip of The Iceberg," *Baxter Economic Service,* April 1986.

17. H.E. Soderling, *National Observer,* September 1974.

18. "Cut Billions From Federal Pensions?" *U.S. News and World Report,* Jan. 16, 1984, 11; Martin Lefkowitz, "Federal Employees Are Paid Too Much," *Human Events,* March 24, 1984,9.

19. Dean Alfange, "My Creed" *This Week,* 1954.

20. Ivan R. Bierly, Ph D., in a privately circulated memorandum to the Board of Trustees, William Volker Fund, Burlingame, California, 1962.

21. Verna M. Hall, *The Christian History of The Constitution of The United States* (San Francisco: Foundation for American Christian Education, 1966), iii.

22. Whittaker Chambers, *Witness* (New York: Random House, 1952), 17.

Chapter 3

1. Justice Leonard Hand

2. F.A. Hayek, *The Constitution of Liberty* (Chicago: University of Chicago Press, 1960), 17.

3. Leonard C. Read, *Accent On The Right* (Irvington-on-Hudson, Foundation for Economic Education, 1968).

4. Thomas Wolfe.

5. Leonard C. Read, *Deeper Than You Think* (Irvington-on-Hudson, Foundation for Economic Education, 1967),16.

6. Felix Morley, *The Christian History of The Constitution of The United States* (San Francisco: Foundation for American Christian Education, 1960),ix.

7. Verna M. Hall, *The Christian History of The Constitution of The United States* (San Francisco: Foundation for American Christian Education. 1960), iii.

8. Noah Webster, *An American Dictionary of The English Language* (New York: S. Converse, 1828). Facsimile edition published by Foundation for American Christian Education, 1967.

9. Rosalie J. Slater, *Teaching and Learning America's Christian History* (San Francisco: Foundation for American Christian Education, 1965), 61.

10. Frederic Bastiat, *The Law* (Santa Ana, Calif.: Register Publishing Co.), from *Harmonies of Political Economy,* vol. 2, 215-217, translated from the original French by Dean Russell, 1945 (Foundation for Economic Education, 1950), 24.

11. F.A. Harper, *Liberty: A Path To Its Recovery* (Irvington-on-Hudson, Foundation for Economic Education, 1949),27.

Chapter 4

1. The very finest definition of the full spectrum of love in all its dimensions and properties is found in 1 Corinthians 13:1-13. An excellent dissertation on that passage of Scripture is Henry Drummond's little essay, *The Greatest Thing in the World.*

2. It is not a matter of being lowbrow, or anti-art, or anti-music; it is a matter of being for the right of each individual to decide to support such cultural activities. Let those who love the arts support the arts to the extent they wish; let those who feel otherwise be free to support their personal pleasures—whether they be bowling or basket-weaving or doing nothing at all.

3. F.A. Harper, *Liberty: A Path To Its Recovery* (Irvington-on-Hudson, Foundation for Economic Freedom, 1949), 147.

4. R.J. Rushdoony, *The Nature of The American System* (Nutley, N.J.: Craig Press, 1965),8.

5. The Constitution of These United States, Article X.

6. In his book *A Worthy Company,* Dr. M.E. Bradford demonstrated conclusively that fifty, and perhaps fifty-two, of the fifty-five framers of the Constitution were practicing Christians.

7. Frederic Bastiat, *The Law* (Irvington-on-Hudson, Foundation for Economic Education, 1950),6.

8. Leonard Read, *Meditations on Freedom* (Irvington-on-Hudson, Foundation for Economic Freedom, 1971), 27.

9. Ludwig Von Mises, *In Brief: The Individual In Society* (pamphlet, Foundation for Economic Education, 1952),8.

10. F.A. Harper, 104.

11. Frederic Bastiat, 73-75.

Chapter 5

1. Rosalie J. Slater, *Teaching and Learning America's Christian History* (San Francisco: Foundation for American Christian Education, 1973), 3.

2. From the Heavenly Father to the earthly father, the head of the household, and from him to the wife and mother and thence to the children, ranked by gender and age.

3. Rev. S. Phillips, as quoted by Rosalie J. Slater, 10.

4. Ibid., 10.

5. Ibid., 11.

6. Rev. R.J. Rushdoony, "The Place of Women," *Position Paper No. 47* (Vellecito, Calif.: Chalcedon, 1986),1.

7. Ibid.

8. Earle E. Cairns, *The Christian in Society* (Chicago: Moody Press, 1973), 156,157.

9. Jose Ortega y Gassett, *The Revolt of The Masses* (New York: W.W. Norton, 1957), 11.

10. Rev. S. Phillips, 17.

11. Dr. Thomas Johnson, "Abortion: A Metaphysical Approach," *The Freeman,* August 1972, 498-505.

12. Dr. Bernard Nathanson, "Abortion Pioneer Now a Top Pro-Life Advocate," *Human Events,* May 7, 1983, 13, 14.

13. Dr. Thomas Johnson.

14. Author's interview with James F. Kappus, American Life Lobby, April 1986.

15. Regarding that 1973 Supreme Court decision, Dr. Nathanson comments: "Some of the key premises are now so outdated, now so anachronistic that the decision itself has been rendered an anachronism... The times, the new data, the new perceptions, and the new science cry out for a change in that decision." On January 22, 1986, 1,100 physicians and surgeons signed their names to a full-page, "1100 M.D.'s Say Human Life Began at Conception," ad in the *St. Louis Post Dispatch* declaring "All medical facts indicate human life begins at conception." And, on June 15, 1983, U.S. Supreme Court Justice Sandra Day O'Connor warned, "The Roe (v. Wade) framework...is clearly on a collision course with itself...it has no justification in law or logic."

16. Jeffrey Hart, *Manchester Union Leader,* August 4, 1984, 14.

17. Dr. Olga Fairfax, "1,001 Uses for a Dead (or Alive) Baby," *A.L.L. About Issues,* American Life Lobby, January 1984.

18. Ibid.

19. Robert Pear, "New, Unashamed Attitude for Women With Abortions," *Washington Star,* April 7, 1975, 1a.

20. Author's interview with James Kappus, American Life Lobby, April 1986.

21. *National Right To Life News,* August 2, 1984, 13.

22. As quoted in *Grace Newsletter,* Tulsa, Okla., April 1986,4.

23. Ibid.

24. M. Stanton Evans, "Social Security: The Continuing Crisis," *Human Events,* April 13, 1985,9.

25. James E. Force, "Abortion, Ignorance & Apathy," *His Church & State,* vol. 2, No.2,1.

26. Dr. Olga Fairfax, *op cit.*

27. Dr. Thomas Johnson, *op cit.*

28. "Women's Liberation, Notes from the Second Year," as quoted in "To Manipulate A Woman," *Concerned Women for America,* Washington, D.C., 1986.

29. Ibid. as quoted from "The Document, Declaration of Feminism."

30. Ibid. as quoted from Los Angeles Times, Part 1, 3, 19-20.

31. Ibid. as quoted from *Saturday Review of Literature,* March 1973.

32. Michael P. Farris, "A Constitutional Lawyer Examines The ERA," *Concerned Women for America,* Washington, D.C., 3.

33. Ibid., 5; also, "Massage Parlors, Laspino v. Rizzo" (1977), as cited in "The Facts About Existing State ERA Laws," *Concerned Women for American Education & Legal Defense Foundation,* Washington, D.C., 1986.

34. Senator Orrin G. Hatch, *The Equal Rights Amendment,* (Washington, D.C.: Savant Press, 1983).

35. James J. Kilpatrick, "The ERA's Hidden Impact," *Universal Press Syndicate,* June 8, 1983.

36. Ibid.

37. Ibid.

38. Phyllis Schlafly, *Alert,* National Christian Action Coalition, as cited in *Foundations Digest,* Rochester, Minn., March-April 1984,4.

39. Douglas Johnson, "State ERA Invalidates Abortion Funding Law," *National Right to Life News,* March 22, 1984,1.

Chapter 6

1. Reverend R. J. Rusdoony, *The Messianic Character of American Education* (Vallecito, Calif.: Ross House Books, 1972), 322.

2. William B. Ball, Esq., as quoted in "On the Mandate for Christian Education," *Letter from Plymouth Rock,* Plymouth Rock Foundation, May 1986,3.

3. Dr. W. David Gamble, "Is Public Education Necessary?" *Letter from Plymouth Rock,* 3.

4.Verna M. Hall, *The Christian History of The Constitution of The United States* (San Francisco: Foundation for American Christian Education, 1966), 240b.

5. Robert A. Peterson, "Education in Colonial America," 1979.

6. Ibid.

7. Rev. R.J. Rushdoony, "The Place of Women" *Position Paper No 47,* Vallecito, Calif.: Chalcedon, 1986.

8. Samuel L. Blumenfeld, *Is Public Education Necessary?* (Boise, Idaho: The Paradigm Company, 1985).

9. Gamble, *op cit,* 4.

10. William B. Ball, "On the Mandate."

11. John Adams, in a letter to his wife, 1775.

12. Reverend Billy Graham, *California Assembly Daily Journal,* July 6, 1971, 64, 68.

13. "Religion in American Public Life," *Brookings Institute,* Washington, D.C., 1986.

14. Ronald Schiller, "How Religious Are We?" *Reader's Digest/Gallup Survey,* May 1986, 102-104.

15. "Textbooks Ignore Religion: New Study," *The Pathway News,* March 1986,11.

16. James Kilpatrick, "Textbook Publishers Keep God Out Of The Classroom," *Universal Press Syndicate,* as reprinted in *Home School Journal,* April 1986,9.

17. Ibid.

18. William Bole, "History Texts Ignore Religious Liberty Tradition, Group Says," *Religious News Service,* April 18, 1986.

19. Haven Bradford Gow, "Education Young People For The Responsibilities Of Freedom," *American Sunbeam,* Jan. 13, 1986,3.

20. Dr. Robert Simonds, president, *National Association of Christian Educators,* Costa Mesa, Calif., a letter, May 1986.

21. Rev. R.J. Rushdoony, *The Messianic Character of American Education* (Vallecito, Calif.: Ross House Books, 1972),323.

22. Michael J. McHugh, "We Hold

These Truths To Be Self-Evident?" *Christian Liberty Academy,* 1986, 2,3.

23. William Jasper, "Showdown in Santa Monica," *The New American,* March 10, 1986, as reprinted in *The Forerunner,* March 1986, 7-9.

24. Ibid.

25. Pastor Ron Norris, press release, Feb. 1986.

26. Ibid.

27. Gene Ragle, *Star Free Press,* May 21, 1986.

28. Jose Ortega y Gasset, *The Revolt of The Masses* (New York: W. W. Norton, 1957), 23.

29. John Matthew, *Washington Star News,* Nov. 18, 1974.

30. Ibid.

31. Jenkins Lloyd Jones, "This Is Literature?" *Washington Star News,* Feb 15, 1975.

32. Ibid.

33. Ibid.

34. Barbara Morris, *Change Agents In The Schools* (Upland, Calif.: Barbara Morris Reports).

35. As quoted in *A Psychiatrist Looks At Sex Education,* Up With Families, Clovis, Calif., 1981.

36. Gordon Gaylord Simpson, as quoted in the *Oroville Mercury,* Dec. 18, 1972.

37. "Creation/Evolution Rift May Go To Supreme Court," *The Rutherford Institute,* Jan/Feb. 1986, 14.

38. Henry M. Morris, "Introducing Creationism Into The Public Schools," *Institute For Creation Research,* Impact Series #20.

39. Ibid.

40. Dr. D. L. Cuddy, "Scientific Evidence Exists Both for and against Evolution," *St. Louis Globe Democrat,* May 27, 1986, as reprinted in *The Christian News,* June 2, 1986, 13.

41. Dr. Pierre P. Grasse, as quoted in "Why Science Questions Darwin,"

Paul Kroll, *The Plain Truth,* May 1986, 20.

42. David Raup, as quoted in "Why Science Questions Darwin," *op cit.*

43. Henry M. Morris, "Introducing Creationism Into The Public Schools," *Institute for Creation Research,* Preface.

44. "School Expenditures By Type of Control and Level of Instruction, 1960-1986," *Statistical Abstract of The United States,* 1986, 128.

45. Ibid., 128.

46. Ibid., "Public Elementary and Secondary School, Number and Average Salary of Classroom Teachers, 1960-1985," 139.

47. "Public and Private Elementary and Secondary School Enrollments," Facts and Figures on Government Finance, 1986, Tax Foundation, F31.

48. As quoted in *The Capsule,* Cameron, Mo., May 1984.

49. Ibid.

50. Ibid.

51. "A Nation At Risk: The Imperative for Education Reform," *The National Commission on Excellence in Education,* April 1983, 5.

52. "Tuition Tax Credits," *Conservative Digest,* July 1983,12.

53. Barbara M. Morris, *Tuition Tax Credits, A Responsible Appraisal* (Upland, Calif.: The Barbara M. Morris Report, 1983).

54. Thoman A. Shannon, *School Board News,* July 1981, as quoted in "Tuition Tax Credits, A Responsible Appraisal,: op cit, 26.

55. Leonard Read, *Government, An Ideal Concept* (Irvington, N.Y.: Foundation for Economic Education, 1948), 116.

56. A.A. Hodge, *Popular Lectures on Theological Themes,* as quoted by R.J. Rushdoony in *The Messianic Character of American Education* (Vallecito, Calif., Chalcedon, 1972), 335.

57. Leonard Read, *op cit,* 115.

58. R.J. Rushdoony, *The Nature of The American System* (Nutley, N.J.: Craig Press, 1964), 21.

59. Samuel L. Blumenfeld, NEA: *Trojan Horse in American Education* (Boise, Idaho: The Paradigm Company, 1985), 262.

60. *Hayward Daily Review,* Aug. 27, 1973.

61. Leonard Read, *op cit,* 114.

Chapter 7

1. Archbishop Fulton J. Sheen, *New York Journal American,* May 7, 1961.

2. Fred G. Clark and Richard Rimanoczy, "Christianity and Capitalism," *Bulletin,* July-August 1952.

3. F.J. Sheen, *op cit.*

4. It would not be far off the mark to suggest that the root of this nation's economic woes, and the precarious state of its financial structure, can be directly traced to the rejection of God's sovereignty and the violation of His laws and turning away from biblical principles.

5. "Comparative International Studies," *Statistical Abstract of The United States,* 1986; "World Population and Area," 837; "Gross National Product of Nations," 1975-1983, 842.

6. Ibid.

7. Ibid., "World Motor Vehicle Registration," 844; "Communications," 845.

8. Ibid., "Average Poverty Levels...," 430.

9. Ibid., "Percent of Population with...4 Years of High School and More...," 135.

10. Ibid., "High School and College Graduates, 1950 to 1983," 149.

11. Ibid., "Median Money Income of Families...," 453.

12. "Facts and Figures on Government Finance, 1986," Tax Foundation, Washington, D.C. 11c, 8d.

13. Warren Brooks, "Urban Institue Study Debunks Harvard's Hunger-Hype," *Manchester Union Leader,* February 1986.

14. "Cash and Non-cash Benefits..." *Statistical Abstract of The U.S.* 1986, 357.

15. Ibid., "Governmental Employment and Payrolls By Level of Government...," 284.

16. David Whitman and Jeannye Thornton, "A Nation Apart," *U.S. News and World Report,* March 17, 1986, 18-21.

17. Ibid.

18. John Chamberlain, "Moyer's Great Documentary," *Manchester Union Leader,* March 16, 1986.

19. Luix Overbea, "Conservative Professor Challenges Fellow Blacks on Power Concepts, Moral Values," *Christian Science Monitor,* February 7, 1986, 1, 36.

20. Ibid.

21. John Chamberlain, op cit.

22. Whitman and Thornton, "A Nation Apart," *op cit.*

23. Ibid.

24. Ibid.

25. "Employed Persons by Sex, Race and Occupation," *Statistical Abstract of The U.S.* 1986, 402-403.

26. Ibid.

27. Ibid.

28. Whitman and Thornton, "A Nation Apart," *op cit.*

29. "Employed Persons by Sex, Race and Occupation," *Statistical Abstract of The U.S.,* 1986, 402-403.

30. Ibid.

31. Walter E. Williams, *The State Against Blacks* (New York: McGraw-Hill Book Company, 1982), 35.

32. Prof. Jacob Mincer, as quoted

by Walter E. Williams in *The State Against Blacks,* 35.

33. Henry Hazlitt, "The Story of Negro Gains," *The Freeman,* Nov. 1971, 697.

34. John F. McManus, "Stop Financing Communism," *Tax Reform Immediately,* March 1983, 5.

35. Honorable John Gorton, as quoted in "The Good Things About the U.S.A. Today," *U.S. News and World Report,* Sept. 2, 1968.

36. Frederic Dewhurst, as quoted by Lawrence Fertig, in *Prosperity Through Freedom* (Chicago: Henry Regnery Company, 1961), 12.

37. "Comparative International Studies," *Statistical Abstract of The U.S.,* 1986, 8390845.

38. Ibid.

39. Ibid.

40. Charles Horton, "The Failure of Socialism," as reprinted by *Christian Anti-Communism Crusade,* July 15, 1985, 1.

41. Earl Nightingale, "The Old Story," *Our Changing World.*

42. R.E. McMaster, Jr., "The USSR: Made By USA, Inc." *The Reaper,* April 24, 1986,4.

43. Nightingale, *op cit.*

44. Mc Master, *op cit,* 2.

45. "Making Covenants With God's Enemies," *Biblical Principles of Government,* (Plymouth, Mass.: Plymouth Rock Foundation, 1984), 154.

46. Senator William Armstrong, remarks in U.S. Senate, April 1982.

47. Richard M. Nixon, *Real Peace* (Boston: Little, Brown and Company, 1984),11.

48. McMaster, *op cit,* 6.

49. Ibid.

50. Archbishop Fulton J. Sheen, *op cit.*

51. Carl A. Keyser, "Freedom's Bounty," *The Freeman,* Sept. 1974, 563.

Chapter 8
1. "Alternate Measures of... Product," *Facts and Figures on Government Finance,* 1986, Tax Foundation, Washington, D.C., 10b.

2. "Median Money Income of Families..." *Statistical Abstract of The United States,* 1986, U.S. Department of Commerce, 453; "Facts and Figures on Government Finance," *op cit,* 156.

3. "Disposable Income In Current Dollars," Tax Foundation, *op cit,* 14b.

4. Ibid.

5. "Capital Investment Per Production Worder in Manufacturing," Tax Foundation, *op cit,* 30b; "Savings and Investment of Corporate Business," 46b.

6. Ibid., "Federal Finance and Gross National Product," 7c.

7. Ibid., "Government Employees by Level of Government and Major Category," 221.

8. Ibid., "Gross Debt of Federal, State and Local Governments," 20a.

9. Ibid.

10. Donald Lambro, *Fat City: How Washington Wastes Your Taxes* (South Bend, Ind.: Regnery/Gateway, 1980),87.

11. Economic Report of the President, 1974, 324.

12. Lambro, op cit, iv.

13. *Human Events,* as cited in *National Review,* June 6, 1986, 16.

14. Charles H. Smith Jr., "The Future Price of Neglect," *Vital Speeches of The Day,* October 1974.

15. "Parathion More Deadly Than DDT It Replaced," *San Rafael Independent Journal,* September 27, 1972.

16. Richard Sennett, "The Hidden Injuries of Class," *Time,* Nov. 4, 1974,102.

17. "The United States Budget in Brief, Fiscal Year 1987," *Office of Management and Budget,* 11.

18. "Unit Labor Costs and Productivity in Manufacturing in Selected Countries," Tax Foundation, *op cit,* 28b.

19. Ibid.

20. Dean, Boissevan and Thomas, "Productivity and Labor Cost Trends in Manufacturing, 12 Countries," U.S. Dept. of Labor, *Monthly Labor Review,* March 1986, 807.

24. Lawrence Fertig, *op cit,* 46.

25. Ibid.

26. Bureau of Labor Statistics, U.S. Dept. of Labor, as cited by National Institute for Labor Relations Research, 1986,

27. Ibid.

Chapter 9

1. R.J. Rushdoony, *Revolt Against Maturity* (Berkeley, Calif.: Ross House Books, 1977), 216-222.

2. Ibid., 221.

3. Milton Mayer, *What Can a Man Do?* (Chicago: University of Chicago Press, 1964), 39,40.

4. Russell J. Clinchy, "Charity, Biblical and Political," (Foundation for Economic Education, 1964), 12.

5. Ibid., 10.

6. Dr. Alfred J. Haake, "Is Private Enterprise Compatible with Christianity?" speech before the Economic Club of Detroit, 1950.

7. Ibid.

8. Is not the term Socialist Christian in itself a contradiction of both fact and purpose? Can a socialist be a Christian? How? The socialist puts the state above God. Socialism is paganism, a form of Moloch worship.

9. Reverend Reinhold Niebuhr, addressing the Fellowship of Socialist Christians.

10. Reverend Edmund Opitz, speech before the mine Farm Bureau, Portland, Maine, Novermber 16, 1959.

11. Ibid.

12. Ibid.

13. Mrs. Cindy Rocker, "The Kingsburg, California, Community Assistance Program," *Chalcedon,* May 1986.

14. Leonard Read, "If Government Doesn't Relieve Distress, Who Will?" *Cliches of Socialism* (Foundation for Economic Freedom, 1954).

15. "Public Aid Recipients...," Statistical Abstract of the U.S., 1986,380.

16. "Public Assistance Payments," *Facts and Figures on Government Finance,* 1986, Tax Foundation, Inc., Washinton, D.C., 50. Assistance for the elderly, aid to the blind and permanently and totally disabled, Aid to Families with Dependent Children, general assistance. Does not include some food, housing, or medical benefits.

17. "Social Welfare Expenditures..." Statistical Abstract of the U.S. 1986, 354-356.

18. "State and Local Employment..." Statistical Abstract of the U.S., 1986, 296; "Paid Civilian Employment, Federal Government," 325.

19. Steve Huntley, "Charity's Life in the Fast Lane," *U.S. News and World Report,* June 2, 1986, 16,17; "Aid To Families With Dependent Children," Statistical Abstract of the U.S., 1986, 382.

20. "Public Aid Recipients, AFDC," Statistical Abstract of the U.S., 1986, 380.

21. Statistical Abstract of the U.S., 1986.

22. Henry Hazlitt, "Welfarism Gone Wild," The Freeman, May 1972, 267.

23. Brian Summers, "Charity and the Welfare State," *The Freeman,* December 1971, 712.

24. Morris C. Shumiatcher, "Welfare Fifty Years Hence," *The Freeman,* March 1974,174.

25. Steve Huntley, "Charity's Life in the Fast Lane," 16,17.

26. "Private Philanthropy Funds," Statistical Abstract of the U.S. 1986, 385.

27. Ibid., "Percent Adult Population Doing Volunteer Work," 383.

28. James Underwood, letter, Christian Fiancial Services, 1974.

Chapter 10

1. The *first* (fruits) tithe (10 percent) is not on our capital but on our income, or increase (Exod. 34:30; Num. 3:13, 44-51; 8:18). When the *second* (rejoicing) tithe (Deut. 14:22-27) and the *third* (poor) tithe (Deut. 14:28,29) are added, the average annual tithe is about 16 percent. (Reverend R.J. Rushdoony, *Tithing and Dominion,* Ross House Books.)

2. "Sources of Government Receipts in Relation to National Income and Product,: *Facts and Figures on Government Finance,* 1986, Tax Foundation, 13b.

3. "Federal, State and Local Expenditures," *op cit,* 11a.

4. "Balanced-Budget Amendment Loses by 1 in Senate," Human Events, April 5, 1986,5.

5. John Rees, "Peter Grace: An Interview," *The Review of The News,* May 30, 1984, 39-52.

6. "Federal, State and Local Tax Receipts," Tax Foundation, *op cit,* 16a.

7. Ibid.

8. Ibid.

9. "Tax and Spending Quiz," *Tax Limitation News,* National Tax Limitation Committee, Spring 1986, 8. Answers to "quickie quiz: (1)D. The average private wage in 1983 was $19,273; the average federal wage was $25,357—31% higher. (2) About three million (this does not count the some 13 million employed by state and local governments or the thousands of consultants employed by private firms but paid by federal tax dollars). (3) B. Every decade since the 1940s (4) C. From 1970 to 1980, the Consumer Price Index rose 224%. A 1970 dollar was worth 47 cents in 1980. (5) C. The 70s. (6) C. One dollar in 1967 was worth 32 cents in 1984. (7) D. One dollar in 1980 was worth 78 cents four years later. (8) A. California collected $43.7 billion in state revenues in 1983. In 1960, all 50 states took in total receipts of $32.8 billion. (9) D. Total state tax revenues in 1950 were $13.9 billion; in 1980 they totalled $276.9 billion. Three years later, total state revenues were $357.6 billion. (10) A. Two percent.

10. "Wealth, Taxation and Fiscal Policy," National Association of Manufacturers, Sept. 1982.

11. In 1937 "the maximum tax any person could have paid was $30 a year—1 percent on the first $3,000 of his yearly wages—for each of 13 years from 1937 through 1949. (The employer was matching those payments.) In 1950 he might have paid 1.5 percent on $3,000 and in 1951 through 1953, 1.5 percent on $3,600. Thus, if he had earned the maximum taxable income in each of those 17 years, he might have paid a total of $597 in Social Security taxes. His employer would have matched that amount, bringing their combined total to $1,194.

"If that person had retired on January 1, 1954, having reached the age of 65, and if his wife had also passed her 65th birthday, they would be eligible for benefits of $127.50 a month. Thus, within 10 months, that man and his wife would receive more in Social Security benefits than both he and his employer could possibly have paid as Social Security taxes for his account over the 17 years since the program was initiated. But life expectancy at the age of 65 is more than 10 months—about 13 years more, in fact. By what twist of logic or of morality does any person expect to get from 10 to 15, or even more, times the benefits for what he has paid? At whose expense, and why?" Paul L. Poirot, "Social Security," Foundation for Economic Education (FEE).

12. M. Stanton Evans, "Social Security: The Continuing Crisis," *Human Events,* Dec. 3, 1983,11.

13. M. Stanton Evans, op cit.

14. Shirley Hobbs Scheibla, "New Social Security Laws Make Some Americans Second-Class Citizens," *Human Events,* Dec. 3, 1983,11.

15. "Social Security and The Taxing of Churches," *Biblical Principles* (Plymouth, Mass.: Plymouth Rock Foundation, October 1984), 249.

16. Ibid., 249.

17. Pastor Kent Kelly, "A Minority Report," *Christian Schools of North Carolina,* December 1983.

18. "Pennsylvania Church Declares Social Security Challenge," *AACS Newsletter,* American Association of Christian Schools, March 1984, 1-5.

19. "Religious Liberty," Plymouth Rock Foundation, *op cit,* 204.

20. Ibid.

21. "Old Age, Survivors, Disability & Hospital Insurance: Tax Rages and Maximum Tax," Tax Foundation, *op cit,* 58c.

22. "Larger Social Security Levy Worries Some,: *USA Today,* April 8, 1986, 6B.

23. M. Stanton Evans, *op cit.*

24. "Social Security and The Taxing of Churches," Plymouth Rock Foundation, *op cit,* 245.

25. "Payments Under Social Security Insurance," Tax Foundation, *op cit,* 27a.

27. As quoted in "Will House Again Panic On Social Security Cuts?" *Human Events,* April 12, 1986, 5.

28. Henry Hazlitt, *Economics in One Easy Lesson* (New York: McFadden Books, 1962)48.

29. "Overhead," *Newsweek,* June 2, 1986, 17.

30. Warren T. Brookes, "Privatization Would Cut $122 Billion in FY87," *Human Events,* Feb. 2, 1986, 17.

31. Rev. Joseph C. Morecraft, III, "Privitization, The Wave of The Future," *Counsel of Chalcedon,* May 1986, 5-8.

32. Ibid.

33. Hazlitt, *op cit,* 48.

34. The wages of public extravagance far exceed the economic sphere. There is a definite relationship between inflation and rising juvenile delinquency, not only in the inner city but also in the suburbs. As more and more mothers are forced to seek employment to help make ends meet, more and more children are left unattended after school and on weekends. Unsupervised and with no one to care, many become easy prey for mischeif, drugs, and promiscuity.

35. "Panel Urges $500 Billion in Cuts," *United Press International,* Jan. 13, 1984.

36. Editorial, Radio Station KNX, Los Angeles Calif., April 15, 1974.

37. As cited by F.A. Harper, *Liberty: A Path To Its Recovery* (Irvington, N.Y.: Foundation for Economic Education, 1949), 107.

38. Leonard C. Read, "Cliches of Socialism, Number 5," Foundation for Economic Education, 1956.

39. L.D. Thurow and R.E.B. Lucas, "The American Distribution of In-

come: A Structural Problem," *Joint Economic Committee,* March 17, 1972.

40. Irving Kristol, "Of Populism and Taxes, " *The Public Interest,* Summer 1972, 5.

41. Reverend R.J. Rushdoony, *The Nature of The American System* (Nutley, N.J.: The Craig Press, 1965), 9.

42. Ibid., 16.

Chapter 11

1. Henry Hazlitt, *What You Should Know About Inflation* (Princeton: D. Van Nostrand Co., 1965), 11.

2. Lawrence Fertig, "The Political Costs of Price Inflation," *The Freeman,* February 1975, 138.

3. Wilhelm Roepke, *A Humane Society: The Social Framework of the Free Market* (Chicago: Henry Regnery Co., 1961), 101.

4. Tom Rose, *Economics: The American Economy from a Christian Perspective* (Mercer,Penn: American Enterprise Publications, 1985), 31.

5. Gary North, *An Introduction to Christian Economics* (Nutley, N.J.: The Craig Press, 1974), 20.

6. Harry Browne, *You Can Profit from a Monetary Crisis,* 42.

7. Leonard Read, "How To Stop Inflation," *The Freeman,* November 1973, 675.

8. Henry Hazlitt, *Economics in One Easy Lesson* (New York: Mc-Fadden Books, 1965), 115.

9. Gary North, *op cit,* 6.

10. Lawrence Fertig, *Prosperity Through Freedom* (Chicago: Henry Regnery Company, 1961), 187.

11. Most congressmen will try to disown the actions of the Federal Reserve, saying that what it does is beyond their control. That's a cop-out. Congress has the power to strip the Federal Reserve of its authority and to regain the Constitutional powers assigned to it anytime its members have enough courage to take on the big bankers.

12. As quoted by North, *op cit,* 12.

13. Ibid., 13.

14. *Economic Education Bulletin,* American Institute for Economic Research, Great Barrington, Mass.

15. Ibid.

16. Morris J. Markowitz, "Is Inflation Here to Stay," *The Freeman,* April 1974,238.

17. Ibid.

18. Gary North, *op cit,* 24.

19. Garet Garrett, *The People's Pottage* (Caldwell, Idaho: Caxton Press, 1953), 1,3,4.

20. Ibid., 101, 102.

21. Hans Sennholz, "The Causes of Inflation," *The Freeman,* May 1072, 284.

22. Lawrence Fertig, "The Political Costs of Inflation," *The Freeman,* March 1975, 138.

23. Hans Sennholz, "Two Digit Inflation," *The Freeman,* Jan. 1975, 23.

24. Ibid., 28.

25. Gary North, *op cit,* 8.

26. Henry Hazlitt, *What You Should Know About Inflation, op cit,* 126.

27. Jack Kemp, M.C., as quoted in "Money, Morality and Gold," *Biblical Principles* (Plymouth, Mass.: Plymouth Rock Foundation, Oct. 1984), 173.

28. Hans Sennholz, "Gold Is Honest Money," *The Freeman,* Sept. 1972, 541.

29. Vermont Royster, *Wall Street Journal,* as quoted in *Biblical Principles,* 174.

30. Charles E. Weber, "A Closer Look At Gold," *The Freeman,* Sept. 1972, 541.

31. Dr. Howard Kershner, "God,

Gold and Government," *Christian Economics,* Christian Freedom Foundation, 1950.

32. Lewis Lehrman, as cited in "Money, Morality and Gold," Plymourth Rock Foundation, *op cit,* 176.

33. Hans Sennholz, "Gold Is Honest Money," *op cit.*

Chapter 12

1. "Crimes and Crime Rates," *Statistical Abstract of the U.S., 1986,* 166; "Police Memorial," *USA Today,* June 1986, 1B

2. "Law Enforcement Officers Assaulted (and Killed)" *Statistical Abstract, op cit,* 172.

3. "Ford Takes a Hard Line," *Washington Star,* May 2, 1975.

4. "Capital Punishment," *Biblical Principles* (Plymouth, Mass.: Plymouth Rock Foundation, Oct. 1984), 16

5. Ibid.

6. Ibid.

7. "Running Out Of Room," *Newsweek,* June 30, 1986, 45.

8. Dorothy L. Sayer, as quoted by Dr. James Roy Smith in *God Still Speaks in The Space Age,* 60.

9. Ibid., 230.

10. Robert G. Clouse, "The Christian, War and Militarism," *The Cross and the Flag* (Carol Stream, Ill.: Creation House, 1972), 230.

11. Report, Department of Defense, as cited in *Soviet Military Supremacy: The Untold Facts,* Quentin Cromelin, Jr., and David Sullivan (Los Angeles, The Defense and Strategic Studies Project, University of Southern California, 1985), iv.

12. Senator Barry M. Goldwater, in letter to President Reagan, March 5, 1982.

13. "Reagan Makes Case For Defense Budget," *Human Events,* March 8, 1986,3.

14. "Congress Prepares To Slash Military Spending," *Human Events,* March 8, 1986,6.

15. Ibid.

16. Crommelin and Sullivan, 31.

17. Senator Steve Symms, *Introduction,* Soviet Military Supremacy, *op cit.*

18. John Rees, "The Soviets Loot Us With Our Own Money," *Conservative Digest,* July 1986, 51-52.

19. Crommelin and Sullivan, *op cit,* "Authors' Notes," 3.

20. Ibid., 52.

21. Ibid., iv.

22. Ibid., 61, 62.

23. Ibid., 118.

24. Ibid., 25.

25. Richard M. Nixon, *Real Peace* (Boston: Little, Brown and Company, 1984), 11.

26. Loenid Breshnev as quoted in *The Economics of Detente and U.S.—Soviet Grain Trade* (The Heritage Foundation, 1976), 102.

27. Plymouth Rock Foundation *op cit,* 150.

28. Joseph Finder, *Red Carpet* (New York: Holt, Rinehart and Winston, 1983),8

29. Robert G. Clouse, *op cit,* 230-231.

30. Rep. Jack Kemp, *Congressional Record,* March 25, 1975.

31. Senator William Armstrong in Foreword to *We Must Defend America: A New Strategy for National Survival* by Lt. Gen. Daniel O. Graham (Chicago: Henry Regnery, 1983), 9.

32. Robert J. Jastrow, *How to Make Nuclear Weapons Obsolete* (Boston: Little, Brown and Compay, 1985), 15-16.

33. As quoted by United Press International, September 26, 1984.

34. Winston Churchill, speech

broadcast to the British people on the eve of the Battle of Britain, 1939.

35. John Chamberlain, "A Reviewer's Notebook," *The Freeman,* Nov. 1974, 463.

36. "Few Friends in The UN," *USA Today,* May 16, 1986, 4A; "Walters To UN Colleagues: Vote With Us or Lose Aid," *Associated Press,* May 14, 1986.

37. Lucille Sollenberger, *Christ In Genesis,* vol.1, *Living The Life Home Bible Studies,* 72,73.

38. Ibid.

39. Burton Pine, "A United Nations Assessment Project," Heritage Foundation, 1985.

40. Dr. Charles W. Lowry, *Communism and Christ,* 101.

41. Whittaker Chambers, *Witness* (New York: Random House, 1952) 17.

NOTE: Some new notes and sources were added to these notes just prior to publication. For an updated copy of the NOTES, please send a SASE to the Plymouth Rock Foundation, P.O. Box 577, Marlborough, NH 03455. Mark envelope "END NOTES." Thank you.